PRAISE FOR *IN HOFFA'S SHADOW*

"It's fair to say that the last thing the world was itching for in 2019 was another speculative account of Hoffa's final days. Which is precisely why Jack Goldsmith's gripping hybrid of personal memoir and forensic procedural lands with the force of a sucker punch. More than just another writer chewing over the same old facts and hypotheses, Goldsmith turns out to have a uniquely intimate connection to the case that gooses him along on his hunt for the truth."
—Chris Nashawaty, *The New York Times Book Review*

"*The Irishman* is great art ... But it is not, as we know, great history ... [Frank Sheeran] surely didn't kill Jimmy Hoffa ... But who pulled the trigger? ... For some of the real story, and for a great American tale in itself, you want to go to Jack Goldsmith's book, *In Hoffa's Shadow*."
—Peggy Noonan, *The Wall Street Journal*

"The unlikeliest riveting read of the year ... [Jack Goldsmith is] always worth reading on any topic on which he opines. But I wasn't prepared to be transfixed by a D.C. 'backstory' unlike any out there ... This is a National Book Award nominee waiting to happen. And though Hoffa did not go gently into the night, his abrupt and final exit is as dark as any tragedy."
—Hugh Hewitt, *The Washington Post*

"[An] emotionally powerful and utterly compelling book ... *In Hoffa's Shadow* is highly impressive not only as a nonfiction murder mystery but also as a work of profoundly apologetic filial love."
—David J. Garrow, *The Washington Post*

"So much has been written about Jimmy Hoffa, the former Teamster boss who vanished from a Detroit suburb in 1975, but a new book about him still contains surprises—not least because of who wrote it ... *In Hoffa's Shadow* is several books in one—an attempt to piece together the enduring mystery of Hoffa's disappearance, a glancing history of the labor movement, a reflection on the government's surveillance powers and, underpinning it all, a memoir of Goldsmith's relationship with his stepfather [Chuckie O'Brien] ... The book's pacing is steady and unrelenting, as Goldsmith toggles between his own careful narrative voice and Chuckie's off-the-cuff wiseguy vernacular."
—Jennifer Szalai, *The New York Times Book Review*

"Goldsmith has produced a wonderful book about the complicated relationship between a deeply flawed stepfather [Chuckie O'Brien] and the adopted son he loved deeply and forgave unconditionally for casting him aside ... Goldsmith doesn't excuse O'Brien's misdeeds. But he comes to view his stepfather's experience as a target of then-Attorney General Robert F. Kennedy through the prism of his own experiences reviewing the legality of new surveillance powers granted after the 9/11 attacks." —Seth Stern, *The Christian Science Monitor*

"This is an incredible story, plainly rebutting the clear understanding of many that Charles O'Brien drove Jimmy Hoffa to his death, and offering a profoundly beautiful recognition of the nature of paternal love. This book will make you weep, repeatedly, for the injustice, and for the love." —Lawrence Lessig, professor at Harvard Law School and author of *They Don't Represent Us* and *Republic, Lost*

"*In Hoffa's Shadow* is a masterpiece and a page-turner—I couldn't put it down. Brilliant, suspenseful, and deeply moving, it offers a personal view of one of the greatest unsolved crimes in American history. At the same time, it offers startling insights into organized crime, the labor movement, and the surprising origins of today's surveillance state. Beautifully written and full of unexpected turns, this book is gripping and revelatory from start to finish."
—Amy Chua, professor at Yale Law School and author of *Battle Hymn of the Tiger Mother* and *Political Tribes: Group Instinct and the Fate of Nations*

"A thrilling, unputdownable story that takes on big subjects—injustice, love, loss, truth, power, murder—and addresses them in sentences of beauty and clarity informed by deep thought and feeling. Jack Goldsmith, one of the finest minds of his generation, has told an insane tale with a storyteller's flair. This is one of the best works of autobiography that I've read in a very, very long time." —Bill Buford, former fiction editor of *The New Yorker* and author of *Heat* and *Among the Thugs*

"I am one of the world's experts on the July 30, 1975, murder of Jimmy Hoffa. And now, Jack Goldsmith—with his brilliant research and beautiful writing style—comes along and tells me a whole bunch of things I never knew about that day. Satisfying his curiosity about his stepfather's alleged role in the crime, and through his own personal integrity, Goldsmith has advanced the state of evidence of this unsolved mystery, bringing us closer to a final resolution."
—Dan E. Moldea, author of *The Hoffa Wars*

"This is an extraordinary, muscular adventure story about what's happened to our nation and what's possible for its future. A must-read."
—Ron Suskind, author of *Life, Animated* and *The One Percent Doctrine*

Martha Stewart

A NOTE ABOUT THE AUTHOR

Jack Goldsmith is the Henry L. Shattuck Professor of Law at Harvard University and the author of *The Terror Presidency* and *Power and Constraint*. From October 2003 to June 2004, he was the assistant attorney general in the Office of Legal Counsel. He lives in Newton, Massachusetts.

IN HOFFA'S SHADOW

IN
HOFFA'S
SHADOW

A STEPFATHER,

A DISAPPEARANCE IN DETROIT, AND

MY SEARCH FOR THE TRUTH

Jack Goldsmith

PICADOR | FARRAR, STRAUS AND GIROUX | NEW YORK

Picador
120 Broadway, New York 10271

Maps and graphics designed by Kerri L. Ruttenberg and produced by Kim Levine.
Base maps © OpenStreetMap contributors (openstreetmap.org).

Portions of the afterword were previously published in "How *The Irishman* Maligns
My Stepfather," *The New York Times* (January 3, 2020), by Jack Goldsmith.

Library of Congress Control Number: 2019020254

Picador Paperback ISBN: 978-1-250-75799-9

Designed by Richard Oriolo

1 3 5 7 9 10 8 6 4 2

For Charles Lenton O'Brien

CONTENTS

INTRODUCTION 3

1. CHUCKIE AND ME 11

2. TWO LOYALTIES 42

3. UNIONISM, HOFFA-STYLE 69

4. BOBBY, JIMMY, AND CHUCKIE 96

5. SURVEILLANCE BACKUP 122

6. THE CONDITION 152

7. "HE GOT NUTS" 185

8. THE DISAPPEARANCE 213

9. LEADING SUSPECT 227

10. TRAGEDY OF ERRORS 244

11. FAILED VINDICATION 263

12. OMERTÀ 287

AFTERWORD TO THE PAPERBACK EDITION 307

APPENDIX 315
NOTES 323
ACKNOWLEDGMENTS 343
INDEX 347

IN HOFFA'S SHADOW

INTRODUCTION

O NE EVENING IN EARLY DECEMBER 2003, I found myself alone in a brightly lit, cavernous office on the fifth floor of the United States Department of Justice, reading a stack of Supreme Court decisions about the Fourth Amendment's prohibition on unreasonable searches and seizures. At the time I was serving as the assistant attorney general in charge of the Office of Legal Counsel, a position that made me a senior legal advisor to the attorney general and the president. A few weeks earlier, I had concluded that President George W. Bush's secret two-year-old warrantless surveillance program, Stellarwind, was shot through with legal problems. I was working late that night because I was under a deadline to figure out which parts of the program might be saved.

The stakes were enormous. The program's operator, the National Security Agency, was picking up what its director would later describe as a "massive amount of chatter" about al-Qaeda plans for "catastrophic" operations in the Washington, D.C., area. I was certainly anxious based on the threat reports I was reading. And yet I increasingly believed that large parts of the program could not be squared with congressional restrictions on domestic surveillance—a conclusion I feared would risk lives and imply that hundreds of executive branch officials, including the president and the attorney general, had committed crimes for years.

My thoughts that stressful December evening began with a crisis about national security and presidential power but soon veered to a different turbulent period of my life. One of the cases in my "to-read" pile was a 1967 Supreme Court decision, *Berger v. New York*, that restricted the government's use of electronic bugs to capture private conversations by stealth. As my tired eyes reached the end of the opinion, two citations leapt off the page like ghosts: "*O'Brien v. United States*, 386 U.S. 345 (1967); *Hoffa v. United States*, 387 U.S. 231 (1967)."

I looked up, incredulous. Neither case was in my stack. So I turned to my computer and printed them out.

The *Hoffa* case involved the pension fraud conviction of James Riddle Hoffa, the autocratic leader of the International Brotherhood of Teamsters who would later vanish, on July 30, 1975, in what remains one of the greatest unsolved crimes in American history. The *O'Brien* decision concerned the conviction of Charles "Chuckie" O'Brien, also a Teamsters official, for stealing a marble statue of St. Theresa from a U.S. Customs warehouse in the Detroit Harbor Terminal. The Supreme Court vacated both convictions so that lower courts could determine if the government had eavesdropped on Hoffa and O'Brien in possible violation of a new governmental policy and developing Supreme Court jurisprudence. The *Hoffa* and *O'Brien* cases were important in their day, but by 2003 had become mere footnotes in the long struggle for legal control over electronic surveillance. That's why they weren't in my stack.

After reading the decisions, I immediately saw their connection to each other, and to me. In the 1950s and 1960s, Jimmy Hoffa was the nation's best-known and most feared labor leader at a time when unions were consequential forces in American life. Chuckie O'Brien met Hoffa at age nine and later served as his most intimate aide for more than two decades. O'Brien helped Hoffa bulldoze his way to the presidency of the Teamsters. He was Hoffa's trusted messenger to organized crime figures around the country, and was by his side during his seven-year battle with Bobby Kennedy that ultimately sent Hoffa to prison. O'Brien escorted Hoffa to his jailers in March 1967, helped secure Richard Nixon's commutation of Hoffa's sentence in December 1971, and stuck by Hoffa as he struggled to regain control of the Teamsters during his post-prison years.

But in 1974, he and Hoffa had a falling-out. They barely spoke in the eight months before Hoffa disappeared. Soon after Hoffa vanished, O'Brien became a leading suspect. He was closely connected to the men suspected of organizing the crime. Based on a slew of circumstantial evidence, the FBI quickly concluded that O'Brien picked up Hoffa and drove him to his death.

I knew this history well because Chuckie O'Brien is my stepfather. His relationship with my mother, Brenda, was one of the reasons he broke with Hoffa in 1974. I was a pimply twelve-year-old in braces when Chuckie and Brenda wed in Memphis, Tennessee, on June 16, 1975, forty-four days before Hoffa vanished. Ever since Hoffa disappeared, my life has been colored by the changing implications of my relationship to the labor icon, and to Chuckie, whom Hoffa treated as his son, and whom I knew as "Dad."

CHUCKIE AND I were very close when I was a teenager, during the height of the Hoffa maelstrom. He was a great father despite his lack of education, the oppressive FBI investigation, and an angry, excessive pride. Chuckie smothered me in love that he never received from his father, and taught me right from wrong even though he had trouble distinguishing the two in his own life. In high school I idolized Chuckie. When I set out on my professional path in law school, however, I renounced Chuckie out of apprehension about his impact on my life and my career. We had barely spoken for two decades by the time of my service in the Justice Department.

I left government in 2004 to become a professor at Harvard Law School, and soon afterward Chuckie and I patched up and once again grew very close. During the next eight years, we often discussed his trying experiences with Jimmy Hoffa and the government juggernaut that since 1975 had sought to pin the disappearance on him. Chuckie had always denied any involvement in Hoffa's death. Over the decades he had been consumed with resentment as the government hounded him and tarnished his reputation through incriminating leaks to the press based on evidence that Chuckie was never able to examine or contest. He watched with bitter frustration as hundreds of newspaper stories and nearly a dozen books were published with supposed insider revelations about the crime and his role in it.

"What's bothered me my whole life," Chuckie once told me, "is that the government through their devious assholes in the Justice Department turned me into something worse than Al Capone." Yet every time Chuckie tried to explain his side of things on television and radio, he ended up looking worse for the effort.

My conversations with Chuckie made clear why he had been such a poor advocate for himself. He wasn't eloquent and his explanations about his role in Hoffa's disappearance sometimes seemed guarded, self-serving, or mendacious. This did not surprise me. Since I was twelve I had often experienced, and frequently laughed at, Chuckie's tendency to hedge or fib. The FBI viewed it as a reason not to believe Chuckie's alibi on the day of Hoffa's disappearance. In a 1976 memorandum analyzing the case, the Bureau noted, "O'BRIEN is described by even his closest friends as a pathological liar."

The more Chuckie and I talked, the more I came to understand that his adversarial relationship with the truth was influenced by his commitment to Omertà, the Sicilian code of silence that he embraced at a young age. Chuckie had a lifelong hatred of rats—people who broke the code and betrayed their honor—and he was alive to speak to me only because he was adept at keeping his mouth shut about certain things. One coping mechanism to ensure that he didn't speak out of school was to shade the truth. "I never told anybody what was right," Chuckie once told me, trying to be truthful. "I always used what I had to use to divert it."

The conversations with Chuckie drew me into a thicket of ambiguity—about Hoffa's disappearance and much more—in which fact and fiction were hard to distinguish. As I tried to make sense of Chuckie's stories and began to study the public evidence against him, I started to doubt that he was involved in Hoffa's disappearance. But I also developed an inkling that Chuckie knew much more than he had told me—and even that he might know the whole story about the disappearance.

"Why don't I write a book about this?" I asked at the end of one of our chats, in early 2012. I was drawn by the mystery of the disappearance, by Chuckie's complicated relationship with the enigmatic Hoffa, and by the fascinating characters that Hoffa and Chuckie had bumped into during their quarter of a century together. I also believed that no matter what came of the project, I could give Chuckie a fairer shake than history had thus far. And I hoped that doing so might make up, at least a bit, for our long estrangement.

I assumed Chuckie would jump at my offer, since he was so distraught about his reputation and legacy. "It pisses me off that I'm gonna die, go away, and my grandchildren will never know nothing—the good things that I've always done for labor and everyone else," he had told me the day before.

But Chuckie didn't jump at my offer. "I gotta think about it," he said after a long silence. He finally assented after a few days of reflection because, as he told me, he was bitter about what he viewed as the government's crooked hounding of Hoffa and him and his Italian friends, since the 1950s. He also hoped that I could use my legal training, academic skills, and Justice Department connections—none of which he really understood—to exonerate him from the charge that he was involved in Hoffa's death. I doubted I could do this. But I pledged to him that I would try my best to tell his story well, on one condition.

"You have to tell me the truth."

I HAD MANY reasons to think the truth would be elusive, and not just because of Chuckie's evasions. As one FBI agent who worked the case in the 1970s told me, much of what the public knows about Jimmy Hoffa's disappearance is "science fiction." For forty-five years, public knowledge has been shaped by unreliable informants, tendentious government leaks, credulous journalists, or aging (and now-dead) mob figures looking to make a buck. Book after book and article after article has provided different theories of Hoffa's death, almost all of which involve Chuckie. And yet there is still not one single piece of direct evidence about what happened to Hoffa on the afternoon of July 30, 1975.

It is apt that my main source for trying to solve this perfect crime is an unreliable chronicler with a stake in the outcome of the events he lived through. For several years I pushed Chuckie in hundreds of hours of conversations—as a son wanting to learn the family history; as a scholar interviewing the person most closely connected to the Hoffa disappearance and its leading characters; and as a cross-examining prosecutor testing the witness's credibility. Our conversations were often maddening, comical, or both. Chuckie inhabits a different linguistic and conceptual universe than I, and rarely provided the direct or intellectually tidy answers I sought. He also hesitated, at first, to discuss some of the legally dubious episodes in his life. Over time, he grew more comfortable in our discussions. He did not "tell all," but he did reveal a great deal of new and fascinating information about important historical events that he lived through, including the Hoffa disappearance.

I also spent a great deal of time trying to corroborate or correct what Chuckie told me. I dug deeply into thousands of pages of unpublished or unexplored government records, including thousands of pages of transcripts from illegal bugs that recorded Chuckie, his mother, and Detroit crime family members in the early 1960s. I did research in archives in more than a dozen libraries. And I interviewed dozens of people, including journalists and historians who are experts on Hoffa and the Teamsters, the four primary FBI agents originally assigned to the Hoffa disappearance, and a dozen other investigators and prosecutors who worked the case thereafter—including those currently assigned to it.

My investigation did not uncover the specifics of what happened to Jimmy Hoffa on July 30, 1975, but it did help me to figure out why the forty-five-year-old conventional wisdom that Chuckie was involved in Hoffa's disappearance is almost certainly wrong. Despite my acknowledged interests, I believe the pages that follow cut through decades of obfuscation and set forth the most objective, fair-minded, and revealing assessment of Hoffa's disappearance to date—one that sheds authentic light on the case and the era in which it happened.

This book started off as an effort to understand Chuckie's role in Hoffa's disappearance, but it grew to be about much more. It is about how a hapless blabbermouth with famously terrible judgment served as a close aide to both Hoffa and a top Detroit mob figure, both of whom trusted him with their most intimate secrets. It is about how an uneducated serial lawbreaker with mob values nourished his vulnerable stepson at a crucial stage in his life to set him on a path that led to the Justice Department and Harvard Law School. It's about Chuckie's life, and mine, in the forty-five-year vortex of the Hoffa disappearance, and my changing thoughts, over the course of my life, about these events. And it is about what I learned about truth-telling, honor and pride, and paternal and filial love and treachery—from Chuckie's tragic ensnarement between two ruthless father figures and implacable government investigators, and from my relationship with Chuckie.

The book is also about the complex legacy that Jimmy Hoffa bequeathed to the American labor movement and American justice. Hoffa is remembered today as a union autocrat who broke the law and worked closely with organized crime. That's true. But as Chuckie taught me, Hoffa also protected the Teamsters from the mob, and his actions were motivated to help workers, which he did with wild success. Hoffa was a labor-organizing genius who leveraged his union's power to lift many hundreds of thousands of people from poverty to the middle class. He was on the verge of even greater labor accomplishments when Robert Kennedy's seven-year assault destroyed him in a manner that was more responsible than has been appreciated for the steady decline in union power ever since. Kennedy's investigations of Hoffa involved excesses approaching criminality and an expansion of the surveillance state for which no one in the government was ever held accountable. They also had an improbable, reverberating impact on subsequent American legal culture, spanning from progressive surveillance reform in the late 1960s to the post-2001 "war on terrorism."

My conversations with Chuckie helped me to understand all of this, and altered my views on matters as far afield as unions, government surveillance, and the basic fairness of American institutions. They also helped me to better understand Hoffa's—and Chuckie's—worldview. "My ethics are very simple," Hoffa once explained. "Live and let live, and those who try to destroy you, make it your business to see that they don't and that they have problems." This philosophy worked for the decades when Hoffa had more power than his many adversaries. In the end, after he lost that power, Hoffa was killed.

Chuckie was raised on and lived by Hoffa's ethics, which informed all our conversations. He also lived by Omertà, which was also present in our conversations, and which in the end clashed with his commitments to Hoffa. I often pressed Chuckie to reconcile his harsh moralistic condemnation of law enforcement abuses against Hoffa and organized crime with his own tales of unregretted violence and frequent lawbreaking that both Hoffa and Omertà seemed to invite. "It's maybe not ethical in a way you understand," he told me. "But we had to do things to win. If we didn't do it, they would do it to us. And that's just the way life was."

Chuckie never persuaded me on this point. But on plenty of others, he did. The uneducated union man, it turned out, had a lot to teach the professor.

What follows is an account of what I learned.

CHUCKIE AND ME

C HUCKIE WAS MY THIRD FATHER, and my best.

My biological father, Jack Goldsmith Jr., grew up in the Gayoso, a hotel in Memphis, Tennessee, that his father owned and that was located adjacent to the family department store his father ran. Jack Jr.'s work-aholic father and alcoholic mother neglected their only child and delegated his upbringing and protection to a black man from rural Arkansas named Andrew. "Andrew was hired because of threats during labor problems at the store and for years he slept in my room, drove me to school where he sat there all day and waited for me, and pretty much spent every second with me," my father told me, late in his life.

Jack Jr. despised his parents but idolized Andrew, who took him hunting and fishing, to the movies on Beale Street two blocks from the hotel, and to Negro League baseball games. Andrew also permitted Jack Jr. to indulge in the vices offered by downtown Memphis in the 1950s. There were no children at the hotel, so my father hung around the bellmen, who taught him how to shoot craps and play cards. A bellman named Shorty once urged Andrew to fix my twelve-year-old father up with one of the hookers loitering at the hotel. "I thought it was a great idea, and after a month of begging and swearing to take it to my grave, Andrew sent me to a room one day, and lo and behold, the deed was done," my father recalled. "Other than my mother and father, life was grand."

After spending most of his teenage years having fun with Andrew, Jack Jr. met Brenda Berger, my attractive but naïve mother. Brenda was a former beauty queen—Miss Teenage Arkansas, 1958—who grew up on the top floor of her parents' West Memphis nightclub. The Plantation Inn, as it was called, was a well-known Mid-South locale where Brenda's alcoholic father, Morris, hosted a popular all-night live radio show that featured such famous early R&B figures as Isaac Hayes and the Newborn Family.

"The Plantation Inn was a family place, in the way a swing joint run by the Addams Family might be," says the historian Robert Gordon. "There were many places a person could get wild and drunk, but with blacks and whites in the same room, even if separated by the proscenium, the PI provided a peek behind the wall erected by society." As a little girl, Brenda worked the hat-and-coat-check stand. When she was a teenager, she took in money at the front door, $2.40 per couple. "We tried to stick to couples to keep any fights down," she later told me.

Brenda thought she had escaped the coarse world of the Plantation Inn when she eloped with the son of a well-to-do Memphis businessman when she was twenty-one and my father was eighteen. I was born ten months later, in Memphis, on September 26, 1962.

My father didn't warm to marriage or fatherhood, however. Within two years Jack Jr. abandoned me and Brenda, and they divorced. But he returned a few months later and remarried my mother. My two younger brothers were the happy consequences of the second marriage, but the rest was wretched.

I was seven years old and we were living in Union City, Tennessee, when my father left again, this time for good, just a few weeks after my youngest brother, Steven, was born. I wouldn't see Jack Jr. again until I was twenty-one, and we have spoken only a few times in five decades.

I remember almost nothing about my time with my father as a boy. But after he disappeared the second time, in late 1969, I vividly recall riding in the black back seat of an orange Dodge Charger Daytona as my mother, crying without explaining why, drove me and my brothers 120 miles down Route 51 from Union City to her mother Clemmye's home in West Memphis, Arkansas. My grandmother Clemmye was a tough, blue-eyed Mississippi girl. She managed the Plantation Inn before it closed in 1964, and ran the other family enterprises, including firework stands, a pool hall, and two liquor stores. She was also my rock of solace when misfortune befell my mother, as it often did.

After we arrived in West Memphis my brother Brett and I played in Clemmye's backyard while my grandmother tried to comfort my distraught mother. About forty-five minutes later, Clemmye asked me to come to her living room and sit on the overstuffed large beige couch where she and I would often watch TV or wrestle playfully. We were alone in the room, and she held both of my hands and looked at me intently with her bright, piercing eyes.

"Your father is gone and not coming back," she said. "You have to be the man of the family now." It took me several seconds, maybe longer, to process what my grandmother had said. I then leapt up, ran to the guest bathroom, and locked the door. I cried wildly for several minutes, thinking, without fully understanding why, that my world had come undone. But after a while I stared into the mirror and calmed down. And then I pledged to myself to follow my grandmother's directive.

My mother's relationship with her second husband, a neurosurgeon in Lafayette, Louisiana, wasn't great either. Dr. Robert Rivet was a distant but stern stepfather. I mainly remember him drinking vodka and grapefruit juice, and yelling at my mother. The marriage to Rivet ended within a few years after Brenda, suffering from postpartum depression following a miscarriage, tried to kill herself with an overdose of sleeping pills. It was 1973 and I was eleven years old at the time. Clemmye gave me the bad news on the same beige couch in her West Memphis living room. I had another bawling fit, then resolved again to be mature.

WHEN MY MOTHER got out of the hospital, she and my brothers moved to a small apartment near Fort Lauderdale, Florida, where I attended a nearby military boarding school called Florida Air Academy. We had little money, since Brenda couldn't work, my father never paid alimony, and his wealthy father ignored us. Clemmye paid for military school and our apartment and ensured that we lived relatively comfortable lives. But my mother struggled to maintain her health and at the same time raise me and my younger brothers. After less than a year on her own, and desperate, she telephoned a man she knew—Chuckie O'Brien.

Brenda had gotten to know Chuckie because Clemmye was friends with his mother, Sylvia Pagano. Sylvia was a dark Sicilian beauty born into a Kansas City crime family who later became a consequential figure in labor and organized crime circles. She and my grandmother met at a hotel pool in North Miami Beach in the early 1960s. They hit it off immediately and remained close until Sylvia's death in 1970.

Just after Brenda's second divorce from my father, Sylvia introduced Brenda to Chuckie. He says he fell in love at first sight. "I knew the day I met your mother that I wanted to spend the rest of my life with her," he once told me. Brenda remembers things differently. With three young children, no income, and mental health struggles, she longed for stability. Chuckie was going through a divorce of his own, and he seemed preoccupied with Teamsters work. At the time, the Louisiana neurosurgeon, Bob Rivet, courted her more aggressively and seemed a safer bet.

It was only after that bet failed that Brenda—depressed, broke, and alone with three young boys—telephoned Chuckie in late 1974. This time he was more focused. He flew to meet her the day he received her message. The two saw each other only a few times during the next six months, but in June 1975, while our family was visiting Clemmye in West Memphis, Chuckie and Brenda wed.

"I think I would have said yes to anyone who asked, 'Will you marry me?'" my mother later told me. "I was that distraught."

Brenda would become much more distraught after July 30, 1975, when the Hoffa disappearance enveloped our lives and the attendant stress ruined what was left of her health. Brenda's marriage to Chuckie nonetheless proved to be a large blessing for me.

Despite Brenda's divorces and attempted suicide, and the lack of a loving father, I remember my childhood before Chuckie in a relatively sanguine light. My main early memories are of fun-filled days building tree houses, shooting snakes, roaming cornfields, and playing football and baseball. I attended church as a boy, but my sense of right and wrong came less from the Bible than from wanting not to be like my biological father. My early education can be summed up by the fact that I learned to read so I could understand the handicapping books at Southland Greyhound Park, the West Memphis dog track where our maid, Bertha Smith, and I would place nightly bets for Clemmye. I loved to watch "the puppies" run from my perch atop Bertha's car in the parking lot. I dreamed of being one of the boys who put colorful jackets on the wispy greyhounds and escorted them to their chutes.

Through and despite these filtered remembrances, I recall growing much happier, even joyful, after Chuckie arrived, seemingly from nowhere, a few months after my twelfth birthday. I had no inkling at the time how much he yearned to succeed as a father—perhaps because his law-skirting father abandoned him when he was a young boy; or because he had just had a breach with his lifelong father-substitute, Jimmy Hoffa; or because he had been a less-than-reliable father to his two children in his first marriage, in part because of his all-absorbing duties for Hoffa. Nor did I understand that he viewed his marriage to my mother as a chance to atone for the many personal failures in his life to that point. I also didn't know that his mother, Sylvia, doted on me when she visited Clemmye, and often talked to Chuckie about me.

All I knew was that a gregarious brown-eyed man with a potbelly, long dark sideburns, an inviting smile, and the biggest forearms I had ever seen had suddenly glommed on to me with love and attention that I never received from Jack Goldsmith Jr., or Dr. Bob Rivet, or anyone else.

WHEN JIMMY HOFFA vanished from the Detroit suburbs in the early afternoon of July 30, 1975, I was 775 miles away on a lake in Hot Springs, Arkansas, fishing for crappie and brim with my mother, Brenda, and my two younger brothers, Brett and Steven.

We had spent the summer at Clemmye's home in West Memphis. We usually fished in one of the local floodplain lakes. But this was a special occasion, as Brenda wanted to celebrate her recent marriage to Chuckie. A few weeks after they wed, Chuckie had driven his 1975 Teamsters-issue black two-door Lincoln Continental from Detroit to West Memphis in anticipation of our family move to South Florida, where Chuckie would soon begin a new Teamsters job. He stayed with us for a bit and then flew back to Detroit in late July to clean out his office and say good-bye to friends.

Within a few days Brenda, my brothers, and I piled into Chuckie's car and headed to Hot Springs to have some fun while he was away. My grandmother Clemmye later joined us there. Ironically for my tale, the resort town known for its 147-degree natural thermal springs was once a famous gangster outpost, a place where Al Capone, Lucky Luciano, Meyer Lansky, and Frank Costello would go to get away from it all.

We spent the next few days fishing from a rented boat on Lake Hamilton, where Bill Clinton used to have fun as a boy. At the end of our third day on the lake, we returned in the late afternoon to the nearby Holiday Inn. Clemmye, who had stayed in, was animated as we walked into her ground-floor room.

"The news said Mr. Hoffa is missing!" she exclaimed. It was the first time I ever heard Jimmy Hoffa's name. His disappearance had just become public.

"I called Tony—he said he saw Chuck, and he is okay," my grandmother said next. "They don't know where Hoffa is. They are trying to figure out what happened."

"Tony" was Anthony Giacalone, a reputed Detroit underboss who would soon, along with Chuckie, become a leading suspect in the disappearance. Chuckie had known "Uncle Tony" since he was a teenager, and was as close to him as he was to Jimmy Hoffa. My grandmother knew Giacalone well from her trips to Detroit to see Sylvia Pagano, who began working with Giacalone in the 1940s.

We returned to West Memphis the next morning, August 1, 1975. Chuckie joined us from Detroit a few days later. He was not mentioned in the extensive news about Hoffa's disappearance that first dominated the headlines. But on August 5, as we were about to hit the road for Florida, the FBI announced that it wanted to interview Hoffa's "foster son." Chuckie flew back to Detroit the next day to meet with the FBI.

In his interview with the FBI, Chuckie acknowledged that he had been in the parking lot where Hoffa's car was found on the morning that Hoffa disappeared. He also told the FBI that he had borrowed a 1975 maroon Mercury Marquis that day from Joey Giacalone, Anthony's son, to deliver a fresh salmon from the Teamsters' Detroit headquarters to the home of a senior Teamsters official. The FBI impounded the car a few days later. The August 10 headlines said that the FBI discovered bloodstains in the back seat, but the papers reported the following day that the blood was from a fish. A few days later, however, the FBI announced that dogs had detected Hoffa's scent in the back seat and trunk of the same car. The government was also telling the press that Chuckie had given "conflicting accounts" of his movements on the day Hoffa disappeared.

By late August 1975, the FBI had formed a theory about Hoffa's disappearance that has been conventional wisdom ever since. The Mafia killed Hoffa, the FBI believed, to prevent him from returning to the presidency of the Teamsters and exposing the mob's cushy relationship with Frank Fitzsimmons, Hoffa's successor. The hit was organized by Anthony Giacalone, whom Hoffa believed he was meeting the day he disappeared, and by Anthony "Tony Pro" Provenzano, a New Jersey Teamsters official, a captain in the Genovese crime family, and a man Chuckie had known for almost as long as he had known Giacalone.

Chuckie's role, the FBI believed, was to pick up Hoffa and deliver him to his executioners under the guise of driving to a get-together with Giacalone.

The FBI doubted that Chuckie knew in advance that he was driving Hoffa to his death. But it thought he participated in and had direct knowledge of the disappearance. The FBI also believed Chuckie owed Giacalone "a large sum of money," as its official report put it, and that Fitzsimmons had rewarded him for his defection from the Hoffa camp with the lucrative new Teamsters job in Florida.

Things looked bad for Chuckie. He had a motive to help Giacalone and Fitzsimmons; he admitted he was in the vicinity of the crime on the day it happened; Hoffa's scent was detected in the car he was driving that day; and he had given inconsistent accounts of his activities. On September 2, the FBI announced that it believed Chuckie had used the Mercury "to facilitate an abduction of Hoffa."

Appearing before a federal grand jury in Detroit the following day, Chuckie refused to answer questions, pleading his Fifth Amendment right against self-incrimination. It is "appalling when a man like this claims to be a 'foster son' and still withholds information needed by the authorities," charged Hoffa's son, James P. Hoffa, Chuckie's lifelong rival for Hoffa's affection. Chuckie's silence, "coupled with his continued refusal to take an FBI-administered lie detector test, makes it absolutely clear that he was involved in some way with my father's disappearance," added the younger Hoffa. Most observers drew the same conclusion.

I would later learn how angry and impotent Chuckie felt in the face of what he viewed as a mammoth frame job. But to my twelve-year-old mind he seemed stoic. My mother, by contrast, was reeling. Her mental health was fragile when she married Chuckie in search of peace and security. Now she was sucked into his fast-collapsing life.

Reporters from around the nation descended on West Memphis, turning our quiet neighborhood into an embarrassing circus. Brenda's high school picture appeared on the front page of the Memphis *Commercial Appeal* in a story about the new bride of the lead suspect in the Hoffa case. The FBI questioned her and our relatives aggressively in our West Memphis home. The Hot Springs newspapers reported that FBI agents were dredging Lake Hamilton in search of Hoffa's body. And *Time* magazine implied that Brenda caused Chuckie's rift with Hoffa when it reported that his recent marriage to a "go-go girl"—an unflattering reference to Brenda's days at the Plantation Inn—"did not receive the full blessing of Hoffa, who has his puritanical side."

When we left West Memphis for Florida toward the end of August, my mother hoped she was putting the Hoffa trauma behind her. But as we approached Tampa—Chuckie driving the black Lincoln, my mother in the passenger seat, my brothers and I in the back—a radio newscast reported the latest rumors about Chuckie's role in Hoffa's disappearance. My mother snapped. I remember her screaming wildly, and Chuckie pulling over at a rest stop to try to calm her down. "I just lost it, I couldn't take it anymore," Brenda would later say, describing her nervous breakdown.

IN EARLY SEPTEMBER 1975, a week or so after we arrived at our rented apartment in Plantation, Florida, Chuckie flew to Detroit to face the grand jury investigating the Hoffa disappearance. He pleaded the Fifth Amendment and told reporters afterward that it was "a lead-pipe cinch" he would be indicted. He wasn't. But soon the grand jury subpoenaed my mother to testify. Presiding judge James P. Churchill declined to enforce the subpoena after being convinced by doctors that Brenda suffered from "hysterical neurosis" and might suffer "an emotional collapse" if she were forced to testify.

Brenda was not feigning. The Hoffa turmoil had deepened her severe depression, and she spent the fall of 1975 undergoing 1970s-style electroshock therapy, made famous in the movie *One Flew Over the Cuckoo's Nest*, which premiered as she was taking the treatment. The marriage that was supposed to be a new dawn for Chuckie and Brenda had within months become a horror show.

"Mr. Hoffa had disappeared and the whole world was chasing me and then I saw what those shock treatments did to your mother," Chuckie later told me. "She got the full jolt. The maximum. It looked like her eyes were coming out of her head. Terrible. That's the worst thing I ever went through in my life." It was terrible not just because of my mother's situation, but also because Chuckie believed he was responsible.

My brothers and I were shielded from much of this. In September 1975 I returned to Florida Air Academy for eighth grade. For the first time, my brothers, Brett and Steven—ages nine and five—joined me at boarding school. It was a rough and in many ways abusive place, and was especially hard on my brothers, who were in fourth grade and kindergarten. But Brenda was in the hospital and then incapacitated for several months, and Chuckie was dealing with the Hoffa storm and traveling all over the South with his new job. We didn't have other options.

Despite these circumstances, and despite Chuckie's many troubles with the law, he was a large, stable, affectionate presence in my life, and we grew very close. I can hardly fathom now how he made time for his three new stepchildren with everything else going on. But he did—he devoted every spare moment to us.

When he took us once to see my dazed and barely responsive mother in a cold, all-white hospital room, I grew very sad. "She will get better," Chuckie assured me as he placed his thick arm around me and kissed me on the head just as we left the room. Cloaked in his physical strength, I believed him.

Chuckie visited me and my brothers frequently at military school and brought us comic books and baseball cards and candy. He showed up at my military parades and athletic events. And every Friday afternoon he would pick us up from school and take us home for a fun weekend during which he spent all his time cooking for us, playing with us, talking about sports, and catering to our many demands. It was the first time I had ever experienced fatherly affection or male attention, and I lapped it up.

When Teamsters work prevented Chuckie from visiting us at military school, he asked Anthony Giacalone and his elegant wife, Zina, who spent winters forty miles away in Miami, to come see us. Once, after they took me and my brothers to lunch, my youngest brother, Steven, then age six, asked to go to a gift shop to get my mother a "get well" card. Steven picked one out, and Uncle Tony, as I began to call him, pulled out his wallet to pay for it. But Steven insisted on buying the card out of his allowance. "Sir, if you pay for that, it won't be from us," my brother said. The tall, immaculately dressed, straight-backed man smiled gently and acquiesced.

The rest of the world knew Giacalone as the probable mastermind of the Hoffa disappearance and a gangster whose "propensity for violence is legendary in Detroit," as an FBI report written at about this time put it. But to me he was a charming, generous, and loving man, and part of my new family.

The new family became official in 1976, when Chuckie adopted me and my brothers, and I proudly changed my name to "Jack O'Brien." We left the military school the following year to attend Pine Crest, a private school in Fort Lauderdale. Now that I lived at home with Chuckie, he and I did everything together—except homework, since "book learning" was not his thing. At least once a week, often more frequently, we went together to get his car washed. Every third Saturday we went to his Italian barber ("Tony," naturally) for a shampoo, haircut, and bullshit session.

Chuckie took me to professional sports events, where he seemed to know the players and coaches and, despite his perpetual money problems, always had great seats. He drove me to faraway comic book stores so I could build up my fledgling collection. He gave me a car at age sixteen (a silver Mercury Zephyr), and rushed to the scene and wasn't angry when I crashed it a few months later. And he was heavily involved in my high school sports life. He went to all my football and baseball games. He knew and hung out with my coaches. And he was famous among my teammates for his night-before-a-game feasts that featured thickly sliced prime rib and piles of his specialty, veal Milanese.

I grew closer to and even more dependent on Chuckie as my mother suffered physical challenges on top of her mental ones. In 1977 she almost died from a botched hysterectomy and had to be operated on a second time. That same year she was diagnosed with a vascular disease. And the following year she had a dangerous pancreas operation.

While Chuckie was dealing with all this and keeping us together, his finances—precarious for all his adult life—collapsed entirely. Chuckie always spent more than he had. But now the IRS had put a lien on his Teamsters paycheck, leaving him only $200 a month. My grandmother Clemmye paid for school and helped us get by. But without Chuckie's income, we had to abandon the "dream house" that he had foolishly built for Brenda with a large chunk of his pension savings, and move into a small apartment nearby. It must have been humiliating for Chuckie. But I was used to moving around, all was otherwise well in my life, and I barely noticed the change.

The Hoffa matter loomed. The FBI continued to believe Chuckie was involved, but it never had enough evidence to indict him for the crime. So it instead brought unrelated charges against him and other suspects, in the hope, as *The New York Times* reported in 1976, that they would feel pressure "to consider plea bargaining and to become witnesses for the state in the [Hoffa] case." In 1978 Chuckie was convicted of what he described as two "bullshit charges" for accepting a gift from a firm where he represented workers and for inflating his income on a bank loan application. He served his time in the minimum security federal prison on Eglin Air Force Base beginning in February 1979.

NONE OF THIS altered my affection for Chuckie, whose worldview I had entirely absorbed. He always spoke reverently of the "Old Man" or "Dad" or "Mr. Hoffa," and would often tear up over his disappearance. "If I were with him that day they'd have had to kill me first," he would often say.

I thought of Jimmy Hoffa as the grandfather I'd never met, and I couldn't imagine Chuckie had anything to do with his murder. The FBI agents who hassled Chuckie were "lying motherfuckers" who abused their power, Chuckie said at the time. The "bullshit" criminal charges that sent him to jail were government efforts to "squeeze" him to get information about Hoffa. The supposed infiltration of the Teamsters by the Mafia was "horseshit." The Mafia "doesn't exist," Chuckie would say. It was a "creation of the government's imagination" designed to facilitate harassment of kind men like Uncle Tony, whom we would visit for holiday meals in his Miami apartment.

Also kind was "Tony Pro" Provenzano, whom I also called "Uncle Tony." During our many visits to Provenzano's house in Hallandale Beach, Florida, I became obsessed with the beautiful carved wooden pool table in his den. Tony Pro called Chuckie out of the blue one day and gave it to me. "Get this fucking pool table and give it to your boys," he said. To this day I think of Tony Pro when I play pool.

As a teenager I grew to venerate the Teamsters union. Two summers after Hoffa vanished, when I was fourteen, our family went to the Contemporary Resort at Disney World for the twenty-fifth meeting of the Southern Conference of Teamsters, the umbrella organization in which Chuckie represented workers in the construction and moviemaking industries. I spent three days in the amusement park with a pocketful of ride tickets paid for by truckers' dues. I was nervous but honored to meet Frank Fitzsimmons, Hoffa's portly successor, and other Teamsters luminaries, including future presidents Jackie Presser and Roy Williams.

These burly, unfit-looking men seemed glum as they walked out of business meetings in their polyester suits and wide-collared shirts. They were much happier in golf shorts on the courses that dotted Lake Buena Vista, which is where they spent most of their time. I got to play in a golf "tournament" with three amiable Teamsters executives, and brought home a two-foot trophy even though I hacked around the course. I had no idea at the time that the mob had been gorging on the Teamsters' pension funds in the two years since Hoffa had vanished, or that the union was under a massive federal investigation for fraud and mob ties. Everyone seemed to be having a good time, and I felt important being there.

It was thrilling to be associated with the Teamsters union in an era that glorified trucker defiance of authority. A musical hit in 1976 was C. W. McCall's "Convoy," a song about truckers driving around the country using CB radios to outwit the police. *Smokey and the Bandit*, a film released the next year, featured Burt Reynolds, Sally Field, and Jerry Reed illegally hauling four hundred cases of Coors beer in an eighteen-wheeler on an extended high-speed chase from Texas to Georgia. In 1978, Sylvester Stallone starred in *F.I.S.T.*, a film based loosely and sympathetically on Hoffa's life in the Teamsters.

I identified Chuckie—who typically wore jeans, cowboy boots, and a Teamsters jacket—with the law-defying heroes of pop culture. Truckers seemed to me the greatest Americans, and Chuckie knew them and helped them organize and be strong. I prized no piece of clothing more than a navy cotton T-shirt with a gold Teamsters emblem of two horse heads over a six-spoke wheel.

Far from being ashamed of Chuckie, I was proud of him and proud to be his son. I attributed his misfortunes to his notorious bad luck and to the government malfeasance he never stopped railing against. Friends, coaches, and teachers at my high school in Fort Lauderdale seemed to like him (though I never knew what they really thought). And having a father reputedly associated with the Mafia had a kind of edgy cool—or so it seemed. I barely noticed Chuckie's rough language, malapropisms, and lack of education. These things were in the background. In the foreground were his charming smile, his unconditional love for me and my brothers, and the comforting security of his physical strength.

Chuckie was far from perfect. He always had money problems. His tendency to confound truth and fiction was sometimes frustrating. He liked more than anything to please, and to tell people what they wanted to hear—often without regard to facts or his ability to follow through. As a boy I got used to these defining elements of Chuckie's personality and learned when to discount what he said. He often promised more than he delivered, but he always meant well. Sometimes he seemed like a bullshit artist, but that was part of his charm. The most important thing was that he loved me dearly, and I loved him the same.

"We were just a normal family," Chuckie told me, late in his life, describing our time together during my teens. I chuckled, and then a few seconds later wept. We were hardly a normal family given our circumstances. But I know what he meant. Chuckie had never had a constant family life—not when he was growing up, and not during his first marriage, where he failed as a husband and father because he was always away with Hoffa. Nor had my mother, brothers, and I ever been a stable family. But with Chuckie we were close-knit, we loved each other, and we had fun.

"I always told your mother we'd make it if we stick together," he later told me. It was Chuckie who held us together, under the most difficult possible circumstances. He remained devoted to my mother and adored her no matter what her difficulties. And he was an extraordinary father to me and my brothers. I always wanted to please Chuckie, who, like his hero Jimmy Hoffa, frowned on drinking, drugs, and "screwing around." I listened attentively when he conveyed that Hoffa despised "ignorant oil"—his term for alcohol—and had seen it ruin the lives of many Teamsters and trucking executives. I avoided the many vices readily available to a teenager growing up in Fort Lauderdale because Chuckie had impressed his old-school values on me and I didn't want to disappoint him.

I was devastated when Chuckie went to prison in the middle of my junior year of high school. In August of that year, a few months before Chuckie was released, my best friend and I visited the colleges we might apply to that fall. It was quite a trip: two seventeen-year-olds crisscrossing the southeast in a huge Lincoln Continental Mark V, talking to truckers about speed traps on our CB radio. I fell in love with Washington and Lee University in Lexington, Virginia.

But the highlight of the trip came on the way home, when we stopped in the Florida Panhandle at Eglin Air Force Base to visit Chuckie during prison visiting hours. It was frightening to enter the facility and even more frightening to wait for Chuckie in the cramped visiting room surrounded by sex-starved, handcuffed convicts groping their girlfriends and wives. But I was thrilled to see Chuckie when he appeared, if only for forty-five minutes. And he was thrilled to see me.

MY ATTITUDE TOWARD Chuckie began to change about a year after he was released from prison, when I went to college in the fall of 1980. I had been an unmotivated and mediocre student in high school. The summer before college, I decided to get serious about my studies and my life. Washington and Lee reciprocated with extraordinary teachers who would become life-long mentors. My ambition to be an accountant didn't survive a freshman introductory literature class, and I would go on to major in philosophy. I worked very hard, became a good student, and developed a love of ideas and learning and argument. By my senior year I had decided to go to law school with the vague notion of becoming a law professor.

In college I read for the first time some of the books about Hoffa's disappearance. The Mafia, I learned, did exist. And Chuckie, it turned out, had close relationships with many organized crime figures (including several people I knew), as well as a history of criminal acts ranging from assault to theft. He was also universally portrayed as the man who drove Hoffa to his death. During my sophomore year, as my unquestioning belief in Chuckie's version of his life began to wane, a hefty, thuggish repo agent knocked on my door and in front of my housemate demanded the keys to the car that Chuckie had given me to use for college. It was the first time that Chuckie's financial irresponsibility concretely affected me. I began to think I couldn't rely on him and might be hurt by doing so.

I also started to feel embarrassed in Chuckie's presence. On his first visit to see me at Washington and Lee, during my sophomore year, I took him to a student performance of William Wycherley's play *The Country Wife*. I cringed at his rough manners and poor grammar when I introduced him to one of my professors before the play. All the men in the audience wore coat and tie. Chuckie wore jeans and a poorly fitting coat over a Teamsters shirt that barely covered his belly. I used to revel in Chuckie's union identity. But that night, it humiliated me. I was relieved when he left, bored and probably sensing my discomfort, at the end of the first act.

I soon began to show open disrespect to the man I once idolized. As a teenager I laughed off Chuckie's exaggerated claims to be friends with movie and sports stars. In college, I started to call him a liar. I also began to tell the man who had an instinctual hatred of the Justice Department since his clashes with Bobby Kennedy in the 1950s that I planned to go to law school and become a government prosecutor. And I started to make fun of Chuckie for mispronouncing words and botching grammar.

I now know how much my cruel barbs hurt him. But at the time, he seemed to take them remarkably well. He referred to me as "the educated idiot" and poked fun at my interest in philosophy and lack of street smarts. But he continued to be sweet to me, and to do things for me (whether I asked or not), and to try to participate in my life.

By my senior year, however, I was growing wary of his involvement. A few months before graduation, about the time I accepted an offer to attend Yale Law School, I began to worry that the association with Chuckie might jeopardize my legal career. During college I had grown close to my grandfather, Jack Goldsmith Sr., who was learned, intelligent, and worldly, and who saw in me what he had hoped for but never found in his son, my father.

Why, I began to wonder, should I go through life burdened with my accidental relationship to Chuckie and Jimmy Hoffa? Why shouldn't I retake the name I was born with, especially since the association with Chuckie was so fraught?

When Chuckie came to my college graduation in June 1984, I barely talked to him. The following week I started a summer job in Memphis, where eight years earlier I had changed my name to O'Brien. During my first week in Memphis, a few months shy of my twenty-second birthday, I hired a lawyer to change my name officially back to Jack Goldsmith III.

I telephoned Chuckie from Memphis to tell him of my plans. He was quiet on the phone. I then sent him this disingenuously upbeat letter for Father's Day, dated June 14, 1984:

> Dear Dad:
> This letter is your father's day card! Dad, I know you are probably upset and hurt because I'm changing my name, but please, please, *don't* let it affect our relationship. I'm not changing my name out of any allegiance to the Goldsmiths, nor am I playing games and trying to get money. There are different burdens that go with both names, and if I'm going to carry the burden of a name, I want it to be the one I was born with.
> What you must understand and believe is that I love you very much; this whole business changes nothing. More than anyone in the *world*, you have helped Mom, Brett, Steven, and myself. Without you, we never could have made it. I mean that from the bottom of my heart. The love you have shown us all is more genuine and more selfless than any of our "true" relatives. I want you to know that despite the name change, you are still my father, and I hope you still consider me your son.
> Dad, I love you very much, and I hope my name change doesn't affect your love for me or make you resent me. In three months, it won't make any difference.
> I love you truly. You're the only father I ever had.
> Have a *great* father's day.
> Love,
> Your Son,
> Jack

Two weeks later I received an eight-page letter, dated June 27, 1984, in Chuckie's whimsical looping cursive handwriting on the stationery of the Southern Conference of the International Brotherhood of Teamsters. Chuckie is not at home in the world of words. This document, he told me thirty years later, was by far the longest he ever penned. He spent several full days working on it in his Hallandale Beach, Florida, Teamsters conference room, rewriting draft after draft on tracing paper with spelling and grammar assistance from his boss, Teamsters vice president Joe Morgan. Here is what he wrote:

> Dear Jack:
>
> The fact that you took the time to sit down and write a letter to me means a great deal. I have read it over many times, and each time I become more confused.
>
> Nothing could change my love for you. Love isn't something that can be turned on and off at the drop of a hat—it is something that grows as two people grow together, sharing good times, hard times, laughter, tears, joy, and sorrow.
>
> A child or a son or daughter can never know the love a parent has for him or her until that child becomes a *parent*.
>
> Good parents continue to love their children, seeing their good points, as well as their faults. That love sometimes brings sorrow, hurt and heartache, as in our present situation.
>
> But more often than not that love brings happiness and love in return.
>
> Jack, if I live a hundred years I will never be able to understand your reason for changing your name. If you really feel as you say you feel that I am your father why don't you want my name? Why do you want your name to be different from your mother's name and your brother's [sic] name? If I am truly the only father you ever had why then do you want to change your name to that of a man who has given you no love, no consideration and who has played no part in your life except to bring trouble and heartache to your mother and all of the boys? These things I cannot understand. Neither can your mother understand.

In three months it *will* make a difference, it will still make a difference in three years or in thirty years. To think that you do not want the O'Brien name, for whatever reason, *hurts*—makes me sad—even makes me angry at times—but I still love you.

I cannot say that the *name change* will not affect our relationship. It cannot help but affect the relationship. That hurt will not go away easily—the pain will be there each time I see or hear "Jack Goldsmith"—it will ever be present.

I can handle it—I've had to handle many, many unpleasant things in my lifetime. I've endured heartache and sorrow—and although it won't be easy, I can handle this one more burden, so to speak.

However, your two younger brothers don't have the maturity to handle this. They are deeply hurt and concerned. The two little boys have watched your accomplishments and achievements wide-eyed, so proud of you, hoping they could follow in your academic footsteps. Now they are disillusioned. They don't know what to think. If this is love, do we need it? They are asking, how can you do this to your family? They wonder whether you want to be a part of our family any longer.

Like I said before, I can handle most anything. I have to. At this point in my life I try to stay calm and accept most anything. I have to. I'll try to stay calm and accept whatever comes my way.

Jack, your mother deserves more than this from you. Brenda Lou has all but given her life for you boys; she has made sacrifices very few mothers have had to make. Both material and physical, to say nothing of the emotional strains that have been put upon her. If ever a mother merited consideration, kindness, love and devotion, your mother does.

I hope you come to the realization of what effect this is having on her and I hope that realization comes before it is too late. You are a grown man, it is time in your life for you to make your own decisions. You must strive to make the right decisions, not only for you, but for those whose lives you touch.

Just remember, this one act touches many who love you and you
are the one who will have to live with your own decision—whether
it be right or wrong. It's your face you'll look at each morning in the
mirror. Be certain you can look into that mirror with pride, happiness
and few regrets. No one makes the right decision all the time. Your
goal should be to make as few wrong decisions as possible, especially
those decisions affecting the ones who *love you most*.

I love you with all of my heart and you will always be my son Jack.

Love your Dad (Chuck)

I read the letter quickly when it arrived, and it didn't move me. Chuckie
made clear that my name change was painful to my mother and brothers as
well as to him. But I was indifferent to his pleas. I was an entirely self-absorbed
twenty-one-year-old, focused on my prospects, my girlfriend, and not much
else.

My breach with Chuckie would not end with my name change; it would
go much deeper. I saw him only once on a brief trip home during the two
years I attended Oxford University before law school. When I attended
Yale in the fall of 1986, I didn't telephone him, and I was curt when he
called me.

I grew politically more conservative during my professionally formative
three years at Yale. I thought at the time it was a reaction to the political correctness in the New Haven air, and that was certainly part of it. But another
part, I now realize, was my unconscious effort to establish an identity contrary to Chuckie's. When I took a labor law class, I found myself rooting for
employers rather than workers and unions. I also became attracted to market
economics, which viewed labor unions as an inefficient cartel. And I came
down firmly on the side of law and order in my criminal procedure classes, a
disposition that made me think poorly of Chuckie's dismissive and contemp-
tuous attitude toward the "asshole" cops, "lying" FBI agents, "cocksucker"
prosecutors, and "no-good son of a bitch" judges who he believed ran the
legal system.

At Yale I began to think concretely about my career aims. I hoped to be a judicial clerk, a practicing attorney and law professor, and possibly a government lawyer. These ambitions were all informed by my desire not to be like Chuckie. And they seemed jeopardized by my association with Chuckie—an association that increasingly angered me, and one that, I told myself, I never sought.

One step to distance myself from him, at least psychologically, came in my choice of jobs after my second year in law school. I wanted to work in Washington, and because I was at Yale and had done well, I had lots of law firm offers for the summer. I chose Miller, Cassidy, Larroca & Lewin with Chuckie clearly in mind. Three of the four named partners in the firm had been intimately involved with Bobby Kennedy's efforts to put Hoffa in jail when I was an infant. (Miller supervised the Hoffa prosecutions as the head of the Criminal Division in RFK's Justice Department; Cassidy was in the labor and racketeering unit that investigated Hoffa; and Lewin was a brilliant young attorney on the prosecution team that convicted Hoffa.)

I never told anyone at Miller, Cassidy about my connections to Hoffa or Chuckie. But I got a thrill working among the men who were on the side of justice in putting Hoffa away. When I helped draft a brief for Nat Lewin, the Hoffa prosecution's "intellectual-in-residence," I believed that I was traveling a path that would take me as far from Chuckie as possible. And indeed I was.

A few months after my summer at Miller, Cassidy, and thinking about my future as an attorney, I decided to cut Chuckie out of my life completely. At that point I stopped visiting my mother when Chuckie was around. Every time he was named in the press in connection with Hoffa's disappearance or organized crime, I excoriated Brenda for being married to him. She divorced Chuckie in the late 1980s under pressure from me and other family members who detested the association (though she and Chuckie never separated, despite the nominal divorce). I never talked to Chuckie other than to ask to speak to my mother when he answered the telephone. Any time he came up in conversation with my mother or brothers or friends, I attacked him as a bad person—unreliable, criminal, stupid, and dishonest.

Chuckie had done nothing affirmatively to hurt me, and indeed had only ever shown me love. But ambition augmented by feelings of moral superiority blinded me to my true motives or to the effect of my actions on him or my family.

THE FIRST TEST of how my break from Chuckie would affect my career came more quickly than expected. After graduation from law school, I served as a law clerk for federal judge J. Harvie Wilkinson in Charlottesville, Virginia. The day I arrived for the job in August 1989, Judge Wilkinson asked me to work on a case involving a CIA officer accused of lying to federal investigators about the Iran-contra affair.

The case involved classified information, and to work on it I needed a security clearance. The security clearance forms asked about aliases and stepfathers. I listed Robert Rivet and Charles O'Brien, and noted that my name was "Jack Rivet" from age 8 through 13, and "Jack O'Brien" from age 13 through 21. I did not mention that "Charles O'Brien" was "Chuckie O'Brien," a central suspect in the Hoffa disappearance.

The FBI figured it out. On September 21, 1989, I went downstairs from Judge Wilkinson's chambers in the Charlottesville federal building to the local FBI office for what I thought was a standard security clearance interview. Decades later I would learn that the week before the interview, a search of my mother's name in the Justice Department's Organized Crime Information System tied me to Chuckie and set off alarm bells within the Bureau. The FBI director's office ordered a "Special Agent with experience with Organized Crime/Labor Racketeering" to interview me about my connection to Chuckie and his Italian friends. It also ordered the agent to ask whether I would be "willing to submit to a polygraph examination to dispel any concerns developed in this investigation regarding [Organized Crime] matters which might subject [me] to undue influence or coercion."

I had no inkling of what was about to happen when I walked into a windowless conference room where two baleful FBI agents in white shirts and blue ties rose to greet me. "Why didn't you disclose on your forms who Charles O'Brien was?" one of them asked, accusingly, as soon as I sat down. I was stunned, and assumed I was cooked because I had withheld pertinent information from the FBI.

After collecting myself, I explained that I had answered the questions fully and honestly, and did not know that I was supposed to say more about Chuckie. The agents then grilled me for several hours with aggressive questions about Chuckie's relationship with Anthony Giacalone and Anthony Provenzano, the details about my interactions with them (including a description of their homes and why Tony Pro had once given me a pool table as a gift), everything Chuckie had ever told me about Hoffa or his disappearance, and anything I remembered about every Teamsters official or organized crime figure I had ever met.

I don't remember much about what I told the FBI during that uncomfortable interview. But decades later I got my hands on the FBI official report about the interview:

> GOLDSMITH advised he lived with his mother and two brothers . . . when his mother married O'BRIEN. The candidate . . . accepted O'BRIEN as his father and even took the name O'BRIEN as his own last name.
>
> O'BRIEN was kind to GOLDSMITH, his mother, and brothers. However, O'BRIEN had no influence over GOLDSMITH since his value system was firmly in place by this time, according to GOLDSMITH.
>
> As time passed, GOLDSMITH stated his association with O'BRIEN turned to total disdain and disgust. He finally was very instrumental in causing his mother to divorce O'BRIEN. . . .
>
> O'BRIEN has introduced GOLDSMITH to TONY PROVENZANO, aka Tony Pro, and TONY GIACALONE. . . . GOLDSMITH did not know who they were at the time, being the late 1970s. GOLDSMITH advised that he had dinner at PROVENZANO's and GIACALONE's homes.
>
> The candidate advised he has no contact with O'BRIEN except if O'BRIEN should happen to answer the telephone when he (GOLDSMITH) is calling his mother. . . .
>
> GOLDSMITH stated "CHUCKIE" O'BRIEN has a complete disrespect for the law and the U.S. legal system to which he

(GOLDSMITH) is devoted. . . . GOLDSMITH advised he hopes he never sees or talks to "CHUCKIE" O'BRIEN again.

GOLDSMITH stated O'BRIEN totally denies the existence of the organization known as "the mob" or the Mafia. O'BRIEN has never discussed JAMES HOFFA's disappearance with GOLDSMITH. GOLDSMITH advised that O'BRIEN held HOFFA in a position of "almost reverence," and spoke most admiringly of him.

GOLDSMITH further stated that he would do almost anything to cause his mother and family to be relieved of any contact whatsoever with O'BRIEN. GOLDSMITH stated as a prosecutor he would like nothing better than to prosecute O'BRIEN for any illegal activities of which O'BRIEN could be found guilty.

GOLDSMITH advised he was so adamantly opposed to and angry at O'BRIEN that he would be most willing to do anything necessary to prove his feelings, including taking a polygraph examination to satisfy any investigation of himself regarding his allegiance or lack of allegiance to "CHUCKIE" O'BRIEN.

The FBI did a thorough investigation and my story checked out. It concluded that since my relationship to Chuckie was so well known, my breach with him so public and credible, and my character references so positive, I posed no threat as a blackmail target or subject of undue influence. I had tossed Chuckie under the bus. And to my amazement, I received a "Secret" security clearance in return.

Over the next thirteen years, my career progressed through a Supreme Court clerkship, private law practice in Washington, D.C., and law professorships at the universities of Virginia and Chicago. During this time I avoided speaking with Chuckie. In 1996, I eloped with Leslie Anne Williams, whom I met in Charlottesville. We had a small church wedding a few months later. I invited Brenda but not Chuckie, whom I continued to avoid even though my relationship with him was professionally irrelevant.

I finally spoke to Chuckie again at my mother's home in Boca Raton, Florida, in March 2001. Leslie and I were visiting Brenda with our eight-week-old son, Jack IV. During our prior visits to Brenda's home, Chuckie had made himself scarce out of respect for my wish not to see him. But this time Brenda insisted that Chuckie not leave the house because he was in such bad shape. Since I had last seen him, a government review board had expelled him from the Teamsters because of his ties to organized crime figures, depriving him of not only his livelihood but also big chunks of his identity and pride. He had suffered from diabetes for more than a decade, and the year before I saw him he had undergone quadruple bypass heart surgery. I could hardly ask Chuckie to leave the house under these circumstances, and I was keen for Brenda to meet her grandson. So I acquiesced.

"Hi, son," Chuckie said to me with enthusiasm as I walked into the house. He was standing in the entranceway, clearly thrilled to see me. I was shocked at how wan, thin, and timid he had grown. "Hi, Chuck," I said, awkwardly avoiding his attempt to hug me.

My mother-in-law, who was also in Boca Raton at the time, later reproved me for my behavior. "I couldn't believe how rude you were to Chuckie," she said. When I wasn't being rude, I kept my distance. And from that distance, I witnessed Chuckie's puppy-dog sweetness that I had experienced as a child. He helped bathe the baby, he was constantly in the kitchen preparing favorite meals, he ran errands incessantly, he made special dinner reservations for me and Leslie, and more.

It was hard to maintain anger in Chuckie's kind presence, especially because he had grown so frail. Indeed, it seemed hard-hearted to do so. For the first time since college, I began to question why I was treating him so badly. "He loves you so much, you should be kinder to him," said my wife, who couldn't understand why I was so angry.

I nonetheless maintained radio silence with Chuckie. I was glad I did when the following year I took a leave of absence from the University of Chicago to join the Bush administration as a special counsel to the Pentagon's top lawyer. For my work in the executive branch I needed a "Top Secret" security clearance. Hoping to avoid a repeat of my experience thirteen years earlier, I noted on the security forms that my former stepfather, Charles "Chuckie" O'Brien, was a suspect in Hoffa's disappearance but that I had barely seen or spoken to him in fifteen years.

Months passed after I turned in the forms, and I did not receive my clearance. I began to worry that I had a problem. Then one evening in December 2002, I answered a telephone call in the cramped apartment in Alexandria, Virginia, where we were living.

"Mr. Goldsmith, my name is Andrew Sluss," said the caller in a gruff but friendly voice. "I'm a Special Agent for the FBI in Detroit. I'm calling about your father, Charles O'Brien."

Sluss explained that he was assigned to the Hoffa case and that he believed that Chuckie was not involved in the disappearance. He had somehow learned that I was a lawyer, and he wanted my help in convincing Chuckie to take a lie detector test that, he said, would help clear his name.

I panicked. Getting a security clearance was vital to my job and to my growing ambition to be a top government national security lawyer. And now I was getting a call from an FBI agent who assumed that Chuckie was my father and that I was close enough to him to want to help clear him from suspicion in the Hoffa matter.

I first wondered, with a touch of paranoia, whether the improbable call was a trick by my background investigators to discern my true relationship with Chuckie. In the next instance I thought that even if Sluss had no connection to my background investigation, his assumption about my closeness to Chuckie was one I didn't want anyone in the government, especially in the FBI, to have. I thought for a moment about trying to help Chuckie. But my main impulse was to protect myself, and above all to make sure I got that clearance.

"Charles O'Brien is not my father," I said curtly to Sluss. "He's my former stepfather, and I've barely seen him in the last fifteen years." I added, "I'm sorry, I can't help you. Please don't call again." I hung up.

After the call I contacted my mother and tried to help her find a criminal defense attorney to advise Chuckie about whether he should take a lie detector test. But I did not contact or help him myself.

A few months later, I received the security clearance. Another bullet dodged. Career track preserved.

After eight months of service in the Department of Defense, President Bush's counsel, Alberto Gonzales, invited me to the White House to interview for the head of the Office of Legal Counsel in the Justice Department.

Previous occupants of the prestigious office included the Supreme Court justices William Rehnquist and Antonin Scalia, and I was thrilled to be considered. My interviewers for the job—Gonzales; Vice President Cheney's counsel, David Addington; and Gonzales's deputy, David Leitch—grilled me about national security law. At the end of the interview, Gonzales said that he intended to recommend that President Bush offer me the job. He then asked a standard question: Would anything in my background embarrass me or President Bush during the Senate confirmation process?

"There's one possible thing," I said. "My former stepfather is the leading suspect in Jimmy Hoffa's disappearance and has long been associated with the Mafia."

The three men's jaws dropped and their eyes bulged. I quickly explained that I had barely spoken to Chuckie in fifteen years and that the association with him had not prevented me from getting security clearances in the past. I nonetheless feared Chuckie would be a political deal-killer for such an important Senate-confirmed position, or might prevent me from receiving the much higher-level security clearances I needed for the job.

My fears proved to be groundless. The FBI did a thorough investigation and had no concerns, in large part, again, because my break with Chuckie had been so public and had persisted for so long. President Bush nominated me for the OLC job, the Senate confirmed me by unanimous consent, and I got the security clearances.

SOON AFTER I started the OLC job, I discovered to my astonishment that the government's enhanced interrogation and warrantless surveillance programs—two of the most important Bush administration initiatives in the fight against al-Qaeda—rested on defective legal foundations. I spent a harrowing nine months trying to bolster those foundations in the face of ongoing counterterrorism efforts and White House threats that my actions would get Americans killed.

The situation I faced was unprecedented, as were the actions I took. I eventually withdrew two of my predecessors' memos justifying "enhanced interrogation techniques." Those decisions caused understandable alarm in the White House and Central Intelligence Agency, since the ongoing program had been previously legally vetted and was deemed vital. The reaction to my legal decisions about interrogation paled next to the reaction to my conclusion that parts of the warrantless surveillance program were legally flawed and needed to cease. This decision led to historical constitutional clashes with Vice President Cheney, Alberto Gonzales, and other senior Bush officials—clashes that played out in the White House and at the foot of Attorney General John Ashcroft's bed in the intensive care unit at the George Washington University Hospital. It was by far the most difficult and stressful period of my life.

Throughout this ordeal I thought a lot about Chuckie and began the jagged process that would lead me to seek his forgiveness. An important step in the process was my accidental encounter with *O'Brien v. United States* from the Justice Department perch that I had reached only because I had renounced Chuckie. When I was a teenager, Chuckie had harshly criticized Attorney General Robert Kennedy for his abusive prosecutions and surveillance tactics against him, Jimmy Hoffa, Chuckie's mother, and his organized crime friends. He claimed that the Justice Department Kennedy ran was a self-serving institution staffed by Ivy Leaguers who under the guise of enforcing the law often broke it in secret and without consequence. As a teenager I swallowed this story whole. But in law school I had dismissed it as the baseless musings of a criminal.

Eight weeks into my job at OLC, I began to think that Chuckie's description of the early 1960s Justice Department was a generally apt description of the post-9/11 Justice Department. (I would later learn that his take on RFK also had a large element of truth.) I was knee-deep in a controversial government surveillance program that was difficult to square with congressional restrictions on government action but that was shielded from public view because the executive branch preferred it that way.

I had also just read an old Supreme Court decision that had vindicated Chuckie's claim of secret governmental overreaching not unlike what I was witnessing up close myself. It turned out that the Justice Department, as Chuckie had always said, was a dangerously powerful institution with surveillance and prosecution powers that, in pursuit of a righteous cause, were easy to abuse. Chuckie was not the tendentious ignoramus I once dismissed. And I was not nearly as smart as I had supposed.

Nor was I as virtuous as my condescending attitude toward Chuckie had assumed, as I began to realize when some people questioned the ethics of my own actions. My Justice Department job required me to dirty my hands with hard decisions about the meaning of complex laws on torture and surveillance. I pushed back against the White House in unprecedented ways on interrogation, information collection, and presidential power. Some important people at the time, starting with Cheney, thought I went way too far and was endangering national security. But I also suspected that other people outside government would think I had not pushed back enough, since I approved some elements of controversial programs. I also believed that my reputation would be jeopardized by mere association with these programs, no matter what I did.

These predictions all proved true. I would eventually be praised in many quarters for the actions I took in the Justice Department. But in the first few years after I left the Justice Department, when most of my decisions were not publicly known, I was excoriated as a lawbreaker, war criminal, and torture facilitator, and some of my new Harvard colleagues questioned whether I should have been hired. I was deeply distressed by these charges, which were so at odds with my self-image and what I thought I had done in government. But for several years I could not defend myself due to classified information and other restrictions.

The ironic connection between my predicament and Chuckie's was obvious. If I had not broken with him in what I increasingly realized was a self-serving effort to maintain my reputation and advance my career, I wouldn't have reached a pinnacle of power that now seemed possibly destructive to my reputation and my career. It wasn't long before I was identifying with Chuckie's decades-long fight to salvage his reputation in the face of what he viewed as baseless public charges. Despite what the FBI and the Hoffa books said, and despite his questionable associations, I never believed Chuckie was involved in killing the man he so obviously revered. But Chuckie lacked the rhetorical, financial, and other tools needed to fight back against the public charges against him. I began to appreciate

Chuckie's frustration, and to understand, at least in a small way, what he had been through.

Other forces led me to question my renunciation of Chuckie. I had been a weak-tea Christian all my life, but during my agonizing time in government I began to pray intensely and regularly, and to read the Bible with more focus. "Judge not, that you be not judged" was one of Jesus Christ's central messages. I began to obsess about the speck of sawdust I had seen for nearly twenty years in Chuckie's eye and the rather large plank I was now noticing in my own.

I also began to recognize that Chuckie had been right, again, when he had said in his 1984 letter that "a child or a son or a daughter can never know the love a parent has for him or her until that child becomes a *parent*." Over the years my mother had made clear to me how deeply I had hurt Chuckie by breaking with him. But it was my primal love for my young sons, and the joy and vulnerability that love brought, that really caused me to understand how devastating my renunciation of Chuckie must have been. Fatherhood on top of everything else led me to feel terrible about what I had done to the man who had been a wonderful father to me and who was now growing old.

My reconciliation with Chuckie came quietly during Christmas vacation in 2004, six months after I resigned from the Justice Department, when my wife and I and our two sons visited Brenda in Florida. Chuckie was there, and this time I was kind. I gave him a hug when I saw him, we spoke frequently during the visit, we cooked and shopped together, and I indulged (rather than criticized) his malapropisms and puffed-up anecdotes. My toddlers had begun to call him "Pappy," the perfect name for the tough guy who once pummeled scabs and ran Hoffa's interference but who was now gentle and vulnerable.

The night before we returned to Boston, Chuckie and I were watching *Seinfeld* in the white-tiled television room in my mother's condominium in Boca Raton. During a commercial, I turned to Chuckie and apologized.

"I was wrong and selfish to treat you as I did all these years," I said, without preface. "I hope you will forgive me."

Chuckie looked at me for a bit, seemingly puzzled, his ashen face quivering and his hollow eyes watering.

"You don't need to apologize, son," he said. "I understand why you did what you did."

And that was that. Chuckie accepted me back into his life without qualification, rancor, or drama. For the rest of his life, he acted as if those twenty years hadn't happened.

TWO

LOYALTIES

C HUCKIE AND I SAT DOWN for the first of hundreds of conversations for this book in the spring of 2012, in the same television room where we had reconciled years earlier. He was wearing cut-off sweatpants and a University of Tennessee T-shirt, lying in a black leather recliner with a medical boot on to protect his diabetes-damaged left foot. I was in my mother's white upholstered reading chair to Chuckie's right, angled toward him. Across from us was a thirty-two-inch television embedded in a wall crowded with three long shelves of variously sized photographs of family and friends.

By this point Chuckie and I had grown close again—as close as we were when I was a boy, though in a different way based on our very different stations in life. I didn't worship him in the innocent way I had as a teenager. Yet I loved him more deeply than ever—for what he had done for me when I was a young man, and for his forgiveness, untiring love, and ineffable goodness despite his many flaws.

Chuckie, in turn, teemed with pride to be my father again. He had little patience for "egghead" professors and even less for former Justice Department officials. The only law he believed in was the law of the street. But for me he made an exception. He started wearing a Harvard baseball cap and would often brag about his son who taught there.

At the outset I understood little about Chuckie's life. We had talked a lot over the years about the Hoffa disappearance. But I didn't know enough then to ask the right questions. And I had only a scattered sense about the four-decade backstory to the disappearance—Chuckie's upbringing, how he came to know Hoffa and scores of organized crime figures, and his relationships with both. I also had no expectation about what broader themes might emerge from our talks.

One large theme, it would turn out, was staring at me from the sea of picture frames. On the bottom shelf to the right of the television, squarely facing Chuckie's eyeline, was a picture of Jimmy Hoffa. It was taken outside his cottage in Lake Orion, Michigan, near Detroit, about a year before he disappeared. Hoffa wore a close-fitting yellow sports shirt that emphasized his unusually thick chest and shoulders. His short graying hair was brushed back, and he wore a proud grin on his still-chiseled face as he hugged his dazed-looking wife, Josephine. Next to his head, in the lower left corner of the frame, Chuckie had decades earlier placed a small Catholic devotion. "Cease, the heart of Jesus is with me, Sacred heart of Jesus thy Kingdom come," it read.

Two shelves above Hoffa's picture, and also turned to face Chuckie's recliner, was a larger photograph of Anthony Giacalone. It was taken in the late 1970s, a few years after he allegedly arranged for his old friend Jimmy Hoffa's disappearance. Giacalone was standing tall behind a dinner chair, wearing a sienna-brown three-piece Brioni suit, a dark brown pocket handkerchief, and a multipatterned brown-and-white tie. He wore a sinister half smile on a face dominated by a high, bald forehead and oversize darkened glasses that made him look remarkably like Junior Soprano.

These were pictures of the two father figures and major influences in Chuckie's life. Chuckie met both men when he was nine years old, when the Teamsters union and La Cosa Nostra were just developing into national powerhouses, and at a time when Hoffa and Giacalone were beginning a decades-long friendship that would benefit both organizations. The two men represented the worlds of labor and organized crime that Chuckie successfully straddled from the time he was a boy until those worlds collided on July 30, 1975, with ruinous consequences for both, and for Chuckie.

CHUCKIE HAD EVEN more complex father issues than I did—starting with questions about his father's identity.

Chuckie told anyone who asked that he did not know his father, "Frank," who Chuckie claimed was killed on a picket line when he was three years old. Most people who knew Chuckie thought this was a ruse. "O'Brien was generally considered by Teamster officials, underworld figures, and government agents to be Hoffa's real son," notes Dan Moldea in his 1978 book *The Hoffa Wars*.

For most of my life I wasn't sure, since Chuckie always spoke about Hoffa in worshipful terms and always deflected questions about his father. I finally learned the truth when I dug up Chuckie's birth certificate, his parents' marriage license, and other historical records. And only then did Chuckie tell me, with a mixture of pride and shame, what he remembered and was told about his father.

Chuckie's father was also named Charles Lenton O'Brien. Charles was the son of a St. Louis boilermaker whose family emigrated from County Cork, Ireland, in the early nineteenth century. He was a naughty boy, first arrested at age five after he stole a neighbor's horse and buggy. Charles committed dozens of petty robberies and other misdemeanors over the next decade until, at age fifteen, he was convicted for assault and robbery involving the shooting of a policeman. That crime led him to be incarcerated for five years in the Reform School for Boys in Boonville, Missouri, a juvenile detention institution infamous for taking in young criminals and making them much worse.

Charles was released from Boonville at age twenty, one year into the Great Depression. He was a quiet man with few talents beyond the rudimentary Sicilian he learned from some of his friends at Boonville and an aptitude for whistling tunes that earned him the nickname "Bing." But Charles would land on his feet, at least for a bit. "My father was a tough little motherfucker," Chuckie told me. "He would put your lights out in two seconds, and that's why they sent him to Kansas City." Chuckie never explained who "they" were. But the city across the state from St. Louis was a natural choice for a young man with Charles's skill set.

Kansas City in the early 1930s was a lawless meld of machine politics, gambling joints, all-night saloons, and outlaw refugees. It was also an outpost for Italian organized crime, which emerged there just after the turn of the century much as it did across the nation. More than four million poor Italian and Sicilian immigrants arrived in the United States from 1880 to 1924, clustered in major cities around the country. In Kansas City they usually arrived via the port of New Orleans and settled near the Holy Rosary Church on the North End. A handful of the new immigrants smuggled in the old country's criminal traditions. At first they preyed on fellow Italians with extortionist letters marked with a bloody dagger in a black hand and backed up by credible threats of murder. The North End was known around the country as a center of Black Hand crime.

During National Prohibition, from 1920 to 1933, Black Hand gangs in Kansas City and other cities developed into disciplined criminal organizations. Because booze was outlawed, its distribution and sale depended on an elaborate system of underworld governance enforced by private violence and largely tolerated, usually for a price, by upperworld cops and prosecutors. The same factors undergirded gambling, prostitution, and other vices.

When Charles arrived in Kansas City in 1930, he fell in with a young crime soldier named Charlie Binaggio. A 1963 FBI memorandum described Charles as Binaggio's "chauffeur," but Chuckie has a richer description. "My father was protecting Binaggio," Chuckie told me. "He was a bodyguard. He was a shooter. And a driver." Charles also helped Binaggio with his gambling operations in Kansas City and elsewhere, and as a front pumped gas at a service station Binaggio controlled near Little Italy.

Charles got to know Chuckie's mother, Sylvia Pagano, when she would walk by the service station where Charles sometimes worked on her way from Manual High School to her home in the North End of Kansas City. Sylvia was an olive-skinned, dark-haired girl who wore elegant dresses made by her mother, a seamstress at Woolf Brothers. She also had blood connections to the Italian families who ran the gambling and loan-sharking operations in Kansas City.

"My mother had a grandfather and an uncle that were old-time moustache guys," Chuck recalls. A "moustache guy" is Chuckie's term for a "moustache Pete"—an elderly traditionalist, usually born in Italy, who is strong in a crime family. "We used to call them that when we were kids and didn't know too much," he explained to me. "Later we'd call the old-time guys 'short coats' because they were little guys and their suits had short coats."

Sylvia's short-coat grandfather, Paolo Campo, was a cheesemaker from the Old Country who also served as a "mediator" to settle grievances between Sicilian clans. "My great-grandfather had a tremendous reputation of honor," Chuckie told me. So too did Sylvia's uncle Mariano Scaglia. The earliest Mafia memoir recounts that Mariano and other relatives, following a violent crime family dispute in Colorado in 1922, "fled to Kansas City seeking the protection of the local *capo*." Scaglia eventually became a "big man" in Kansas City during Prohibition, Chuckie told me.

It must have been unusual for a Sicilian girl with these relations to wed the Irish Charles, even with his Sicilian connections. The marriage license indicates that the couple married on November 4, 1932, when she was eighteen and he was twenty-two. They almost certainly eloped, since a justice of the peace in a rural town forty miles south of Kansas City performed the service on a Friday, the same day that they applied for their license.

A few days before his eighty-second birthday, I told Chuckie I had discovered the circumstances of his parents' marriage. He was in a private room at the Cleveland Clinic hospital in Weston, Florida, where he had been hospitalized due to complications with his diabetes. I had found him there in a blue mood.

"Was my mother pregnant with me?" he asked with an anguished mien that revealed seventy-five years of cumulative ignorance, confusion, and dishonor about his father.

I was happy to report that the answer to the question was no. Chuckie's birth certificate states that he was born thirteen months later, on December 20, 1933, in St. Vincent's Hospital in Kansas City. It lists his parents as Sylvia Pagano and Charles Lenton O'Brien.

Chuckie has few memories of his father, who skipped town forever when Chuckie was seven years old. Sylvia never talked about why Charles left, and Chuckie doesn't remember him leaving. He simply vanished, just as my father did when I was Chuckie's age. Chuckie's aunt Rosella told him that his father ran into trouble with some of Binaggio's colleagues and fled to the West Coast. In 1947 Charles was found hanging from the loft in a Beverly Hills apartment. The coroner deemed it a suicide. Chuckie bristled at this account since it made his father seem unmanly. With the picket-line story blown, he reverted to claiming that Charles was murdered in retaliation for deeds done in Kansas City.

Soon after her husband disappeared in the late 1930s, Sylvia moved to Detroit, whose Motor City economy was reviving after the Depression, in search of a new life and better job opportunities. In a pattern that would recur throughout Chuckie's childhood, Sylvia sent her young son to live with relatives—on this occasion, in Denver—while she focused on business. The pretty granddaughter of Paolo Campo used an introduction from Uncle Mariano to get a job in the office at the produce terminal of William "Black Bill" Tocco, one of the founders of Detroit's Italian crime family. But the job at Tocco's was temporary, and Sylvia needed to find her own way.

"My mother was in the business of wanting to make money, and you didn't make money with some square company," Chuckie told me. She was smart, charming, and resourceful. But her defining characteristic—one she developed during her years married to Chuckie's father—was her grit.

"She was a lady, but she was tough, and whatever it would take to get it done, she would do it," Chuckie told me. "My mother had big balls. In those days most women were intimidated. She wasn't—I don't care who it was. If she had to do something, if somebody asked her to do something, she wasn't suicidal, but she'd get the job done."

These qualities attracted Owen "Bert" Brennan, a fierce former truck driver from Chicago who had become a Teamsters union organizer in Detroit in 1934. Brennan probably met Sylvia when he was trying to organize truckers and loaders at Tocco's terminal. He hired her to do the types of union jobs then available to women—clerical work, walking picket lines, and "salting," the term for gaining employment in nonunionized workplaces with the aim of organizing from the inside.

"In those days we didn't have all the shit that unions now have to go through," Chuckie told me, alluding to the legal intricacies that weigh down modern labor law. "My mother would get a job in the bakery, in A&P and Kroger's, or in a potato chip factory, and start signing people up."

Through this work Sylvia met Brennan's brash young Teamster colleague, Jimmy Hoffa, whom she would soon introduce to her new Sicilian friends.

HOFFA WAS BORN on Valentine's Day, 1913, in Brazil, Indiana, a coal mining town of about 10,000. His mother, Viola, raised him, his brother, and his two sisters alone after Hoffa's father, John, a Pennsylvania Dutch coal prospector, died of a black-lung-induced stroke when Hoffa was seven.

Viola was stern and moralistic—a "staunch Baptist mean motherfucker," according to Chuckie, who knew her well. She held three jobs after her husband died, including a home laundry business, and never sought or accepted handouts even though the family lived from meal to meal. Jimmy helped with the laundry by splitting kindling for the stove, filling the coal scuttle, and collecting and delivering loads. He and his brother gathered wild fruit and hunted birds, rabbits, and squirrels for the dinner table.

The poor neighborhoods where Hoffa did these tasks were grim even by the standards of the day. "The culture of Brazil expressed the pain and desperation created by its economy," says the historian Thaddeus Russell. Hoffa's blue-collar neighborhood in Brazil was dotted with saloons, and "violence, suicides, drunkenness, prostitution, and gambling were common features of everyday life." The Little Italy area of nearby Clinton, Indiana, where Viola moved her family in 1922, was no better. Clinton was a bootlegging center during Prohibition that developed in the 1920s into "one of the roughest towns in the Midwest," according to Russell. It is probably where Hoffa first encountered Italian organized crime, which operated there, and labor strikes, which the United Mine Workers often called, usually with an armed response from management and the cops.

In 1924, Viola moved the family to Detroit in search of the same things Sylvia Pagano would seek sixteen years later: a steadier job and better wages. Viola worked long hours polishing radiator caps at the Fisher Body plant and washed laundry in her spare time. Hoffa worked odd jobs on weekends and evenings to help his mother. He also got in fights. When he first moved to Detroit, a group of Polish boys taunted him and his brother, Billy. "We learned that unless you were willing to fall into line and accept the pecking order of an existing clan, you had to establish your right to maintain your own private domain," Hoffa later recalled. "This was accomplished by bloody noses and shiners, but finally we won acceptance into the neighborhood youth's social order." The same philosophy would later guide Hoffa in his confrontations with recalcitrant employers, rival unions, and the federal government.

The young Hoffa also absorbed his mother's Protestant ethic. He loved to work from the time he was a child, and he would always live frugally, even in the years when his Teamsters office looked out on the nation's capital and he was surrounded by suitcases full of cash. Hoffa never smoked or drank, and he looked down on others who did. He embraced what he described as his mother's "remarkable independence, responsibility, resourcefulness, and steadfastness."

It is little surprise that a young man with these values, in his family's circumstances, would quit school after ninth grade and go to work full-time. In 1927, the fourteen-year-old Hoffa began work as a stock boy at Frank & Cedar's Dry Goods and General Merchandise, earning $12 each week for sixty hours of work. He loved the job and his co-workers. His bosses told him he had great prospects there, and the future labor leader dreamed of running the store one day.

But then the stock market crashed in October 1929, hitting Detroit harder than any city in the country. The automobile industry collapsed, and with it the city's jobs. One-third of the Detroit workforce was unemployed within a year, and Hoffa's prospects at Frank & Cedar's suddenly looked bleak. Taking the advice of a co-worker that the food business was a more secure place to work because people had to eat, Hoffa got a job through friends at a Kroger warehouse near his home.

If Hoffa's happy days working at Frank & Cedar's would later inform his sometimes-cozy relationship with employers, his job at Kroger at the height of the Depression would teach him the need for unions and make him a labor leader. He worked the night shift, unloading freight cars of fresh produce at thirty-two cents per hour. With Detroit's economy still shrinking, with tent cities, public begging, and garbage-eating growing, and with no public welfare to cushion the blow, Hoffa was lucky to have a job. But conditions were gruesome. The workers lacked job security and were paid only for the hours they loaded and unloaded, which meant that they often hung around the warehouse all night for just a few hours' pay.

Making matters much worse was the foreman, Al Hastings, a cruel, dictatorial screamer who took pleasure in taunting the workers and firing men on a whim—"the kind of guy who causes unions," as Hoffa later said. Hoffa and the other workers tolerated Hastings's "outrageous meanness" because the alternative—joining long lines of starving men and women begging for a few hours of paid work—seemed worse. But by the spring of 1931, after Hastings fired two workers for no apparent reason, the situation had become intolerable. Hoffa and four other workers decided to form a union.

The idea was risky to the point of irresponsible. Unions aim to establish a cartel among workers at a firm in order to extract from employers wage, benefit, and workplace protections above what the free labor market would provide. This was not a popular idea in 1931, especially in Detroit, which a contemporary observer described as "the open shop capital of America." Nor was it easy to achieve, since unions at the time had no legal protections, and employers, backed by politicians, police, and hired strikebreakers, fiercely resisted nascent union movements. If Hoffa and his friends had simply presented their grievances, Hastings would have quickly fired and easily replaced them.

The men went forward in a different way. One hot May evening, on

Hoffa's cue, they stopped transferring crates of fresh strawberries from a refrigerated car into a trailer, and left them on the loading docks. Hastings barked orders and threatened to fire the men. But the strikers stood firm. As the strawberries began to wilt, Hastings folded and called his supervisor, who agreed to meet with Hoffa over the men's grievances if they returned to work. Over the days that followed, the five "strawberry boys" negotiated a one-year contract that recognized their union, guaranteed a half-day's pay, and established modest work rules.

Hoffa spent the next few years working at the warehouse and for the fledgling Kroger union until he and Hastings had a final confrontation that caused Hoffa to leave. The next day, Joint Council 43 of the International Brotherhood of Teamsters, which had been trying for years to organize the Kroger warehouse, offered him a job as a business agent for Detroit Local 299. The union had emerged at the turn of the century to represent the rough-and-tumble teaming trade. By the early 1930s it had developed into a fragmented and poorly run affiliate of the American Federation of Labor with 40,000 members nationwide, most of whom were inner-city haulers of specialized products (like coal and ice) transitioning from horse-drawn to motor vehicles. Local 299 had only a few hundred members and was near bankruptcy. It offered Hoffa no salary, but rather a portion of the dues of each new member he signed up.

At age twenty-one, and still living with his mother, the squat, muscular Hoffa—by then a dense five feet six inches and 170 pounds—had found his calling. He had worked for a mean-spirited boss and experienced what he later described as the workingman's "constant insecurity, his pointless frustrations, his perpetual submersion in a pool of hopelessness." For the rest of his life Hoffa identified with struggling workers and possessed an angry intensity about righting power imbalances in the workplace.

HOFFA JOINED THE American labor movement at a propitious time. The movement had lost millions of union members during the prosperous 1920s and had weakened further during the first three years of the Depression. But American unions changed direction sharply in 1934, and would triple their membership in the next six years. An unprecedented militancy among workers instigated the era. In every industry and trade, desperate men and women at the height of the Depression banded together to wield economic and physical power, often through violence, to overcome the traditional tools of business resistance on shop floors and picket lines.

The New Deal architects sought to channel this militancy into peaceful industrial relations. The key legislation was the 1935 Wagner Act, labor's "Magna Carta," which recognized workers' rights to form unions and bargain collectively, outlawed unfair employer labor practices, and established an administrative body to guarantee these and other worker protections. "President Roosevelt wants you to join a union," declared John L. Lewis, the head of the United Mine Workers, following passage of the Wagner Act, and millions of workers did so. That same year, Lewis helped found the progressive Congress of Industrial Organizations, an umbrella group that rejected the AFL's orientation toward skilled craft workers and sparked huge increases in the unionization of mass production workers.

In the decade of labor's resurgence, the trucking industry grew rapidly in step with advances in motorized and refrigerated vehicles, the pneumatic tire, and the expansion of surfaced highways, which surpassed the million-mile mark in 1938. But truck driving was brutal work. "It grinds you down and takes your body apart," Chuckie once explained. Both the roads and the trucks were life-threateningly hazardous, even after the pneumatic tire became prevalent. So were the loading and unloading that truckers typically had to do. Driving required constant concentration. And over-the-road trucking, which was increasingly prevalent, was lonely because long haulers typically spent weeks at a time on the road.

Hoffa had an affinity for the individualistic and resilient workers typically attracted to such jobs, and an unusual talent for organizing them and improving their lives. In the 1930s he rose to dominate the Teamsters union in Michigan, whose ranks swelled from a few hundred short-haul truck drivers at the beginning of the decade to more than 20,000 drivers of every sort, and other workers, by the dawn of World War II. "By 1942, less than a decade after its origin as a struggling, rough-and-tumble outfit, the Detroit Teamsters organization had become a force in the Motor City rivaled only by the United Automobile Workers," writes Russell. Hoffa was rewarded with the positions of president of Local 299 in 1937, negotiating chairman of the Central States Drivers Council in 1940, and president of the Michigan conference of Teamsters in 1942.

Hoffa's success had little to do with the legalisms of the Wagner Act, for which he had little patience or need, or the birth of the CIO, with which he would often clash. It was attributable, rather, to skills and tactics for which he would later become famous—convincing personal pitches to the rank and file, intimate knowledge of trucking economics, dictatorial centralization of collective bargaining, relentless expansion of the bargaining unit, and a preternatural talent for negotiation. But more than anything else in the 1930s, Hoffa succeeded because he learned to deploy violent force successfully.

In no city was the labor militancy of the 1930s more violent than Detroit, and no union in Detroit was more violent than the Teamsters. Hoffa's elders taught him that an efficient way to organize a nonunion trucking company was to threaten to blow up its rigs or terminals and then follow through if necessary. Hoffa and his Teamster friends also used baseball bats, chains, and fists against the thugs whom companies hired to resist his unionization efforts. "Mob guys had muscle, and where in hell do you think employers got the tough guys when they wanted to break a strike?" Hoffa once noted. "They hired thugs who were out to get us, and Brother, your life was in your hands every day," he said another time. "There was only one way to survive—fight back. And we used to slug it out on the streets."

The fights also usually involved the police or National Guard, which invariably sided with management. "The police would beat your brains in for even talking union," Hoffa said. "The cops harassed us every day. If you went on strike, you had your head broken." Hoffa was not exaggerating. He was frequently beaten, often arrested, and sometimes convicted in the 1930s, which the historian Arthur Schlesinger Jr. accurately described as "a savage decade for labor."

The distinctive lessons that Jimmy Hoffa learned from his brutal early labor experiences would guide him for the rest of his days. He learned that "respectable" employers used hired heavies in labor disputes, and he would soon adopt the same tactic himself. He learned that the courts and cops were the enemies of labor, and were often on the take.

But more than anything else, he learned that "every day of the average individual is a matter of survival," as he explained to the newscaster David Brinkley in 1963. "If by chance he should go from home to work and have an accident, lose an arm or a leg or an eye, he's just like an animal wounded in the jungle. He's out. Life isn't easy. Life is a jungle."

This outlook spawned in Hoffa an unvarnished social Darwinism that led him to pursue superior power—especially economic and physical power—at all costs. Hoffa was nonideological in the pursuit of power, and he believed that the ends of enhancing the union's strength (and his own) justified any means. He would trade for power in any currency, with any person, from any quarter, if it brought him an advantage. "He didn't care what it would take to do it or who he had to use," Chuckie told me. "He would say to me, 'If I had to deal with Hitler, I'd deal with Hitler, when it comes to our members.'"

It was this amoral and opportunistic pursuit of power that led Hoffa to seek assistance from the criminal underworld.

LABOR UNIONS WERE not the only private organizations seeking to bring order to the ravages of laissez-faire capitalism in the 1930s. So too, in a different way, was the criminal underworld. And no underworld group was more successful than the Italians.

The organization that became known as the "Mafia," "La Cosa Nostra," "LCN," or (as Chuckie often calls it) "the Outfit" or "the Company," grew out of Prohibition. In major cities around the nation, as in the Kansas City of Sylvia Pagano's youth, Italian gangs in the 1920s evolved into disciplined entrepreneurial groups that peddled liquor and other vices. The most notorious ones in this era included Al Capone's in Chicago and those of the Sicilian old-timers Salvatore Maranzano and Giuseppe Masseria in New York. Toward the end of the decade, these groups had violent clashes with their Jewish and Irish competitors, and internecine clashes as well, in efforts to consolidate power. A defining battle, known as the "Castellammarese War," began in New York in 1930 between the Maranzano and Masseria clans. Dozens of gangsters in both groups were killed in combat until the thirty-three-year-old Charles

"Lucky" Luciano brought peace in 1931 by arranging for both leaders to be killed.

Lucky Luciano was the most consequential mafioso in the twentieth century. He was born in Palermo, Sicily, and came to New York as a young boy. Unlike the generation of leaders he knocked off, the pockmarked, scar-faced Luciano spoke English and valued profits and order over clan affiliation. Building on an initiative by Maranzano, Luciano recognized New York's five independent Italian crime families, one of which he headed. He and Capone then organized a meeting of leaders from around the country in Chicago in late 1931. The men decided to recognize the independence of each family and set their membership sizes at 1931 levels in order to preserve rough equality. They also established a national governing structure known as "the Commission."

The Commission originally consisted of the heads of New York's Five Families, Capone, and Stefano Magaddino from Buffalo. It had "no direct executive power," but was rather "an agent of harmony" that "could arbitrate disputes brought before it," as Joseph Bonanno, the head of the eponymous New York family and an original Commission member, later explained. Each family had a boss or "Father," an underboss, an advisor-mediator known as the consigliere, managers called caporegimes, and soldiers who, in exchange for status, protection, and dispute resolution, paid upward much of the cash generated from their various criminal enterprises. The Chicago gathering also agreed to norms borrowed from the Old Country that each family, with local variations, adopted. Membership was restricted to Sicilians or southern Italians and was governed by strict rules of loyalty, honor, and manliness, the most important of which was Omertà.

The Mafia emerged from Prohibition at the height of the Great Depression brimming with cash, confidence, and a disciplined organizational structure that would generate billions in secret profits over the next five decades. It continued to dominate the liquor industry even after alcohol became legal in 1933, and it expanded its gambling, narcotics, prostitution, and loan-sharking businesses as the upperworld economy disintegrated. Another major and growing source of income came from its connections with the American labor unions, which were also rising to national power. Italian criminal organizations had long hired out muscle to businesses trying to break union strikes and, less often, to unions trying to fight back. But the real value of unions to the mob, and the primary basis for their long-term relationship, lay in the ways that unions could facilitate racketeering.

A "racket" is the catchall phrase for a corrupt business enterprise infiltrated by organized crime, including shakedowns, protection, forced participation in an employer organization, mob takeovers, and the like. Rackets tend to flourish in decentralized low-wage industries like warehouse work, groceries, fresh food, garments, laundry, construction, garbage, and trucking. These and similar trades require little skill or capital for entry. Competition is savage, and profits paper-thin. These circumstances created a great demand from employers and workers alike for order, and presented endless opportunities for the mob to use coercion and extortion to tame the market and reap profit. "One must remember that in the economic sphere one of the objectives of a Family was to set up monopolies as far as it was possible," said Bonanno.

When employers invited hoodlums to eliminate cutthroat business competition or threats from unions, the hoodlums sometimes stayed on, "not as hired specialists but as partners," as the historian Humbert Nelli explained. Other times the mob muscled its way in by creating an employers' association that businesses in a territory were forced to join for a fee that the mob pocketed along with its skim of the resulting monopoly returns. Many employers and workers—the ones who survived—were pleased to pay for the stability the mob brought to prices and the market. In these and other ways, rackets were, as the journalist Walter Lippmann put it in 1931, "perversions of the search for economic security, a diseased compensation in the lower reaches of capitalism for the instability of proletarian life, and the terrific struggle for existence." They brought a kind of order to the lower reaches of society that the state was unable to achieve.

This order grew most menacing when the mob sought to pervert unions to assist in its monopolistic aims. Control of a union local gave a mobster access to its dues-filled coffers. Unions also served as a "legitimate" vehicle to coerce businesses by threatening labor strikes or slowdowns. The Teamsters union was especially attractive to the mob. Its locals were relatively easy to infiltrate because they had unusual autonomy from the national organization. And just about every industry where rackets prevailed relied on trucking services that LCN could deploy as leverage points. Several Teamsters union locals came under mob control toward the end of Prohibition. Before he went to prison for tax evasion in 1932, Al Capone co-opted a few Teamsters locals in Chicago, which he used to extract revenues from industries ranging from milk delivery to dry cleaning to hotels. In New York, the Lucchese family was most rapacious in infiltrating Teamsters unions to control rackets in industries ranging from airport services to garments.

The family in Detroit was mostly an exception to the labor racketeering trends in New York, Chicago, and elsewhere. It emerged in 1931 when Black Bill Tocco's eastside "River Gang" defeated its westside Italian rivals by arranging for the murder of their leader, Chet LaMare. Tocco's friend Joseph Zerilli became Detroit's boss when Tocco went to prison for tax evasion in 1936. The Detroit family in the 1930s focused heavily on gambling and loansharking, and also on drugs and prostitution. But it did not have close relations with the fledgling labor unions in town. To the extent it got involved in labor matters at the time, it was to hire out its muscle in labor disputes, initially to employers. Which was how it encountered Jimmy Hoffa.

ALMOST EVERY ACCOUNT of how the Detroit family first linked up with Hoffa and the Detroit Teamsters attributes the introduction to Chuckie's mother, Sylvia. Sylvia had become close to the leaders of the Detroit family through her connections in Kansas City and her entrée at Tocco's produce warehouse. She made the introduction, according to Chuckie, during a famous labor battle in Detroit in 1941. The Teamsters had called a strike in April after the Detroit Lumber Company refused to grant union recognition, and sympathy strikes soon shut down construction work in the city. Fights broke out at construction sites and lumberyards as nonunion drivers sought to move through picket lines. The scabs had plenty of company-hired help, including, Chuckie says, a crew of Sicilian men led by twenty-two-year-old Anthony Giacalone.

Uncle Tony was born in an Italian neighborhood on the east side of

Detroit on January 19, 1919, the first of his Sicilian immigrant parents' seven children. As a boy during Prohibition, Giacalone worked with his father, Giacamo, who peddled fruits and vegetables. "Uncle Tony's father had a wagon with produce on it," Chuckie told me, "and he would sell to all the millionaires going up Jefferson Avenue, the Fords, the Chryslers, and all them." Giacalone was probably introduced to the Detroit family through his father's cousin, who was a member of the River Gang during Prohibition. As a teenager Uncle Tony ran errands for family bookmakers. By his early twenties he was an occasional driver for boss Joseph Zerilli. He was also a street enforcer who, among other things, organized the dirty work when companies paid his bosses to break up strikes.

"Uncle Tony was young and they were kicking the shit out of the strikers and bringing the trucks out," Chuckie told me. On May 12, 1941, a Teamster picket named Arthur Queasbarth was killed by a brick thrown at his head, probably by someone in Uncle Tony's crew. The event quickly became a test of Hoffa's leadership, not just because of Queasbarth's death and Hoffa's fight with the lumber companies, but also because a rival union backed by the increasingly powerful CIO was trying to poach Teamsters drivers and loaders as part of its campaign to destroy the union altogether.

"He knew that the only way he could win was to get an army together and he did it and he didn't care a shit who he'd deal with," Chuckie told me. "But he didn't have the financial money to buy people."

Chuckie says that Hoffa sought advice from Bert Brennan, his chief lieutenant and closest friend. Brennan advised Hoffa to talk to "Facci," the Sicilian word for "face," which was Sylvia's nickname on account of her beautiful visage. Hoffa did so. Sylvia then set up a meeting between Hoffa and Detroit family figures (probably Angelo Meli and Santo Perrone), and advised Hoffa about how to act. "Being a hillbilly, he thought all that Italian shit was pokydory," Chuckie told me. "He didn't understand all the formalities and all that, he thought it was all bullshit."

Chuckie doesn't know where the baby-faced but burly twenty-eight-year-old labor leader met the minatory gangsters. Nor does he know exactly what transpired. But he says the Italians agreed to help Hoffa rather than his enemies. And in exchange Hoffa allowed them to grab an occasional scab truck that he let leave the yard. "When you got a full load of lumber, that was big money in those days," Chuckie told me. With the help of his new friends, Hoffa won the lumber strike with better wages and work conditions, crushed the CIO offensive, and went on to other productive arrangements. And thus was born a fateful new relationship—fateful for Hoffa, for the American labor movement, and for Chuckie.

Hoffa's lifelong indifference to the taboos associated with organized crime was shaped by his early experiences fighting thugs hired by employers. "I've never been able to understand why the finger is pointed at us in the Teamsters—and only at us—that we knew mobsters and hoodlums," he said late in his life. "Mob people are known by employers and employers' associations much better than we ever knew them and employers always were the first to employ them." This understanding that Hoffa formed in the 1930s stuck with him. For the rest of his life Hoffa self-servingly but genuinely viewed attacks on his increasingly dense mob associations as discriminatory and hypocritical.

IN TELLING THE tale of Sylvia's introduction of Jimmy Hoffa to the Detroit Mafia, many writers refer to Sylvia as Hoffa's former mistress.

"Never happened," Chuckie told me many times.

"It would be better for our story if it did," I once joked.

"Yeah, but it didn't happen," he replied. "He was so bashful around women; as tough a leader as he was, he was very shy. My mother would be very particular if she is going to have an affair with somebody, and it ain't going to be him."

There is no way to know for sure, but the cold facts appear to support Chuckie. Hoffa was diffident around women, both before and during his marriage to Josephine Poszywak in 1936. In the years when the affair supposedly took place, Hoffa was organizing around the clock in Michigan, and Sylvia was a teenager in Kansas City with a new husband and their infant son. I have found no evidence that she was in Detroit during this period, or that he was in Kansas City.

The rumors about Sylvia and Hoffa, like the ones about Chuckie's paternity, appear to be mistaken inferences from their very close relationship over many decades. A more likely explanation for their closeness is that Hoffa admired Sylvia's take-charge grit and found her extraordinarily useful. She was useful because she could organize workers in difficult circumstances. She was useful because she introduced Hoffa not just to the family in Detroit, but later to other Italian families around the country, and also to the Jewish gangster Moe Dalitz, to whom Hoffa would lend Teamsters pension funds to build much of Las Vegas. And she was useful because she took care of the busy Hoffa's wife.

Josephine was a shy, frail woman who suffered from undulant fever, and later severe alcoholism, both of which left her weak and unable to care for herself. Sylvia looked after Josephine and kept her company during Hoffa's long periods away from home. And she protected Josephine when people made fun of her simple ways. "A lot of people would shit on Ma Jo behind her back," Chuckie told me. "Once my mother went over and told one of them, 'If you don't stop that shit, I'll knock your fucking head across the street,' and that ended all that shit." Hoffa valued Sylvia's loyalty and toughness; and Sylvia and Josephine became close friends.

At the same time that Sylvia was becoming close to the Hoffas, she continued to help the Detroit family. "They trusted her, they knew that my mother was strong and never opened her mouth about anything," Chuckie told me. Among other things, Sylvia kept the books for the gambling operations that Giacalone was running in the 1940s. "She worked for Uncle Tony. She had an apartment at the Whittier, and across the hall from her she had another apartment, and that was where the layoffs all came through." Sylvia kept records on flash paper that dissolved on exposure to water, and once when the cops raided her apartment she flushed everything down the toilet and "saved the Outfit, Uncle Tony and all, from going to jail," according to Chuckie.

Sylvia Pagano, Jimmy Hoffa, and Anthony Giacalone were young adults, insignificant twentysomethings, when they first met in the early 1940s. Over the next quarter century, Hoffa would rise to the apex of American labor, and Giacalone would become powerful enough in the Detroit family to attend the infamous 1957 national summit of Sicilian crime leaders in Apalachin, New

York. Sylvia's role as liaison between Hoffa and the mob grew in step with these men's expanding power and mutual interests.

As a busy single woman navigating the intersection of two dangerous worlds in the 1940s, Sylvia had little time for her only son. "My mom was always away working, and I was always stuck with somebody," Chuckie told me. From the age of eight through eighteen, he bounced between two military boarding schools, his uncle Dante's house on Detroit's east side, and his mother's parents' home in Kansas City. Chuckie venerated his mother, always claimed to understand why she consigned him to relatives and friends, and denied any resentment toward her for doing so. "My mother was a saint," he told me dozens of times, whenever I raised the subject—but usually with a clipped, conversation-changing tone that implied a painful remembrance.

Chuckie didn't live with his mother, but he grew up in her worlds. His friends at military school were the sons of the top guys in Detroit. By age twelve he had figured out their business. He soon had a job collecting tickets for their numbers game from the workers exiting gates 12 and 14 of the Ford Motor Company's enormous River Rouge plant, which he would place in bags and take to a nearby rooming house. "The basement was long, really long," Chuckie told me, "and it had these ping-pong tables all the way down and the guys that were working for the Outfit were counting the money, the coins and the dollars and all that, and it just piled up all the way down, maybe ten or twelve tables just filled with money."

Chuckie developed a romantic view of the Detroit and Kansas City crime families and their leaders, whom he knew as a boy. The old-timers he admired most—his uncle Mario and Joseph Filardo in Kansas City, and Black Bill Tocco and Joseph Zerilli in Detroit—were modest, dignified gentlemen with legitimate businesses who seemed to Chuckie to embody the Old World ethos of honor, discretion, manliness, and loyalty. The fatherless boy idealized these men and their families. He embraced their principles as part of his heritage and as a mainstay in his scattered life.

The central principle Chuckie learned, the one he would clutch all his life, was Omertà. "On the Sicilian side you're taught, if you see something happen, you don't talk about it," Chuckie explained to me. "I learned that rule in Kansas City. But I learned it more from Uncle Tony."

Anthony Giacalone was the person in LCN whom Chuckie admired the most by far. Giacalone was in his midtwenties when Chuckie met him. He was a tall, imposing man who already possessed the dignified air, beautiful clothes, and menacing blue-eyed glare for which he would later be famous. "Uncle Tony, when you met him, you saw a gentleman of stature and respect," Chuckie told me. Giacalone was the person Sylvia would send the youthful Chuckie to see for discipline when he got out of line. Chuckie revered him, listened to him carefully, and obeyed his every word.

"The person who instilled loyalty in me, and who taught me to don't say nothing, was Uncle Tony," Chuckie told me. "Uncle Tony, since I was a kid, he hated anybody that was a snitch. He told me to never, no matter how bad it is, rat anybody out, because people like that, time will take care of them. He told me in Sicilian."

Chuckie's favorite scene in the movie *Goodfellas* is when Jimmy Conway praises the half-Irish, half-Sicilian teenager Henry Hill, who kept his mouth shut when the cops nabbed him selling cigarettes illegally. "He told him you never rat your friends out," Chuckie explained. "And it just brought back memories of when I was young. I pictured Uncle Tony there talking to me. It was true, you never rat your friends out."

Uncle Tony's Omertà edict was a looming presence in my conversations with Chuckie. I once pressed Chuckie to explain to me some of the tasks he performed for Giacalone over two decades.

"Jack, I ain't telling you," he replied.

"I want to know," I said.

"I can't do this, Jack—I'm laying my ass on the line," Chuckie said. "I'd rather be honest with you. I mean, there are still people around that . . ."

"Say no more," I said.

It took me a while to understand Chuckie's Omertà commitments. Though he sometimes spoke of being killed if he told me too much, that concern evaporated when examined. Chuckie's secrets about organized crime were more than four decades old. Everyone who cared enough to retaliate had died a long time ago. And Omertà in the 2010s wasn't what it used to be. Dozens of wiseguys had for several decades talked publicly about old mob secrets, almost all with impunity. A few had even written autobiographies. Chuckie abhorred this trend. He despised those who told secrets in books in order to "go to their grave with a few bucks." And he had special loathing for people who finked on their bosses to avoid jail.

"There was no honor among some of these guys, especially the younger ones," Chuckie explained to me. "People of honor became rats. They didn't want to go to prison." The example Chuckie usually invoked was Salvatore "Sammy the Bull" Gravano, the violent underboss of the Gambino crime family who ratted out his boss, "Dapper Don" John Gotti. "How could a guy this tough, killed nineteen people, turn on Gotti and bury him?" Chuckie asked, shaking his head. "He didn't want to go to jail, that's the problem." But as Chuckie also acknowledged, Gravano defied his witness protection, wrote a book about his experiences, and often appeared on television, all without consequence.

I eventually came to understand that Chuckie didn't resist telling me what he knew about LCN for fear of punishment. He resisted simply because he thought it was wrong. The people "still around" whom he worried about were the families and associates of the old-timers he knew in Detroit, Kansas City, and New York. He worried not about what these people might do to him, but rather what they would think of him.

"I just can't do it, Jack, it's not right," he insisted.

Chuckie took his Kansas City heritage, his mother's values, and his teenage pledge to Uncle Tony more seriously than any other obligation in his life.

"Every time I think about what I want to do to help you understand, Jack, my mother's right in front of me," he once told me, referring to the embodiment of his Sicilian conscience.

For Chuckie these obligations were a matter of identity, not calculation. It would be shameful if he blabbed, no matter what benefit it might bring him.

"I could have ratted people out, but I never did," he once told me. "I was that way my whole life, even with the Old Man," he added, referring to Hoffa.

Yet despite his obligations, Chuckie eventually told me a lot. He did so because his guarded and limited answers to thousands of questions over the years added up in the aggregate. "I'm trying to remember what I can't tell you," he once said in response to a question—and sometimes he misremembered.

And Chuckie told me a lot because I told him that his story would be more credible to the extent he could tell me more. "I got to figure out how to get there" was his frequent refrain. Where he drew the line kept shifting, though his secrets, and the deflections, persisted to the end.

CHUCKIE ABSORBED OMERTÀ and every other element of Sicilian loyalty, but he could never fully be part of Uncle's Tony's world. He was Sicilian in looks and attitude and self-understanding. But like Henry Hill, he couldn't be a wiseguy because his father was Irish. And so Chuckie's ambitions migrated elsewhere, in the direction of the other great male influence in his life, Jimmy Hoffa.

Chuckie met Hoffa soon after he met Giacalone, probably in 1943, when he was nine years old. Sylvia introduced him to Hoffa and Josephine one evening at their home at 16154 Robson Street in northwest Detroit. From this first encounter Chuckie remembers Hoffa's toothy smile, his intense green-gray eyes, and his "tremendous forearms, and shoulders, for his size." The thirty-year-old labor leader, whose son, James P. Hoffa, was an infant, immediately took a shine to Chuckie. "When he flashed his heartwarming smile at me and began talking, I knew we were going to be close," Chuckie recalls.

In the early summer of that year, on a Friday, Sylvia brought Chuckie and a packed suitcase to Hoffa's office at Teamsters Local 299 on Trumbull Avenue. "Get in the car, we're going to the Lake," Chuckie remembers Hoffa snarling. "He used to drive like a maniac, we used to call him 'lead foot.' In the old days with those roads going out there, it was a thrill."

Hoffa drove Chuckie forty miles to the very modest "cottage" he had recently purchased on Square Lake in Lake Orion, Michigan. "The Lake," as everyone referred to the cottage, the lake, and its environs, would serve as Hoffa's sanctuary until the day he disappeared. The shallow, sand-bottomed body of water was ideal for children, and Hoffa played in it that weekend with Chuckie, his five-year-old daughter, Barbara, and his son, James.

"We'd fish, he'd get the boat and we'd row the boat all over with Barbara and Jimmy in it," Chuckie said. "And then he'd pounce in the water and rope it off, and the rule was that anybody that came out there couldn't go past the ropes."

Chuckie would go to the Lake several more weekends that summer, and grew close to the Hoffas and their children. For the next decade he would visit the Lake for weeks every summer, playing with Barbara, taking care of Jimmy, helping Josephine, and pining for Hoffa to arrive on the weekends. Sometimes his mother would join, especially on holidays like the Fourth of July, and cook a massive Sicilian feast that Hoffa loved. It was Chuckie's happiest time as a boy—the only time in his youth he felt he had a real family.

Hoffa did not raise Chuckie, as many (including Hoffa) have claimed. He was working too hard and on the road too much during this period to be said to have raised even his own children. And Chuckie never moved in with the Hoffas as a boy except for the weeks in the summer at the Lake. But Hoffa took him hunting with his Teamsters buddies, taught him how to drive, advised him about life, and in general showered him with affection whenever they were together. Perhaps Hoffa was thanking Sylvia. Or perhaps he identified with Chuckie because he lost his father at a similar age. Whatever his motivation, Hoffa grew very fond of Chuckie, and treated him like a son—"my other son," whom he considered "one of our family," as Hoffa would say in his 1970 autobiography.

Chuckie was defenseless against any male attention and yearned to connect with every man he met, many of whom he called "Uncle." But the tender, intense attention from a man with Hoffa's outsize charm and personality was like nothing he had ever experienced, and it struck him like an arrow. "He was my fuckin' hero," Chuckie told me. "He had a heart as big as a building but nobody knew it 'cause he didn't want anybody to know it."

Chuckie's affection for Hoffa quickly morphed into an ambition to be like him. As a kid he would help Hoffa and his mother on picket lines. One weekend when he was about twelve he joined Hoffa and other Teamsters to assist Myra Wolfgang, an organizer for the Hotel Employees and Restaurant Employees Union, with a strike at a White Tower hamburger joint. When Hoffa arrived at the strike's headquarters at the seventeen-story Hotel Wolverine across the street from the restaurant, he took Chuckie to the roof. "We got up there and they had cases of eggs, all these eggs, and we started throwing eggs at the people coming out of the restaurant." The mischievous fun in pursuit of the cause was intoxicating.

During his high school years in Kansas City, Chuckie drove a dump truck for a company run by "Uncle Cork and Uncle Nick" Civella and another truck for a wholesale plumbing company. He proudly joined Teamsters Local 541 in the hopes of impressing the Old Man. When he graduated from Glennon High School in Kansas City in 1952, he married his sweetheart, Mary Ann Giaramita, and moved to Detroit. He joined Teamsters Local 299 because he drove trucks for two different companies, one delivering bakery goods and the other handling theater products.

But his real ambition was to be an organizer like Hoffa, who by then was the top Teamsters official in Michigan. On weekends Chuckie, Mary Ann, and their young son would have dinner at the Lake with the Hoffas, and Chuckie started to pester the Old Man for a job. To Chuckie's disappointment, Hoffa deflected these requests for eight months. He gave various excuses. Chuckie was too young. Or he needed more experience as a driver. Chuckie finally sought help from Bert Brennan. "I asked Uncle Bert to convince the Old Man to hire me," Chuckie said, and "a couple of weeks gone by, the Old Man called me."

Hoffa was thirty-nine years old and one of the most powerful Teamsters union officials in the country when he telephoned Chuckie. He had come to dominate the union in the Midwest, where he organized drivers, ran strikes, and directed locals through his control of the Central States Drivers Council. He was also making impressive inroads in the hard-to-organize South. In a few months he would be elected the youngest international vice president in the union at its national convention.

Chuckie went to see the "biggest small man in Detroit," as Teamsters president Dan Tobin called Hoffa, in the office that Hoffa shared with Brennan on the second floor of Local 299 on Trumbull Avenue. As he entered the dark, mahogany-paneled room, Hoffa looked up from his burgundy leather chair behind his large desk.

"Why do you think you could make a pimple on a business agent's ass?" Hoffa asked.

"I think I can, but I can't prove it until you give me a chance," Chuckie replied.

After a brief, chortling deliberation with Brennan, Hoffa gave his decision. "I've decided to put you on as an organizer, for 299, but you're not going to sign any contracts," he said. "You're going to organize and you'll go to every meeting when there is a contract, and I want you to learn everything in this local—car haul, freight, contracts—learn it all."

Chuckie assented, thanked Hoffa profusely, and left the office. He was thrilled. At the age of nineteen, he felt his goal of being like Jimmy Hoffa was on track.

His desire to be close to the Company was also proceeding as well as could be expected. At about the same time that Hoffa offered him the job, Uncle Tony, by then a capo, invited Chuckie to the Grecian Gardens, a popular Detroit Greektown restaurant where some elements of the Detroit family would hang out and do business. Giacalone brought Chuckie to a small back room, where sitting around a table were boss Joseph Zerilli and a few other tough-looking top guys from Detroit.

The gentlemen rose to greet Chuckie, then sat down. Anthony Giacalone spoke. "Tell them what you told me," he said.

Chuckie hesitated, looked nervously around the room, and then said, "On my honor I will never betray any relationship I have with all of you." At which point the men rose again, thanked Chuckie, and hugged and kissed him. And then they had dinner together.

This brief, odd episode was no initiation ritual. Chuckie did not take a blood oath or burn the card of a saint in his hand. He couldn't become a made man because his father was Irish, and he took on no formal obligations beyond the pledge he made. The entire event was a favor to Sylvia, whom the tops guys adored and who wanted to fortify her son's Sicilian connections and identity.

But the event made a lifelong impact on Chuckie. In his mind he became "part of the Outfit as an 'associate,'" a catch-all designation for people who aren't made men but who provide assistance to the Outfit. "It meant I could be trusted because of my background," Chuckie told me. It also deepened the Omertà values that he had grown up with in Kansas City and Detroit, and that Uncle Tony had been schooling him in for years.

Sixty years after these business meetings, across from the photographs in my mother's television room in Boca Raton, I asked Chuckie to explain his relationships with Hoffa and Giacalone.

"Hoffa through labor, and like a father," he said. "Labor-wise I was close to the Old Man because I tried to copy his labor ability, everything he taught me. Labor was my dream."

Chuckie was also very close to Giacalone, but theirs was "a Sicilian relationship." Giacalone was more "like a godfather" than a father, Chuckie said. "Uncle Tony looked at me from a different outlook. He would study if I was advancing or not advancing, and he knew who was trying to jack around with me and trying to screw me around. If it got to a point that somebody was not right, he let that person know."

Chuckie's assessment of his two father figures was reflected in the warm, affectionate photograph of Jimmy Hoffa and the stern one of Anthony Giacalone that he chose to place on his wall of fame. Since Chuckie was a teenager, Hoffa had been his love and his ambition, and Uncle Tony his identity, his conscience, his protector.

THREE

UNIONISM, HOFFA-STYLE

IN THE FALL OF 2012, I taught a seminar at Harvard Law School called "The Rise and Fall of the American Labor Movement." "The main but not exclusive focus will be on the International Brotherhood of Teamsters and its leader from the 1940s–1960s, Jimmy Hoffa," read the course catalog. "Topics examined will include changes in labor laws, globalization, changing social norms, labor democratization movements, the influence of organized crime, government takeover of unions, and more. The seminar will include outside speakers."

Chuckie was the outside speaker on October 2. He was no labor scholar, but he was qualified by experience. He had closely witnessed Hoffa's approach to labor. He had lived through labor's steep decline from its zenith in the 1950s to its dismal state in the second decade of the twenty-first century. And he had firsthand knowledge about the issue of labor corruption. I hoped my students would get a kick out of meeting a labor old-timer, not to mention an alleged abettor to Hoffa's murder. And I knew that Chuckie would be thrilled to do it. He frequently wears Harvard Law School paraphernalia, and with a straight face tells anyone who asks that he graduated in the class of '58.

When Chuckie entered room 3011 of Wasserstein Hall, he was wearing jeans and a royal-blue jacket with a huge bright-gold Teamsters emblem on the back and the insignia of Local 299, the Detroit union he grew up in, on the front. "I never thought I'd make it back to Harvard," Chuckie told my students after I introduced him.

Chuckie wasn't joking this time. He actually had been to Harvard Law School once before, five decades earlier, when, as he told the class, "I brought Mr. Hoffa here to speak and have a debate." The date was March 30, 1962, six months before I was born, and the event was a speech by Hoffa at the law school titled "Area Contracts and the Teamsters," with critical responses by John Dunlop, then the chair of the Harvard economics department and a prominent labor economist, and John Meyer, a specialist at Harvard in transportation economics.

Hoffa had a reputation by that time as a law-defying bully, and the buttoned-down students on campus did not receive him well. "As we were walking into the school," Chuckie recounted to my students, "all these kids were up in trees, and they're going, 'Hiss, hiss, hiss.' And Mr. Hoffa said to me, 'What the hell's wrong with these kids? Don't they know how to boo?'"

My students and I chuckled. I later dug up a recording of the debate in the Harvard archives. Hoffa had begun with a detailed (and, Chuckie says, unscripted) thirty-minute defense of the tactics he deployed during the last decade in his quest for a national labor contract for truck drivers. He then bested the two Harvard professors when they challenged him, leaving the impression—as he often did in his many campus debates—that the eggheads knew little about the real world of unions.

"I watched a guy that never went to college, had to leave school after ninth grade, and he cut those guys into pieces," Chuckie told my students, his voice cracking, holding back tears. "And when we were leaving, the students were not booing—they were clapping." Hoffa's biographer Arthur Sloane says of the evening that "an initially hostile audience wound up giving him a standing ovation."

After recounting this tale, Chuckie gave a meandering hour-long talk about Hoffa's labor philosophy. "Mr. Hoffa always said the union was a business," Chuckie explained. His narrow goal was to sell labor in the marketplace at the highest price possible. Some elements of the labor movement, especially in the 1930s and '40s, sought to use unions to transform American capitalism and bring radical social change to the United States. But Hoffa "didn't believe in all that social shit like that wacky commie Walter Reuther," Chuckie told my students.

Hoffa wanted to exploit the free market, not kill it. But due to the brutal experiences of his youth and the labor battles of the 1930s, he also believed that the market was rigged. Hoffa "regarded capitalism as a racket that the strong manipulated to their own advantage—a system in which everyone was on the take, morality was bullshit and no holds were barred," as Arthur Schlesinger Jr. put it. He thought nothing of serving himself or his union by circumventing laws or courts, which he believed systematically privileged employers and the government. He saw nearly every encounter in life as a market opportunity to enhance his power in which the only questions were currency and price. For him, negotiating a labor contract was at bottom the same enterprise as buying off politicians and cops, running lucrative side businesses with his employers, or partnering with underworld crime figures when it brought him an advantage.

Hoffa's ingenious manipulation of American capitalism made him one of the most powerful and consequential labor figures in the twentieth century. The trucking industry grew steadily throughout his career, especially in the period after the war, when the economy grew much more dependent on their deliveries of goods via the expanding, federally subsidized network of superhighways across the country. At the height of his power in the early 1960s, Hoffa had organized truckers and related workers into the largest union in the country, whose control over transportation gave it enormous influence over the national economy.

Hoffa might have used his organizing acumen and control over transportation networks to lead the American labor movement in a very different direction than the one it in fact traveled. But his neglect of society's rules of etiquette—and especially his many criminal associations—would destroy him, with tragic consequences for all of labor.

WHEN HOFFA ASCENDED to the presidency of the Teamsters union in 1957, the rest of the American labor movement was beginning to stagnate. At the end of World War II, unions were wealthier and more powerful than ever. But they overplayed their hands with waves of controversial strikes in 1945–46 that sought sharp postwar wage increases. The disruptive strikes on top of labor's historic gains since 1933 attracted a coordinated postwar backlash by business groups and conservative politicians who sought to demonize unions as too powerful and harmful to the economy. The 1947 Taft-Hartley Act, a product of this backlash, imposed harsh new restraints on organizing tactics.

Despite Taft-Hartley, in the early 1950s unions seemed to be doing fine. The United Auto Workers negotiated deals with the giant car manufacturers at the beginning of the decade that gave workers novel cost-of-living adjustments and health and pension benefits. The contract between General Motors and the UAW, dubbed the "Treaty of Detroit," was widely copied in other industries and led to sharp wage and benefit increases, and industrial harmony, as the postwar economy boomed to the steady benefit of many blue-collar workers.

The merger of the AFL and the CIO in 1955, which seemed to herald Big Labor ascendancy, actually marked the start of its decline. Many unions were becoming sclerotic bureaucracies run by a professional class that had grown distant from rank and file and less interested in organizing new members. Most of labor would also be hurt by a steady decline in blue-collar workers and, in large part because of Taft-Hartley, by difficulties unionizing the South and the growing white-collar sector. Union membership peaked at 35 percent of the workforce in 1954 but would drop to 31 percent by 1960. "We are going backward," Reuther proclaimed that year.

Hoffa defied these trends. In the decade before he became president of the union in 1957, he increased membership sharply in the Midwest and even in the South, where union-busting right-to-work laws decimated other unions. The Teamsters continued to grow and prosper throughout the nation when he assumed the top job. In the year ending May 1959, he added 132,000 members even though the economy was in recession. He would continue to expand the size, power, and wealth of the nation's largest union throughout his reign. The Teamsters' power was even greater than its large numbers suggested because it could make or break other unions' strikes, or destroy businesses, simply by stopping or slowing deliveries.

There are many reasons why Hoffa succeeded when the rest of labor was slowing. He had a superhuman work ethic, and he was a shrewd bargainer. He rejected labor's complacent attitude toward organizing drives. He also defied the Teamsters' traditional craft limitations by organizing every possible type of worker—not just truckers, but hundreds of thousands of workers who produced, loaded, and unloaded many of the items they delivered. "If it moves, organize it" was his motto.

This characteristically pragmatic attitude led Hoffa to organize African American and women workers more forcefully than other unions during the period. In April 1958 Hoffa wrote to remind every Teamsters local of the union's "policy of non-discrimination because of race, color, or creed," and to urge them "to take positive action" toward this goal. Chuckie told me that Hoffa had real empathy for the civil rights movement and especially Martin Luther King, whose work Hoffa supported generously and with whom Hoffa corresponded. But while Hoffa may have identified with King's struggles against the government, his approach to civil rights was motivated mostly by a desire to grow his union's numbers and thus its power. For similar reasons, the radical-hating Hoffa had no qualms about working with Harry Bridges, the communist leader of the longshoremen's union, when necessary to avoid jurisdictional conflicts at the docks.

The truck freight industry remained the most important one for Hoffa to organize, since control there helped build power in other areas. The challenge was that the industry consisted of many thousands of small and medium-size firms that the journalist Paul Jacobs described in 1957 as "a rough, brawling, extremely competitive battle royal." Hoffa played his disorganized adversaries against one another. He understood trucking routes and transportation economics better than trucking company executives. And he spent a lot of time learning about the weaknesses of the men he exploited at the bargaining table. "He knew the trucking company guys better than their own wives," Chuckie told me. "He knew who was screwing around or drinking too much, he knew who would choke at the bargaining table, he knew who would get tired and sign the contract."

Hoffa also perfected what the labor economists Estelle and Ralph James described as "ingenious" organizing techniques that allowed him to leverage economic power in one region or industry to advance a bargaining aim in another. In 1957, as Hoffa was spreading his influence to the South, a North Carolina trucking company run by Malcolm McLean balked at a Teamsters contract. Hoffa ordered the loading docks he controlled up and down the East Coast not to admit or unload McLean's trucks. With his business fast collapsing, McLean signed the Teamsters contract. Hoffa once explained his approach as follows: "First, we close down this guy's outfit where the trouble is. Then, if he won't settle, we close him down [i.e., prevent him from doing business] in the surrounding states. Then if he still won't settle, we close him down across the whole goddam country."

Hoffa's power grew as his control over the densely interconnected U.S. transportation system expanded. That is why he devoted his career to negotiating with trucking companies on an ever-wider and eventually national scale. The main obstacle to national bargaining came less from employers than from fiercely independent local Teamsters union bosses. Wages in some areas, especially large cities, were higher than others, especially in the South. To achieve the overall advantages to the union from bargaining on a national scale, Hoffa had to convince locals in the wealthier parts of the country to give up bargaining power to him and to forgo wage increases until he could bring up wages and benefits in other parts of the country. This was not an easy task, and when persuasion didn't work, Hoffa turned to controversial tactics. He sometimes responded to recalcitrance in the locals by threatening their leaders or placing them in receivership. Other times he turned to his Italian friends for help.

Hoffa did not believe in union democracy, and his authoritarian control was deeply unpopular with the local and regional union leaders who saw their power wane. Yet while he cut down the local barons, Hoffa "always put the members first," as Chuckie told my students. He won large and often huge wage increases. He secured for truckers better hours and better equipment, including air-conditioned rigs and power steering. He also won impressive health, pension, and vacation benefits. As Chuckie said at Harvard, Hoffa brought hundreds of thousands of truck drivers and other "lowly" workers into the middle class and gave them "a dignity they never imagined possible."

Hoffa also displayed what the labor reporter Sam Romer described as a "single-minded dedication to spending almost all his waking hours in the union's vineyards." Chuckie was usually with Hoffa as he faithfully visited locals around the country to be with "the boys who pay me" and to hear and resolve their complaints. He gave his office and home telephone numbers to members, who would call him collect day and night. He was an untutored but bewitching orator who studied Billy Graham's sermons and roused members with candid, fiery, extemporaneous speeches. Teamsters members reciprocated Hoffa's personal attention, great contracts, and lived working-class values with an enthusiastic allegiance that had no parallel in modern labor history.

Many of Hoffa's happy union members assumed that "Jimmy got some on the side" from employers, which he did. When Hoffa organized Michigan grocery stores and bars in the 1940s, for example, he exacted tributes from the store owners to keep deliveries coming, and demanded as well that his syndicate friends be given space for their profitable vending machines (candy, cigarettes, and jukeboxes), from which he also drew a cut. "The Old Man went in and he choked 'em like a chicken," Chuckie said, explaining how Hoffa enforced these deals against store owners.

"Do you think that's fair?" I once asked. "Why should the grocery stores have to pay extra to Hoffa, since the workers are already getting higher wages?"

"When you're getting your ass whipped by Hoffa you would say it wasn't fair, but when you looked at what he was doing for the union member, you understood," Chuckie replied. Chuckie claimed that Hoffa used the piles of cash he amassed from deals of this sort on the workers. "He would give money away, he would pay for favors, he would buy people off," Chuckie insisted—all with the aim of building Teamsters' power.

This is a plausible contention, since Hoffa often did in fact use the money in this way, and the Teamsters' lot was improving when he was in charge. To the coerced employers and to outsiders, Hoffa was making corrupt deals and lining his own pockets with cash. But the vast majority of Teamsters were sanguine. "I don't care what Jimmy Hoffa does with my four dollars a month—he can shoot craps on the White House lawn if he wants to—so long as he keeps up the present conditions," said one typical Teamster in 1958. The workers trusted Hoffa, he took good care of them, and he seemed to use his illicit gains not for personal use, but rather to enhance his power, and thus theirs.

Even many of the employers whom Hoffa regularly whipped admired him. Hoffa was the toughest of negotiators. But his push toward national bargaining helped consolidate the trucking industry, and thus allowed trucking companies—with assists from the Interstate Commerce Commission and a trucking industry exemption from antitrust laws—to pass most of the cost of higher wages and benefits to their customers. The larger trucking firms that were the biggest winners in these organizing campaigns came to like and trust Hoffa despite his warts. Hoffa's sensitivity to the needs of employers often invited the charge of sweetheart deals. But Hoffa's overall record of wage and benefit improvements and the enthusiastic support he enjoyed from union members always spoke for themselves.

Hoffa spent his first seven years as Teamsters president racing around the country cajoling, bargaining with, and strong-arming local unions and trucking companies to get in line with his efforts to achieve a nationwide labor contract for truckers. "To get a national contract, he would go himself personally and make speeches like you couldn't believe, and the membership believed him that he was not trying to screw them," Chuckie says.

Hoffa finally realized his ambitious vision for the Teamsters on January 15, 1964, when he concluded the first national labor contract in the trucking industry. "It took Mr. Hoffa six years to get it done, and he did it with no strike, without a day lost," says Chuckie. The agreement won large wage, pension, and health-care benefits for nearly 400,000 truckers and was "one of the most significant labor developments of the postwar period," reported *The New York Times*. It was a "personal triumph for the union's president," the *Times* explained, that would "tighten Mr. Hoffa's grip on the union and . . . increase his power in dealing with the industry."

THE PHOTOGRAPH THAT memorialized the national freight agreement—versions of which were reproduced in national newspapers and on the cover of the February 1964 *Teamster* magazine—portrays a tired but jubilant Hoffa shaking hands with a bemused C. G. Zwingle, the trucking companies' chief negotiator, outside the eighth-floor suite in Chicago's Edgewater Beach Hotel, where they concluded the contract. In the dead center of the picture, standing between and a few feet behind the two men, is the thirty-year-old Chuckie, staring blankly through heavy eyelids into the distance like Forrest Gump photoshopped into one of the great labor pacts in American history.

"Mr. Hoffa insisted that I be in the picture to thank me for my help," Chuckie told me.

The Edgewater Beach Hotel photo exemplifies Chuckie's relationship with Hoffa during the height of Hoffa's power, as do the many similar newspaper photos of Hoffa and Chuckie that he had collected and shown me as a teenager. From 1952, when he went to work for the Teamsters, until 1967, when Hoffa went to jail, Chuckie "hardly left Hoffa's side," Hoffa's daughter, Barbara, told the FBI in 1975. He was with Hoffa during his important labor negotiations and grievance sessions. He sat near Hoffa in the Caucus Room of the Senate Office Building during years of congressional investigations. During all but one of the criminal trials the U.S. government would bring against Hoffa, Chuckie was on most days seated in the first row, just behind the counsel chair.

In my teens I imagined that Chuckie was providing Hoffa with important counsel in these gatherings. Many outsiders drew the same impression at the time. In his novel *The Godfather*, Mario Puzo modeled Tom Hagen—the brainy, level-headed, quietly powerful Irish orphan (played in the movie by Robert Duvall), whom Don Corleone raised and eventually made his consigliere—on Chuckie. "Tom is sort of a rough model on a guy called

O'Brien in Detroit who was like a son to Jimmy Hoffa," Puzo told an interviewer two weeks after the novel was published in 1969.

But Puzo, and I, were mistaken. "I didn't advise Hoffa, he advised me," Chuckie made clear in our conversations. The relationship was "more father-son than a business relationship," he continued. "I'd be with him. If something had to be done, I did it."

The labor journalist Victor Riesel accurately described Chuckie as Hoffa's "intimate companion, driver, bodyguard and special troubleshooter." Chuckie picked up Hoffa and drove him around. He ran errands. He delivered and received messages and money. He watched Hoffa's back. He made sure that Hoffa, and whomever he was meeting, were well fed. He collected signatures for contracts. He did intelligence work in the union. He gathered the names of officers and charter dates for Hoffa's speeches at union locals. When the two men traveled together, which they often did, they shared a suite. Chuckie was the last to see Hoffa before bed, usually at 10:00 p.m., and the first to see him in the morning, usually at 6:00 a.m., newspapers in hand. He helped Hoffa select his clothes to wear at the beginning of the day. And the two men would typically watch the evening television news together before bed.

Chuckie first assumed these roles soon after he joined the Teamsters as a teenager in 1952. Hoffa assigned him to apprentice in Detroit with his 1930s mentor, Al "Pop" Squires. But he also invited Chuckie to join him on his frequent weekend trips to speak at union locals, to dine with organizers, or to dedicate a new union hall. Chuckie got a rush tagging along with his idol in his late teens and early twenties, studying at the master's feet and "doing anything the Old Man asked me to do." He learned a great deal from Hoffa—about labor and more. "Mr. Hoffa helped me a lot teaching me to read," Chuckie explained. "Most people don't read, my generation. He got me in the habit of reading *The Wall Street Journal*. I didn't know what *The Wall Street Journal* was until Mr. Hoffa said, 'You read this, you read *Time* magazine, *Newsweek*, and find a book and read it and you'll be able to handle yourself with anybody.'"

After a few years alongside Pop Squires, though, Chuckie wanted real labor organizing responsibilities, like Hoffa had at his age. More than anything else, Chuckie wanted to be an officer in Hoffa's home Local 299 in Detroit. "My boyhood and lifelong dream was to be on the board of 299 and maybe get a chance to work my way up one day and become the president," he told me. Hoffa didn't help Chuckie advance in Local 299, however, and he saw to it that Chuckie received only trivial labor assignments in and around Detroit—mostly organizing gas stations, tire companies, and riverfront transportation services.

On Friday, October 4, 1957, Hoffa made clear to Chuckie that he would not soon have a leadership role in Local 299. The two men were in Miami Beach. It was the day that Hoffa realized *his* dream by being elected president of the Teamsters union. After Hoffa's acceptance speech at the Miami Beach auditorium, Chuckie walked to the stage through a swarming crowd and found Hoffa, who hugged and thanked him, and invited him to dinner. At 7:00 p.m., Chuckie found himself in the dining room of the Fontainebleau hotel, alone at a small corner table with Hoffa and Josephine.

"I'm making you assistant to the general president," Hoffa told Chuckie with clear pleasure, just after they ordered dinner. It was a big promotion and an important title for the twenty-four-year-old business agent.

"You don't need to do that," Chuckie replied meekly, before thanking Hoffa profusely.

But Chuckie was quietly distraught about the new position, which sounded good but implied that he would remain Hoffa's gofer. "It was like a death sentence," he explained to me later. Chuckie knew that he would be given few if any independent labor organizing tasks and that his union identity would be subsumed entirely in Hoffa's. And to make matters worse, the new title generated resentment among many Teamsters officials. "It was like putting a light bulb in a dark room," Chuckie explained. "I was a young little shit. All these motherfuckers on the outside are looking at a twenty-four-year-old kid becoming an assistant to the general president. There were guys that would have given their left nut for it and I didn't look for that. I just wanted 299."

It would take Chuckie decades to grasp why Hoffa didn't help him advance on his own as a labor official. His main theory at the time, and in our conversations half a century later, was that Hoffa simply wanted Chuckie by his side. "He didn't want to lose me, he wanted me around," Chuckie often said. There was an element of truth in this assessment. But another truth—obvious to nearly everyone in the Teamsters, uncomfortably implicit in our conversations, but too painful for Chuckie to see, or at least talk about—was that no one, including Hoffa, thought Chuckie was up to the task.

Chuckie studied Hoffa closely. "I tried to copy my style on how Mr. Hoffa ran meetings and dealt with members," he once explained. "I patterned my ability through him." But Hoffa was one of the most talented labor leaders in the twentieth century. He combined "the business sense of an industrial tycoon with the political instinct of a big city boss and the showmanship of a vaudeville entertainer," according to Estelle and Ralph James. He mastered every detail, commanded every situation, and always followed through on his word.

Chuckie lacked these skills. His time at Hoffa's side gave him "much knowledge of [the Teamsters] organization and affairs," as Frank Fitzsimmons, Hoffa's successor as Teamsters president, told the FBI in 1975. And Chuckie ran a few small organizing campaigns over the course of his three-decade Teamsters career and was effective on picket lines. He was also one of the earliest union officials to try to organize professional sports teams.

But Chuckie didn't grasp the finer points of labor organizing or union finances, he wasn't a charismatic speaker, he often didn't follow through on commitments, and he lacked good judgment. He had a knucklehead charm and undoubted goodwill, and most people liked him despite his shortcomings. But when he tried to mimic Jimmy Hoffa, Chuckie often fell on his face.

"In organizing campaigns and stuff, I would always get in a spot," Chuckie once acknowledged. Others were less kind. Chuckie "would screw off" in union matters, according to Frank Fitzsimmons. Chuckie often misspent union funds, such as when he treated the entire Detroit Red Wings team to an expensive evening at the Roostertail restaurant or when he chartered a plane to bring Johnny Cash to a disaster relief rally, neither of which was authorized or closely connected to union business.

In the late 1950s, Chuckie was in an organizing fight with the Seafarers International Union on the Detroit River. SIU business agents cruised the river on a small boat, approached vessels, dropped a ladder, and made the union's pitch. Chuckie was "pissed off because we didn't have a boat," he told me. His solution was to use union funds to buy an expensive all-steel cruiser—not to compete for members, but rather "to run these SIU mother-fuckers over in the river and sink them." Bert Brennan stopped the scheme at the last minute. But Hoffa, two old-timers told me, defended Chuckie. "What's wrong with that?" he asked with a chuckle when he learned about the scheme. "That's a pretty good idea."

It wasn't just union men who took a dim view of Chuckie's antics. Many Detroit underworld figures did as well. In the early 1960s, Chuckie used union funds to buy a new car for Frank Meli, the brother of the Detroit con-sigliere Angelo Meli. The Detroit family was not pleased when Frank, along with Chuckie, was indicted for labor law violations—though it eventually helped both men beat the rap. Frank's son, Vince, who himself would later rise to the rank of underboss, described Chuckie to the FBI as a "bullshit art-ist" who "talks a lot about things he knows nothing about." Chuckie's just "a big show-off, always putting on a big act," said another Detroit crime lieuten-ant, Dominic Peter Corrado, to the FBI.

Chuckie was similarly unhelpful in Hoffa's many legal fights. His os-tensible job during Hoffa's trials was, he told me, to "guard the files" and bring them to and from the courtroom. But since he was so close to Hoffa, he invariably got involved in more. Hoffa's longtime lawyer, Morris Shenker, noted that Chuckie displayed "extreme loyalty" to Hoffa, but complained that during trial preparation sessions Chuckie would "furnish information relative to witnesses and other matters in connection with the defense" that Shenker would invariably later determine to be false. Hoffa "condoned this action," Shenker noted, "always defending O'Brien and stated he never would intentionally lie."

Chuckie was no Tom Hagen, and Jimmy Hoffa knew it. Yet Hoffa kept Chuckie at his side, defended him despite his failings, and invariably bailed him out. "If I had a problem, he was there," Chuckie told me.

Chuckie had a lot of problems, and Hoffa was there a lot. "Any fuckin' thing Chuckie wanted to do, he could do, and Hoffa would laugh like a proud father," explained Michael Bane, a Teamsters colleague who knew Hoffa and Chuckie well. "If he took a car and ran over ten fuckin' people, Mr. Hoffa would say, 'Why the fuck didn't they get out of the way?' Chuckie could do no fuckin' wrong."

Jimmy Hoffa was a deadly serious man who suffered no fools and in labor matters surrounded himself with learned professionals. Why, then, did he abide Chuckie? One explanation is that Chuckie was an effective factotum. Another, simpler explanation is that Hoffa loved him deeply. From the time he met Chuckie as a boy and continuing into his adult years, Hoffa showed Chuckie solicitude, patience, and affection that he showed no one else in his life except for his daughter, Barbara.

Hoffa's improbable, singular affection for Chuckie is one reason so many people assumed that he was Chuckie's real father. "Everybody thought Chuckie was more like a son than an employee," said Mike Bane. "Hoffa loved Chuck as a true son and Chuck loved Hoffa as a father," said Jackie Presser, who led the Teamsters in the mid-1980s. Charles Ashman, a Los Angeles journalist who spent a lot of time with Hoffa in his last two years, said that Hoffa "completely trusted" Chuckie and treated him "like a son." Many others said similar things, and Hoffa himself often referred to Chuckie as his son.

Chuckie also had traits that Hoffa found attractive. He boxed in high school, and had powerful arms, a quick temper, and a disposition toward violence. On a few occasions, he roughed people up at Hoffa's request. He also took care of Warren Swanson, a madman who tried to assassinate Hoffa during Hoffa's 1962 trial in Nashville for alleged labor law violations. Swanson entered the courtroom and from a pellet gun fired three shots that bounced harmlessly off Hoffa's upraised arms and chest. Chuckie, sitting a few yards away, leapt at Swanson and hit him in the head with his right fist, knocking him to the ground.

"Then I grabbed his hair and I'm bouncing his head off that marble floor, crushing him, and blood is spouting all over and I'm just beating him and beating him," Chuckie later told me. "I wanted to kill him because I thought he killed the Old Man." A Nashville newspaper reported that Chuckie "started stomping and kicking the assailant about the face and body with such force" that Hoffa ordered him to stop. The beating was so savage, according to the Nashville journalist Jim Ridley, that "spectators who had previously feared for their own lives now feared for Swanson's." Hoffa proudly told the press, "My man Chuckie O'Brien held that fellow down. I raised that kid."

Another quality that Hoffa prized—the one that made Chuckie such a great father to me decades later—was his absolute devotion. The neglected little boy grew into a young man who yearned for affection and who sought it by loving those he cared for with intense fidelity and by doing his all to please them. Chuckie loved Jimmy Hoffa more than anyone and would do anything he asked.

"Mr. Hoffa knew that I would never say no to him," Chuckie told me. "A lot of people would run away because they didn't want to get involved. He knew he could count on me."

Chuckie dutifully carried out even the craziest of Hoffa's directives. Hoffa complained incessantly about the sharp attacks on him and the Detroit Teamsters by *The Detroit News* in the early 1960s, and asked Chuckie to do what he could to stop it. Chuckie and a Teamster colleague paid a friend in the Wayne County Morgue $1,000 for a cadaver's head that they put in a box, wrapped in Christmas paper, and had delivered to Martin Hayden, the editor in chief of the paper.

"If I had to go through a wall for him, I would try," Chuckie told me. As the government bore down hard on Hoffa and his associates in the late 1950s and early 1960s, say Estelle and Ralph James, personal loyalty became Hoffa's "paramount consideration, surpassing competence." No one was more loyal to Hoffa than Chuckie.

Hoffa also counted on Chuckie to take care of his family. When Hoffa moved to Washington after he became president in late 1957, he was overwhelmed with running the union and dealing with what would become dozens of government investigations and several criminal trials. His wife, Josephine, would sometimes join him in Washington, but his teenage children, James P. and Barbara, remained in Detroit. And so Hoffa asked Chuckie to move his own young family into the Hoffas' home on Robson Street and watch over Barbara and James, and Josephine when she was in town.

Chuck complied without question. "I knew that the Old Man was on a course that he didn't have the time to do all that," he explained. The Robson house had four small bedrooms. Two families were a tight fit, but by all accounts no one complained. "We call it our Puerto Rican boarding house," Barbara Hoffa cheerfully told a journalist in the early 1960s. "It gets pretty crowded sometimes." Chuckie was on the road with Hoffa most days, so the everyday task of raising the Hoffa children fell to Chuckie's mother, Sylvia, and his wife, Mary Ann, who was only a few years older than Barbara. When Chuckie was not with Hoffa, his main task was to take care of Hoffa's family, to whom, Barbara would tell the FBI in 1975, Chuckie was "highly devoted." Barbara and James P. Hoffa viewed Chuckie as a "fun-loving and personable surrogate older brother who was never too busy to take their mother to the doctor or to do an endless variety of other errands," says Hoffa's biographer, Arthur Sloane. And Chuckie's mother was Josephine's closest friend.

The intimacy between Chuckie's family and Hoffa's was apparent at Barbara Hoffa's grand wedding to Robert Crancer in the Central Methodist Church in Detroit on October 21, 1961. Sylvia made all the arrangements, including helping Barbara find a dress and ordering the eighteen-layer, eight-foot cake next to which a beaming Hoffa and his daughter appeared in a front-page photo in the *Detroit Free Press*. Chuckie's son was an usher at the wedding. Chuckie's wife was Barbara's matron of honor. And Chuckie's then four-year-old daughter, Josephine—named after her godmother, Hoffa's wife—was the flower girl.

Just before the procession began, the father of the bride and much-feared labor leader tried to move young Josephine to a position beside him. "She stamped her foot and refused," reported the *Free Press*. "The Teamster chief's most eloquent pleas didn't move the four-year-old a foot."

CHUCKIE'S LOYALTY, STRENGTH, and devotion were important assets to Hoffa. But there was another reason why Hoffa held him so close. Following in his mother's footsteps, Chuckie was a conduit between Hoffa and the Italian syndicate.

In Hoffa's home base, the Detroit family had continued to do regular business with Hoffa ever since he gave them that first truckload of lumber in exchange for muscle in the labor wars of the early 1940s. It sold enforcement power to him when he needed help on picket lines or with employers. And it did mutually beneficial business with Hoffa in other ways.

"We go to him when we need favors," Anthony Zerilli, the son of the Detroit don Joseph Zerilli, explained to Anthony Giacalone on a hidden FBI microphone in 1963. "We have no ties with him."

The relationship between Hoffa and the Detroit family was ad hoc and contractual, not one of obligation or control. "The Outfit had influence," Chuckie explained. "People on the outside, we didn't look at them as gangster mob guys. They all had legitimate businesses and they called us when they had a problem and needed some help or assistance. And so did we."

Hoffa had quite different relationships with families in other parts of the country, however. When he began to expand beyond the Midwest, he needed the support of locals in big cities on the East Coast, both for votes at the national convention in 1957 and for help slowing down wages to facilitate his national contract dream. But unlike in Detroit, organized crime controlled many locals in the East. Long before Hoffa arrived on the national scene, the Five Families in New York exploited unions, including many Teamsters locals, as vehicles for bribes, extortion, kickbacks, embezzlement, price-fixing, and other rackets. By the 1950s, the mob-controlled locals had become a significant power within the international union because they controlled the delegates that elected the president.

"If you think New York and Chicago didn't put the okay on whoever become the president of the Teamsters, then you're fuckin' dreaming," Chuckie explained.

Hoffa couldn't realize his ambitious labor goals without confronting the reality of mob-controlled unions, especially in the East. "The Old Man learned what he needed to become the general president," Chuckie says. "He learned that Chicago and New York are the keys to your strength."

If Hoffa had been straitlaced, he might have narrowed his ambitions or fought it out. The latter option, however, was not realistic. "You couldn't come in there flexing muscles," Chuckie explained. "You would have to get the okay, even Hoffa." And the former option never occurred to him. He had worked with the mob for a long time closer to home. He knew what he wanted to accomplish in the East, and he had no compunction about striking a deal.

"You can't choose your associates," Hoffa once said. "You associate with whomever you need to make you a winner."

The conventional wisdom is that Hoffa's entrée into New York came through a pact he struck with Johnny Dioguardi, a capo in the Lucchese crime family. Johnny Dio was "a great guy," according to Chuckie, but the rest of the world knew him as a violent labor racketeer who hired a thug to throw sulfuric acid in the face of the labor journalist Victor Riesel, blinding him, on April 5, 1956. (Chuckie doubts that Dio ordered the Riesel attack, but the evidence that he did is pretty solid.) At about the time of the attack, Hoffa arranged for Dio to set up nearly a dozen New York City Teamsters "paper locals"—fake union locals that were typically vehicles for extortion and sweetheart contracts—in exchange for those locals' support for his run at the Teamsters presidency in 1957.

Chuckie says that Hoffa's foray into the metropolitan New York was more complicated. At first Hoffa was flummoxed about how to proceed, since each of the Five Families had tentacles in different, uncoordinated locals, making impossible the unified regional action he sought. Sometime in the early 1950s Hoffa contacted several heads of important locals, "but 'fuck him,' they won't even answer him, because they don't fuckin' listen," explains Chuckie.

With Sylvia's help, Hoffa arranged a meeting in a New York hotel, probably in 1954, with LCN members who controlled unions. The men were "Tony Pro" Provenzano, who was then a Genovese capo and a rising business agent in Teamsters Local 560 in Union City, New Jersey; Matthew "Matty the Horse" Ianniello, another Genovese family member who controlled transit unions in New York; Johnny Dio, who at the time ran several corrupt United Auto Workers locals in and around New York; and Dio's Lucchese family superior, Antonio "Tony Ducks" Corallo, who also had unions in the area.

The meeting was a disaster. The wiseguys argued among themselves and Hoffa grew irritated because none had the authority to speak for all Teamsters in the New York area. "Hoffa wanted to know where the power was, who could decide this thing," Chuckie says. "He wanted to separate the rat shit ^ from the raisins. He wanted to know who the boss was."

Tony Pro provided an answer. "Jimmy, we'll get this straightened out," he said.

Provenzano grew up on New York's Lower East Side and was an amateur boxer and Teamsters union truck driver until he was befriended by a neighbor, Tony Bender, a Genovese family lieutenant who ran labor rackets on the New York and New Jersey waterfronts. Bender helped Tony Pro become a made man, and by 1950 had set him up as a business organizer for Local 560 in Union City, New Jersey, which several years later elected him president. Chuckie had known Tony Pro since he was a young boy, when his mother introduced him.

"Was he a good organizer?" I once asked, early in our conversations, before I fully understood what Tony Pro was about.

"He never organized anything," Chuckie replied.

"Why was he in charge of the local?" I continued.

"He came up and took over," Chuckie explained. "Nobody wanted to fuck with him—I mean, if you had any brains." In 1961, Provenzano put a hit on a not-so-smart rival at Local 560, Big Anthony "Three Fingers" Castellito, whose body was never found.

Chuckie says Tony Pro—who had a short, squat, powerful build not unlike Hoffa's—was the most uncontrollably violent man he ever met in his life. "He was a beautiful guy, but he had a temper and a short fuse like dynamite," he told me. "It was lights out with him."

Pro's tendency toward violence influenced his organizing tactics. "Tony Pro ran a muscle union," Chuckie explained. "I mean old school. You get in his fuckin' local, you live by whatever contract they negotiate and there is no shit, he didn't want to hear it. He don't want no whiny. And if an employer didn't sign the contract or didn't agree with him, he'd send a couple of his guys over there and they agreed."

By the late 1950s, Provenzano had extended his power from Local 560 to Joint Council 73, a statewide conglomeration of New Jersey locals. This gave him control over all freight being trucked through New Jersey, which meant he could charge trucking companies for passage through the state and filch cargo when he liked.

Such were the Teamsters locals that Hoffa had to deal with when he sought to expand to the East. These were not locals that, as in Detroit, had beneficial but formally arm's-length relations with organized crime. "All of labor in New York was controlled by the Outfit," Chuckie explained to me. "Hoffa found these people in charge. They'd been there a long time."

When Tony Pro told Hoffa that he and his friends would "get this straightened out," Chuckie knew what he meant. "They're going to sit down and talk to all the heads of the Five Families," Chuckie explained. Chuckie doesn't know how the Commission decision was made, though he says that the young Provenzano played a role. The Five Families decided they would do what they could to support Hoffa in the 1957 convention and would help him as well in his efforts to control wage increases in the Northeast.

"The deal was, they wanted something back," Chuckie told me. Chuckie didn't tell me everything Hoffa had to give in return. It involved cash. It involved promotions and power for LCN union men like Tony Pro, who a few years later would become a vice president and the first wiseguy on the Teamsters International Executive Board. The paper locals to Johnny Dio were also part of the deal. "We need a local for a candy maker, we need a local for this, we need a local for that," Chuckie explained, mimicking the mob's requests. "Hoffa didn't give a shit, he issued the charters."

"So the reason the Outfit wanted the locals was because they could go to the employers—were they organizing people?" I asked.

"They fuckin' shake them down, Jack!" Chuckie said. "That's all they were doing. They didn't give a fuck about employees."

"Why did they need a local to shake them down?" I continued.

"Because you've got a threat then, Jack. You've got the International Brotherhood of Teamsters Local 237 coming to you, not one of the Company guys walking in with a ball bat and saying, 'Look, motherfucker, this is what you're going to do.'"

Hoffa made many accommodations to exercises of criminal power in his union's name—not just in New York, but in Chicago, Kansas City, Philadelphia, and other cities. He was remarkably candid in defense of these arrangements. He always claimed he was simply adapting his labor goals to the power reality on the ground. As he said in a report to the Central Conference of Teamsters in 1958: "Why don't the investigators inspect the product where it really counts—the wages and conditions under which our members work?" He also continued to charge that complaints about his criminal associations were hypocritical. "Twenty years ago the employers had all the hoodlums working for them as strike-breakers," he told a reporter in 1959. "Now we've got a few and everybody's screaming."

WHERE HOFFA WENT far beyond simply accommodating organized crime, however, was in his promiscuous doling out of the Teamsters' massive financial funds. Beginning in 1949, Hoffa gave the administration of the Midwestern Central Conference of States health and benefit insurance account to a small insurance company in Chicago run by a former marine named Allen Dorfman.

Chuckie describes Dorfman as a "classy guy and great dresser who played the shit out of golf." The rest of the world knew him as the stepson of Paul "Red" Dorfman, a labor racketeer with close ties to the Chicago Outfit who in Tony Pro fashion took over the Chicago Waste Handlers Union in 1939. Red met Hoffa a few years later when he was trying to organize Michigan's scrapyard industry, and he introduced Hoffa to the Chicago Outfit. Hoffa awarded the Teamsters' insurance business to Red's handsome, athletic stepson. The business generated millions of dollars of service fees and was the first of many favors in exchange for Chicago's support.

The insurance service fees were small beans compared to the cash generated by the employer-funded Central States Pension Fund that Hoffa negotiated for and established in 1955. "The pension fund, that's the whole ball of wax," Chuckie emphasized. "The Company made a lot of money with the pension fund. They didn't give a fuck about the union; the only thing they cared about was being able to get money out of the pension fund."

The fund accumulated $10 million in its first year, and by the time Hoffa went to jail a dozen years later it was taking in more than $6 million each month. It was the largest private pension fund in the country at a time when such funds were barely regulated. At first Hoffa let banks manage the money in the fund. But by 1958, he began investing from the fund himself with the approval of a twelve-member board of trustees—half employers, half union men—that Hoffa was on and dominated. He also headquartered the fund in Chicago and eventually arranged for Allen Dorfman to manage it. The pension fund offered loans at below-market interest rates and usually invested in real estate, especially hotels, resorts, and shopping centers. Hoffa used the funds, as he once put it, "to reward friends and make new ones," including friends in organized crime. And Allen became his moneyman and one of his closest aides.

Hoffa loaned generously to LCN leaders and other organized crime figures around the country. But *he* controlled the loans, and he was not intimidated or coerced by the Mafia or anyone else in doling them out. Hoffa drove a hard bargain, and he frequently rejected applications, many by organized crime. "The Old Man often said no and didn't give a reason why," Chuckie says. But the mob couldn't get the money for their highly profitable ventures from traditional banks, and so they were thrilled to do business with Hoffa on his terms.

During the twelve years that he ran the fund, Hoffa made hundreds of loans to finance projects all over the country, but nowhere more so than in Las Vegas. "There would not be a Vegas today if it weren't for the Old Man," Chuckie says correctly. "These stuffed-shirt asshole bankers, because of their reputation of being so legitimate, they couldn't be seen giving money to a gambling person, so we started loaning them all the money."

Hoffa's main but far from exclusive collaborators were the St. Louis businessman Jay Sarno and Morris "Moe" Dalitz, the Cleveland gangster whom Chuckie's mother, Sylvia, introduced to Hoffa when they were all three young and living in Detroit. Hoffa gave out Teamsters' loans for casinos and resorts through front groups run by Dalitz, Sarno, and others, but organized crime families around the country had hidden interests that allowed them to skim untold millions.

Hoffa was delighted by his Vegas investments. He scheduled a Teamsters Executive Board meeting in August 1966 to coincide with the opening of Sarno's Caesars Palace, the lavish faux Roman hotel and casino that Hoffa had juiced with a $10 million loan. Hoffa stayed in the best suite in the hotel and was "hailed like a Caesar," according to Sarno's biographer David G. Schwartz. The prudish Hoffa wasn't drawn to the "orgy of excitement," including "libations, feasting, casting of dice, spinning of wheels, turning of cards, and revelries of entertainment," that the invitation to the opening gala promised. During the inaugural events, he sat bored at the table of honor in the Circus Maximus dinner theater, "refus[ing] all drinks, quietly watching the drunken debauch around him."

But Hoffa had been engaged and excited during the previous two days as he roamed the lobby and casino, chatting with and encouraging the laborers who were putting on finishing touches, and occasionally getting on his knees to help. "I watched the Old Man in the days before Caesars Palace was supposed to open up," Chuckie says. "He would go in and help the electricians screw in wall lights and plug covers and shit because he wanted the hotel to open properly. He was so proud."

Hoffa was pleased with his investments for another reason. Conventional wisdom is that "the Teamsters Union did not participate in the [Vegas] skimming operations," according to an investigative study of the union's history. Hoffa was reportedly rewarded for his loans with the organized crime support he got in elections and when he needed muscle. But Chuckie says that Hoffa himself got a very large piece of the action.

"You had to come up with ten percent of the loan in cash and you never got it back, and that was just for the application," Chuckie told me. Hoffa also got points on the loans and had at least one point with at least eight Vegas casinos: the Desert Inn, Caesars Palace, Circus Circus, the Fremont, the Stardust, the Dunes, the Aladdin, and the Sands. A point amounted to 1 percent on the monthly skim. "A point doesn't seem like a lot, but let me tell you what, it is," Chuckie told me. Both before and during Hoffa's imprisonment, Chuckie frequently flew to Vegas to collect Hoffa's personal cut and then delivered the cash to Allen Dorfman in Chicago.

Hoffa had points on many other loans as well. Just before he went to prison in 1967, he listed every property he owned, along with his take. "He took a pad," Chuckie told me. "'One, two, three, four, five, six, seven, eight, nine, ten. Okay. Caesars Palace.' One point. Boom boom boom. Every one of them that he gave loans to, he got cash." Chuckie speculates that Hoffa accumulated many tens of millions of dollars from his various loans and side deals. He spent the money freely to win friends and buy influence. And what he didn't spend or invest, he parked (among other places) with Dorfman in Chicago and with Calvin Kovens, a Miami real estate developer and one of Hoffa's few close friends outside labor.

Despite Hoffa's elaborate, profitable, long-term relationships with organized crime families around the country, he spent practically no time with wiseguys. He saw mobbed-up union bosses like Anthony Provenzano and Johnny Dio in the course of his labor work. And he had a very close relationship with Anthony Giacalone, whom he saw a lot over many decades—in Detroit and also in Miami Beach, where the two men owned apartments in adjacent buildings. But Hoffa spent his days and nights working on the union. Beyond Giacalone, he had no time and little interest in hanging out with any of the scores of top guys with whom he did business, and he understood very little about their operations.

"He never really jacked around with people on a personal basis," Chuckie says. "Mr. Hoffa loved Italian people, but he didn't understand the Outfit. The only thing he knew about them is that he liked spaghetti. He didn't believe in taking an oath of silence and all that kind of stuff, he didn't understand all that tradition. He didn't know the inner workings, he didn't give a shit about the rituals and rules."

Hoffa was particularly dismayed by the "whole kissing stuff and all that shit," Chuckie says.

"Why they got to kiss each other when they come in a room?" Hoffa once asked Chuckie. "What the fuck's that about?"

It's a "Sicilian belief, that's showing respect," explained Chuckie.

"Well, why can't they just shake your fuckin' hand?" Hoffa responded.

Hoffa had no affinity for the Italian syndicate. He dealt with it for the same reason and with the same philosophy as he dealt with every other organization: it could help him achieve some greater end. And he dealt with it from a distance, through intermediaries.

One of Hoffa's main intermediaries was Chuckie's mother, Sylvia, who helped Hoffa navigate the Sicilian world he never really grasped. "My mother was a person that had the ability to have a friendship with people, and through that friendship she was able to assist Mr. Hoffa in getting the kind of help he wanted," Chuckie says. Sylvia was especially effective in convincing Hoffa to make loans. "When Uncle Tony and them couldn't do it, they'd come to her and she'd do it," Chuckie told me. "My mother could get Hoffa to do anything the Outfit wanted."

Chuckie wasn't puffing. Secret FBI microphone recordings from the early 1960s make clear that Sylvia was in the middle of many loans—not just to the Detroit guys, but to families in Kansas City, Chicago, and New York. She was also tight with the bankroller Allen Dorfman. Sylvia "is your key to Jimmy Hoffa," Anthony Giacalone explains on one recording to a colleague for whom Sylvia had just secured a Teamsters' loan. "What she has done for us and vice versa [in] business there is no money that could pay [for] it."

Over time, beginning in the early 1960s, Chuckie began to take over some of Sylvia's go-between responsibilities. "My mother, God bless her, she started wanting to relax a little bit," Chuckie told me. Chuckie was still in his twenties, and Sylvia was well aware of his strengths and weaknesses. She schooled him on how to behave before top guys and how to avoid surveillance. And she laid down two cardinal rules. One was to never embellish any message. "Make sure when you talk to Uncle Tony you say it the way it is, don't add anything," is how Chuckie remembers her advice. The other was never to question orders from either side. "If something had to be done, I did it," Chuckie explained. "I didn't ask questions. You never ask, Jack."

Chuckie never received specific compensation for his errands beyond the general support Hoffa gave him. "I never asked him for anything. My mother said you don't take anything and I didn't take because Mr. Hoffa took care of my mother. That's all I cared about. I just wanted to make sure that she got whatever would have come to me."

Chuckie was compensated in a different way, however, a way that probably meant more to him than cash. Hoffa was a financial hub whose spokes connected to the top dons around the country. When Chuckie carried messages for Hoffa, he got to meet these revered gentlemen in their inner sanctums. I could never get Chuckie to tell about the content of the scores of messages he delivered, but he did list with pride the many senior wiseguys whom he met.

"I knew every guy in Chicago," he told me, including Paul "the Waiter" Ricca, Anthony "Big Tuna" Accardo, Salvatore Giancana, and Louis "the Tailor"

Rosanova. In New York he met Anthony Corallo, boss of the Lucchese crime family, who controlled most of the labor action in New York. "You can't get any bigger than Tony Ducks," Chuckie told me with pride. He also saw "the little guy in Florida, the little Jew, Mr. Lansky," in Hallandale Beach, Florida. He was a go-between with "Uncle Nick and Cork," the Civella brothers who ran Kansas City, and Russell Bufalino, a Pennsylvania crime boss whom Chuckie used to meet in an old Italian restaurant in Pittston. He also often visited Carlos Marcello, the longtime Louisiana crime boss, in his modest New Orleans office in a motel he ostensibly ran, especially in the 1960s when Marcello was trying to help Hoffa with his legal difficulties.

IN THE 1959 issue of the *Harvard Business School Bulletin*, the labor-union maven James Healy, who taught industrial relations at Harvard, wrote an essay about Jimmy Hoffa and the future of American labor unions. By this point Hoffa had been president of the Teamsters for two years and had suffered through three criminal trials, all resulting in acquittals, and a grueling Senate investigation that had portrayed Hoffa as an evil man who led a mobbed-up union and exploited members for his personal financial gain.

Healy examined Hoffa's record "with some objectivity" in order to "complicate the neat black-and-white picture we have painted of the man." He noted that in contrast to "many other union leaders," Hoffa had "gone out of his way to establish a close rapport with his constituents" and had a "loyal membership following." He also noted that most employers "respect him and view him as a person whose word at the bargaining table is entirely reliable," and that Hoffa had "developed substantial support in the inner circles of many employer groups" with which he bargained. These achievements, on top of growth in membership and worker benefits under Hoffa, led Healy to conclude that despite Hoffa's "schooling in sin," he may "emerge as one of the outstanding labor leaders of all time."

But it was not meant to be. Hoffa's labor accomplishments would be largely forgotten, and the Teamsters union would not lead American labor to the promised land. Hoffa was a brilliant labor tactician who succeeded wildly in improving the lives of working men and women, but at great cost in corruption of various kinds.

As the journalist Eric Sevareid explained on a CBS radio broadcast in late 1958, and as his deep connections with organized crime make plain, Hoffa was also "a man at war, in his heart, with orthodox society" who "accepts [trouble] as the normal and natural element of his existence." Hoffa hated the cops as a kid, Sevareid continued, and as an adult transferred that hate to "the Senate, the courts, the press, the whole sprawling, occasionally majestic apparatus of social order." And so it was inevitable, Sevareid concluded, that he would also come to hate a man naturally at home in that order: "the button-down-collar, Ivy League prosecutor Robert Kennedy."

FOUR

BOBBY, JIMMY, AND CHUCKIE

W HEN I WAS A TEENAGER, Chuckie told me tales about
Robert F. Kennedy's moralizing crusade to destroy Jimmy
Hoffa. His favorite story was about an encounter he had with
the thirty-one-year-old "snot-nosed little piece of shit" early in the Senate
labor racketeering hearings that Kennedy led as chief counsel.

As part of his investigation into Hoffa's corruption, Kennedy in the summer of 1957 issued subpoenas for all books and records in several Detroit
Teamsters locals dating back to 1950. At the time, Hoffa was the president
of Local 299, a vice president of the international union, and the leading
contender to replace President Dave Beck at the Teamsters convention that

fall. Hoffa eventually made photostatic copies of the relevant documents and asked Chuckie, who was twenty-three years old, to deliver them to the federal building in Detroit. "Make sure he signs for every damned piece of paper or don't give them to him," Hoffa commanded. "I don't want some of them getting 'lost' and him claiming we didn't give them to him."

Chuckie followed Hoffa's orders literally. He drove a station wagon full of boxes to the federal building loading dock and insisted to Kennedy's brainy forensic accountant, Carmine Bellino, that he needed a signature and receipt for each document. After a fruitless back-and-forth, a miffed Bellino reentered the building. "Next thing I know here comes Bobby Kennedy storming down with his sleeves rolled up," Chuckie told me. "A typical pompous Ivy Leaguer with his hair uncombed and tie undone."

RFK refused to sign for the individual documents. "I'll send you straight to jail for obstructing justice if you don't release them," he threatened Chuckie in his high-pitched, nasally Boston accent.

"I ain't afraid of that," Chuckie said before climbing into the station wagon and returning to Hoffa's office.

Kennedy quickly hauled Hoffa into court, but the judge agreed with Hoffa's legal team that the request for individualized receipts was reasonable. Chuckie later drove back to the federal building, where he watched with satisfaction as Bellino and other government employees spent several hours "pounding out signatures" for every document.

Chuckie loved to tell this story because in it he bests the loathed Bobby Kennedy. But Chuckie's was a trivial tactical success in a lengthy war that Kennedy viewed in righteous apocalyptic terms. RFK was convinced that Hoffa's labor tactics and ties to the underworld rendered his leadership of the Teamsters a "conspiracy of evil," as he said in his 1960 book, *The Enemy Within*. And he brought to the war many weapons that Hoffa and Chuckie lacked, including inherited wealth, a Harvard education, gilded connections, an influential father, and the clout of two important government jobs his family helped him secure—chief counsel for the Senate Permanent Subcommittee on Investigations in the 1950s and attorney general of the United States in the early 1960s. Hoffa and Chuckie disdained "the little pimple" for these unearned and undeserved privileges. And they came to despise him when he used his government perches to lead a massive, relentless, and ultimately successful seven-year effort to destroy Hoffa.

Chuckie often spewed bile about RFK when I was young. A common theme was that Kennedy and the Justice Department were crooked. "They can break every law there is, but they got backup," Chuckie would say. As a boy I didn't really understand what Chuckie meant by the government's "backup," and by the time I entered my anti-Chuckie, pro-government phase in law school, I no longer cared. Over the next two decades, I avoided learning about Kennedy's assault on Hoffa, probably for the same unconscious reason I never watched the *Godfather* movies until my forties: I wanted to keep my distance from anything associated with Chuckie, good or bad.

Much later in life, I came to understand that by "backup," Chuckie was referring to the government's ability to skirt the law in circumstances of its choosing even as it enforced the law against everyone else. Kennedy had plenty of justification to go after Hoffa, who defied law and conventional morality till the day he died. But Kennedy targeted Hoffa in a personal vendetta probably without parallel in American history. And in so doing, he broke many rules for which he was never held accountable, and did collateral damage to the institutions he sought to protect.

BOBBY KENNEDY'S CHILDHOOD propensity to pick fights had grown "manic" as he approached his thirtieth birthday on November 20, 1955, according to his biographer, Evan Thomas. Kennedy had an innate confidence in his virtue, a Manichaean view of the world, and a large chip on his shoulder. He also possessed a seething desire to right wrongs and do great things. But he couldn't figure out how. In his twenties he ran his brother John's successful 1952 Massachusetts Senate campaign and held inconsequential government jobs, including a brief stint as assistant counsel to Republican senator Joseph McCarthy on the Permanent Subcommittee on Investigations. "Without quite realizing why, he seemed to be searching, with a kind of grim determination, for an outlet for his anger—for an enemy he could attack," says Thomas.

After Dwight D. Eisenhower's reelection in 1956, Kennedy sought to boost both his stature and his brother John's 1960 presidential chances. His guide was the man who defeated JFK for the number two spot on the 1956 Democratic ticket, Senator Estes Kefauver of Tennessee. In 1950–51, Kefauver led sensational Senate hearings about organized crime in fourteen cities around the country that thirty million Americans watched on television. "There is a sinister criminal organization known as the Mafia operating throughout the country with ties in other nations," the Kefauver Committee concluded. Neither Ike nor the FBI nor Congress followed up on this finding. But Kefauver introduced the American people to colorful Mafia figures for the first time and earned a national reputation that propelled him to a vice presidential candidacy.

RFK sought to achieve similar stature for the Kennedy clan with a congressional investigation into the link between labor and the mob. After the 1956 election, Bobby, now the investigations committee's chief counsel, floated the idea to the new chairman, Arkansas senator John McClellan. McClellan was a conservative Democrat from a right-to-work state who saw labor as "the greatest potential threat to our freedom," as he explained in a letter to Eisenhower in 1957. He quickly assented, but to accommodate congressional governance rules he set up a new committee called the Select Committee on Improper Activities in Labor and Management. Eight senators, including John F. Kennedy and Barry Goldwater, joined "the McClellan Committee." Bobby and his staff did the work, and Bobby did most of the questioning of important witnesses. The successes and excesses of the investigation have been remembered, with justification, as his.

When Kennedy began snooping around the union in 1956, he quickly discovered the enemy he had been seeking. He was disgusted when he learned of Hoffa's underworld connections, tough labor tactics, and misused union funds. Even before the hearings began, says Schlesinger, Kennedy concluded that Hoffa had "betrayed honest workingmen and had no object in life beyond money and power for himself."

Hoffa was familiar with government investigations. He had been arrested almost twenty times in the 1930s, mostly for picket-line offenses. A state prosecutor had convened a multiyear grand jury in the 1940s to examine the strong-arm tactics Hoffa used to organize Detroit's grocery stores and other businesses. Hoffa got off the hook by temporizing and then pleading guilty to a trivial offense. In 1953, Hoffa suffered through an investigation led by Michigan representative Clare Hoffman, who accused him of extortion, conflicts of interest, mob ties, and misusing pension funds. But once again Hoffa avoided legal jeopardy when Hoffman's committee abruptly dropped the investigation. Chuckie told me why. "Mr. Hoffa," he said, "put together a program in Michigan politics—all the top guys brought pressure on the committee."

Based on these and similar experiences, Hoffa knew how to handle government scrutiny. He eschewed banks accounts and credit cards and operated solely in cash. He lived modestly. And he made a practice of destroying (or not creating) incriminating documents. "I know what I done wrong and what I didn't," Hoffa told a reporter of his preparation for Kennedy's hearings. "I know what they'll uncover and what they won't. . . . All my life I've been under investigation."

Hoffa and Kennedy met for the first time on February 19, 1957, one week before the hearings began, over dinner at the home of Eddie Cheyfitz, a Washington insider who hoped to smooth relations between the two men. At the time it didn't seem like a crazy thought. Kennedy and Hoffa were in many ways alike: diminutive, candid, charming, mercurial, demanding, intense, inspiring, hardworking, edgy, competitive, authoritarian, vengeful, fearless, moralistic. Both men wore white socks with their suits and both had a puerile tendency to show off their fitness. These odd similarities were entirely irrelevant, however, due to the men's incompatible experiences and commitments. The dinner at Cheyfitz's was "foredoomed," Schlesinger writes, because each man "represented what the other detested most."

Hoffa spent the evening bragging about his toughness and candidly discussing the smash-mouthed world of labor organizing. "I do to others what they do to me . . . only worse," he told Kennedy. The performance triggered every one of Kennedy's many moralistic trip wires. He left the dinner thinking Hoffa was more depraved than he had assumed. Hoffa had an equally severe reaction. "Here's a fella thinks he's doing me a favor by talking to me," he thought after shaking Kennedy's limp hand in Cheyfitz's living room. Hoffa became angrier when Kennedy jabbed him condescendingly with questions about his upbringing, education, and salary. He left thinking Kennedy was prissy, ill-informed, and a "damn spoiled jerk."

The McClellan Committee hearings began a week later, on February 26, 1957, in the ornate marble-columned Senate Caucus Room where Joseph McCarthy had hounded alleged communists a few years earlier. Over the next three years, the committee would issue 8,000 subpoenas in 253 separate investigations and hear 270 days of testimony from 1,526 witnesses. The hearings became a national television spectacle that dwarfed the impact of Kefauver's effort.

RFK drew blood early, a few months into the hearing, when he caught Teamsters president Dave Beck using hundreds of thousands of dollars of union funds on his lavish personal life. Beck announced that he would not run for reelection, and he was later found guilty of embezzlement. More than a dozen others would be convicted for crimes investigated by the committee, and many more would have their reputations sullied. But the man whom Kennedy tried hardest to guillotine in the hearings survived and in some ways was empowered by them, at least in the short term.

Kennedy thought he had taken care of Hoffa even before he testified. A few weeks before the hearings began, a former Secret Service agent named John Cye Cheasty told Kennedy that Hoffa had offered to pay him to get a job on the committee and become a spy. Kennedy quickly hired Cheasty, made him a counterspy, and began feeding Hoffa information through Cheasty under the FBI's watchful eye. The FBI arrested Hoffa on March 13 just after filming him in Washington's Dupont Circle handing Cheasty cash for committee documents. "I never seen so many guys with machine guns in my life," says Chuckie, who was there. A sophomorically giddy Kennedy brought his wife, Ethel, to watch the spectacle of Hoffa's arraignment at 2:00 a.m. the following morning. He was so confident of a conviction that he pledged to "jump off the Capitol" if Hoffa prevailed.

Hoffa's attorney at the trial in July was the thirty-seven-year-old Edward Bennett Williams, a law partner of Eddie Cheyfitz who had grown to fame in recent years representing the likes of Joseph McCarthy and the New York mob boss Frank Costello. Williams, who was friends with Bobby Kennedy, got RFK to admit at trial that he had given sensitive committee documents to journalists prior to hearings so they could write up preview stories about impending disclosures. It was an unethical practice that Kennedy would deploy over the next three years to great effect to tar many witnesses' reputations, often unfairly, before they appeared at the hearing. But at this early stage the tactic backfired. Hoffa testified—almost certainly falsely—that he paid Cheasty as an attorney to help him prepare his testimony, and that Cheasty told him he got the documents from reporters.

"Kennedy's sloppy practices with the press had provided Hoffa with a plausible alibi," notes James Neff, who wrote the definitive account of the Hoffa-Kennedy feud. Hoffa bolstered his alibi with a friendly appearance at the defense table by the boxer Joe Louis in front of a mostly African American jury, and with stories in a local newspaper that portrayed the Teamsters president "as a lifetime friend of the Negro people," as Schlesinger reported. After Williams's brilliant closing argument beatified Hoffa and destroyed Cheasty's credibility, the jury acquitted Hoffa on July 19. At Williams's request, Chuckie bought a parachute from an army-navy surplus store and delivered it to Kennedy's office in room 101 of the Russell Building on Capitol Hill.

It was the first of many times that Kennedy thought he had Hoffa pinned, only to see him wriggle free. Each time, Kennedy's moral outrage grew. "I feel deeply that it is the obligation of people with advantages to lead those who lack them," Kennedy once said, explaining why a Boston blue blood was motivated to save American blue-collar workers from Hoffa's clutches. But after the 1957 acquittal, a different motivation was born and would steadily grow: revenge. With each Hoffa victory, Kennedy got angrier, became more vindictive, and invariably cut more corners.

RFK pulled out the stops to demolish Hoffa during his scheduled testimony before the committee the following month. He blanketed Teamsters offices with subpoenas. Kennedy had also cajoled the IRS to depart from its policies to let him fish through Hoffa's income tax returns looking for wrongdoing without any inkling that a tax crime had been committed. When Hoffa showed up for his first confrontation with Kennedy in the packed Caucus Room on August 20, 1957, Kennedy's aims were to "besmirch Hoffa before a national television audience, reveal him as a crook to his fellow Teamsters, and (assuming he didn't plead the fifth) trap him into committing perjury," writes Neff.

Over a fifth of the witnesses before the McClellan Committee, 343 in all, pleaded the Fifth Amendment—many, according to Chuckie, on Hoffa's advice. Kennedy made these witnesses pay for exercising their constitutional rights. He asked inflammatory, disgust-filled queries and hurled insulting charges, over and over, often with little evidentiary basis, knowing that the witnesses could not challenge his insinuations of guilt without waiving the privilege. He also belittled tough-guy witnesses who took the Fifth as "morally . . . yellow," or "little girl[s]," or lacking "guts."

These tactics, as the historian David Kaiser notes, "were obviously designed, like McCarthy's, to humiliate and disgrace individuals whom law enforcement, for a variety of reasons, was unable to convict." Though not illegal (because of the separation of powers between courts and Congress), they nonetheless did "subvert the integrity of the administration of justice," as the Yale Law School professor Alexander Bickel charged at the time, because their "sole object" was "the destruction of this or that individual" rather than the collection of information for legislation. But because Kennedy was a more attractive figure than McCarthy and because his targets were less sympathetic, his tactics did not attract the same level of renunciation as when McCarthy deployed them.

Edward Bennett Williams urged Hoffa to invoke the Fifth Amendment despite the reputational costs that Kennedy was sure to impose if he did. But Hoffa eschewed the road of implicit guilt by silence and chose the more dangerous road of testimony under oath. He went toe-to-toe with Kennedy, cagey and unapologetic, for seventeen legally fraught hours over four days.

Kennedy first tried to embarrass Hoffa with his long arrest record, but Hoffa proudly noted that most were for picket-line clashes. When Kennedy asked why Hoffa's income exceeded his Teamsters salary, Hoffa chalked it up to gambling winnings. When RFK revealed Hoffa's business interests, some with union-connected firms, Hoffa said they gave him insights as a labor negotiator. Hoffa forcefully defended his union record when Kennedy questioned his labor tactics. He displayed an impressive capacity to avoid perjury by a hair, and to render senators slack-jawed, with obfuscating denials such as "to the best of my recollection I have no disremembrance." And he enjoyed toying with "Bob," whom he treated with open disrespect. Hoffa childishly glared at Kennedy, who childishly glared back, only to receive a Hoffa wink in return.

Kennedy spooked Hoffa, and almost drew him to commit perjury, when he challenged Hoffa's evasive answers about his ties to Johnny Dio with damning recordings of conversations between the two men that a New York state prosecutor had lawfully obtained. In these and other encounters, RFK showed the world that Hoffa engaged in shady union deals and allowed mobsters to run some locals for personal benefit. Hoffa had an explanation for everything, but he came off as complacent about criminality in his union when he refused to say a bad word about the unsavory characters RFK linked to him.

But while Kennedy tarnished Hoffa's reputation in respectable quarters, he did not establish illegal activity. RFK was an inexperienced attorney who lacked the self-discipline, the well-ordered evidence, or the cross-examination skills needed to put the crafty Hoffa away. His helter-skelter, television-focused approach was better designed to shape public opinion than to build a legal case. When the August hearing ended, he had not landed a knockout blow.

Undaunted, Kennedy worked furiously to deny Hoffa the presidency of the Teamsters at the union's national convention six weeks hence. He pressured the Justice Department to bring perjury charges against Hoffa. But many career prosecutors considered the referrals "to be something of a joke," according to Neff. The committee reconvened a week before the convention with four more days of hearings that aired dozens more accusations against Hoffa in an effort to influence the convention's outcome. Many criticized RFK's extraconstitutional zeal. It was inappropriate to use hearings "to campaign against any candidate for office in a labor union," *The Washington Post* declared, especially since the committee was using the "discredited investigating technique" of disclosing details about what it would prove before even taking evidence. *The Wall Street Journal* warned that the committee might "serve the cause" of Hoffa by allowing him to claim he is a "martyr to continued outside persecution."

The *Journal* was right. The charges against Hoffa that seemed so scandalous to Kennedy weren't news to the Teamsters rank and file. The convention delegates and union members cared much more about the thick slabs of bacon that the trusted working-class Hoffa delivered than the accusations hurled by the union-hating Arkansas senator and the preppy Harvard multimillionaire who had never dirtied his hands with real work. Hoffa manipulated the delegate process to favor him at the convention, but it was all overkill. He faced weak opponents, and his already-broad support swelled as a result of the committee's attacks on him. On October 4, 1957, Teamsters delegates elected Hoffa president by a three-to-one margin.

Hoffa's emotional acceptance speech before the raucous crowd in the Miami Beach auditorium included an attack on Kennedy and the McClellan Committee. "Something is wrong when a man may be judged guilty in a court of public opinion because some enemy or some ambitious person accuses him of wrongdoing by hearsay or inference," he said to deafening applause. "Destruction of the basic principles of due process and the use of the lawmaking function to smear a man's reputation without the protection of judicial processes is one of the greatest threats to freedom and the rights of the individual that America has faced in our lifetime." Jimmy Hoffa was an improbable defender of the American Constitution. But in this instance, he was right.

Hoffa and Kennedy would slug it out twice more in 1958. Kennedy continued his scattershot charges against Hoffa and continued to draw open inferences about Hoffa's criminal guilt when mob figures and criminals associated with Hoffa—including Anthony Provenzano—took the Fifth. Kennedy also continued what the historian Robert Caro describes as "a steady stream of inflammatory press releases and the use of friendly reporters to propagate the image of Hoffa that he himself saw." And to undermine Hoffa's support, RFK expanded IRS queries in 1958 to cover 3,500 individual tax returns in all, casting what Neff describes as "a dragnet, working backwards from suspicions about people and companies connected to Hoffa, the Teamsters,

and mob figures." This unethical practice crossed the line to a criminal violation, never redressed, when Kennedy's team put some of the confidential IRS
information into the congressional record.

To Kennedy's amazement and despair, Hoffa survived the onslaught.
During the first two years of the McClellan Committee, Hoffa also endured
two criminal trials in New York for alleged illegal wiretapping, an indictment
for perjury in connection with that trial, expulsion of the Teamsters by the
AFL-CIO, a judicial monitor to redress irregularities in the 1957 election,
and a thorough investigation by the Justice Department of his McClellan
Committee testimony. In the face of the government barrage and despite
the 1957–58 recession, Teamsters union membership and coffers increased
sharply during the first eighteen months of Hoffa's command.

Hoffa was strangely empowered by Kennedy's efforts. "The more they
hammered him, the more his power grew," Chuckie told me. The New York
Times's venerable labor reporter A. H. Raskin privately interviewed nearly
two hundred Detroit Teamsters in terminals and loading docks in late 1958,
after the brunt of RFK's charges had been aired. All but two pledged fealty
to Hoffa, declaring "with every indication of sincerity," as Raskin wrote, that
"Hoffa had done a standout job on wages, welfare, grievances and every other
phase of union service."

Bobby Kennedy left the McClellan Committee in September 1959. But
his campaign to destroy Hoffa had long-term consequences for the American labor movement. When the hearings began in February 1957, union
density—the percentage of American employees in trade unions—was near
its historical peak. The month before, support for unions among the American people had hit its all-time high, 75 percent, in the Gallup polls.

But February 1957 would be a high point in the history of American labor.
By September, in a poll taken soon after Kennedy's widely watched four-day
grilling of Hoffa, support for unions had dropped to 65 percent. And that was
just the beginning. As the labor historian Nelson Lichtenstein has noted, the
committee's hearings would go on to have a "devastating impact on the moral
standing of the entire trade-union world" and "marked a true shift in the public perception of American trade unionism and of the collective-bargaining
system within which it was embedded."

The blame for this shift lies largely with Hoffa. His amorality and righteousness about the labor cause blinded him to the risks of his corrupt methods and to the need for obeisance to public morals. Hoffa truly believed, as Chuckie puts it, that "everything he did was for the workers"—that the violence, mob deals, piles of illicit cash, and coziness with employers ultimately served the members' interests and thus were legitimate. He came to the McClellan Committee thinking the government used law as a tool to suppress workers, an opinion reinforced by his experience with RFK. But his defiant embrace of criminal tactics and associations allowed Kennedy and the anti-labor members on the committee to paint him as a subversive force. Hoffa's resilient Teamsters would flourish for another decade after the McClellan Committee hearings, but his performance tarnished the entire labor movement, with consequences that persist to this day.

Bobby Kennedy also bears a share of responsibility for the committee's pernicious impact on American labor. Kennedy never credited Hoffa's improvement of the lives of hundreds of thousands of workers. He manipulated the print press and nationally televised hearings to exaggerate even Hoffa's and the Teamsters' sins. In his single-minded vendetta to get Hoffa, Kennedy tended to ignore the bad acts of employers, who were often willing participants on the other side of some of the illegal activities he attributed to Hoffa. He made the public think that Hoffa and the Teamsters had established an internal conspiracy to subvert the American economy, and that unions had grown into dangerously powerful institutions that threatened not just America's economy but also its moral sense.

Kennedy's McClellan Committee performance gave the postwar conservative critique of American unions a broad public audience and a credibility that anti-labor forces in the business community and Congress never could have achieved. For a decade before Kennedy got going, conservatives had with middling success been trying to paint unions as corrupt, too-powerful, dangerous threats to American society. They had been assisted in this effort by the Kefauver hearings in 1950–51 and the airing of On the Waterfront in 1954.

But it was Kennedy, the righteous Boston liberal, who used a massive investigation, McCarthyite techniques, and extensive coverage by a fawning press to firmly identify the American labor movement with the scary and

impenitent Jimmy Hoffa. The five conservatives on the eight-man committee, all of whom hailed from right-to-work states—McClellan, fellow Democrat Sam Ervin, and Republicans Barry Goldwater, Carl Curtis, and Karl
Mundt—did not always see eye to eye with RFK. But they welcomed and
encouraged his implicit identification of labor power with malfeasance and
ran with the cover he gave them.

Having "depicted the problem of union corruption as intrinsically bound
up in the phenomenon of union power," notes the historian David Witwer,
the McClellan Committee "pursued a political agenda intended to win new
restraints on that power." The immediate consequence was the Landrum-
Griffin Act of 1959. The law began as a reform of union democracy and
finances. But in the anti-labor atmosphere created by the committee, conservatives were able to add provisions that eliminated labor's most successful
organizing and strike tactics, not because they had a connection to corruption, but simply because unions needed to be cut down.

More fatefully, the committee embedded in the public mind, including
the minds of many workers, the idea that unions were flawed institutions
exercising illegitimate power. There are many reasons why union membership fell from its high point in the mid-1950s to its current pitiful state
of 10.5 percent of the workforce, including labor's bureaucratization, adverse legislation (like Landrum-Griffin), global competition, technological
change, and hostile judicial and administrative decisions. But the most fun-
damental reason was the identification of the entire labor movement with
corruption, violence, and bossism—an identification that crystallized with
Bobby Kennedy's singular crusade and that has never receded, even though
the idea was exaggerated at the time and is largely inaccurate today.

RFK BECAME HIS brother John's presidential campaign manager when he
stepped down from the McClellan Committee. But he was not yet done with
Hoffa, who at RFK's urging became a target in the presidential campaign.

"In my judgment, an effective Attorney General with the present laws
that we now have on the books can remove Mr. Hoffa from office," John F.
Kennedy said during a campaign event on September 23, 1960. "And I can as-

sure you that both my brother and myself share a very deep conviction on the subject of Mr. Hoffa." Three days later, in his opening remarks in the famous first debate with Richard Nixon, Kennedy continued the theme. "I'm not satisfied," he said, "when I see men like Jimmy Hoffa—in charge of the largest union in the United States—still free."

Hoffa understood his fate should Kennedy become president, and did everything he could to stop him. He spent freely to help Hubert Humphrey during primary season, to deny Kennedy the nomination on the first ballot at the Democratic Convention, and to support Richard Nixon during the presidential campaign. Nothing worked.

"We got a problem now," Hoffa said to Chuckie when he spoke to him the day after the election, on November 9, 1960. They had a bigger problem when President-elect Kennedy announced five weeks later that he would nominate Bobby to be attorney general. The appointment was controversial—less for its nepotism than for RFK's undistinguished legal career and his reputation as a hothead. For Hoffa it was horrible news. "Mr. Hoffa was not worried because of Kennedy's ability—legally, he couldn't get out of a fuckin' phone booth," Chuckie told me. "But when he became attorney general he put that Hoffa Squad together."

The attorney general is chief prosecutor and thus the fulcrum of American justice. "The prosecutor has more control over life, liberty, and reputation than any other person in America," Attorney General Robert Jackson said in a famous speech in the Great Hall at the Justice Department on April 1, 1940. With the snap of his finger, the prosecutor can start a financially ruinous investigation and then can secure a grand jury indictment based on a "one-sided presentation of the facts." He can also "pick people that he thinks he should get," and then order investigations and search the luxuriant criminal code for a crime.

Jackson warned that these abuses were especially dangerous against persons whom prosecutors find "personally obnoxious" or "subversive." He cautioned that "activities which seem benevolent to wage earners, persons on relief, or those who are disadvantaged in the struggle for existence may be regarded as 'subversive' by those whose property interests might be burdened or affected thereby."

Two decades after Jackson spoke these words, his successor, Robert Kennedy, fulfilled them. "From the moment he was named attorney general, Bobby was determined to prosecute Jimmy Hoffa," wrote Nicholas Katzenbach, the head of RFK's Office of Legal Counsel who later succeeded him as attorney general, in his memoirs. RFK had been shamed by his prior failures to defeat the hated leader of the most powerful union in the nation. He had also been furious in the late 1950s when the enormous pressure that he and McClellan brought on the Justice Department to indict Hoffa bore no fruit. But now that Kennedy was attorney general, satisfying the grudge against Hoffa "became the public policy of the United States," as the law professor Monroe Freedman wrote in 1967. It was a policy RFK himself could now personally implement, with the full backing of his brother the president and the redoubtable resources of the U.S. government.

Bobby set up a "Hoffa Squad" of bright young lawyers and former McClellan Committee investigators and expanded the Justice Department's organized crime section of the Criminal Division. He also revved up the IRS. RFK arranged for his tax law professor at the University of Virginia, Mortimer Caplin, to become the IRS commissioner after extracting a pledge from Caplin that the IRS would be more aggressive in fighting Hoffa and organized crime.

Soon after inauguration, RFK asked the IRS to give the McClellan Committee's accountant, Carmine Bellino, access to all "files, records, and documents requested by him." When Bellino and his staff identified a Teamster or mob suspect, the IRS conducted what Caplin called a "'saturation type' investigation," including wiretapping and bugging, which increased dramatically during Kennedy's tenure. "It made Mr. Hoffa livid that Kennedy got away with shit like this," Chuckie told me, especially since "Bobby Kennedy's dad was a booze guy," a reference to Joseph Kennedy's associations with organized crime during Prohibition.

Kennedy deployed these tools to investigate (and thus harass) anyone closely associated with Hoffa, including the attorneys who represented him in Kennedy-led investigations and trials, regardless of criminal suspicion. RFK also continued to feed the press tendentious information about Hoffa. But now the leaks were designed not to discredit people testifying before

Congress, but rather, more fatefully, to shape the perception of the juries whose votes Kennedy needed to put Hoffa and his friends in jail. Senators and congressmen from both parties, and many commentators and civil libertarians, including the ACLU, denounced these tactics as an abuse of power.

Few law-compliant citizens could withstand this unparalleled onslaught, and Hoffa was very far from law-compliant. RFK first indicted Hoffa in connection with a company called Test Fleet that Hoffa established in 1949 to lease trucks to firms that employed union members. The Justice Department charged that Test Fleet received payments from trucking firms in exchange for favorable labor terms, in violation of the Taft-Hartley Act. The practice was not obviously illegal at the time, and was at worst a misdemeanor. Ramsey Clark, later Lyndon Johnson's attorney general, advised Kennedy against prosecution. Kennedy disagreed, and threw his best lawyers and investigators, and boundless funds, at the case.

"Never in history had the government devoted so much money, manpower and top level brainpower to a misdemeanor case," noted the journalist Victor Navasky. Kennedy left nothing to chance. He chose to prosecute Hoffa in Nashville, which had tenuous connections to the case, in part because his friend and ghostwriter on *The Enemy Within,* John Seigenthaler, was the editor of a local newspaper, *The Tennessean,* that would cover Hoffa critically. RFK also took the inappropriate step of lunching with the presiding judge, William E. Miller, before the trial began. RFK later claimed he did not discuss the Hoffa case with Miller, but there was no other reason for the men to meet.

When Hoffa arrived in Nashville for trial, twenty-five FBI agents coordinated by radio to track Hoffa and his associates by car and on foot. "I knew where he was twenty-four hours a day," said Kennedy's chief investigator, Walter Sheridan, of Hoffa. Hoffa deployed counterintelligence in the person of Bernard Spindel, an electronics surveillance expert who recorded FBI radio communications while agents tailed "The Man," Hoffa, and "the ex-boxer," Chuckie.

Kennedy and his men believed that Hoffa's criminal extremes and prodigious resources justified their very aggressive moves, even in a misdemeanor case. "On the other side, you had a group of criminal defendants prepared to do total and unreserved battle," said Hoffa Squad member Nathan Lewin. "You had to meet that with similar resources and flexibility from the government side."

Whether justified or not, Kennedy's tactics wore on Hoffa, who after five years of relentless pursuit had grown paranoid. His life "was dominated by his fear of 'that little monster,'" according to Ralph and Estelle James, who spent much of the year before the Nashville trial with Hoffa and wrote in detail about it. Hoffa believed that the FBI at Kennedy's direction "tapped his phone, opened his mail, and beamed electronic listening devices on him from half a mile away, aided by invisible powder they had rubbed onto his clothes." And so his team fought back against the Hoffa Squad with every tool it had. "We knew the government spent taxpayer money endlessly and broke every rule there was," Chuckie says. "We went after Kennedy just as hard as he went after us."

The most notorious thing the Hoffa camp did was to tamper with the Nashville jury on a grand scale. Someone claiming to be a reporter from the *Nashville Banner* (a rival to *The Tennessean*) contacted several pro-government jurors to ask questions about Hoffa, thus requiring their dismissal. The president of the Nashville Teamsters Local, Ewing King, sought to bribe a local policeman whose wife was on the jury. Allen Dorfman was in town and making phone calls to find ways to get at the jury.

And then there was the juror Chuckie worked to bribe. He provided the cash and coordinated the effort by an African American Teamsters business agent named Larry Campbell and his uncle in Nashville, Thomas Parks, to attempt to bribe Gratin Fields, the only African American on the Hoffa jury.

Unfortunately for Chuckie's scheme, Judge Miller got wind of these unsubtle bribe attempts and dismissed several jurors, including Fields, before final deliberations in the case began. Two days before Christmas in 1962, the remaining jurors deadlocked seven to five in Hoffa's favor, indicating that he probably would have prevailed against the government's weak case without the bribes. As soon as the jury announced its result, however, Miller ordered prosecutors to convene a new grand jury and investigate "shameful" jury tampering efforts.

Five months later, the government indicted Hoffa along with six others, but not Chuckie, for jury tampering during the Test Fleet trial in Nashville. Although the prosecutors never figured out precisely how the attempted bribe of Gratin Fields unfolded, internal Justice Department documents from the period indicate that they knew about Chuckie's involvement. A Hoffa Squad memorandum dated March 27, 1963, indicates that prosecutors planned to indict Chuckie along with Hoffa and others. But they later dropped him from the indictment, perhaps (as Chuckie speculated) for fear that he would take the fall for Hoffa and testify that Hoffa knew nothing about the scheme.

The government believed that Hoffa was the mastermind of the bribery scheme even if he did not act directly. But it had only one witness who could tie Hoffa to the scheme: Edward Grady Partin.

Partin was the brawny, slick-tongued president of Teamsters Local 5 in Baton Rouge, Louisiana. He was "a great organizer and a real Teamster" who "ran a good local" with a Hoffa-like strong arm, according to Chuckie. In the fall of 1962, Partin faced three criminal indictments: one in Louisiana for kidnapping, one in federal court for embezzling funds from Local 5, and one in Alabama for manslaughter growing out of a hit-and-run the previous Christmas.

The day before Hoffa's trial began, Partin showed up in Nashville at the Andrew Jackson Hotel. The Hoffa entourage—Hoffa, Chuckie, a dozen lawyers, union officials from around the country, and many secretaries and other assistants—had taken over the seventh floor of the hotel as a temporary headquarters. It was a chaotic scene. One large suite was converted into a conference room for legal deliberations. Another was made into an office where Hoffa conducted union business every afternoon after trial, as was his practice. "Every time he got indicted, we'd set up an office in the hotel and bring in two girls and telephones and he ran the union as soon as the court finished for the day," Chuckie says. "He also held meetings, people would fly in." Hoffa and Chuckie and the lawyers also slept on the seventh floor.

Chuckie brought Partin to see Hoffa in his suite and watched him "whine for help" with his legal problems. The impatient Hoffa, who knew about Partin's legal troubles, listened to his pleas for two minutes and then asked him to step outside while he decided what to do. Hoffa characteristically made a snap decision to help out a Teamster in trouble. "Go get twenty," he ordered Chuckie. Chuckie went to the hotel safe where Hoffa kept his cash. "From our defense fund I gave that no-good son of a bitch twenty thousand dollars," Chuckie told me.

It didn't seem unusual when Partin lingered to help out with odd jobs during the trial. As Chuckie told me, Partin "was one of several guys—from Cleveland, Detroit, all over—that came there and just hung around to support the Old Man for the trial." No one suspected that Partin was working for the government. "If you knew the guy you couldn't think he's a rat," Chuckie explained. "You don't think a guy that's a Teamster is gonna do that."

But Partin was a rat, or perhaps more accurately, a mole. A month earlier he had contacted local government officials from his cell in the East Baton Rouge Parish jail, claiming that Hoffa had told him of a plot to assassinate RFK. "I know a way to get out of here," Partin told his cellmate. "They want Hoffa more than they want me." After failing and then passing a lie detector test about the assassination claim, Partin reached an agreement with the Hoffa Squad. He would "report to the federal authorities any evidence of wrongdoing that he discovered" in the Hoffa camp during the Nashville trial. In return, the government would eliminate or defer the charges against him and make child-support payments to his ex-wife.

Partin thus approached Hoffa as a paid government agent looking for crimes, and was lurking in the background on the seventh floor of the Andrew Jackson Hotel as Hoffa and his attorneys prepared witnesses and discussed trial strategy. He often spoke with many of the Hoffa associates, including Chuckie and Ewing King, and Hoffa's lawyers. And then he would dutifully report what he learned, on an almost daily basis, to Kennedy's lead investigator, Walter Sheridan.

Fifty years later Chuckie was still enraged by Partin's double cross. Perhaps he felt responsible for Hoffa's troubles since he had on his own initiative undertaken the Fields bribe attempt, and told Hoffa about it. Or maybe he imagined that subsequent events might have turned out differently, for Hoffa and for him, had Partin not showed up in Nashville.

"Fuckin' Partin, I should have killed him that night, and I almost did," he once told me. Chuckie was referring to an evening during the Nashville trial, very near the time that he pummeled the crazed drifter who tried to assassinate Hoffa with a pellet gun. In the distrustful atmosphere of the Test

Fleet trial, Chuckie often roamed the halls in the evening with a .410 shotgun. One night at about 10:00 p.m. he noticed that the door to the suite that served as Hoffa's on-the-road Teamsters headquarters was open and there was movement inside. He entered and saw someone crouching behind a desk and threatened to shoot if he didn't rise with his hands up. Partin arose and claimed he was looking for Hoffa. "I should have blown his fuckin' head off," Chuckie told me. But instead, Chuckie told Hoffa what happened. Despite his paranoia about RFK's tactics, Hoffa let it slide. "The Old Man thought so much of Partin as a union guy and how tough he was in Louisiana, he didn't suspect him."

Hoffa's trial for tampering with the Nashville jury began across the state in Chattanooga, Tennessee, in late January 1964, just a few weeks after Hoffa had concluded his historic National Master Freight Agreement. As the trial meandered for several weeks without any testimony tying him to the undoubted evidence of attempted bribes in the Test Fleet case, Hoffa grew confident of yet another victory over Kennedy. But when the government called its surprise witness, Hoffa exclaimed, "My God, it's Partin." He then grew "frozen and pale, white as a sheet," as Chuckie remembers. "It shocked him. The whole courtroom was shocked."

Partin testified for five days. The gist of his testimony was that Hoffa asked him to stay in Nashville to help with the jury-bribing scheme, and spoke specifically about the juror whose husband Ewing King had bribed and about having "the colored male juror in my hip pocket."

Chuckie begged Hoffa to let him take the stand to take the fall for the Fields bribe attempt, but Hoffa wouldn't let him. "I argued over and over that I was the only one involved in anything the government might have considered illegal, but the Old Man wouldn't hear it," he explained. "Till the last day of my life I will wonder why."

On July 26, 1964, after hunting Hoffa for seven years, Bobby Kennedy finally snared him when the Chattanooga jury announced that Hoffa was guilty on two counts of jury tampering in the earlier trial. The conviction had nothing to do with the labor abuses or mob connections that Kennedy had been railing about since 1957. It was, rather, an own goal by the Hoffa side. Hoffa and his team had been lucky and resourceful in avoiding legal jeopardy in six previous trials and in the face of more indictments. But in Nashville they had grown exhausted, cocky, and neglectful in their illicit behavior even though they knew that RFK would use every trick.

Hoffa was stunned by the verdict. In his hotel suite thirty minutes later, surrounded by lawyers and union officials, he asked Chuckie to join him and a few others in his bedroom. "It was the most worried I had ever seen him," Chuckie told me. "He closed the door of the suite and he said, 'We've got a problem and it's going to take a miracle to fix it.'"

Hoffa then gave Chuckie an assignment. He asked him to stay in Chattanooga and work with Hoffa's local attorney, Harold Brown, to "dig up dirt" on anyone related to the trial—prosecutors, judge, jurors, marshals—in order to help Hoffa win on appeal or get a new trial. "I need you to help me here more than I ever have," he told Chuckie. He then gave him $250,000 in cash, and told him to "use Spindel," the electronics expert, "when you need him."

Chuckie would come to view his Chattanooga assignment as the most demanding and senseless one he undertook for Hoffa, and his execution of it as the clearest sign of his unquestioning loyalty. For much of the next eighteen months, he was stuck in Chattanooga, away from his family and Hoffa and the Teamsters, miserably executing Hoffa's desperate open-ended order. Chuckie approached every juror and FBI agent he could find, and anyone who knew the jurors or the judge, or who worked in the hotel where the jurors were sequestered. He eventually garnered affidavits from hotel bellboys who said that marshals delivered liquor to the jurors and from prostitutes who said they had sex with jurors and marshals during the trial, all supposedly with the aim of influencing the jury. He also elicited an affidavit from a prostitute who claimed that the trial judge told her over drinks that he was out to destroy Hoffa. These affidavits did not withstand scrutiny when later presented to a judge.

As Chuckie was trying to dig up dirt in Chattanooga, Hoffa faced a different trial two months later in Chicago, Illinois, this time for fraud and conspiracy in connection with alleged kickbacks on a Central States Pension Fund loan connected to a real estate development in Florida. Four months later, a jury once again found Hoffa guilty. As in Chattanooga, very little concrete evidence tied Hoffa to the crime. And once again, the conviction had nothing to do with Hoffa's organized crime connections—a point Allen Dorfman made to Chuckie's mother, Sylvia, as the FBI learned from a secretly implanted listening device in Sylvia's apartment a few months after the trial. "Hoffa wouldn't be in this trouble if he would have stayed away from the ten-cent moochers," Dorfman told Sylvia, according to an FBI summary. "He never had any trouble when he was dealing in New York and Chicago," he added, referring to the crime families in those cities.

ONE HUNDRED DAYS before jurors in Chattanooga returned a guilty verdict for Jimmy Hoffa on March 2, 1964, Lee Harvey Oswald shot and killed President John F. Kennedy from a sixth-floor window in the Texas School Book Depository in Dallas. When Robert Kennedy learned the news in a telephone call from FBI director J. Edgar Hoover on a sunny afternoon by the pool at his Hickory Hill estate in Virginia, he immediately suspected that Hoffa might be involved. He asked his closest aide, Walter Sheridan, to scour every back channel for Hoffa's involvement. For the same reason, he ensured that one of his Justice Department attorneys, Charles Shaffer, was placed on the staff of the Warren Commission.

Many critics viewed the Warren Commission as a whitewash because, despite Shaffer's involvement, it did not seriously pursue the possibility that Hoffa or the mob was involved in JFK's death. Many authors have filled the commission's gap by garnering stray circumstantial facts to cook up conspiracy theories about Hoffa's involvement.

Hoffa hated the Kennedy brothers. He threatened violence against Bobby, in public and in private. He would have benefited from the assassination. He had close connections to the two underworld figures most often linked to the Kennedy assassination, Carlos Marcello of New Orleans and Santo Trafficante of Tampa. He also went way back with Chicago mobster Red Dorfman, who was a childhood acquaintance of Oswald's assassin, Jack Ruby, and in whose union Ruby briefly worked. And in the two months prior to the assassination, Ruby placed telephone calls to several Hoffa Teamsters associates, including Barney Baker, a muscle organizer with many links to organized crime.

Chuckie acknowledges that Hoffa was pleased about Kennedy's assassination. "Bobby Kennedy is just another lawyer now," he told reporters the weekend after the assassination. "One prick gone, maybe we'll get lucky with the second one" was his reaction to Chuckie. But Chuckie always laughed at the thought that Hoffa had anything to do with the Kennedy murder. "It's all bullshit," he told me many times.

It is unlikely that Hoffa was involved without Chuckie knowing about it—not just because he was Hoffa's intimate, but also because he was his conduit between Hoffa and Marcello. Chuckie does, however, claim that he and Hoffa knew Jack Ruby—a claim bolstered by James P. Hoffa's assertion that Ruby was "the kind of guy everybody knew," including his father.

Chuckie met Ruby briefly through his mother in Detroit, where Ruby's brother ran a well-known dry cleaner's that Chuckie frequented. He describes Ruby as a "wacko knockabout guy, a street person hustling to make a dollar." Chuckie speculates that Ruby might have called Barney Baker for professional reasons. "Ruby was managing juke joints with the naked girls going up and down the poles," Chuckie told me, referring to Ruby's Dallas strip clubs. "He probably had a labor problem, which Barney was good at fixing."

The House of Representatives did a do-over of the Warren Commission investigation of Kennedy's assassination, beginning in 1976. It looked closely at Hoffa's involvement and reached an assessment similar to Chuckie's. Its 1979 report noted that Hoffa's links to the underworld, combined with his hatred of the Kennedys, gave him "the motive, means and opportunity for planning an assassination attempt" on JFK. But the committee said that it "uncovered no direct evidence that Hoffa was involved in a plot on the President's life, much less the one that resulted in his death in Dallas in November 1963." The committee "strongly doubted" that Hoffa would risk such a plot given the intense government scrutiny he was under. And the committee supported Chuckie's conjecture about Ruby's telephone calls, attributing them to Ruby's need for "assistance in a nightclub labor dispute." Its final conclusion was that it was "improbable that Hoffa had anything to do with the death of the President."

In the months between his brother's assassination and Hoffa's first conviction, Bobby Kennedy had calmed down about Hoffa's complicity. He had also begun his fabled transformation from the ruthless, overbearing, and hateful Bobby who pursued Hoffa to the ground, into the gentler, more mature, and compassionate Bobby who would emerge as the great liberal hope in 1968 and beyond, in the remembrance of many. At the Hoffa Squad's celebration after Hoffa's Chattanooga conviction, Kennedy sat "silent, melancholy," according to Robert Caro. "I'm tired of chasing people," he said later that day. After Hoffa's convictions, he didn't show much interest in Hoffa or the seven-year scorched-earth battle to destroy him.

BOBBY MAY HAVE lost interest in Jimmy Hoffa after his brother died, but the legacy of his prosecutorial hounding of Hoffa, like his McClellan Committee legacy for organized labor, outlived him. In a pattern familiar in American justice, decisions that the government thought in the passion of the times were justified to meet extreme threats proved self-defeating, and established precedents and policies that took on a life of their own, with unexpected and often pernicious consequences.

Bobby Kennedy assumed that putting Hoffa in jail would be a blow to the union's cozy relationship with the mob and its pension loans for mob projects. But he misunderstood the relationship and would be proven tragically wrong about the impact of Hoffa's removal. The Teamsters' business dealings with LCN grew under Hoffa, who had no compunction about accommodating wiseguys when necessary or when it brought him benefit. But the union and its pension fund remained under Hoffa's control, and Hoffa often declined to support mob projects or requests that he believed did not serve his or Teamsters' ends.

When Hoffa went to jail in March 1967 to serve his eight-year sentence, however, the wall between the mob and the union, and especially its pension fund, collapsed altogether. Hoffa's weak successor, Frank Fitzsimmons, "allowed existing rackets to flourish and new ones to start with no credible prospect of IBT [International Brotherhood of Teamsters] interference," stated a 2002 study of organized crime in the Teamsters. And even more consequentially, the study concluded, "with Fitzsimmons at the helm of the IBT, Allen

Dorfman and his mob associates enjoyed virtually unfettered control over loans." The sharpest irony of RFK's crusade against Hoffa is that it opened the door for the mob to infiltrate and leech off the union like never before.

RFK's drive against Hoffa also had unfortunate legal and political consequences. His targeting of Hoffa is the paradigmatic case in American history of wielding prosecutorial power to destroy a person rather than pursue a crime. Under RFK's command, the Department of Justice determined that the evil Hoffa needed to be brought down and then conducted a comprehensive inquisition into every aspect of his life in order to pin on him a crime, any crime, using every tool of governmental coercion. It also used the same tools against his colleagues and associates in an effort to undermine Hoffa. Even RFK loyalists in the Justice Department who otherwise defended his extreme tactics acknowledged that he veered toward persecution and vendetta in the inordinate focus and resources he allocated to nailing Hoffa.

One need not be naïve about criminal justice to agree with this assessment. Prosecutors have deployed "pretextual prosecutions" against the Mafia since at least 1931, when the federal government put away Al Capone not for his bootlegging endeavors or frequent murders, but rather for income tax evasion. The ideal of prosecuting the crime and not the man is just an ideal. Despite Robert Jackson's warnings, our system of justice has long tolerated flexible uses of the government's manifold legal tools to put away dangerous criminals.

But RFK's relentless, very public, and obviously vengeful campaign to put away a single man at any cost was alarming precisely because the same techniques could be used to destroy just about any citizen who draws the ire of the state. It also belied the appearance of evenhanded justice that is so crucial to the legitimacy of prosecutorial power, especially since RFK was the brother of a president who had pledged to put Hoffa away. It is impossible to assess RFK's actual impact on public perceptions of future Justice Department actions. But his "Get Hoffa" campaign was widely invoked (or decried) as a precedent in the two subsequent notorious instances of prosecutorial excess—Ken Starr's pursuit of Bill Clinton in the late 1990s and John Ashcroft's pursuit of Islamist terrorists in 2001–2002.

It is easier to trace the pernicious effects of the Kennedy brothers' reorientation of the IRS for political ends. Earlier administrations had sometimes used the IRS to serve non-tax goals, including in law enforcement. But RFK's political litmus tests for top appointments, and his systematic integration of the IRS into non-tax-related investigations against Hoffa and the mob, marked a significant departure from past practice. Once the Kennedys got a taste of what IRS files could do, they used them aggressively for other non-tax-related prosecutions. They also established the Ideological Organizations Project, which examined the activities of disfavored groups with an eye toward diminishing their power through punitive audits or removal of tax-exempt status. The Kennedys did not go as far as Richard Nixon, who used the IRS more promiscuously to destroy his political opponents. But they paved the way for Nixon's excesses, which he modeled on their use of the IRS.

Chuckie's condemnation of Kennedy's seven-year pursuit of Hoffa and his organized crime friends—that "they can break every law there is, but they got backup"—was hyperbole, since Kennedy secured jury convictions against Hoffa and dozens of organized crime figures that courts ultimately approved. And yet Chuckie's criticism, I have come to realize, contained an important kernel of truth. In his McClellan Committee extremes, his exploitation and transformation of the IRS, and the Hoffa Squad, Bobby Kennedy and his government colleagues neglected, elided, or interpreted away ethical and legal restrictions that are supposed to channel and constrain the federal government's colossal power to destroy one's reputation and liberty.

The Kennedy men did not set out to break legal and ethical rules, which they, unlike Hoffa, believed in deeply. RFK viewed himself as a virtuous vindicator of law's majesty, which Hoffa and his thuggish associates mocked and defiled.

And yet as Justice Louis Brandeis once wrote, "the greatest dangers to liberty lurk in insidious encroachment by men of zeal, well-meaning but without understanding." Kennedy and his investigative agencies believed they were at war with Jimmy Hoffa and that the nation's fate was at stake. But as has happened so often in other wars, the imperative to defeat the enemy skewed the government's understanding of the proper limits on its actions. In no context was this more true than in its abuse of its secret surveillance powers—as I would come to understand when Hoffa's and Chuckie's legacies and my own government work became entwined.

FIVE

SURVEILLANCE BACKUP

MY BOSS FOR A YEAR in the Department of Justice, Attorney General John Ashcroft, was as unlike his predecessor Robert Kennedy as Kennedy was unlike Jimmy Hoffa. Ashcroft was a country boy from a family of modest means that lacked political connections. He began his career in public office as Missouri state auditor and slowly worked his way up the Missouri political ladder as a social and fiscal conservative to become governor and senator before George W. Bush nominated him for U.S. attorney general in January 2001. Though he attended college at Yale University, Ashcroft, like Hoffa, had a natural mistrust of Ivy Leaguers, especially of the progressive variety.

And yet after the attacks of September 11, 2001, Ashcroft modeled his approach to defeating terrorists on Robert Kennedy's approach to defeating Jimmy Hoffa and organized crime. "Forty years ago, another Attorney General was confronted with a different enemy within our borders," Ashcroft told a gathering of U.S. mayors in October 2001. "Then, as now, the enemy that America faced was described bluntly—and correctly—as a conspiracy of evil," he added, using Kennedy's phrase to describe Hoffa's Teamsters. Ashcroft praised Kennedy's aggressive use of "all of the available resources in the law to disrupt and dismantle organized crime networks." A month later, Ashcroft spoke at the ceremony to dedicate the Justice Department building to RFK. Ashcroft's first note of praise was for Kennedy's "extraordinary campaign against organized crime that inspires us still today in the war against terrorism."

Ashcroft deployed the Kennedy model aggressively to find and incapacitate the 9/11 enemy. The Justice Department he led took hundreds of undocumented immigrants from the Middle East and South Asia off the streets for immigration violations. It deployed criminal laws to jail or hold "material witnesses," usually with little proof of terrorist ties. It approved aggressive interrogations bordering on torture. And it signed off on the legality of Stellarwind, President George W. Bush's post-9/11 surveillance program that intercepted the telephone calls and email messages of Americans and collected metadata in bulk.

President George W. Bush secretly approved Stellarwind in the Oval Office on the morning of October 4, 2001. According to an official government report, a few hours later the legal authorization for the program was "pushed in front of" Ashcroft by an unnamed person "and he was told to sign it." Ashcroft had not been "read in" to the classified program before October 4, and he had done no research on its legality.

Three weeks earlier, on the morning of September 12, President Bush had interrupted the first National Security Council meeting following the 9/11 attacks and looked at Ashcroft. "Don't ever let this happen again," Bush said, appearing to place responsibility for the most devastating terrorist attack in U.S. history on his attorney general. Ashcroft took this remark "personally" and made it his "guidepost" in the war on terrorism. Years later he would invoke the president's words in urging me to go as far as the law would allow in approving aggressive counterterrorism actions. I imagine that he had this guidepost in mind when he dutifully signed the papers for Stellarwind after being told that the program was "critically important" to keeping Americans safe.

Ashcroft's signature on the authorization was critically important as well. The intelligence bureaucracy charged with executing Stellarwind had good reason to worry that it violated criminal restrictions on domestic surveillance. Ashcroft's sign-off solved that problem. As a practical matter, Justice Department approval of an intelligence operation precludes the Department from prosecuting anyone involved in implementing it, even if the program is later deemed to violate the law. It's an extraordinary power.

It's also another example of what Chuckie—who knows nothing about surveillance law but a lot about government double standards—calls "backup": the government's ability, in secret, to determine the limits on its actions and thus to skirt legal rules that bind everyone else. Surveillance backup did not begin with John Ashcroft's signature on the Stellarwind authorization. For the six decades prior to 9/11, presidents and attorneys general, under pressure to find and defeat various "enemies" in American society, had secretly blessed surveillance practices that would be declared illegal when they came to light years later. One such illegal surveillance program took place during Bobby Kennedy's tenure as attorney general and would ensnare Chuckie, Anthony Giacalone, Sylvia Pagano, and perhaps Jimmy Hoffa.

ON JULY 26, 1917, the godfather of the American surveillance state, the twenty-two-year-old J. Edgar Hoover, joined the Department of Justice. It was a disquieting time, three months after the United States entered World War I and four months before the Bolsheviks' October Revolution. The patriotic Hoover quickly ascended to the head of the Department's Alien Enemy Bureau and spent World War I and its aftermath zealously hunting for the thousands of anarchists, communists, disloyal citizens, and other enemies of the state that he and his subordinates would round up and incapacitate. Hoover had a conspiratorial bent and was a master at using the many secrets he amassed to enhance his power. He became director of the Justice Department's Bureau of Investigation in 1924, and remained there, through its 1935 rechristening as the FBI, until his death in 1972.

During Hoover's fifty-five-year career ferreting out the ever-changing security threats that he so often defined, the telephone wiretap and the microphone bug were two of the FBI's most valuable tools. Since the invention of the telephone and the microphone recorder, the government has used these technologies to listen in on private communications. Hoover developed an insatiable appetite for the private information the FBI gathered from wires and bugs without the targets' knowledge. Congress and courts intermittently imposed legal restrictions to control the obvious threats to privacy this appetite posed. And Hoover and his executive branch colleagues, in turn, became adept at circumventing those restrictions.

The Supreme Court imposed one important restriction in late 1939, when it interpreted a federal law to bar the government from using wiretap evidence in court. Attorney General Robert Jackson, Hoover's nominal boss, concluded that the decision required the executive branch to stop tapping wires. "Justice Department Bans Wire Tapping," read the *New York Times* headline on March 18, 1940.

Hoover acted quickly to have Jackson's decision reversed. Adolf Hitler had been gobbling up countries in central Europe and was preparing for war against the United States. The FBI, with President Roosevelt's endorsement, was scouring the country for Nazi spies and saboteurs. When Hoover conveyed to Roosevelt that Jackson's ruling blinded the Bureau to the Nazi menace, FDR overruled his attorney general and ordered domestic wiretapping to continue.

In a secret memorandum to Jackson explaining his decision, FDR acknowledged that "under ordinary and normal circumstances wiretapping by Government agents should not be carried on for the excellent reason that it is almost bound to lead to abuse of civil rights." But, he weakly reasoned, "I am convinced that the Supreme Court never intended any dictum . . . to apply to grave matters involving the defense of the nation." Jackson acquiesced and government wiretapping continued. Jackson's successor, Francis Biddle, later announced this interpretation publicly, but the scale of the government's secret wiretapping would not become known until the 1960s.

Roosevelt's and Hoover's circumvention of the Supreme Court established a pattern. Whenever a legal obstacle to electronic surveillance arose, Hoover would agitate his White House or Justice Department superiors about the dangers to the nation of going dark. These officials had a constitutional duty to comply with the law. But since many national security and law enforcement actions never made it to court, the attorney general and, ultimately, the president, had to interpret the law for themselves. This unavoidable process has always carried the danger of opportunism, especially when the stakes are high. Even the finest executive branch lawyers, acting in good faith, have a tendency to interpret away constraints on actions deemed important by the president, especially when the actions take place outside of public scrutiny. Such tendentious resourcefulness in secret is the essence of backup.

Hoover's next major need for surveillance backup arose in connection with microphone bugs, which the FBI had been using with the knowledge of attorneys general since at least 1940. The FBI often had to break into a home or office to implant a bug before listening in. In a 1954 case called *Irvine v. California*, Robert Jackson, now a Supreme Court justice, made clear that this practice "flagrantly" violated the Fourth Amendment. Hoover quickly asked Dwight D. Eisenhower's attorney general, Herbert Brownell, for guidance. He also gave Brownell an "informal draft" of the authorization he hoped for, which emphasized the dangers to national security should the Bureau not be able to use bugs.

Brownell got the message. He considered the Supreme Court's *Irvine* decision but nonetheless secretly authorized Hoover to bug "espionage agents, possible saboteurs, and subversive persons," including by physical invasion. Brownell explained that "considerations of internal security and the national safety are paramount and, therefore, may compel the unrestricted use of this technique in the national interest." And just like that, the executive branch had again secretly flouted a Supreme Court limit on electronic surveillance.

Before the mid-1950s, the FBI used wiretaps and bugs to look for the agents of foreign powers—mostly Nazis and communists—with whom Hoover was obsessed. These were the spies, saboteurs, and subversives whom

Brownell had in mind. Beginning in the late 1950s, Hoover pushed his secret surveillance powers—especially microphone bugs—much further to include a different threat by a different enemy: the domestic criminal activities of gangsters.

Hoover had previously downplayed the threat posed by the Mafia. During Kefauver's hearings on organized crime in 1951, he testified that the problem was mostly limited to local gambling and should be resolved by local police. The FBI "is not authorized to conduct any investigation of what is strictly a local violation," he told the committee. Even after sensational hearings around the country led the committee to conclude that organized crime was a national problem extended beyond gambling to labor racketeering, prostitution, and narcotics, Hoover continued to resist. One theory was that he feared that pursuit of the mob might corrupt his G-men just as it had many state and local police forces around the country.

Hoover's odd passivity allowed the mob to flourish in the quarter century after Lucky Luciano founded the Commission in 1931. But Hoover's indifference to the mob ended on November 14, 1957. On that day, state police in the rural southern New York town of Apalachin stumbled upon a conclave of more than sixty mob leaders and advisors from around the country at the 130-acre country spread of Joe "the Barber" Barbara, a lieutenant in the Buffalo crime family.

The men had gathered at New York boss Vito Genovese's request for a sitdown about LCN governance following a bloody civil war in New York that the Commission had been unable to prevent. When the cops surrounded the estate, dozens of the top guys in the country fled by car, only to be nabbed in roadblocks, questioned, and identified. (Many others—including Detroit's boss Joseph Zerilli, and his lieutenant, Anthony Giacalone—escaped detection by fleeing through the woods.) The ensuing publicity about the Mafia's scope and strength forced Hoover to act quickly to learn how it was organized and operated.

Hoover ordered his agents to use all of the Bureau's tools, including telephone wiretaps, informants, and physical surveillance. But bugs were the most effective for gathering intelligence. "One microphone was worth a thousand agents," said FBI agent William Roemer, who installed the first one against the Italian Syndicate, in July 1959, in the obscure Chicago tailor's shop where it congregated.

Before Hoover could deploy bugs against the mob, however, he had to overcome the highest legal hurdle yet. Brownell's secret 1954 authorization for bugs extended only to national security threats like the underground communists or Soviet spies. Brownell had drawn the line at foreign agents because the president had special constitutional authority to prevent foreign threats to national security. But the president had no conceivable constitutional authority to authorize break-ins to plant bugs on suspected domestic criminals. That was at the core of what the Fourth Amendment prohibited.

Hoover's FBI nonetheless went there after Apalachin. It did so by interpreting Brownell's passing acknowledgment in his 1954 memorandum that bugging foreign threats furthered "national safety" into an authorization to plant bugs in purely domestic "criminal cases" involving the mob, which the Bureau had deemed to threaten "national safety." This was a preposterous interpretation of an already-questionable secret executive branch ruling. Eisenhower's attorney general at the time, William Rogers, was aware of what the FBI was doing and under what authority, and he acquiesced. But no one in Congress or the general public knew about it.

Rogers's successor, Robert Kennedy, continued this "don't ask, don't tell" approach to government bugs for organized crime. RFK had long viewed the FBI as too passive in its pursuit of organized crime, and he made clear from his first day in office that the Bureau must be more aggressive in confronting it. He "pushed, ordered, cajoled and successfully enticed the FBI into the fray," writes Victor Navasky, "so that eventually it was a full-fledged if somewhat eccentric participant in the fight to destroy the syndicates."

On May 4, 1961, Hoover wrote a memorandum to Kennedy's deputy, the future Supreme Court justice Byron "Whizzer" White, with whom RFK had daily contact. The memo sought to advise Kennedy as he prepared for upcoming congressional testimony on pending surveillance legislation. Hoover explained that the Bureau was using "microphone surveillances" on the basis of Brownell's 1954 authorization. He said that the FBI used bugs "even though trespass is necessary"—not just for spies and communists, but also "in connection with our investigations of the clandestine activities of top hoodlums and organized crime." And he emphasized that "from an intelligence standpoint, this investigative technique has profound results unobtainable through other means."

Kennedy later denied any knowledge of the FBI's use of bugs. But a great deal of other evidence in addition to Hoover's memo to White strongly suggests that the attorney general, who regularly consumed the fruits of the organized crime bugs, knew about and approved of the practice. And as Navasky notes, "To the extent that Kennedy was ignorant of the FBI's bugging practices, it was an administrative failure so flagrant that Kennedy is morally chargeable with the consequences of his ignorance."

DURING KENNEDY'S YEARS as attorney general, the FBI conducted 842 wiretaps and installed 374 bugs, most of which involved break-ins. These figures represented a sharp rise in the use of both techniques from the Eisenhower administration even though the Red Scare had abated.

The federal government did not acknowledge anything approaching this scale of electronic surveillance—especially with regard to bugs. But rumors of electronic snooping by the government abounded, and sparked feverish concern about "Big Brother." Newspapers and magazines were filled with stories about newfangled miniaturized microphone devices, radio transmitters, and what Justice Potter Stewart described in 1961 as other "frightening paraphernalia which the vaunted marvels of an electronic age may visit upon human society."

In this milieu, Hoffa believed the federal government was always listening in on him. In the early 1960s, Chuckie at Hoffa's request bought thousands of copies of George Orwell's 1984 and distributed them to union locals around the country. "Some of these poor guys, the only thing they knew was how to drive a truck or work at a warehouse, they didn't have the knowledge of the electronic shit," Chuckie told me. "Mr. Hoffa wanted them to read that book, and said that this is what's going to happen to not only us but to everybody—and exactly what he's predicted has happened."

During Hoffa's trials in 1964, Hoffa and his team became even more certain that they were being wiretapped and bugged. Both Chuckie and Marvin Berke, one of Hoffa's attorneys during his 1964 trial for jury tampering, told me they heard strange noises during their phone calls; that they found recording devices in their workspaces, which they turned over to local police; and that the government anticipated their legal tactics as if they had been in the room during deliberations. These beliefs "were very real to Hoffa and his associates, and greatly influenced their behavior," say Ralph and Estelle James, who were with Hoffa in the run-up to his trials.

The Department of Justice always denied these allegations. Hoffa was never able to provide credible witnesses or evidence to support his anxieties, and courts ultimately rejected Hoffa's appeals and motions based on allegedly illegal electronic surveillance. Government documents not available when courts were deciding Hoffa's fate, however, suggest that the Department might not have been entirely candid about the matter.

The most damning one is a memorandum that FBI assistant director Cartha DeLoach wrote to FBI associate director Clyde Tolson—Hoover's longtime intimate right-hand man—on June 14, 1966. DeLoach was informing Tolson about an ethically dubious conversation he had with Supreme Court justice Abe Fortas about a case involving FBI surveillance pending before the Supreme Court. When the conversation turned to one of Hoffa's appeals then before the Court, Fortas asked DeLoach if he "knew of any irregularities on the part of Bobby Kennedy in connection with the Hoffa case?" DeLoach replied that RFK "on one occasion had specifically asked an FBI representative to place a microphone on an attorney by the name of Haggerty." James Haggerty was Hoffa's lead legal counsel in the Nashville and Chattanooga cases.

We will never know for sure whether—as Hoffa and Chuckie believed, but as the Kennedy men denied—the Justice Department illegally wiretapped or bugged Hoffa during his trials. Some people at the time thought that Kennedy's overkill maneuvers against Hoffa—especially the incessant physical surveillance of him and his associates during trial, and the mole inside his camp—constituted intrusions on Hoffa's privacy comparable to bugging and wiretapping even if they did not cross a legal line.

But even this assessment understates the government's intrusion into Hoffa's life. During the period of Hoffa's trials, the FBI gained enormous insights into Hoffa's travails through illegal electronic surveillance on a massive scale of those closest to Hoffa, including his wife, Josephine; Anthony Giacalone; Sylvia Pagano; and Chuckie.

ON JANUARY 21, 1961, the FBI broke into and placed a bug in the office in Giacalone's headquarters in the Home Juice Company at 6341 East Palmer Street—his "legitimate" business front that he and his brother, Vito, won in a barbut game. Uncle Tony was forty-two years old and running the Detroit family's lucrative businesses in numbers, sports betting, and high-stakes card and dice games. He was a well-known figure in Detroit due to almost twenty arrests since 1937 for gambling violations, bribing cops, and using threats and violence to collect debts. Giacalone was tall and a famously stylish dresser.

He also possessed a reputation for violence and intimidation. Kurt Luedtke, who as executive editor of the *Detroit Free Press* aggressively covered Uncle Tony's illegal antics, described his first encounter with the "fabled Giacalone stare" as a hard-eyed, hateful assessment. "He wanted to be rid of me, and only self-control and the setting were preventing him from using his fists to accomplish that," Luedtke told me.

Two months after the FBI broke into the Home Juice Company, the Supreme Court reiterated that electronic eavesdropping in a criminal case "accomplished by means of an unauthorized physical penetration into the premises" is "beyond the pale" and a clear Fourth Amendment violation. But the FBI—still operating with backup—ignored the decision and kept on listening. In addition to the bug it placed in Uncle Tony's office, the FBI also illegally entered and placed a bug in the living room of apartment 606C in the Alden Park Manor in Detroit's Gold Coast, where Chuckie's mother, Sylvia Pagano, lived at the time. Sylvia was a target because of her connections to made men in Kansas City, Chicago, Cleveland, New York, New Jersey, and Detroit. She was also, by that point, in a relationship with Uncle Tony.

For almost three years, FBI agents listened to every conversation the bugs picked up. They recorded everyone in the room. They did not focus only on discussions about Mafia organization and operations, or even on criminal activity. They swept up everything, the full range of human conversation on every mundane matter, including sex, family and health matters, political and religious opinions, and personal secrets.

FBI agents dutifully transcribed and summarized the recorded conversations, redacting little. When they learned something of conceivable professional interest, they wrote a memorandum that summarized the conversation and then circulated it in various ways around the FBI. To conceal the legally dubious source of the information, they attributed the intelligence to an "Informant" of a "sensitive nature" and cautioned that "care should be utilized in the dissemination of this information." Transcripts and reports based on these bugs were not included in the FBI's main files, but rather were kept in a secret file called "JUNE" to avoid scrutiny inside and outside the Bureau.

In research for this book, I read thousands of pages of the JUNE electronic surveillance transcripts related to Hoffa and his associates, all based on bugs planted during Kennedy's tenure as attorney general. They provide an illuminating window on the intertwined relationships among Hoffa; his wife, Josephine; Chuckie; his mother, Sylvia; and Giacalone at the height of Hoffa's travails with Kennedy. Before I read the transcripts, Chuckie had portrayed these relationships in the idealized way that he wanted to remember them. The Old Man and his mother went way back and were very close. Uncle Tony and Hoffa were great friends and business partners. Josephine and Sylvia were like peas and carrots. And Hoffa and Josephine were deeply in love despite her occasional struggles with alcohol.

But the FBI transcripts revealed a quite different reality: a drama of striking characters in dysfunctional relationships that was unsettling for me to absorb.

AT THE CENTER of the drama was Jimmy Hoffa, who was living through the busiest and most demanding years of his busy and demanding life: micromanaging the union as always; dealing with several criminal trials; racing around the country to cut deals with employers or strong-arm Teamsters to support him; and negotiating the historic National Master Freight Agreement in Chicago. Hoffa was under unfathomable stress and rarely in Detroit. His voice was never picked up in thousands of hours of recordings. But though offstage, Hoffa was the protagonist—the object of everyone's interest and solicitude. Sylvia, Giacalone, Chuckie, and Josephine needed and depended on him in different ways. They constantly tracked his whereabouts, and they frequently tried, and always failed, to get him on the telephone to discuss a pressing matter.

In the transcripts, Chuckie has a starring role as the intermediary to Hoffa. When he is at the Home Juice office or in Sylvia's apartment, Uncle Tony and Sylvia implore him for information about Hoffa. When he is on the road with Hoffa, they leave him messages for Hoffa and (along with the FBI) learn from him what Hoffa is saying, thinking, and doing, including about his trials. Chuckie is also heard facilitating Hoffa's business deals. He arranges one of the meetings between Hoffa and Giacalone over what would become a large loan to the Detroit family to buy the Frontier casino in Las Vegas, and he carries messages between the two men.

While Uncle Tony clearly trusted Chuckie, his hard-handed, one-legged younger brother, Vito, a Cosa Nostra colleague, took a dim view of Chuckie's talents that would be relevant a decade later when Chuckie supposedly helped the Giacalones knock off Hoffa. In one conversation in February 1964, Vito criticized an associate as a "miniature Chuck O'Brien" in this respect: "Anything you ask, he says, 'Yeah, I can do it,' but he can't do it." Two months later he compared Chuckie to a hapless soldier in the Detroit crime family. "Trouble seems to follow both of them around no matter what they do," Vito told his brother.

When Chuckie was in Detroit and not with Hoffa, he often took care of Hoffa's wife, Josephine. "Mama Jo," Chuckie told me, was a "shy, sweet person." She was also the tragic character in the play. By the early 1960s, with her husband never around, Josephine was bitterly lonely and struggling with the worst period of her decades-long alcoholism. "When she'd get some of that sauce in her she got crazy and it was hard to hold her down," Chuckie said. "She liked Crown Royal. She would down two or three of them and she'd get all screwed up."

In the early 1960s, Josephine spent several periods in Grace Hospital in

Detroit due to alcoholism, tranquilizer addiction, and, at least for the hospitalization in August 1963, a nervous breakdown. Josephine "is in a state of shock, her mind snapped," Sylvia tells Chuckie's wife, Mary Ann, on August 14, 1963. "They got her under heavy sedation, they got her strapped down, . . . her eyes are rolling." Out of the hospital in January 1964, Josephine wanted to join Hoffa in Chicago. But he was in the final week of negotiations for the national trucking contract, and Hoffa pushed her off.

"She can't stand it no more [be]cause she is all by herself," Giacalone tells his brother, Vito, on January 9, 1964. Tony then appears to suggest that they invite Josephine to dinner. "I would like to see you bang her," he tells Vito, for then "we would have her eating right out of our hands." Four days later, while Hoffa and Chuckie were in late-night negotiations in Chicago, Vito tells his brother that he "had dinner at the Living Room Lounge" with Josephine and then "took her to a motel and had intercourse with her three times."

When Josephine is subsequently hospitalized in February 1964, in the middle of Hoffa's Chattanooga trial, Uncle Tony tells Chuckie's wife that Josephine "belongs in an institution." He further claims that Hoffa "is hurting this woman" by not putting her in a specialty hospital where "she can get the proper care." On the tapes, Hoffa comes across as brutally indifferent to Josephine's plight. "He was very busy with important matters," Chuckie told me.

Hoffa delegated the task of dealing with Josephine mainly to the steadfast Sylvia, who shopped, dined, and traveled with her. Sylvia's main task, however, was coping with Josephine's alcoholism—dealing with doctors, checking her in to the hospital, paying medical bills, and trying to control her drunken behavior. Sylvia had affection for her ward. "I love you, Josephine," she says in one phone conversation during a hospital stay. "I don't want anything to happen to you." Sylvia defended Josephine to Chuckie one morning, arguing that "if Josie didn't drink she wouldn't be the way she is."

But Josephine did drink, a lot, and Sylvia grew irritated and then bitter playing the role of substitute husband trying to deal with Josephine's irrational alcoholic behavior. "I could have beat the shit out of her today," she tells Tony in a typical conversation in the summer of 1963. "I've had it, Tony, I must have nerves made of steel. I have to do . . . fucking everything, everything." Giacalone later tells Sylvia, "You can't watch her all the time because this woman is going to put you out of your mind. . . . There is nothing that anybody can do."

Because Uncle Tony was close to Sylvia, he was close to Josephine as well. He and Jo often spoke on the phone. He sent her lobster and steak when she was in the hospital. And he introduced her to Anthony Cimini, a low-level Detroit family member, to help her fight loneliness. Josephine and Cimini had a fiery affair from the summer of 1962 until late 1963. "I love you," she tells him, at 5:39 p.m. on Friday, July 26, 1963, in Sylvia's apartment. He sent her a dozen roses under a pseudonym when she was once in Grace Hospital.

Josephine's affair with Cimini ended when two members of the Detroit family told Giacalone that he, Sylvia, Josephine, and Cimini were spotted checking into a hotel together. The encounter sparked a conflict within the Detroit family. When Giacalone asked the men for the source of their information, they refused to tell him. Giacalone then kicked the dispute up to his "confessor," Anthony Zerilli, the son of boss Joseph Zerilli. "Caporegina Tony" acknowledged in the Home Juice office that the two men should have revealed their source to Giacalone because "one of the first requisites of a friend of ours is that you cannot lie to another friend of ours."

Zerilli told Giacalone that Cimini's affair with Josephine could be a problem if Hoffa had a formal relationship with the Detroit family. But "we are not connected with Hoffa in any way," Zerilli says, so "it makes no difference." He added that if Hoffa "were your partner or my partner then it would be a different situation." That different situation would be that Cimini would be killed for violating the Detroit family's rules of honor. Zerilli was not denying that the family did business with Hoffa—only pointing out that Hoffa was not under its control.

The most important business transactions concerned the large loans that the Detroit family wanted from the Teamsters Central States Pension Fund. The bugs revealed in detail the elaborate dance that Giacalone and his Detroit associates went through to get a $10 million loan, in the midst of Hoffa's Chattanooga trial, to finance the Frontier casino in Vegas.

Hoffa also helped out in more personal ways, such as when he assisted

Uncle Tony after he was arrested in June 1963 for bribing a cop. The topic came up late one evening in Hoffa's Washington, D.C., apartment. Giacalone was in town to talk to Edward Bennett Williams about his case, and he took Josephine to dinner with another of Hoffa's attorneys, Larry Burns. As Giacalone later recounted to his brother, Vito, in a conversation overheard by the government, Hoffa arrived home at 10:00 p.m. from New York to find Giacalone and Burns with his passed-out wife, Josephine. Unfazed, Hoffa asked Giacalone to spend the night, but he declined.

The two men then discussed how to deal with Giacalone's criminal charges. "I don't like to do anything by law," Uncle Tony once told Chuckie. "I never won anything by law in my life." So Giacalone naturally took the non-law route and asked Hoffa to "talk to Gillis"—Joseph A. Gillis, the judge in his bribery case. Hoffa claimed to have later paid $15,000 to Gillis, who delayed the case for years until Uncle Tony won an acquittal.

Hoffa wouldn't accept immediate repayment for his favor. As Giacalone told Vito, Hoffa advised him to "wait till this thing is over with then . . . we will straighten it out. . . . I've done you a favor, I'd like a favor from you."

The dapper Giacalone often did wardrobe favors for the plain-dressed Hoffa. The recordings reveal Sylvia delivering Hoffa dozens of shirts with two-button cuffs and "French boxers" with snaps that Hoffa liked but that were out of style. Chuckie says that Uncle Tony's tailor made both based on Hoffa's old shirts and underwear that Chuckie "snitched." Giacalone also came up with a solution to the infamous white socks that Hoffa wore with his suits because his feet were allergic to dyes, but that offended Giacalone's sartorial sensibility. "Uncle Tony had his guy in New York make socks with black, blue, and brown tops and the bottoms were white, which ended all that bullshit," Chuckie told me.

But of course Hoffa wanted much more than underwear and socks in return for keeping Giacalone out of jail. The recordings do not reveal what he sought, but Giacalone makes clear who typically got the better of the deal: There "ain't nobody sharp enough for Jimmy Hoffa . . . in this town or any other town. He's going to use everybody, every SOB in the world." When Tony Zerilli once flippantly suggested that the Detroit family should "grab that Jimmy Hoffa" because he wasn't giving them everything they wanted, Giacalone made clear who had the upper hand in the relationship. "Jimmy Hoffa is the type of a guy you can't bulldog," he said to his brother, Vito, criticizing Zerilli.

The person who was by far the most successful in convincing the head-strong Hoffa to do favors for the Outfit was Sylvia. "Sylvia is the only person . . . around this country that can handle Jimmy Hoffa," Giacalone boasted on the tapes to a colleague for whom Sylvia had just secured a Teamsters loan. Chuckie always told me that Sylvia influenced Hoffa through persuasion. My mother "had a way of saying 'Jimmy' that he'd melt," Chuckie told me, aping Sylvia's firm, suggestive voice. "And then she would talk to him and he would listen." The bugs suggest that Sylvia's access and influence over Hoffa were a form of payback for brokering relationships and loans with organized crime figures around the country, but especially for lifting Josephine's enormous burden from his shoulders so he could do his work.

Josephine grew more difficult as Hoffa grew more distant and preoccupied. When Sylvia started to think she was getting the bad end of the bargain, her decades-long relationship with Josephine transformed from one that was partly contractual and partly affectionate into one that was exploitative. In January 1964, Sylvia and Uncle Tony began to discuss ways they could rob Hoffa's cash-stuffed safe in the bedroom closet in his Washington, D.C., apartment. Every scheme involves taking advantage of Josephine's alcoholism.

A few weeks later, Giacalone and his brother, Vito, discussed how they might rob the Washington apartment while Hoffa was busy with his Chattanooga trial. The men relied on the fact that Hoffa would think Josephine "got drunk and gave the money away." Anthony speculated about how much money Hoffa has collected from "loans with the 10 percent." His brother then says that Hoffa "must have at least half a million." Anthony later proposes that he will rob the safe while Vito and Josephine "zoop it up." Everything goes according to plan until the keys that Uncle Tony had made to open the safe did not work. So Uncle Tony grabbed the cash lying outside the safe and left.

But the brothers were not done. Plan B involved robbing Hoffa's safe in his Miami Beach apartment, which was in a building adjacent to an apartment that Uncle Tony owned. A few months after the aborted robbery in Washington, Uncle Tony succeeded in getting into Hoffa's Miami Beach safe while Sylvia and a drunken Josephine were out having dinner.

THESE ARE BUT a few shards of insight that the FBI gleaned from the many thousands of hours of JUNE recordings at Uncle Tony's and Sylvia's places. Hundreds more organized crime figures and associates in Detroit and around the country disclosed similarly intimate information via bugs in their homes and offices. The bugs helped the FBI paint a rich and detailed picture of the Italian Syndicate's organization and operations. And though not aimed directly at Hoffa, the bugs in Detroit and elsewhere gave the FBI extraordinary insight into his whereabouts, actions, beliefs, and travails during the period he was under investigation and on trial.

The FBI bugs on organized crime figures were a clear violation of the Fourth Amendment and state trespass law, and they would cease a few years later when they became public. Constitutional law arguments aside, they were also a gross invasion of the privacy of everyone involved—both at the time and especially in their permanent transcribed archival form. This is one reason why they were the most painful of all the difficult topics Chuckie and I discussed.

I struggled with whether I should tell Chuckie about the recordings that so clearly belied his idealized remembrances. I tried to imagine how my beliefs about family and friends and their relationships with one another, and with me, would change if I had encountered years of secret recordings of their unguarded conversations. I also tried to picture how painful it would be to read my own unwary conversations, which certainly would not comport with my sentimentalized sense of self and others. And I tried to contemplate how painful it would be to read and discuss the ugly truths so many years after the events, after having endured—as Chuckie had—so many other personal humiliations for so long.

After considering these dreadful possibilities, I began to absorb the evil in the government's indiscriminate and illegal recordings, even in the context of chasing the mob. The government had spent many thousands of hours listening in to the lives of those in Chuckie's circle—and probably hundreds of thousands of hours making illegal recordings of the lives of countless others.

The topic of the FBI recordings finally came up when Chuckie and I were discussing the government's 1976 leak to *The Detroit News*, a year after Hoffa's disappearance, of fragments of these recordings, in an attempt to discredit Chuckie and Uncle Tony, both suspects in the disappearance at the time. Chuckie at first dismissed the recordings as a fictional government conspiracy. "They made all that bullshit up," he said. "They can write down anything they want for the papers."

But when I told him that I had the authentic transcripts on which the *Detroit News* stories were based, he asked to see them. I handed him a highlighted transcript that included a passage in which Uncle Tony and his mother plotted to rob Hoffa. Sitting in his recliner in our usual spot in my mother's TV room—facing photos of Hoffa, Giacalone, and Sylvia—Chuckie read the highlighted portions with a blank expression for two minutes. And then he winced as if he had broken a tooth, and he threw the papers across the room. "I don't want to read this shit," he said, scowling, "and I don't want to talk about it."

We didn't discuss the bugs for a long while. But we eventually did, a bit. The robbery plots embarrassed Chuckie. "I knew about it and I got mad about it," he said. "It was wrong and I told my mother to stop, that she was hurting me. She did it for Uncle Tony." Mr. Hoffa never noticed the missing cash in his Miami apartment, Chuckie says, probably because he had so much on hand and because (as Sylvia had theorized) Josephine and Sylvia had done a lot of shopping that week. "He would have flipped his fuckin' lid if he found out," Chuckie told me.

Of Josephine's drunken dalliances with Cimini and Vito, and his mother's and Uncle Tony's enabling roles, Chuckie was even more circumspect. "That shit never should have happened," he told me with a mixture of anger and humiliation. He refused to discuss the episode between Vito and Josephine. But he says Hoffa did find out about Josephine's affair with Cimini, though he does not know how. "There's not a fucking thing I can do about it," a physically and mentally shattered Hoffa told Chuckie in late 1963, as he was in the midst of preparing for the historic National Master Freight Agreement negotiations and his fourth criminal trial in six years, both of which would occur in the next few months. "I got all I can handle right now."

Chuckie wouldn't explain how the revelation affected Hoffa's relationship with Josephine, Sylvia, or Uncle Tony, or whether Hoffa ever discussed the matter with them. But he did say that Hoffa understood clearly how difficult Josephine was to control when drunk. "The Old Man had so much going on trying to save himself, he couldn't deal with it," Chuckie said.

The goings-on with Josephine while Chuckie was on the road with Hoffa were the greatest crisis in Chuckie's life to that point. For the first time, he was caught awkwardly between the labor side and the Sicilian side. "My mother taught me a lot," Chuckie said, trying to explain the dilemma. "She taught me about respect for Company guys, and loyalty. And she taught me never to give your friends up. She was big on that. No matter what happens." But now Chuckie's loyalties to his mother, and Uncle Tony, and Jimmy Hoffa, were in conflict. Chuckie managed the conflict by trying to persuade his mother to stop exploiting Josephine, but otherwise by staying out of it.

It was clear in my conversations with Chuckie about these matters that his primary concern and anxiety at the time, and fifty years later, ran to Jimmy Hoffa. Indeed, Chuckie is the only person on the recordings who displays affection for Hoffa. He often talks to his mother and Uncle Tony about the strain Hoffa is under due to his criminal trials. Just after Hoffa is twice indicted in what would become the Chicago and Chattanooga trials, Chuckie is furious that some members of the Teamsters Executive Board are starting to jockey to push Hoffa aside.

"They don't care about Hoffa, they don't care if Hoffa lives or dies," Chuckie lamented to his mother in the living room of her Alden Park Manor apartment at 6:04 p.m. on Thursday, June 13, 1963, as FBI agents Bernard A. Schweder and Gerald R. McVittie secretly, and illegally, listened in.

THE SURVEILLANCE ABUSES that took place on RFK's watch were some of the worst in American history. They were mainly the work of Hoover, who had used surveillance tricks in an expanding array of contexts for decades with the secret imprimatur of prior attorneys general. But RFK did nothing to stop the abuses and presided over their expansion. His heavy hand on the FBI to gather evidence on the mob allowed the Bureau to amass "more resources, more power, and more latitude to use bugs and wiretaps," notes Larry Tye. The Senate Church Committee reformers of 1975 had Kennedy in mind as one of "those officials at the highest levels of government" who "had a duty to control the activities of the intelligence community" but who "sometimes set in motion the very forces that permitted lawlessness to occur" through a combination of sharp demands for results, failure to establish guidelines or oversight, and willful blindness about questionable practices.

When the Church Committee looked back on this period, they focused most critically on RFK's approval, on October 10, 1963, of the electronic surveillance on Martin Luther King and the Southern Christian Leadership Conference—an authorization Hoover's men would use to try to destroy King's marriage, discredit him publicly, and blackmail him into quitting the civil rights movement. It also focused on RFK's wiretap authorizations that included congressional staff, executive branch officials, reporters, a lobbyist, and a law firm. But the committee said barely a critical word about the colossal illegal surveillance by bug of the hundreds of unsympathetic organized crime figures that swept up so much information about Hoffa when he was under investigation.

Kennedy's excesses, unlike Hoffa's, were never subject to government accountability beyond their limited exposure during his lifetime and more so after his death. The law-and-ethics-skirting acts—especially on surveillance—were impossible to challenge because they took place in secret and because the Department controlled law enforcement, which it rarely turns against itself, especially at the highest levels. Kennedy was not the only person to avoid accountability. Not a single person in the federal government was ever held criminally accountable for decades of illegal surveillance through the 1960s that affected many thousands of U.S. citizens.

The man who took some of the most important steps to bring the executive branch to account was Senator Edward Long of Missouri. Long was a civil libertarian who sponsored the landmark Freedom of Information Act in 1965 and wrote a bestselling book about government invasions of privacy, *The Intruders*, in 1966. He used his chairmanship of the obscure Subcommittee on Administrative Practice and Procedure to hold hearings, beginning in February 18, 1965, on the "armory of electronic snooping devices" that he believed the executive branch was using against the American people.

Long's achievements are legion, but his motives were complex. His obsession with exposing secret governmental surveillance might have been stoked by the tens of thousands of dollars in "referral fees" that he received in 1963 and 1964 from Hoffa's attorney Morris Shenker. In 1967, *Life* magazine charged that the fees were meant to encourage Long to use the hearings to discover evidence of government wiretapping that would help clear Hoffa. (The FBI apparently leaked the story to *Life* in retaliation for Long's investigation and proposed wiretapping legislation—part of a multiyear effort to manipulate Long via secret surveillance of his connection to Hoffa and others.)

Long began by asking every federal agency about its surveillance programs. The request set off panic in the Justice Department and FBI, which were keenly aware of the dubious legal foundations for their practices, especially microphone recordings via black bag jobs, which FBI assistant director William Sullivan described in a confidential 1966 memorandum as "clearly illegal." The FBI was already on edge due to the discovery of its bugs in the office of Edward Levinson, the owner of the Fremont casino in Las Vegas, from whom it was learning about skimming operations in connection with a Hoffa-arranged pension fund loan. When Levinson's attorney, the ever-present Edward Bennett Williams, sued four FBI agents, the Bureau quickly settled the case and promised not to prosecute Levinson in order to keep the matter quiet. But now Long was threatening to blow the lid off hundreds of surveillance operations throughout the government.

In the midst of this gathering storm, with exposure of decades of illegal surveillance operations imminent, RFK's successor, Attorney General Nicholas Katzenbach, at the direction of President Johnson, ordered an end to bugging and wiretaps against organized crime. "The AG apparently feels that he is on solid ground in approving microphones and wiretaps in national security cases, but he is fearful of the Long Committee and attorneys such as Edward Bennett Williams with reference to the use of microphones in the organized crime field," FBI assistant director A. H. Belmont explained to his boss, Clyde Tolson, in September 1965.

Belmont was right. There was an arguable legal justification for break-ins for microphone surveillance against foreign national security threats, but no plausible legal justification for such tactics against domestic criminals. Hoover acquiesced in Katzenbach's ruling but told him that he was "extremely concerned" about the loss of microphones in organized crime cases, which "has produced extremely valuable intelligence data."

Despite Long's investigation and the Las Vegas discovery, the government's wiretaps and bugs remained out of public view until the following spring. On May 24, 1966, Solicitor General Thurgood Marshall confessed to the Supreme Court that in 1963, when RFK was attorney general, the FBI had bugged a hotel suite of the Washington lobbyist Fred Black and had overheard conversations between Black and his attorney. The revelation caused a stir because Black's prosecution was part of a tax fraud investigation that had snared LBJ's longtime Senate aide, Bobby Baker.

The stir grew when the justices ordered Marshall to reveal who approved the bugging and under what authority. The FBI, the Justice Department, and former attorney general Kennedy then had a very public spat over whether RFK had approved Hoover's bugging adventures. Kennedy, then a senator from New York, denied that he approved the Black bug (true) but suggested that he did not know about or give tacit approval for FBI bugging (almost certainly false). The wily Hoover arrayed internal memos that indicated that the FBI bugging operations were carried out with RFK's (and previous attorneys general's) knowledge and approval.

Two months later, Marshall told the Supreme Court and the world about the FBI's secret bugging and wiretapping practices going back decades. He acknowledged that "no specific statute or executive order" supported microphone surveillance of Black. Using careful, responsibility-minimizing language, he stated that "for years prior to 1963" and "continuing into 1965," the Justice Department authorized Hoover to bug in several contexts, including cases involving organized crime. "FBI Had Sanction in Eavesdropping," read the front-page *New York Times* headline, more directly. The Justice Department and the Bureau had been exposed as "Lawless Lawmen," concluded

The New Republic. Senator Long pounced on the admission, which he called "an example of how far government has gone in invading the privacy of citizens."

The Long hearings and the revelations in the Black case precipitated a revolution in the Supreme Court's jurisprudence on electronic surveillance. The Court's first step was to overturn Black's conviction and order a new trial, to give Black a chance to challenge any illegally obtained evidence used against him. Suddenly, dozens and maybe hundreds of federal prosecutions were in jeopardy on the grounds that they might be tainted by illegal wiretapping or bugging. "An extensive review is presently being conducted in order to determine the instances in which there might have been monitoring affecting a case," Marshall assured the Court in November. His office later pledged that it would disclose all evidence of illegal electronic surveillance that gave the government "any information which is arguably relevant to the ligation involved."

Chuckie himself would be a beneficiary of that review. In August 1962, at the urging of "Mr. Sam" Finazzo, the family member who ran the Detroit boxing scene, Chuckie had paid a worker guarding the salvage of the SS *Montrose* for several items on the British ship that had sunk in the Detroit River the previous month. Chuckie's main prize, which cost him $25, was a damaged alabaster statue of St. Theresa that he gave to Monsignor Kern, the renowned "labor priest" at the Holy Trinity Church in Detroit. He also took cases of marble slabs and brass valves. The Hoffa Squad found out about the transactions and issued what Chuckie described as a "bullshit indictment" for illegally removing items from a bonded customs warehouse.

"I didn't steal nothing and that wasn't a bonded warehouse," Chuckie insisted to me five decades later. "They said they were going to throw that shit away, and I bought it." Chuckie was found guilty at trial, but when the case reached the Supreme Court, Thurgood Marshall told the Court that the FBI had overheard Chuckie talking with his lawyer Larry Burns about his case on the bug installed in Uncle Tony's Home Juice office. The Court vacated Chuckie's conviction and ordered a new trial, which the government never initiated.

Chuckie had lucked out in *O'Brien v. United States* and assured his tiny place in the annals of the Supreme Court's criminal procedure jurisprudence.

Jimmy Hoffa was less fortunate. The existence (though not the contents) of the JUNE file of secret FBI recordings came to light in August 1969 during one of Hoffa's many efforts to overturn his conviction for jury tampering. The courts concluded that the recorded conversations disclosed by the government were not pertinent to Hoffa's trial and thus legally irrelevant. The government never disclosed JUNE file information it gained from the bugs at Uncle Tony's Home Juice offices and Sylvia's apartment.

Hoffa also lost in his efforts to overturn his conviction in Chattanooga based on the treacherous testimony by Edward Partin. Supported by the ACLU, Hoffa argued in the Supreme Court that Partin was an illegal human listening device planted in Hoffa's hotel suites in violation of Fourth Amendment prohibition on unreasonable searches. Many commentators believed that the Court would rule for Hoffa, since it had been giving greater rights protections to criminal defendants generally, and since its recent jurisprudence in this context had been hinting at some restrictions on the use of government informants.

But it was not meant to be. Partin "was not a surreptitious eavesdropper," reasoned the Court, since he was in Hoffa's suite "by invitation, and every conversation which he heard was either directed to him or knowingly carried on in his presence." The Court concluded that the Fourth Amendment affords no protection to Hoffa's "misplaced belief that a person to whom he voluntarily confides his wrongdoing will not reveal it."

Chief Justice Earl Warren sharply disagreed in a famous dissent. Given Partin's instructions from federal authorities to report "anything illegal" or "anything of interest," Warren maintained, Partin "became the equivalent of a bugging device which moved with Hoffa wherever he went." He added, "No conviction should be allowed to stand when based so heavily" on the testimony of a man with the "incentives and background of Partin." And he noted that "if a criminal defendant insinuated his informer into the prosecution's camp in this manner he would be guilty of obstructing justice." Warren concluded that what happened to Hoffa was not in "keeping with the standards of justice in our federal system."

We'll never know for sure why the Court ruled against Hoffa. Justice Abe Fortas's law clerk at the time probably captured the Court's sentiment when he wrote in a memorandum to his boss that "although many of the practices in this case are troubling, this is the kind of case—trial of an alleged jury tamperer perfectly capable of tampering again and of intimidating witnesses and jurors alike—that excessive Government supervision and breathing down the neck can be tolerated." The ends of putting the evil Hoffa away, in other words, justified tolerance of government tactics that "pushed to the limit of propriety in its well-known campaign to 'get' Hoffa," as Justice Harlan's law clerk put it. Or as Nat Lewin, who argued the Hoffa case in the Supreme Court for the government, told me, "It is very likely that the Court came out the way it did because it was Jimmy Hoffa."

Hoffa's failure to convince the Court that Partin was a human bugging device was an exception to the comprehensive surveillance reform in the late 1960s. A few months after letting Chuckie off the hook, the Court decided two landmark decisions that imposed new Fourth Amendment restrictions on electronic wiretapping, expressly outlawing it in cases like organized crime investigations absent a judicial warrant. The following year, in 1968, Congress enacted a statute with wide-ranging restrictions on wiretaps and bugs, including a requirement of a judicial warrant. These transformations of American surveillance law would be followed, a few years later, by the Church Committee's airing of the government's electronic surveillance abuses stretching back five decades. And not just electronic surveillance abuses: break-ins, mail openings, subversion campaigns, illegal drug testing, violations of freedom of speech, and much more.

Courts and Congress still had work to do after 1975 in cleaning up the mess of decades of executive branch surveillance malfeasance. One outstanding issue was whether the president could continue to order electronic surveillance without judicial approval in national security cases, as FDR had determined in 1940. In 1972 the Supreme Court ruled that judicial warrants were necessary for surveillance in cases involving threats to "domestic security." The Court declined to address the original FDR exception for warrantless electronic surveillance where there was a "significant connection with a *foreign* power." Congress finally addressed that issue in 1978, in the Foreign Intelligence Surveillance Act, a landmark law that required a judicial warrant by a secret court for electronic surveillance even of foreign agents. This was the law that I would confront a quarter century later, when I began poring over cases and documents related to the two-year-old Stellarwind program.

"TAKE A LOOK at this!" an agitated Jim Baker said as he handed me a piece of paper with scribbled signatures on it. It was an early December afternoon in 2003 in my Justice Department office. Baker was in charge of an office that sought national-security-related warrants from the secret court in accordance with the 1978 FISA law. He was an expert on surveillance law and one of the most outstanding government lawyers I knew—smart, careful, fair-minded, and perpetually worried. As he walked into my office, Baker's face expressed more unease than usual under his close-trimmed, fast-graying beard.

At the time, I was trying to figure out whether I could approve Stellarwind. Baker had learned about the program a month after it began, and he didn't like it. The basic problem was that it authorized surveillance activities by the National Security Agency in the United States against suspected terrorists and citizens without the judicial warrants that FISA, on pain of criminal penalty, required. The program had been approved by Attorney General Ashcroft in October 2001 and by my predecessors in OLC every six weeks or so since the fall of 2001. But it was hard to square with the law.

The paper Baker handed me was a memorandum, dated October 7, 1963, for Attorney General Robert F. Kennedy from FBI director J. Edgar Hoover. The subject line read: "Martin Luther King, Jr., Security Matter—Communist." Hoover wrote that King was a "wholehearted Marxist" in addition to his position as president of the Southern Christian Leadership Conference. "In view of the possible communist influence in the racial situation," Hoover wrote, "it is requested that authority be granted to place a technical surveillance on King" at his office and anywhere else, for an unspecified period of time. Robert Kennedy's signature appears in the approval line of the document, dated October 10, 1963. At the time I was amazed to learn that Kennedy had authorized Hoover to wiretap King, without a warrant and without limit, based on a factually unsupported link between King and communists, the "enemy within" that preceded gangsters and terrorists.

"*This* is why we have FISA," Baker explained, jabbing his finger into the document. He saw the King surveillance as a cautionary warning about abuses of secret unilateral electronic surveillance. "If they think FISA is cumbersome or too slow, we can get rid of it," he said, referring to the law's requirement of judicial approval before surveillance. "But do we really want to go back to these days?"

I certainly didn't want to go back to those days. But I also didn't cherish upending a vital intelligence program at a time when everyone in the government feared another attack. I was bound by a presumption that my predecessors' legal judgments were sound, and I could find no example in American history in which the attorney general or his delegate (which is what I was) had withdrawn legal support for an intelligence program in the middle of a war. And yet in March 2004, I concluded that the Stellarwind legal opinions contained fatal legal flaws, rested on a misunderstanding of how the program worked, and couldn't be squared with FISA and other laws. I disapproved parts of the program for which I could find no plausible argument and upheld the parts I thought could be supported by plausible ones.

Ashcroft and his deputy, James Comey, agreed with my analysis, and agreed that the Justice Department could not reauthorize Stellarwind when it came up for renewal on March 12, 2004. The White House disagreed. "If you rule that way, the blood of the hundred thousand people who die in the next attack will be on your hands," shrieked David Addington, Vice President Cheney's counsel, in a White House meeting about a week before the next approval for the program was due. White House counsel Alberto Gonzales, though calmer, was also unhappy. These were understandable reactions, since the Justice Department had signed off on Stellarwind for years.

What followed was a series of now-famous events. Ashcroft was stricken with severe gallstone pancreatitis and would be heavily sedated for the next few days as the doctors waited for the inflammation in his pancreas to subside before operating on him. In several meetings, White House and senior intelligence officials, and Vice President Cheney, sought unsuccessfully to change my mind and Comey's, or at least delay our decision, until Ashcroft was well. When that tack failed, I witnessed Gonzales and White House chief of staff Andrew Card approach a weak and heavily sedated Ashcroft, in his intensive care hospital room a few hours after gallbladder surgery, only to be rebuffed by Ashcroft. President Bush then decided to continue Stellarwind without Justice Department approval. But he changed his mind the next day and accepted our legal objections and proposed constriction of the program after learning that many of his senior officials were on the verge of resigning.

President Bush's last-second decision averted a historic constitutional crisis and executive branch meltdown. The episode showed that while the president has the legal authority to overrule his attorney general on a matter of law—as Roosevelt had done in overruling Jackson at the dawn of World War II—his ability to effectuate his legal interpretation depends on the willingness of subordinates to carry out his wishes (as Jackson had done when Roosevelt overruled him). "Your office is expert on the law and the president is not," then FBI director Robert Mueller told me at the time, explaining why he had threatened to resign rather than abide by the president's overruling of my decision.

For the unprecedented steps I took in narrowing Stellarwind and in standing up to the White House, I would later be hailed a "hero" in some quarters. In other quarters I was censured as "political" or "opportunistic" for not having the courage to support the president across the board. And critics on the other side complained about the parts of Stellarwind I had reapproved. They accused me of contorting the law and even committing a crime. There was no perfect solution to the mess I faced, but after thinking about it for fifteen years I'm still not sure I should have done anything differently.

I did not fully realize it at the time, but the efforts I made to uphold parts of the program were not unlike the ones made by past attorneys general and their advisors who, faced with enemies within, approved and sometimes expanded ongoing surveillance programs to meet the threat. This was especially true in the part of my ruling that made an alternative argument to support continued warrantless wiretapping based on the president's war and national security powers. It was an argument that traced its pedigree to Roosevelt's overruling of Jackson so that Hoover could continue looking for German spies. In fact, I cited the Roosevelt precedent and its pedigree.

Roosevelt's ruling was "backup" made possible because he interpreted his own presidential authorities in secret, without judicial review. And that is what I was doing in 2004 as well. I was acting in a long tradition—a tradition that included Bobby Kennedy's inheritance of surveillance practices that had been approved by his predecessors and deemed vital to domestic security, and that he too was loath to stop, especially since he was so keen to put away his enemy.

I thought often about Chuckie during the Stellarwind mess. His complaints about the abuses of secret government surveillance and opportunistic government "backup" when I was a teenager haunted me on the fifth floor of the Justice Department. I was witnessing how the imperative to bring down the enemy, combined with the enticing power of secret surveillance, could lead government officials acting in good faith to cut legal corners.

I also thought about Chuckie because there was an improbable connection between Stellarwind and Jimmy Hoffa. My Stellarwind opinion concluded that the government's collection of metadata did not violate the Fourth Amendment. The 1979 decision I invoked for this conclusion, *Smith v. Maryland*, had in turn relied on the Supreme Court's 1966 ruling that Edward Partin's presence in Hoffa's hotel suite was not the equivalent of an illegal bug. The Court in 1966 reasoned that Hoffa could not complain about what Partin told the government because he, Hoffa, had voluntarily conveyed information to Partin about bribing jurors. The *Smith* case extended this principle to hold that persons lose Fourth Amendment protections when they voluntarily reveal "to" and "from" information to their communication providers. And I in turn relied on this "third party" doctrine in my Stellarwind opinion. That doctrine is today under attack, but it still allows the U.S. government in many circumstances to collect the metadata of American citizens without individualized suspicion, much less a warrant.

We can never know whether the Court in 1979 in *Smith* would have ruled differently if the *Hoffa* case in 1966 had come out differently, as many at the time thought it should have. And I cannot lay my opinion upholding the legality of part of Bush's secret surveillance program at the doorstep of the *Hoffa* case. Other decisions also supported my conclusion, and tracing the counterfactual path of the law is impossible.

But whatever might have happened if Hoffa had prevailed in his constitutional complaints about Partin, the legal fingerprints of RFK's Hoffa Squad were nonetheless present in the *Smith* decision and in my reliance on that decision to uphold Stellarwind—one of many bizarre connections between Chuckie's and Hoffa's ordeals with RFK's Justice Department and my ordeals in the same Department a half century later.

SIX

THE
CONDITION

RICHARD NIXON HATED Bobby Kennedy for his wealth and privilege, his efforts to deny Nixon the presidency as John F. Kennedy's campaign manager in the 1960 election, and his part in tax and criminal investigations of Nixon and his family in the early 1960s, which Nixon described as an "abuse of the Internal Revenue Service and the Justice Department for political purposes."

Bobby Kennedy was also the candidate whom Nixon feared most in the 1968 presidential election, and some historians believe that Kennedy, had he lived, would have won the Democratic nomination and defeated Nixon. Sirhan Sirhan eliminated that possibility when he assassinated Kennedy, five months before the election, at the Ambassador Hotel in Los Angeles following Kennedy's victory in the California Democratic primary. Nixon defeated the eventual Democratic nominee, Hubert Humphrey, in the 1968 election. And as a result of these events, Nixon developed a fateful relationship with Jimmy Hoffa.

Nixon never knew Hoffa personally. "I feel a little bit denied that I was one of the few people in government who never met Hoffa," he proclaimed, half seriously, in a 1972 Oval Office conversation with his special counsel and dirty tricks maven, Chuck Colson. When Nixon was vice president in the 1950s, he was once on a commercial flight when Hoffa walked by him in the aisle. "Fellow sitting there in the seat next to me said, 'You know who that was? Jimmy Hoffa,'" Nixon recalled, in a different Oval Office conversation. Nixon later "looked him up." Despite his virulently anti-labor disposition at the time, Nixon liked what he saw in Hoffa—a manly, pragmatic labor leader who often supported Republican candidates and causes.

By the time of the 1960 presidential election, Nixon and Hoffa were scratching each other's backs. Through intermediaries Hoffa secured money and Teamsters support for Nixon in the 1960 election against John F. Kennedy, whom both men hated. In return, Vice President Nixon arranged for the Justice Department to stop two criminal investigations against Hoffa, including the Test Fleet matter that Bobby Kennedy would revive after the 1960 election. In the hope that Nixon would spring him with a pardon, Hoffa made sure the 1968 Nixon presidential campaign received lots of cash from the Teamsters union and his casino friends in Las Vegas.

Nixon was sympathetic to Hoffa's plight. "Some people hate [Hoffa], but that's because of Bobby Kennedy," he told his secretary of the interior, Rogers C. B. Morton, in the Oval Office on Christmas Day, 1971. "Edgar Hoover told me last night that . . . [Hoffa] was really railroaded. I think he was guilty, but there's being guilty and being railroaded too."

As chief executive, Nixon possessed unreviewable power to pardon Hoffa or reduce his sentence through clemency. But Nixon acted on cold political calculation, not sympathy. It would take three years of maneuverings before he had extracted the political and financial benefits that he viewed as the price for Hoffa's freedom. And when he finally set Hoffa loose on December 23, 1971, he conditioned the release on Hoffa's never returning to the

Teamsters union—a condition that set in motion events that led to Hoffa's disappearance three and a half years later.

THE TANGLED PATH that led to Nixon's condition on Hoffa's release from jail began a decade earlier. It started with a coin flip at Bert Brennan's funeral in the Oakwood Cemetery in Saline, Michigan, on May 31, 1961.

Brennan was Hoffa's closest aide and friend as well as the man who'd brought Sylvia Pagano into his circle. He was also a business partner in the Test Fleet Corporation that was the subject of the bribe-filled Nashville trial. And he was one of thirteen vice presidents on the Teamsters Executive Board whose support Hoffa needed for his major union initiatives. Hoffa wept as he helped carry Brennan's casket before the three hundred people who attended the funeral. But as soon as Brennan was buried, Hoffa set about replacing him on the Teamsters board.

The choice came down to Hoffa's two other old Detroit comrades, Bobby Holmes and Frank Fitzsimmons. Hoffa had been close to Holmes since they conspired together in the strawberry strike at Kroger in 1931. Holmes was the widely respected leader of Detroit Local 337 who, though no saint, had ascended in the Detroit Teamsters hierarchy with few of the questionable associations that had characterized Hoffa's rise. "Bobby never dealt with the Outfit," Chuckie told me. His upright reputation, intelligence, and English accent from childhood years in Yorkshire made him one of Hoffa's favorite conduits to the press and public.

Hoffa and Fitzsimmons also went way back, to 1937, when Hoffa "pulled him off of a truck and brought him in as a business agent," in Chuckie's words. Fitzsimmons was a pudgy, colorless, chain-smoking Hoffa loyalist who earned his stripes in the labor wars of the 1930s and 1940s and served dutifully in the 1950s as Hoffa's vice president and paper pusher in Detroit's Local 299 when Hoffa turned his ambitions to the national stage. "Fitz was a very docile old-time Irish guy," said Chuckie, "the most lazy son of a bitch I knew." Fitzsimmons showed up late for work at Local 299, took long lunches, and did Hoffa's bidding.

Hoffa was torn between Holmes's competence and Fitzsimmons's obedience. His Italian friends helped break the tie. "Bobby was a great labor person, but he was a square," says Chuckie. "The Old Man knew Bobby's ability and wanted to keep him out front in the union. But the Outfit, though they respected Bobby, didn't trust him. They never thought they could go to Bobby and get what they wanted if they needed it."

By contrast, Anthony Giacalone knew and had worked quite a bit with "the puppet," as he often called Fitzsimmons, and admired his pliancy. Uncle Tony told Chuckie that the consensus "on the outside," especially in Detroit and Chicago, was that Fitz was the right choice. "Fitz is a nice man and this is what we hope Jimmy does" was the message Chuckie conveyed. Hoffa "thought it was the right choice too," Chuckie said. "The Old Man was always gaming out possibilities years ahead, and in the back of his mind he thought that elevating Fitz might help if Kennedy ever nailed him."

Hoffa was notoriously hesitant to bring bad news to friends and didn't have the heart to tell Holmes the truth. But Uncle Tony had a plan. After Brennan's casket was lowered into the ground, Hoffa asked Holmes and Fitzsimmons for a private chat. The men walked from the grave site and huddled under a tree, with Chuckie, as ever, in the shadows about twenty yards away. Hoffa recounted their days together, told each man how much he loved him, and said he had to make a choice. Then he pulled out a nickel and said that Fitz gets the job if it's heads, Bobby if it's tails.

What Fitzsimmons knew that Holmes didn't was that Uncle Tony—who ran the Detroit family's gambling operations—had, through Chuckie, given Hoffa a two-headed nickel. The Teamsters president flipped the coin, and Fitz had a spot on the board. "I was not with them when they flipped, but I was not too far away because I wanted to get that fucking nickel and get rid of it," Chuckie told me.

The coin flip at Brennan's funeral changed the direction of Fitzsimmons's life. He had been a Teamsters organizer for a quarter century but never had a large profile in the national hierarchy. He lacked Hoffa's intelligence, charm, or work habits. But as Hoffa's prospects of jail increased over the next six years, he began to see Fitzsimmons as a plausible caretaker in his absence for the same reasons that he originally put him on the board: he was loyal, he was dutiful, he took orders well, and he lacked ambition. Hoffa also thought Fitzsimmons was best suited to deal with the Outfit. "Hoffa knew who Fitzsimmons was going to be faced with throughout this country—guys who controlled locals, the Company people who controlled trucking companies," Chuckie told me. "Fitz would handle that the proper way, no commotion."

In the summer of 1966, nine months before he went to jail, the wildly popular Hoffa was reelected by acclamation to a five-year term as president of the Teamsters union. He pushed through changes to the union's constitution that allowed him to remain president if he went to jail, and that created a new post of general vice president, filled by Fitzsimmons, to run the union in the event of his absence.

That eventuality materialized nine months later, on March 7, 1967. At 8:30 a.m., Hoffa stood in his Teamsters office in Washington, D.C., with Fitzsimmons, Chuckie, and a few others, making final preparations for jail. He had elaborately tutored the amenable Fitzsimmons on running the union and on how to push the government to get him out of jail. "I'm counting on you, Fitz," Hoffa said as he and Chuckie left the office. Chuckie then drove Hoffa and his lawyers through the cold drizzling rain to the federal courthouse half a mile away. Hoffa was unusually quiet during the ride, but Chuckie was distraught. "I was sad, fucking crying," he recalled. "My life was leaving me."

Chuckie parked in front of the courthouse and marched alongside Hoffa through the crush of screaming newspaper and television reporters. When the crowd jostled Hoffa and grew too dense for him to pass, he paused and gave an impromptu press conference. "I know you all have jobs to do, for which I hope you're getting paid union wages . . . which I doubt if most of you are," he joked. But then his face hardened. "The government has wire-tapped, room-bugged, surveilled and done everything unconstitutional it could do" to put him away, he said. "I hope and trust that those who have been a part of this conspiracy will realize that it's not just Hoffa they are doing this to," he added. "If they can do this to Hoffa they can do this to any citizen." Hoffa pledged that if his health held, he would return to the union.

Federal marshals drove Hoffa in handcuffs and leg chains to the federal penitentiary at Lewisburg, Pennsylvania. From the outset, the warden, J. J. Parker, was worried about Hoffa's surprisingly fragile health. Hoffa suffered from mild diabetes and had almost died in January 1966 due to a hernia that caused him to lose eight pints of blood over ten days.

Lewisburg officials also worried about how Hoffa would cope in prison. Hoffa's "chief concern was about his adjustment in the institution and particularly about his relationships with other inmates," associate warden J. J. Clark learned in his entrance interview. Lewisburg was an overcrowded prison where rapes and violence were commonplace. Hoffa feared prisoners looking for favors, but he feared more those he might have crossed. Hoffa "is certain that he has some enemies here," Clark wrote, but he "doesn't know at this point who they might be."

Hoffa had protectors too. "He had a lot of friends from the East that were in there," said Chuckie. One was Anthony Provenzano, Hoffa's old friend from New Jersey and another target of Robert Kennedy's ire, who was serving a four-year sentence for extortion. After a few years in the can together, Tony Pro and Hoffa would have a famous dispute over Hoffa's ability to lift restrictions on Pro's Teamsters pension fund. But at first, and for a long time, Provenzano saw to it that Hoffa ate well, had privacy, and stayed safe.

From the day he arrived at Lewisburg, Hoffa worried that Fitzsimmons was not up to snuff. Hoffa complained to prison officials that Fitzsimmons "is not capable of handling some of the situations that Hoffa himself could handle," according to a summary of his prison entrance interview.

It turned out that the caretaker didn't even try. "Fitz was no taskmaster and didn't like to make decisions," Chuckie said. "He liked to delegate." What many people saw as Fitzsimmons's lethargy was a preference for staying out of harm's way and letting others take the credit—and the heat. "Everybody said he was a dumb Irishman," Chuckie said, "but he wasn't going to stick his head in the screen door, he always told me that." Fitzsimmons operationalized his leadership-from-behind by devolving power to local and regional union leaders, many of whom were Executive Board members. "I don't think I can judge what happens in Boise, Idaho," he said, justifying the change.

Hoffa loyalists, including Chuckie, viewed Fitzsimmons's moves as signs of weakness. But even Hoffa had struggled to control the vice presidents in recent years, and everyone thought they would devour Fitzsimmons. Fitzsimmons had no interest in local meddling or infighting with his board. So he made a virtue out of necessity. The crusty Teamsters vice presidents who had bridled under Hoffa's yoke loved their new freedom and the power and perks it brought. They began to respect the man who gave them these things, especially after he raised their salaries. "Most Teamster officials are happy with the way Mr. Fitzsimmons is running things," *The New York Times* reported, five months after Hoffa went to jail.

After a while, "people wanted Fitz to stay as general president, because their life changed," Chuckie told me. Those "people" included organized crime leaders whom Hoffa had accommodated when necessary or when it brought him advantage, but otherwise kept at bay from both union opera- tions and the pension fund. Under Fitzsimmons's passive rule, however, the wall that Hoffa had maintained between the Teamsters union and organized crime collapsed. Crime families in many cities made deep new inroads into local Teamsters operations.

Much more significantly, Fitzsimmons ignored the pension fund and "let Dorfman do all that shit," says Chuckie. Hoffa had created the Central States Pension Fund and tightly controlled the hundreds of millions of dollars of loans it doled out, even to the Outfit. "When Fitzsimmons became general president the fucking door was open for everybody," Chuckie said. "He turned the international over to certain people in different areas." Fitzsim- mons was fine with this arrangement. The union was running itself and he was enjoying the perks of the Teamsters presidency, including the largest sal- ary of any American labor leader and a twin-engine airplane at his disposal. "He liked the fact that he didn't have to put up with any bullshit in 299, and once he started playing golf he liked it even better," Chuckie said.

Fitzsimmons had taken up the sport a decade earlier when a friend told him it would help his ulcers. "Worst golfer in the world," Chuckie told me. "He had a hole in one pocket in his pants, and if he lost a ball, he'd let a ball go through the hole—'Oh, I found the ball, here it is.' Fucking thief."

Hoffa frowned on golf, which Chuckie said he viewed as a "waste of time" by "nitwits walking around with a stick hitting a white ball." But under Fitzsimmons, Teamsters meetings were held at fancy golf resorts and accommodated prime tee times. "Guys are on golf courses that never were on a fucking golf course in their life," Chuckie remembers. "Everybody stopped working."

The only perk of the Teamsters presidency that Frank Fitzsimmons liked more than playing golf was going to Richard Nixon's White House.

FROM THE MOMENT of his slim victory in the 1968 presidential election, Nixon was fixated to the point of paranoia at the prospect that he would not win reelection. One early reelection strategy was to win over the "silent majority" of Americans who shared Nixon's loathing of counterculture protesters and the eastern establishment, and who supported his efforts in Vietnam. Nixon had been anti-labor his entire career, but as president he came to see the white blue-collar workers who had flirted with George Wallace in 1968 as potential allies.

The "strong" and "uneducated working people" represent "what little is left of the character of this god damn country," Nixon ranted to his staff in the Oval Office in July 1971. For the first two years of his administration, they had supported him when he had a "tough problem," including on national security. Nixon knew that most labor leaders "hate us politically." But on other issues he saw an opportunity to wrench the culturally conservative rank and file from the Democratic Party. "There is a considerable chance of a hell of a political payoff among labor," he told his advisors.

Early in his first term Nixon identified the two million "strong, vigorous pro-American" Teamsters as his best prospects, and directed top players in his administration to court Fitzsimmons. Attorney General John Mitchell often met with Fitzsimmons, and George Shultz, Nixon's director of the Office of Management and Budget (and former labor secretary), played golf with him. But the point man for the romance was the cunning Chuck Colson.

Colson began work in the White House in 1969. He became notorious as Nixon's hatchet man who, among other feats, compiled Nixon's "Enemies List," oversaw illegal efforts to discredit Pentagon Papers leaker Daniel Ellsberg, and helped cover up the Watergate break-in. Colson was originally hired to improve relations with unions and other special interest groups, and one of his main jobs was securing Teamsters support for the 1972 election. He was thus in daily contact with Fitzsimmons, whom he made a regular at White House dinners and to whom he gave lots of access to Nixon.

The first Oval Office visit came in December 1970. Nixon and Fitzsimmons hit it off. Fitzsimmons "practically can't string three words together but is a pretty strong guy," Nixon later told his advisors. "I like him, he's a great fellow," Nixon said another time. Fitzsimmons liked Nixon too. "I believe in the president and I believe in what you are doing and I support you," he told Colson.

Chuckie says that Hoffa specifically warned Fitzsimmons about becoming "mesmerized by the fucking whores" in Washington, but Fitzsimmons had done just that. "Fitz got capital fever," Chuckie told me. "He liked his tuxedo and his black tie and to go to all those bullshit things." Fitzsimmons was also pleased when Nixon arranged for his wife, Pat, to join the Arts Committee for the John F. Kennedy Center for the Performing Arts.

The courtship of Frank Fitzsimmons worked. Fitzsimmons got access to Nixon and lots of help in cooling investigations of him and his relatives and union friends. In return, Fitzsimmons gave rambling press conferences and speeches that backed Nixon on Vietnam, denounced marijuana use, complained about lenient judges, and decried countercultural "agitators." He also supported Nixon's anti-inflation policies, brokered relations with other union leaders, and raised piles of money for Republican candidates. "We've been getting a hell of a lot of help from Fitz," Colson reported to the president in November 1971. "God, he has been magnificent."

But the real prizes for Nixon were a Teamsters endorsement and Teamsters cash for the 1972 presidential election. Between Nixon and those goodies stood the fraught question of Jimmy Hoffa's imprisonment.

When Hoffa arrived at Lewisburg, he told the associate warden he "was hopeful that he would not be here very long." (This is probably why he worried so little about putting Fitzsimmons in charge.) Hoffa and the Teamsters union spent millions on lawyers to fight his legal appeals, and on politicians and other supplicants to exert every form of political pressure on the U.S. Board of Parole and Presidents Johnson and then Nixon. But Hoffa could not find a way out of prison. He lost in the courts, and the Board of Parole denied his requests for freedom in 1969. Lyndon Johnson was preoccupied with the Vietnam War and showed no interest in freeing Hoffa. And at first the Nixon administration rejected the pleas from many quarters—including from Frank Fitzsimmons—for Hoffa's release.

With each setback Hoffa coped less well in Lewisburg. All his life he had been the fiercest lion in the jungle. But in prison in his middle fifties, Hoffa was "buried alive," as he later said. For several years, every day, the fireball workaholic was "caged in a little eight-by-eight hole with a paddle, beating fucking mattresses," as Chuckie described Hoffa's prison job. "He'd have to knock them down all day by himself—that's what he did all day, every day." When the hyperactive Hoffa wasn't restuffing mattresses, he spent most of his time in his seventy-square-foot cell, struggling with the physical confinement, the empty time, and the loss of control.

Fitzsimmons remained publicly loyal to Hoffa during this period. When talking to fellow Teamsters he would pull his keys from his pocket and pledge, "These are Jimmy's and I'll return them as soon as he's released," according to Chuckie. He publicly described Hoffa as a "political prisoner" and the failure to pardon him as "horrendous and inhuman." And in the first year of Hoffa's imprisonment, Fitz genuinely tried to get Hoffa out of jail.

But as time passed, Fitz's attitude changed. He grew wary of the cranky second-guessing from "His Nibs," as Fitzsimmons began to refer to Hoffa, according to Chuckie. "It got to a point that the Old Man was sending too much out to direct him, and Fitz got sick of it," Chuckie said. "Fitz had some pride, especially when he's got a lot of cheerleaders around him pumping him up." Fitzsimmons thought he was doing a good job running the union and grew less interested in securing Hoffa's release. Fitz "felt that he was loyal and he was entitled to the job," said Chuckie. This self-assessment was reinforced in his mind by the White House visits and the private plane that at a snap would take him to any golf course in the country.

As Hoffa's avenues out of Lewisburg narrowed, as his jail time lengthened, and as his grip on his union slipped away, Chuckie in his prison visits witnessed Hoffa seethe and then boil with rage—at the Justice Department for putting him there, at prison officials who humiliated him daily, at his lawyers for losing his appeals, and, over time, at the increasingly disloyal

Frank Fitzsimmons. "I saw him change, and at times get very bitter," Chuckie told me. Hoffa told Chuckie over and over again that "Fitz is fucking me."

Hoffa's temper grew shorter and louder, not just with Chuckie, but with all of his visitors, including his wife. "He got tired of being locked up in that cage, he wanted out of that fuckin' prison," Chuckie said. "He just would say to me, 'I've got to get out of here—what are they doing?'" By the third year, Chuckie began to worry about Hoffa's health, as he lost twenty pounds, his cheeks hollowed, and his hair started to turn gray. He also grew concerned about Hoffa's mental condition. "Mr. Hoffa sometimes is not being rational," a prison guard told Chuckie in 1971. "He's getting bitter about a lot of things, griping about this and that, being belligerent, pissed off at the warden."

RICHARD NIXON DIDN'T care about Hoffa's struggles. But he did care about the pressure that Hoffa loyalists—the rank-and-file members who still revered him, the Hoffa family, and a few senior Teamsters leaders—were placing on his pal Fitz. As early as 1970, Nixon advisor John Ehrlichman counseled the president that pardoning Hoffa "made good political sense and was a nice way to stick it to the hated Kennedys," according to the historian Stephen Ambrose. But Nixon's other senior advisors—Mitchell, H. R. Haldeman, and Colson—argued at the time that Nixon would suffer political heat if he released Hoffa. They also noted that Hoffa, once out, would reassume the Teamsters presidency, to Nixon's detriment.

The first recorded discussion of the Nixon White House's deliberations about Hoffa's release occurred on May 28, 1971, in the Oval Office. "Mr. President, we've been playing this game of keeping Hoffa in jail for the simple reason that we can't do anything about getting him out except wrapping a presidential pardon around your neck," Mitchell advised Nixon. He added that Nixon was much better off with Fitzsimmons running the Teamsters. "Fitzsimmons is a good man—plays the game all the way," Nixon agreed. "Hoffa would be a disaster for us."

What Nixon sought was a way to make Teamsters rank and file happy while at the same time preventing Hoffa from regaining control of the union. These were goals that, by 1971, were shared by the increasingly Machiavellian Fitzsimmons and the LCN leadership that was guzzling Teamsters cash. The Nixon White House eventually worked out a solution worthy of its Watergate machinations the following year.

The first step in the White House plan, hatched in secret with Fitzsimmons, was to deny Hoffa's release until Fitzsimmons became Teamsters president. Hoffa's five-year term ended in July 1971, when Teamsters would meet at their national convention to elect a new president. Hoffa wanted to run for reelection. But these plans began to crumble when the Board of Parole denied his second application for parole on March 31. A week after the parole denial, and based on a request that Fitzsimmons made to Mitchell, the Bureau of Prisons granted Hoffa a furlough to visit Josephine, who was recovering from a heart attack in San Francisco. Mitchell made clear to Fitzsimmons, just as the Bureau of Prisons had advised Hoffa, that Hoffa must not conduct union business or create any publicity during the furlough.

Chuckie was in San Francisco caring for Josephine and helped arrange for Hoffa to stay in a suite on the nineteenth floor of the San Francisco Hilton hotel. For the first two days, Hoffa visited Josephine and stayed quiet. But by the third day, Chuckie told me, "All hell broke loose."

For years the only outsiders Hoffa had contact with were his family, his lawyers, and Chuckie. After a few days of semi-freedom in San Francisco, the perpetually restless Hoffa decided to ignore the restrictions and do some business. He telephoned Teamsters officials around the country to get the score on union affairs. Then he told Chuckie to ask Allen Dorfman to come to San Francisco to give him an account of his earnings from various loans and investments. A reluctant Dorfman complied. Hoffa also interrupted Frank Fitzsimmons's golf trip in Miami and asked him to come to the West Coast. Fitzsimmons balked because of his deal with Mitchell. But Hoffa pressed him, on the grounds of Josephine's illness, and Fitzsimmons complied.

"What the fuck is going on here?" Fitzsimmons muttered angrily under his breath to Chuckie when he arrived in Hoffa's suite and saw that Hoffa had also summoned half of the Teamsters Executive Board and was barking commands as if he were still in charge. "I didn't come out here to have a fucking convention."

Fitzsimmons certainly didn't come for a convention run by Hoffa, who before the Teamsters executives was "as assertive as ever, an opinion on every subject and no doubt about the correctness of all of them," as A. H. Raskin of *The New York Times* later reported. "I saw the strength that he got, and he just pushed Fitzsimmons to the side," Chuckie recalls.

After a while Hoffa asked Fitzsimmons, along with Chuckie, to join him in one of the bedrooms in the suite. It was the first conversation the two old friends had had in four years—four long years in which Hoffa from his tiny jail cell had grown deeply resentful about how Fitzsimmons was running his union, and four years in which the once-subservient Fitzsimmons had grown in confidence and had learned to love, and to wield, power.

"I'm going to run for president in July," Hoffa told Fitzsimmons, straight out. Hoffa technically had remained president of the international union while in jail, and was telling Fitzsimmons that he was going to seek reelection from jail, at the July convention.

Fitzsimmons was not happy to hear this, but he was prepared for it. "When I took this job, I took it on the understanding that, if you were cleared, and you came back to the union and took your job, the law permitting, then I would step down," he said. "And if that happens, prior to convention, that's still my understanding with you. But if you're still in prison and you run for president, then get yourself another boy to run for the general vice president."

Fitzsimmons was making it harder for Hoffa to run for reelection because if Fitzsimmons quit, there would be a fight at the July convention for his position—acting president while Hoffa was in jail—that Hoffa might not be able to control to his advantage.

Hoffa was incredulous at Fitzsimmons's presumption and disrespect. But he knew he lacked power over him. "Enough of this," he said angrily, and changed the subject to his prospects for release. Fitzsimmons matter-of-factly itemized what he had done over four years to pressure the Justice Department and White House. But he added that he believed that neither the White House nor the Board of Parole would release Hoffa if he planned to return to the union. "If you don't resign your positions, if you don't agree to stay out of labor, I don't think I can get you out," he told Hoffa.

Hoffa turned red with irritation and pressed Fitzsimmons about the political hurdles to his release. But Fitzsimmons had him. Hoffa's lawyers and several members of the Executive Board with whom he spoke in San Francisco had also told him he needed to cut his ties to the Teamsters to win parole.

"All right," Hoffa said suddenly, in an angry, staccato tone. "I'll give it up." It was an impulsive statement, an abrupt turnaround, but Hoffa had been reconciling himself to the need to resign ever since his Board of Parole setback in March. Fitzsimmons accepted Hoffa's word, quickly left the room, and headed to the airport. Hoffa conveyed the same message at the Hilton to his two closest friends on the Executive Board, Harold Gibbons and Larry Brennan.

The following morning Hoffa returned to Lewisburg after his brief taste of freedom. In the weeks that followed, he sent contradictory signals through his attorneys about his San Francisco pledge. He was struggling with the ghastly dilemma of having to give up his life's work in order to avoid the continuing hell of prison. Hoffa "almost surely would win" reelection from prison if he decided to run, Raskin wrote in the *Times* on May 30. But it was just as clear that "neither President Nixon nor the United States Parole Board would ever cut a single day from his incarceration if the result would be to put him back as the full-time head of the two-million-member union, with its power over the nation's transportation lifeline."

Hoffa's desperation for freedom won out. On June 3, he resigned as president "because of my present legal problems" and endorsed Fitzsimmons. The Executive Board quickly named Fitzsimmons president during a meeting at Miami Beach, pending his formal election at the convention a few weeks later. Nixon drove up from the Florida White House at Key Biscayne to congratulate the Teamsters board on their vote. "My door is always open to President Fitzsimmons," said Nixon next to the beaming Fitzsimmons, who later that day told George Shultz that "it was the greatest moment of his life."

A month later, on the morning of July 8, Hoffa scribbled a sentence on a piece of paper at Lewisburg and gave it to his attorney Morris Shenker to deliver to Fitzsimmons in the hope that it would help convince the Board of Parole or Nixon to release him. The note, signed by Hoffa, read: "'I agree not to be in organized labor as a [sic] officer.'" That afternoon, the delegates to the Teamsters convention in Miami unanimously elected Fitzsimmons to a five-year term.

FITZSIMMONS'S ELECTION WAS an astonishing coup for the White House.

"We have got Mr. Fitzsimmons where he is now the Teamster president, which was worked just the way it should have been," Mitchell boasted to Nixon on August 9, 1971, in the Oval Office, with Haldeman sitting nearby. And "we got Mr. Hoffa out of the business," he added.

"We've won that," Nixon said with satisfaction.

Mitchell turned to the question of Hoffa's fate if the Board of Parole, which was meeting again in eleven days, rejected Hoffa's appeal. "I think we may get down to a question as to whether or not, when, and on what condition, if we should give Hoffa a pardon for Teamster support," he said. After noting that Hoffa had more sway over union members than Fitzsimmons, Mitchell asked, "Do we want to leave Hoffa where he is and go with what Fitzsimmons can deliver, or do we want to talk about down the line sometime, whatever, conditions, circumstances, we might want to come up with a pardon?" Or, the most corrupt attorney general in U.S. history said to great laughter, "Do you want me to indict him again?"

Nixon advised Mitchell to "have a frank talk with Fitzsimmons" about Hoffa. What Fitzsimmons told Mitchell on the links at the La Costa golf course two weeks later, and what he kept telling Mitchell and Colson all fall, was that he did indeed want Hoffa out of jail. On August 20, the Board of Parole had met and once again turned down Hoffa's request for release even though Hoffa had served four and a half years of his prison sentence and had resigned his other union positions. (The *Detroit Free Press* reported that Chuckie had "tears in [his] eyes" when he got the news, and that he "locked himself in an office and would not talk with newsmen.")

Fitzsimmons worried that the situation would look like what it was: a double cross. He was conspicuously close to Nixon and had become president of the Teamsters thanks to Hoffa's resignation and endorsement. Yet

Hoffa still languished in jail. Fitzsimmons feared that if he didn't get Hoffa out, the rank and file might lash out, with unpredictable consequences. He assured Colson that Hoffa had pledged to stay out of labor, and showed him the signed note. But in light of the fiasco in San Francisco, Fitzsimmons wanted a way to enforce the deal. "I don't want him out unless the president has, and plus the government has, the ability to bring him back in," he told Colson. "I hope we can let him out," Fitzsimmons added, "but if he violates any conditions he goes back in."

After a month of extensive White House deliberations about releasing Hoffa, Colson conveyed the stakes to Nixon on the afternoon of December 8. "Fitz wants to get Hoffa out because that's the only way that he can keep control of the pro-Hoffa forces within the Teamsters," he advised. "He is shot down eventually if Hoffa doesn't get out. If Hoffa gets out with no strings attached, Fitzsimmons will undoubtedly, at some point, be in a power struggle and they lose. So he wants him out but he wants him out with strings."

Later that afternoon Nixon asked Attorney General Mitchell whether he could put "strings" or "wraps" on Hoffa "in case he starts to screw around." Colson had previously advised the president that his main leverage if Hoffa broke his word was to indict him on other charges. Mitchell gave similar advice. "There's enough other activity that he's been involved in . . . pension fund and so forth, which we could hang over his head," he said.

That was enough for Nixon to pull the trigger. "The P apparently met with the Attorney General yesterday and agreed to pardon Hoffa," Haldeman wrote in his diary on December 9. After receiving word of Nixon's decision through Fitzsimmons, Hoffa's lawyers on December 16 filed formal papers seeking the decision the president had already made. On top of his personal assurances that he would stay out of labor if released, Hoffa in his petitions for commutation pledged that he had resigned from all Teamsters offices, and, if released, planned to live on his pension and "enter the educational field on a limited basis as a teacher, lecturer or educator."

The order that Nixon signed on December 23, 1971, commuted Hoffa's sentence and released him from jail on the condition that Hoffa "not engage in direct or indirect management of any labor organization prior to March sixth, 1980." The order added that "if the aforesaid condition is not fulfilled this commutation will be held null and void in its entirety."

The origin of this legal condition on Hoffa's post-prison activities, which would become so consequential in the run-up to Hoffa's disappearance, has long been the subject of controversy. But the Nixon archives, Hoffa's legal papers, and documents from Hoffa's subsequent lawsuit against the government attacking the condition make plain what happened. Nixon, Mitchell, Colson, Haldeman, and Fitzsimmons had been searching for months for a way to release Hoffa with handcuffs in order to keep Fitzsimmons in power. As late as December 8, Mitchell and Colson believed the best leverage was a threat to prosecute Hoffa on other charges. The week before Hoffa was released, however, assistant White House counsel John Dean came up with a better idea.

Dean had the pardon portfolio in the White House counsel's office. He had not been a participant in the months-long Oval Office discussions about Hoffa's release, but had gotten wind from Colson that Nixon wanted to restrict Hoffa's labor activities outside of prison and had reached an informal agreement to that effect with Hoffa's representatives. When the Hoffa paperwork was being assembled, Dean researched the possibility of placing a condition on the commutation and discussed it with Mitchell and the Justice Department pardon attorney, Lawrence Traylor.

"The power of the President to grant a conditional pardon or commutation has been upheld in several cases," Dean subsequently wrote in a memorandum to the attorney general on December 21. The memorandum noted precedents dating back to the early nineteenth century, and added that "the Pardon Attorney informs me that he strongly believes that the President has the power to grant conditional commutations." After subsequent discussions inside the White House and with the attorney general, Dean telephoned Traylor and instructed him to add the condition in Hoffa's commutation papers.

The president was pleased when he looked over the commutation papers that Dean had prepared and that Haldeman brought him to inspect just after lunch on December 22. "Now that solves it really," Nixon said, reading the condition out loud. He noted to Haldeman that by extending Hoffa's banishment from labor until 1980, the condition "made it tougher" on Hoffa, because if he had stayed in prison he would have received a mandatory release in 1975 and could have returned to the labor movement without conditions. "So you've put five years more restriction on him than he would have had under the law," Nixon concluded, with satisfaction.

The next afternoon at 4:30 p.m., Hoffa walked out of Lewisburg federal penitentiary in a charcoal gray suit and dark blue tie and met with reporters. After talking about how tough prison was, Hoffa answered questions about his release. "I have no intention of returning to the Teamsters," he said. "The leadership is in good hands. Frank Fitzsimmons is doing a good job." Later that same day in St. Louis, Hoffa claimed not to know about the conditions on his commutation, but expressed no displeasure. "Whatever [the conditions] are, those are the conditions I will live up to," he said. A few days later, back in Detroit, Hoffa discussed the labor condition with his supervising parole officer and stated no objection.

Despite his representations in St. Louis, Hoffa knew he was being let out of prison on the understanding he would not return to labor and would go back to jail if he tried. He agreed to this deal because he was desperate to get out of jail, but he never intended to honor it.

"The Old Man can pretend like he didn't see or hear anything if he wanted to," Chuckie explained, but "he knew what the deal was." And Hoffa was confident he could defeat any restrictions on his release. "I'll get out of this fucking prison, I'm on the streets, I'll turn this motherfucker around," said Chuckie, explaining Hoffa's reasoning. "Ninety percent is bullshit, ten percent I can handle."

THE FOUR YEARS, nine months, and sixteen days that Jimmy Hoffa spent in Lewisburg marked the worst period of Chuckie's difficult life to that point. March 7, 1967, was not just the day that he lost the man he idolized to jail. It was also the day that his always-uncertain position in the Teamsters union became precarious.

Chuckie's nominal title during this period was business agent for Local 299 in Detroit. But in reality he had few real labor tasks. His primary "job" in the union had been to serve Hoffa personally, and that included helping Hoffa maintain autocratic control over the union. Chuckie was Hoffa's boy, and once Hoffa was gone, he inherited the ire of Hoffa's enemies, including many on the Executive Board who liked the way Fitzsimmons ran things. "I was being hammered because of Hoffa," Chuckie told me. "People who would not fuck with me normally would start fucking with me because of the relationship."

Chuckie got along better with Fitzsimmons, at least most of the time. Chuckie's mother, Sylvia, knew Fitzsimmons well and had sometimes parked young Chuckie with his family when she was busy. "As a child O'Brien used to play with my kids and I gave him everything my kids got, meaning toys, parties and the usual youthful gifts," Fitzsimmons would tell the FBI agents investigating Hoffa's disappearance in 1975. Fitzsimmons gave Chuckie his first job after high school: driving a theater company truck. He shared a desk with Chuckie at Local 299 in the 1950s and often went to lunch with him. And the two were in frequent contact during Hoffa's ten years as president. Chuckie viewed Fitz as Hoffa's not terribly competent second fiddle. And Fitzsimmons viewed Chuckie with a combination of affection and wariness. He knew Chuckie had performed delicate tasks for Hoffa and Giacalone, but he viewed him as inept in labor matters.

Chuckie was disappointed when Fitzsimmons tasked him with the care of Josephine in addition to escorting her monthly to Lewisburg. Chuckie was thirty-four years old and tired of caretaking and running errands. He wanted to do what he had been trying to do since he was eighteen years old: real labor organizing work, like his idol Hoffa. But Fitzsimmons knew Chuckie and his limitations well, and was no more inclined to grant his wish than was Hoffa.

As always, Chuckie did what was asked. He took care of Josephine. He made regular trips to Las Vegas to collect Hoffa's cut from hotel loans, which Chuckie delivered to Dorfman in Chicago. And in his plentiful free time, he told me, he did "things to make the Old Man not think he was forgotten." He coordinated the truckers who refused to collect the furniture the inmates made at Lewisburg unless the warden allowed Hoffa to greet them. He also helped organize an airplane flyover with a HAPPY BIRTHDAY, JIMMY sign every February 14.

"Uncle Tony okayed that," Chuckie explained to me. "He said there is nothing wrong with that." Chuckie had not sought Giacalone's permission, just his advice. "I would ask Uncle Tony to protect myself that I was doing the right thing," he explained. "Sometimes I would do stuff and never tell anybody and then my dick was in a wringer."

Chuckie once got his dick in a wringer when he pushed Fitzsimmons too hard. Chuckie often asked the acting general president what he was doing to get the general president out of jail. And he angered Fitzsimmons when he helped whip up rank-and-file support for Hoffa. He coordinated the printing of thousands of FREE HOFFA bumper stickers that appeared on rigs across the nation. He also helped organize a petition seeking Hoffa's release that gathered more than two hundred thousand signatures.

Fitzsimmons bristled at the truckers' persistent and very public preference for Hoffa over him. "It made Fitz go crazy," Chuckie said. He told Chuckie, probably disingenuously, that rank-and-file remonstrations would make a pardon seem like a cave to union rowdies, and thus harder to obtain. "Fitz told me, 'You gotta get everybody to stop this shit, I'm gonna get him out, and I'm working on it, but all this adverse publicity, the bumper stickers and all this shit, we don't need it right now.'" Chuckie stopped circulating the bumper stickers.

Chuckie at first disliked how Fitzsimmons ran the union. Even though the mob was the beneficiary, he hated to see him giving up the centralized power that Hoffa, with Chuckie's help, had fought so hard over so many years to secure. He also hated the golf course mentality that took hold of the Executive Board, and Fitzsimmons's inattention to members' needs. "It pissed me off a lot," Chuckie told me.

As always, Uncle Tony, who was happy with Fitzsimmons as president, helped. "You knew Fitz was easygoing," he counseled Chuckie, adding that sometimes "people get into a position, they're not the same person that you think they're going to be." As Hoffa's years in prison passed, Chuckie began to settle down about Fitzsimmons's leadership style and, at Uncle Tony's urging, to support him. "He's your fucking boss, nobody else," Giacalone told him. "You work as hard for Fitzsimmons as you worked for Hoffa." That is what Chuckie did. And in so doing, he saw no contradiction with his loyalty to Hoffa, since Fitzsimmons seemed to be trying to get Hoffa out of jail, supported Chuckie's visits to Lewisburg, and always gave Josephine anything she needed.

In between the monthly visits to Lewisburg, often a three-day affair, Chuckie didn't have much to do while Hoffa was in prison. His main task in the Teamsters union was to work on its dispute with César Chavez's United Farm Workers over representation of "lettuce and grape" workers around the country. But his life was filled with sadness beyond his alienation from union power and Hoffa's imprisonment. His wife, Mary Ann, divorced him the year after Hoffa went to jail. In his inimitably luckless fashion, Chuckie beat up a man who he wrongly believed was having an affair with Mary Ann, lost the divorce by default because he didn't respond to the legal papers served on him, and later spent a weekend in jail when he missed alimony payments. The divorce and subsequent estrangement from his children with Mary Ann heightened Chuckie's isolation and debt. It was about this time that he first met and fell hard for my mother, Brenda, after Sylvia and Clemmye introduced them. But his life was a mess, and in 1970 Brenda chose to marry the neurosurgeon Bob Rivet instead.

Much more devastating than Chuckie's divorce was Sylvia's unexpected death, in December 1970, of a heart attack. The loss hit him like nothing ever had. "God took her and it broke my heart," Chuckie told me. Sylvia was his only close relative. He had always idolized her. She helped him out of his many scrapes, gave him money during his frequent pinches, and guided his major life choices. Chuckie never had a confident sense about how he should act, about what decisions were right and wrong. And suddenly his main advisor, his champion, the person he knew had his back and guarded his interests, was gone. "I know that she is in heaven and she will help me as much as she did on earth," Chuckie wrote to his friends Marvin and Betty Adell just after Sylvia's funeral. But the reality was that Sylvia, like Hoffa, was no longer there to help.

CHUCKIE WAS NOT much involved in the plot to free Hoffa from prison—until the end, when he says he played a brief but crucial role in the final deal.

There have long been rumors that the Nixon administration received a large payoff from the Teamsters union in exchange for Hoffa's commutation and the ban on his return to Teamsters leadership. Many news stories in the 1970s peddled these rumors. Some claimed that the payoff was made to get Hoffa out of jail; others said that it secured the condition on his release. Many characters over the years, aping these rumors, have claimed to have made a payoff to various people in the Nixon administration—before and after Hoffa's release—in connection with the decision. The money was supposedly used to finance the Watergate cover-up or Nixon's 1972 campaign, or both. The Hoffa team at the FBI and the Watergate investigators scoured financial records in the Teamsters union and the Nixon campaign, resulting in hundreds of pages of legal and financial analysis. But they were unable to find any credible evidence that Nixon or his representatives were paid to release Hoffa.

One basis for the rumors of a payoff was a famous conversation between Nixon and Dean on March 21, 1973, about where to get hush money for E. Howard Hunt and other Watergate conspirators. "What I mean is you could get a million dollars—and you could get it in cash," Nixon told Dean. "I know where it could be gotten. We could get the money."

This statement puzzled the Watergate special prosecutor, who told the Hoffa FBI team that he could "account for almost all of the money involved in the Cover-up" but didn't understand what Nixon was talking about in his reference to a million dollars.

The Nixon archives reveal nothing concrete about a million-dollar payoff for Hoffa's release, but do contain one timely and suggestive conversation. In the late afternoon of December 8, 1971, about thirty minutes before Nixon made his final decision to commute Hoffa's sentence, the president and Colson had a brief, puzzling telephone conversation. Nixon alluded to an arrangement between Mitchell and Fitzsimmons. He advised Colson to tell Fitzsimmons that Mitchell would "handle it" and that Fitzsimmons should reciprocate and "play our game now, boy." Nixon also asked Colson to tell Fitzsimmons that he, the president, "wants it done and done the right way," and that Fitzsimmons should "tell Mitchell everything he wants and that Mitchell will do it." Colson assented. "That's all I need to do," he said to the president. Fitzsimmons, Colson added, "just needs that signal."

This mysterious exchange involves something so shady that Nixon and Colson—who were typically candid in their Oval Office conversations, even about corrupt activities—spoke in code. The exchange could describe a cash-for-commutation deal. It makes sense that Mitchell, a central player in the Watergate break-in and cover-up, would be involved in any such deal. He was Fitzsimmons's oldest ally in the Nixon administration. He had participated in years of deliberations within Nixon's inner circle about whether and how to release Hoffa from prison. He would be the person who formally "recommended" Hoffa's commutation to the president. And a few months after the commutation, he would resign as attorney general to become Nixon's campaign manager for the 1972 election, and thus would likely be the man using Hoffa's cash—either on Nixon's reelection or to pay off the Watergate burglars.

This is all speculation, and no concrete evidence directly supports any of the payoff rumors. Chuckie nonetheless insists there was a payoff. And he says he was the delivery boy.

Chuckie told me that in early December 1971, he received a telephone call in Detroit from Fitzsimmons's secretary, Annie. "Mr. Fitzsimmons would like to see you," she said. Chuckie got on the next plane, flew to Washington, and went straight to Hoffa's former office at the foot of Capitol Hill.

After small talk, Fitzsimmons got to the point. "He's coming home, and it's going to cost this much," Fitzsimmons whispered to Chuckie, raising his right index finger to indicate $1 million. "There will be a package here tomorrow that I want you to pick up and deliver."

The following afternoon, Annie called Chuckie, who was staying at a hotel adjacent to the Teamsters headquarters near the Capitol building. "Mr. Fitzsimmons asked me to tell you that you left your briefcase in his office," she said. Chuckie had not left anything in Fitzsimmons's office, but he quickly went there. Fitzsimmons was not around, but Annie pointed Chuckie to a leather litigation bag next to Fitzsimmons's desk—a "big, heavy old-fashioned briefcase," as Chuckie described it. Chuckie picked up the bag, and Annie handed him an envelope. Inside the envelope was a piece of paper with "Madison Hotel, 7 p.m." and a room number written on it.

It was about 5:00 p.m., and Chuckie took the bag to his hotel room. He had delivered dozens of packages during the past two decades, no questions asked, mostly for Hoffa, sometimes for Giacalone, and very occasionally for Fitzsimmons. But this time was different. Chuckie knew of the strain between Fitzsimmons and Hoffa. He wasn't sure what game Fitzsimmons was playing, especially since Hoffa had not at this point discussed a payoff with him. Chuckie was anxious about what he was getting into. And so he did something he had never done before: he opened the bag.

"I wanted to see what was in the briefcase," Chuckie told me. "I didn't trust these motherfuckers. I needed to look; it could have been ten pounds of cocaine in there and the next thing I know a guy is putting a handcuff on me."

What Chuckie saw was neatly stacked and tightly wrapped piles of one-hundred-dollar bills. He closed the bag without counting the money.

The Madison Hotel, where Chuckie was supposed to deliver the bag, was two miles away, six blocks north of the White House. It "was a very famous hotel" in the early seventies, a place where "political big wheels" and "foreign dignitaries" stayed, Chuckie told me. At about 6:45 p.m., Chuckie took a taxi to the Madison, went to the designated floor, walked to the room (he doesn't remember the number), and knocked on the door. A man opened the door from darkness. Chuckie stepped in one or two feet. He sensed that the room was a suite, but could not tell for sure.

"Here it is," Chuckie said, and handed over the bag.

"Thank you," said the man. Chuckie turned and left.

That was it. The whole transaction, from the time he left his hotel to the delivery on the top floor of the Madison, took less than twenty minutes. The actual drop was over in seconds.

In many discussions over many years I grilled Chuckie about the details of this story.

"Why did Fitz have you deliver the money?" I asked.

"I don't know, Jack. I did a lot of things, and sometimes I now stop and think, what the fuck was I doing it for?"

"Where did the money come from?" I asked.

"From the Old Man," Chuckie answered. "Through Allen Dorfman. It was the Old Man's money. Dorfman had a lot of his money. Fitz wouldn't give you a dime if you were dying."

Chuckie's insistence that Hoffa paid for his own release is telling. None of the public rumors suggested this. A payoff from Hoffa's secret stash, as opposed to from Teamsters sources or the mob, might explain why the FBI was never able to corroborate the rumor. It also makes sense of a confidential FBI report in which an informant at the Lewisburg penitentiary, Charles Allen, claimed that Hoffa said it would "cost him . . . a lot of money" to be released, and that "Fitzsimmons was supposed to give Attorney General Mitchell the money to get Hoffa out." We cannot assess Allen's credibility, and he seems confused about when the money was transferred and to what effect. But in identifying Hoffa as the source of the cash and the involvement of Mitchell, Allen supports Chuckie's story.

"Why didn't you just get the money from Dorfman?" I asked. "Why did you have to go to the Teamsters building?"

"I never asked," Chuckie replied.

"So Fitzsimmons just called you in one day and said, 'Do this for me'?" I asked.

"He would do that a lot," Chuckie said. "'We need to get this done,' 'you've got to go over here,' stuff like that was not a big thing. It never meant nothing to me."

"Did Fitz tell you who you were delivering the bag to?" I asked.

"No. I took the fucking briefcase to where it's supposed to go, I never asked any questions. You never ask, Jack."

"Do you know who was in the hotel door when you opened it?" I asked.

"No," he told me. "Didn't care. It was dark in there."

"Are you sure you're the person who delivered the money?" I asked, half joking, at the end of one lengthy interrogation.

Chuckie blew up. "Jack, you know I'm tired of answering you, I really am," he screamed. "I'll get so fucking mad that I'll hit you with a fucking baseball bat. Who the fuck do you think takes the money? Fitz ain't going to take it. Who could he trust to take it?"

"Don't get mad at me," I said.

"Listen to me, okay? I'm just telling you as a person that is a square. The deal was one million dollars and he comes home, okay?"

Chuckie's story stayed remarkably constant over many years and many conversations. But I still wasn't sure, because I lacked corroboration. My doubts diminished, however, when Chuckie began to regret what he told me. He often spoke in very general terms about money deliveries he made over the years for Hoffa. But in no other context that I learned about were the stakes so large, nor did he reveal so many details. And though talking about the payoff from Hoffa to Nixon did not involve a Sicilian secret, it was still speaking much further out of school about secret business than usual.

"I just wish Uncle Tony was alive," Chuckie said abruptly and with irritation as I was probing for more details in one of our talks about the payoff.

"Tell me why," I said.

"I could talk to him," Chuckie said. "I could talk to him about taking the money."

"You mean to see if it's okay for you to talk about it?" I asked.

"Yeah," he said. "I never told anybody that I did it, that I took it to where I took it, nobody knew that."

Uncle Tony had nothing to do with the payoff, and Omertà did not extend to Hoffa's business with Nixon. But Chuckie worried about giving away a deep secret nonetheless. And after his mother's death, Uncle Tony was the person Chuckie went to for advice when he didn't trust his instincts or judgment.

"What's he worried about?" my mother, Brenda, asked. She was sitting with us during the conversation, only half paying attention, when she noticed Chuckie's discomfort.

"I think he's worried that he's talking about things he shouldn't be talking about," I said. "He's worried about being a rat."

"You're right," Chuckie snapped. He was panicked about revealing secrets in a way that I would witness just one other time, years later. "I really didn't want to talk about this because it shows me being a no-good son of a bitch mistrustful person and that's what bothers me," he added, without artifice. "It shows me as being a rat."

WHEN HOFFA WAS released from prison in December 1971, his drive to remove Fitzsimmons and reassume the presidency of the Teamsters union focused on the 1976 election for the Teamsters top spot. The Nixon bar on his involvement in a labor union until 1980 stood in Hoffa's way. For the first few years out of prison, he took a low-key approach to overturning the ban. In private, he never stopped bad-mouthing Fitzsimmons. But in public, Hoffa praised Fitzsimmons throughout 1972 and into much of 1973.

Hoffa also avoided direct approaches to the Fitzsimmons-friendly White House and instead sought assistance from "anybody else that could help him," Chuckie told me, including "politicians, senators, and congressmen" to whom Hoffa paid a lot of money. "He wasn't bashful about paying," says Chuckie. At the same time, Hoffa's lawyers sought yet again to overturn his jury tampering conviction, using a dubious affidavit from Edward Partin that Chuckie, along with the New Orleans crime boss Carlos Marcello, helped secure. If successful, this tactic might have negated the condition, since Hoffa had already served time on the pension fund conviction.

While Hoffa was pursuing these quiet moves against the Nixon restriction, he burnished his public image. The five years in prison had ground down some of his sharper edges and made him more appealing. He had gray temples and seemed less threatening, perhaps because he no longer commanded two million Teamsters. And his intelligence shone through. In his first television interview after prison, on ABC's *Issues and Answers*, Hoffa spoke confidently about the pathologies of criminal justice, the problems bedeviling American labor, and the political scene. "He put out one of the most impressive performances that I've seen a man on television do," Chuck Colson said to President Nixon of the interview. "He was firm, he was crisp, his words were well chosen. He was quick with his answers. And he gave the impression of real depth. He's quite an interesting guy."

Hoffa didn't publicly comment a great deal on the social issues roiling the nation in the early 1970s. But he did enthusiastically take up the cause of prison reform in talks around the country, testimony before Congress, and press interviews. After his release from prison, "almost no Hoffa interviewer, no matter what the original line of questioning, departed without having heard a lengthy narration about just how bad life in the penitentiary was," said Hoffa's biographer, Arthur Sloane. Hoffa emphasized that drugs, violence, and rape were prevalent in prison, and tended to leave inmates, especially young ones, more crime-prone than when they entered. And he proposed a long battery of reforms.

Hoffa was committed to prison reform, but it was also "a disguise," according to Chuckie, that gave Hoffa a reason other than labor management to travel around the country and meet with the many Teamsters who had never stopped adoring him. "Every city he would go to—you have to understand the magnitude of his personality—he'd be there for prison reform but every fucking guy that was a Teamster, either a member or an officer, showed up," Chuckie told me. And when they showed up, Hoffa spoke to them quietly about the labor issues they faced and sought their support for his return, which they pledged to him. "When he was making those speeches, all the Teamsters are there, and I think he got more and more enthusiastic," Chuckie told me. Everywhere Hoffa went, crowds of people greeted him. Every day he was at the Lake, he received dozens of letters from admirers urging him to return to the union.

The rank and file was enthusiastic about Hoffa's return, but Fitzsimmons was dead set against it. Throughout 1972 he and Hoffa clashed in private even while making nice in public. Fitzsimmons complained to the White House that Hoffa was secretly violating the condition on his release, but the White House had less and less time for these complaints as it became engulfed in historic scandal.

Watergate emerged from the same consuming obsession to reelect Nixon that led the White House to cozy up to Fitzsimmons and cut the corrupt clemency deal for Hoffa's release. Nixon believed that in the 1972 election, "Information would be our first line of defense," as he said in his memoirs. The best tools for gathering information were ones earlier administrations had deployed against communists, gangsters, and other threats: domestic wiretaps, break-ins, and bugging. By the early 1970s, the elderly Hoover, burned by revelations in the 1960s, refused to cooperate. So the Nixon team organized its own spying group. "The president created the Plumbers because he thought Hoover had lost the will to conduct political warfare," notes the journalist Tim Weiner. "Many of the elements of the bill of impeachment drawn up against Nixon three years later grew out of his frustrations with the FBI, his thirst for the secrets Hoover no longer supplied, and the bugging and burglary that followed."

On June 17, 1972, District of Columbia police officers arrested five men who had broken into the offices of the Democratic National Committee at the Watergate complex, carrying a stash of electronic bugging devices. Carl Bernstein and Bob Woodward reported on October 10, 1972, that "the Watergate bugging incident stemmed from a massive campaign of political spying and sabotage conducted on behalf of President Nixon's re-election and directed by officials of the White House and the Committee for the Re-election of the President." But the scandal did not metastasize before the election, which Nixon won in a landslide the following month in part because of an endorsement and loads of cash and assistance from the Teamsters, all of which Fitzsimmons secured. Two months later, in January 1973, the five Watergate burglars pled guilty, and the former Nixon aides G. Gordon Liddy and James W. McCord Jr. were convicted in connection with the burglary.

As Watergate descended on Nixon's presidency, the animosity between Hoffa and Fitzsimmons finally broke into public view. On February 5, 1973, *The New York Times* reported that a "bitter and widening rift" between the two men was complicating Nixon's "politically rewarding romance with the big union."

The president was furious when he read this story. "To what extent is Fitz going to have to be meaner and rougher because of Hoffa breathing down his throat?" he asked his advisor John Ehrlichman. "I just want the message to get out loud and clear that Hoffa can't get back into that thing. Isn't that what the commutation said, that you cannot go back into that?"

Ehrlichman agreed that Hoffa was "gradually violating" the condition and that it was "a problem for Fitz." When Nixon read in *The Washington Post* a few weeks later that Hoffa intended to run for president of Detroit Local 299, he ordered his new attorney general, Richard Kleindienst, to tell Hoffa he was "going to go back to jail" if he followed through. Kleindienst did so, and publicly announced that the government would "move quickly to enforce all aspects of the conditional commutation in the event that Mr. Hoffa does not abide by the conditions imposed upon him."

Nixon and Hoffa were now openly at odds. But Nixon had a weak hand. If he forced Hoffa back to prison, Hoffa might have nothing to lose from telling what he knew about the corrupt circumstances of his release. Nixon became politically much weaker, and much less focused on Hoffa, over the course of 1973—with the resignation of Haldeman and Ehrlichman and Kleindienst, and John Dean's firing, on April 30; the damaging Senate Watergate hearings in the spring and summer; Alexander Butterfield's public revelation on July 16 that Nixon recorded conversations and phone calls in the Oval Office; and Nixon's refusal to turn over those recordings in the form requested by Special Prosecutor Archibald Cox, which resulted on October 20 in the firing of Cox and the resignation of Attorney General Elliot Richardson and his deputy, William Ruckelshaus.

Eleven days before this "Saturday Night Massacre," the Supreme Court denied Hoffa's last effort to have his jury tampering conviction overturned. Hoffa now had only one very long shot at removing the condition on his release: a direct legal challenge to Nixon's authority to impose the condition. Morris Shenker, Hoffa's longtime attorney and the point man in his commutation efforts, balked at taking the case. So Hoffa shopped around and hired the famed civil liberties lawyer Leonard Boudin. As they were preparing for the lawsuit, Hoffa took his feud against Fitzsimmons public. He accused Fitzsimmons of "traveling all over the country to every damn golf tournament there is, when being president of the Teamsters is an eighteen-hour-a-day job." Fitzsimmons responded by firing Hoffa's wife, Josephine, and his son, James, from the Teamsters jobs they had held since Hoffa went to prison.

On March 13, 1974, Boudin brought a suit against Nixon and his then attorney general, William Saxbe. He asked the court to declare the condition illegal as an abuse of presidential power and a violation of Hoffa's rights to free speech and association. Hoffa told the trial court that he was never aware of and did not agree to the condition on his release. "I would not have accepted freedom had I personally been aware of such conditions (the 1980 restriction) at the time of my release," he said in legal papers. He also alleged that the condition was part of a corrupt deal by Colson and others in the White House to keep Fitzsimmons in power in exchange for political favors and campaign donations from the Teamsters. The lawsuit "could produce more of the explosive disclosures that have deepened the crisis of Mr. Nixon's Presidency since the Watergate burglary," reported *The New York Times*, which added that Hoffa had accused government officials "of activities that could be construed as criminal."

Hoffa was right about the Nixon-Colson-Fitzsimmons deal but could not prove it. Mitchell, Colson, and Fitzsimmons swore in depositions that they knew little about the condition on Hoffa's release and nothing about a deal in exchange for it. All three lied, as the Nixon archives make clear. But they weren't the only ones who lied. The lawsuit was premised on a big lie, one accepted by Hoffa's biographer and many others over the years. Despite feigning ignorance about the restrictions on his commutation soon after he was released, Hoffa had pledged many times to many people that he would never return to labor if he got out of Lewisburg, and he knew that Nixon claimed he could enforce the pledge by sending him back to jail for other matters. Some have questioned whether Hoffa knew before his release about the legal condition that the Nixon team inserted into the commutation papers, but it appears that he even knew about that.

It was widely reported long before Hoffa left prison that neither Nixon nor the Board of Parole would release him absent a bar on his organized labor activities. (The Justice Department had in 1970 sought such a legal bar in Congress.) Olymp Dainoff, the Lewisburg parole chief, says he told Hoffa about the actual condition on his release. Hoffa did not appear "particularly displeased," and described the condition as "no problem," Dainoff stated under oath. Morris Shenker, who filed Hoffa's request for commutation, "insisted" that "Hoffa knew prior to his release that his commutation was conditional and provided for some restrictions," according to a 1975 FBI interview summary. Shenker "could not conceive of the government releasing Hoffa without attaching some conditions."

Nor could Hoffa. That is why he pledged to Fitzsimmons, orally and in writing, never to return to organized labor; why his son, James, was rumored to have told the Board of Parole in the summer of 1971 that Hoffa would accept a condition on his parole; why Hoffa stated in his request for commutation that he planned to "live on a pension" and "enter the educational field"; and why he stated upon his release from Lewisburg that he would abide by any

Jimmy Hoffa, left, and his closest aide, Bert Brennan, in a Teamsters meeting in 1946 (Walter P. Reuther Library, Archives of Labor and Urban Affairs, Wayne State University)

Chuckie with Hoffa's wife, Josephine, and children, James P. and Barbara, just after Hoffa's 1957 acquittal for allegedly bribing John Cheasty to spy on the McClellan Committee (Bettmann / Getty Images)

Robert Kennedy, chief counsel for the McClellan Committee, confers with Hoffa in 1957, prior to Hoffa's appearance before the committee, during which the two men famously clashed

(Bettmann / Getty Images)

A celebratory evening in Miami Beach on October 5, 1957, one day after Hoffa's election to president of the Teamsters. Chuckie is seated at the far end of the table, holding his young son, also named Chuckie. Hoffa is to the right, and Hoffa's wife, Josephine, to the left. Chuckie's mother, Sylvia, is next to Josephine. Hoffa's daughter, Barbara, is seated front left, and his son, James, is third from her.

(Reproduced with permission of Charles O'Brien)

Chuckie's mother, Sylvia, left, with the New Jersey Teamsters official Anthony Provenzano and his wife, Maria, in Miami Beach, 1957
(Reproduced with Permission of Charles O'Brien)

Hoffa, seen from behind, at a meeting with trucking industry executives, negotiating the landmark National Master Freight Agreement in January 1964
(International Brotherhood of Teamsters Archives)

Chuckie at the center of the cover of *The International Teamster* after the conclusion of the 1964 National Master Freight Agreement. "Mr. Hoffa insisted that I be in the picture to thank me for my help," Chuckie told this book's author.
(International Brotherhood of Teamsters Archives)

Hoffa and Chuckie at a
working lunch in 1965
(location unknown)
(Frank Dandridge / The LIFE
Images Collection / Getty Images)

Hoffa and his handpicked
successor, Frank Fitzsimmons,
on July 7, 1966, at the
Teamsters convention that
reelected Hoffa to president
and Fitzsimmons to general
vice president, in anticipation
of Hoffa's imprisonment
(Bettmann / Getty Images)

Chuckie looks at reporters as
Hoffa holds an impromptu
press conference at the federal
courthouse in Washington, D.C.,
on March 7, 1967, just before
surrendering to serve his sentence
at the Lewisburg penitentiary.
(Bettmann / Getty Images)

Hoffa speaks with reporters after his release from the Lewisburg penitentiary on December 23, 1971.
(Bettmann / Getty Images)

Teamsters president Frank Fitzsimmons meets with President Richard Nixon at the "Western White House," San Clemente, California, on February 12, 1973. One week earlier, *The New York Times* reported that a "bitter and widening rift" between Fitzsimmons and Hoffa was complicating Nixon's "politically rewarding romance with the big union." (Bettmann / Getty Images)

Chuckie working on the Teamsters' lettuce and grape campaign in July 1973
(Reproduced with permission of Charles O'Brien)

Chuckie with his attorney, James Burdick, after invoking his Fifth Amendment right not to testify before the Hoffa grand jury, September 3, 1975
(Walter P. Reuther Library, Archives of Labor and Urban Affairs, Wayne State University)

Anthony Provenzano speaks to reporters in front of his Hallandale Beach, Florida, home one week after Hoffa's disappearance
(Bettmann / Getty Images)

Anthony Giacalone, right, with his attorney on his way to the Hoffa grand jury, September 8, 1975
(Bettmann / Getty Images)

The author and his brothers with Chuckie at Florida Air Academy, 1976 (Reproduced with permission of Brenda O'Brien)

Chuckie and his new family at a friend's home in Miami, Christmas 1976. From left: Chuckie, the author, Brett, Brenda, Steven (Reproduced with permission of Brenda O'Brien)

The author's graduation from Washington and Lee University in June 1984. One week later, Jack would tell Chuckie he was changing his name from O'Brien to Goldsmith. (Reproduced with permission of Brenda O'Brien)

June 27, 1984

Dear Jack,

The fact that you took the time to sit down and write a letter to me means a great deal. I have read it over many times, and each time I become more confused.

Nothing could change my love for you. Love isn't something that can be turned on and off at the drop of a hat — it is something that grows as two people grow together, sharing good times, hard-times, laughter, tears, joy, and sorrow.

A child or a son or daughter can never know the love a parent has for him or her until that child becomes a parent.

Good parents continue to love their children, seeing their good points, as well as their faults. That love sometimes brings sorrow, hurt and heartache. As in our present situation.

But more often than not that love brings happiness and love in return.

The first page of Chuckie's long letter to the author, responding to the news about the name change

(Reproduced with permission of Charles O'Brien)

Chuckie, in a photo taken by the author in Boca Raton, Florida, September 10, 2018

conditions and had no intention to return to the Teamsters. "The Old Man definitely knew about the condition," Chuckie insists. "He agreed to it to get out."

None of the lies about the condition on Hoffa's commutation mattered in the end, when federal judge John H. Pratt of the U.S. District Court threw out the lawsuit on July 19, 1974, about a year before Hoffa's disappearance. The commutation was proper, he ruled, because previous presidents had put conditions on pardons, and Nixon's was "reasonable" in light of Hoffa's conviction for labor corruption. Pratt added that Hoffa chose freedom with the condition, and could not "complain of the choice he has made"—especially since he was unwilling to return to prison.

Hoffa expected a different outcome. "Nothing is lost until the final round," he glumly told reporters in Detroit. After pondering what to do for several months, Hoffa floated the idea in November 1974 of running for Local 299 but not assuming office unless and until he prevailed in the challenge to his condition on appeal. He knew this plan defied the limits on the restriction, but he assumed that the government would be "unwilling to alienate powerful Teamsters rank-and-file support by moving against" him before the 1976 elections, as *The Detroit News* reported.

But Hoffa had finally gone too far. The Watergate scandal had forced Nixon to resign a few months earlier, and the government was no longer so compromised. On November 29, 1974, two weeks after Hoffa announced his intentions, Henry Petersen, the head of the Justice Department's Criminal Division, wrote to the deputy attorney general, Laurence Silberman, with a plan to "retake and recommit" Hoffa for violating the restriction. Petersen drafted a letter for President Ford's signature that found that Hoffa had "violated the terms and conditions of his conditional commutation," that declared the commutation "void and of no effect," and that directed the attorney general to "take all necessary and appropriate action to apprehend and return Mr. Hoffa to prison to complete the service of his original sentence."

It would have been high political and constitutional theater if the Ford administration had followed through. But it didn't need to. The Justice Department floated its plan to put Hoffa back in jail in the press, and it probably showed his attorneys the papers it had drafted. Hoffa then decided not to run in the January 1975 Local 299 elections. The decision was the death knell of his efforts to win back his union in the 1976 election—and given his age (almost sixty-two), perhaps ever. "Hoffa, a supreme realist, knew in his heart that he would never regain union power," Shenker would tell the FBI eight months later.

Nixon's condition had held. The traitor Fitzsimmons had won. And Hoffa grew angrier, gloomier, and much less rational.

·

SEVEN

"HE GOT NUTS"

O N THE EVENING OF NOVEMBER 30, 1974, Chuckie settled into the couch at the home of his friends Marvin and Betty Adell in Bloomfield, Michigan, to watch an *ABC News Close Up* report called "Hoffa." He was stunned by what he saw.

The program was based on extensive interviews with Hoffa. It began by recounting the bitter feud between Hoffa and Frank Fitzsimmons, and Hoffa's efforts to regain control of the Teamsters union. It then examined Hoffa's links to organized crime through corrupt Teamsters pension fund loans. It said that loans had continued under Fitzsimmons, and that the Feds were closing in on the entire operation. And in connection with the loans, the program tied Fitzsimmons to Louis "the Tailor" Rosanova, who Jim Kincaid of ABC News said was a member of the Chicago Mafia.

Rosanova was indeed a senior figure in the Chicago Outfit. Hoffa and Chuckie knew him from their many dealings in the Windy City. Hoffa once arranged a Teamsters pension loan to help Rosanova build a hotel and golf course in Savannah, Georgia.

Hoffa didn't finger Rosanova as a mob figure on the ABC program. But a viewer might have inferred that Hoffa was a source for the material on the show. Chuckie did, and couldn't believe it. "Big Lou loved this man like you can't believe," he told me.

Rosanova drew the same conclusion. He sued Hoffa (along with ABC News) for libel. "All or some of the information used on said show was supplied and compiled by the defendant, James R. Hoffa," who "reviewed the contents and script used in the said show, [and] approved the same," Rosanova charged in his legal filing.

Rosanova's organized crime friends around the country interpreted Hoffa's involvement in the program the same way. And they were alarmed, since it seemed to confirm rumors that Hoffa was talking out of school, possibly to the government, about LCN and its extensive infiltration of the Teamsters since Hoffa stepped down as president in 1967. "It was the shot heard round the world," Chuckie told me.

Chuckie had seen Hoffa two days earlier, on Thanksgiving Day, at the Lake, where he had joined the Hoffa family for its traditional dinner together. He and Hoffa had a tense exchange just before dinner about Chuckie's longtime ambition to run Detroit Local 299. The FBI later believed that the two men had a falling-out that day because Hoffa had failed to support Chuckie's dream. "At that point, O'Brien became embittered and broke off his relationship with Jimmy Hoffa," concluded a 2002 FBI report. "O'Brien did not communicate with Jimmy Hoffa from approximately Thanksgiving of 1974 through the date of the disappearance," it added. "Jimmy Hoffa attempted a reconciliation, but O'Brien rebuffed these attempts."

There is a misleading sliver of truth in this assessment—an assessment that influenced FBI suspicions about Chuckie's involvement in the disappearance. Chuckie and Hoffa did grow apart during 1974, and their conversation on Thanksgiving Day was one of the reasons. But the two men did not "fall out" on that day. The deterioration in their relationship was at least as much about Hoffa's pushing Chuckie away as it was about Chuckie's leaving Hoffa. It was also a result of Hoffa's increasingly vocal threats to expose LCN influence in the Teamsters. But the clinching event for Chuckie was not his disappointment about Local 299 or Hoffa's irresponsible talk about LCN. It was, rather, my mother's unexpected return to his life.

IN LATE 1971, Chuckie was still working on the Teamsters dispute with the United Farm Workers. When Hoffa was released from prison, however, everyone who mattered wanted Chuckie back at Hoffa's side, though for different reasons.

Hoffa wanted Chuckie around for the same reasons he always had: companionship, errand-running, and intelligence-gathering.

Fitzsimmons wanted Chuckie with Hoffa for a different reason—to keep him preoccupied. "Fitz wanted me to stay with him, go shopping, do things that he wanted done at the Lake, and all that," Chuckie told me. "Don't worry about any assignments," Fitzsimmons counseled. "He is the general president emeritus and we are assigning you to him."

Anthony Giacalone, who represented LCN interests, "told me to stay out there too," at the Lake, to "keep Hoffa happy."

Chuckie was thrilled that Hoffa was out of jail but not pleased to be returning to his role as Hoffa's drudge. He was almost forty years old. His labor career was still stuck in park. He lacked an executive position in the union and he was not in line for one. But at least he had been working on the important and challenging farmworkers fight. Now he was being asked to cut back his time on that assignment in order to babysit the demanding, ornery, union-barred Hoffa.

One of the first things Chuckie and Hoffa did together was to collect some of Hoffa's money. Hoffa had withdrawn $1,740,000 from his Teamsters pension soon after he was released from prison. But he had much more to collect from another source. They twice flew from Detroit to Miami and back in a privately chartered plane. The real estate developer Calvin Kovens met them in Miami with ten large suitcases the first time and five large suitcases the second. Chuckie says the suitcases were full of "tens and twenties, no fifties or hundreds," which was how Hoffa preferred his cash.

"The Old Man didn't like to hand out hundred-dollar bills," Chuckie explained to me. "'It'll come back and bite you in the ass,' he'd always say." Chuckie doesn't know what happened to the cash. "We put it in the car and took it to the Lake and I never asked."

Hoffa had many millions of dollars in cash. But it didn't matter. "Money is just a commodity," he once said. "Power is what lets you eat and sleep." When Hoffa got out of jail, he had no power. And that meant that Chuckie's time with him was quite different than in the heady days in the 1950s and 1960s, when Hoffa ran the world.

The two men spent most of their first two summers after Hoffa's release fixing up the dilapidated cottage where Chuckie played with Hoffa as a boy. "I spent a lot of time out with him at that fucking Lake. I worked my ass off physically and mentally and everything else." They built a new kitchen, master bedroom, and porch; they repaved the road to the cottage; they razed the lawn around it and installed a sprinkler system; and they installed a pony ring and barn for Hoffa's grandchildren.

Hoffa and Chuckie often chatted after work and dinner in rocking chairs on the porch they built. Hoffa was unusually nostalgic about his early days in labor. Chuckie asked "a zillion questions" and lapped up the answers. Once he asked what Hoffa thought of a newspaper story on Joseph Crater, the Tammany Hall–connected state court judge who walked out of a Midtown New York restaurant on August 6, 1930, got in a taxi, and was never seen again despite a sensationalistic nationwide manhunt. "For a clean disappearance like that, he must have gotten somebody very important very angry," Hoffa answered. Later, after Hoffa's disappearance, it would "freak me out that he said that," Chuckie told me.

Most of the time, Hoffa stewed about Fitzsimmons. He would "get crazy, ranting and raving about shit at the Lake when he'd get on that soapbox with me about how Fitzsimmons fucked him," Chuckie told me. Hoffa complained that "the motherfucker" Fitzsimmons double-crossed him, stole the union from him, and "robbed me of a million dollars." Chuckie said little in response. He "just let him run off the fuckin' steam."

But the pressure kept building. As Hoffa pursued legal and political avenues in 1972 and 1973 to get the Nixon condition lifted, his union supporters wound him up about Fitzsimmons's ineptitude.

"He would get calls every fuckin' day on that fuckin' phone at that Lake, every moron would call him, and just get on Fitzsimmons," Chuckie told me. "They would say, 'Fitz is doing this to the union, he's doing that, and look what he did with the freight contract.'"

Hoffa couldn't fathom that his genial subordinate was running the union he built, contrary to principles Hoffa spent decades establishing, while he, Hoffa, was stuck at the Lake with no influence. Hoffa exploded with each conversation. "He was not rational," Chuckie told me. "It reminds me how he got with Bobby Kennedy—he was treating Fitzsimmons the same way." One sign of Hoffa's visceral, almost childlike hatred was that he taped a picture of Fitzsimmons's face under the downstairs toilet seat at the cottage.

Hoffa's rants were not new to Chuckie, who had been hearing them since Lewisburg and had learned to ignore them. But the context was different. Hoffa was now out of jail and taking shots at the man who paid Chuckie's salary and could fire him. Hoffa's threat to Fitzsimmons became official—and more awkward for Chuckie—when he filed suit the following month to seek to overturn the Nixon condition in the hopes of retaking the presidency from Fitz.

But things got really uncomfortable for Chuckie when Hoffa started publicly bad-mouthing Fitzsimmons in Chuckie's presence. On June 13, 1974, Chuckie drove Hoffa to a television interview on WXYZ-TV in Detroit, ostensibly to discuss his views on Richard Nixon and the unfolding Watergate scandal. At one point the interviewer, Dennis Wholey, asked Hoffa about Fitzsimmons's recent claim that Hoffa "should not be allowed back in organized labor." It was a month before the adverse ruling in his lawsuit against Nixon, at a time when Hoffa was confident he was going to be able to run for the Local 299 elections and for the presidency of the union.

"I understand from reliable sources in the international union that Fitzsimmons is seeing a psychiatrist twice a week," Hoffa answered. Fitzsimmons had accomplished little, he continued, and "should be the last to talk about who belongs in organized labor," Hoffa added. He went on to accuse Fitzsimmons of a case of "Potomac Fever" because he had been "rubbing shoulders with bigwigs" in Washington. And for good measure, he suggested that Fitzsimmons's son Richard was an alcoholic.

Hoffa's radio attack on Fitzsimmons stunned Chuckie. "He shouldn't have done that with me being there," Chuckie told me. The two men had a tense conversation on the drive home.

"Fitz is going to fire me," Chuckie said to Hoffa. "He is my boss, and you're killing me."

"Well, he won't be for long," Hoffa replied, implying that Fitzsimmons would soon be out.

"You're leading with your chin," said Chuckie. "You're going to walk yourself right back into the penitentiary."

"Don't worry about my fucking chin," he replied. "I'm in a war, goddamn it."

At this point Chuckie shut up and the two men were silent for the rest of the car ride.

The episode at WXYZ clarified what both Chuckie and Hoffa had understood for a while: he was no longer very useful to Hoffa. Chuckie was with him only with Fitzsimmons's blessing. If he helped Hoffa to unseat Fitzsimmons, he would almost certainly be fired, just as Hoffa's wife and son had been. Hoffa understood this and cut Chuckie out of most of his union comeback efforts. Chuckie would still deliver cash and messages for Hoffa for various investments and paybacks unrelated to union business. But those deliveries were less frequent than before. Hoffa wasn't traveling around the country as often and wasn't doing many things that required Chuckie's services in any event.

Nor could Chuckie help with Hoffa's complex legal battles. There were no trial boxes to watch over or meetings to organize, as in the good old days. And to make matters worse for Chuckie, Hoffa during this period began to rely more and more on his lawyer son, James. Chuckie had for decades been closer to the Old Man than his real son, whom Chuckie helped to raise. He had been in the trenches with Hoffa while James was "getting educated" in the 1960s, when he attended college at Michigan State and law school at the University of Michigan. Hoffa was proud of his son's establishment accomplishments but for a long time kept him at a distance from his business affairs. In the years since Hoffa was released from prison, however, James had grown closer to his father and become one of his chief advisors in fighting the Nixon condition, just as Chuckie and Hoffa were growing apart.

As Hoffa's chances to return to labor waned, so too did his tolerance for Chuckie's antics. In June 1974, Lawrence Adell, the teenage nephew of Chuckie's best friends, Marvin and Betty Adell, was kidnapped in Palm Springs. Chuckie asked Hoffa to make an appeal about the boy's whereabouts to one of the arrested suspects, Angelo Inciso, a former union official and ex-convict whom Hoffa knew. Hoffa agreed but insisted that his help be kept out of the news. On July 20, 1974, one day after he learned that he lost his case against Nixon in the trial court, a dejected Hoffa flew to California and met Inciso in prison.

The following day, a front-page *Detroit Free Press* story reported on the visit. "Hoffa is going to try to see what he can do," said Chuckie, described as Hoffa's adopted son. "When it comes to kids, my dad, well, he's very concerned." The story discussed Inciso's shady background and Lawrence's father's possible gambling connections with "Mafia figures Vito and Tony Giacalone"—exactly the type of publicity Hoffa sought to avoid. Chuckie says Hoffa "got very, very upset with me." (Lawrence's bones would be found a few years later in the California desert.)

Hoffa also grew displeased with the course Chuckie's life had taken. The moralistic family man frowned on Chuckie's divorce from Mary Ann. Hoffa the fitness nut frowned on Chuckie's expanding paunch, which Hoffa viewed as a sign of indiscipline and sloth. And Hoffa the longtime bankroller frowned on Chuckie's worse-than-ever money problems. All of his adult life Chuckie lived far beyond his Teamsters' income. But by the early 1970s he was beyond broke. For years he had been dating a San Francisco Playboy Bunny, Lanie De Pasco, whom he showered with gifts he could not afford. Most of his wages had been garnished for unpaid back taxes. And his home had been repossessed for failure to make mortgage payments. Chuckie was forced to move in rent-free with the Adells, and he lived off their generosity and his travel per diem of twenty-five dollars.

In the past Hoffa had helped Chuckie out of his frequent financial scrapes in dribs and drabs with the copious cash that he always had on hand. "How ya holdin'?" he would often ask, before doling out a thousand dollars here and there. Hoffa also very frequently backed loans and other financial help that his friends or acquaintances gave to Chuckie, and paid them off when, as was often the case, Chuckie couldn't. But by mid-1974, Hoffa was tired to the point of anger about bailing out his increasingly profligate second son.

Chuckie never really grasped Hoffa's frustration with his money mismanagement. And he wondered why the multimillionaire Hoffa failed to set him up with financial security. "He never protected me," Chuckie told me reluctantly, and with embarrassment, near the end of our conversations. "When he made these big deals, I never got anything."

Chuckie was too proud to expect or ask for more than what Hoffa gave him. "I knew what he was doing, he didn't bullshit me when it come to that," Chuckie told me. Hoffa seemed to give Chuckie just enough to keep him afloat but on the line. But beginning in the summer of 1974, for reasons Chuckie could not fathom, Hoffa stopped offering to help even though he knew Chuckie was in desperate financial straits.

For almost twenty-five years Chuckie had served Hoffa loyally, no questions asked, in very difficult circumstances. He had been nourished by Hoffa's approval and support, and the implicit power and prestige that came with it. But now he won little approval or support from the distracted Hoffa, who had little power or prestige to share in any event. And he was feeling heat from Fitzsimmons and his men, who expected Chuckie to keep Hoffa under control. Chuckie was miserable. For the first time, he began to wonder how he could move on with his life.

It was at this low point, in the late summer of 1974, that Hoffa "got out of the normal way he operated, and did some things that I thought he would never do," as Chuckie put it. Hoffa had been frantically seeking support from any quarter of LCN. But almost everyone of consequence in the mob was happy with how Fitz was running things and was unwilling to help. Hoffa had, according to government informants, offered LCN leaders $10 million for support to get the union back. The mob was clearing more than that every year with Fitz in charge. In their eyes, Hoffa was a "'used to be guy,' whose 'obsession' to return to Teamster Union political power had nearly reduced him to pathetic stature," as Hoffa's mob-connected friend Jay Sarno would later tell the FBI. Desperate for a power base in the union and keen to do anything to hurt Fitzsimmons, Hoffa went in league with the union rebels whom he once fought hard on principle. "He was so erratic that last year, he just wasn't himself," Chuckie explained.

These were not the most surprising things Hoffa did, however.

"He asked me to drop a dime on Fitzsimmons and Dickie Bird to the IRS, and all that kind of shit," Chuckie told me. "Dickie Bird" was Fitzsimmons's son Richard, an official in Local 299.

"What does 'drop a dime' mean?" I asked.

"Hello, Uncle Sam, I've got some information, you ought to check Fitzsimmons on his income tax returns, he's lying," Chuckie explained. "Hoffa wanted me to do whatever I could do with the government to screw Fitz and his kid." It was an ironic request because, unbeknownst to both men, Fitzsimmons had been a secret informant to the IRS for several years, dumping harmful information on his nemeses in the union in exchange for relief from his own tax problems.

Chuckie reacted sharply to Hoffa's request. "I thought his trolley came off the track," he told me. Hoffa had always had contempt for the government, and for anyone who ratted to the government, under any circumstances. "He never exposed anybody, I don't give a shit if the guy was caught red-handed, he'd say, 'It's all bullshit.' He hated rats. He hated people that talked." But now Hoffa was asking Chuckie to rat on his boss, a request that went against every instinct that Hoffa, as well as Uncle Tony and his mother, had drilled into Chuckie since he was a teenager.

"I'm not going to do that," Chuckie told Hoffa, without thinking. "I'm not going to do that bullshit, trying to leak something on somebody. I wasn't born that way and you know that. I wouldn't even know how."

It was the first time in his life Chuckie had ever said no to Hoffa. And Hoffa was pissed.

"What are you saying no about, goddamn it?" he barked as he gave Chuckie "that Hoffa look"—a scowling, angry, green-eyed stare.

"It's not right, you never fought that way," Chuckie said.

"I don't give a shit, this is a different kind of war," Hoffa retorted. "I want my union back."

Then things got worse. When Hoffa really got out of character—when Chuckie thought "he got nuts, he lost his mind"—was when he started talking openly about exposing LCN's infiltration of the Teamsters. In 1974, Hoffa began work on an autobiography with Oscar Fraley, who cowrote *The Untouchables* with Eliot Ness. (The book was published just after he disappeared.) Hoffa praised Chuckie in the book and described him as "almost like a son to me." He also devoted the opening chapter to excoriating Frank Fitzsimmons. Among other things, Hoffa said:

> I *charge* him with selling out to mobsters and letting known racketeers into the Teamsters. . . .
> I *charge* him with permitting underworld establishment of a union insurance scheme which in one year was a ripoff to the tune of $1,185,000 in the New York area alone. . . .
> I *charge* him with making vast loans from the billion-dollar Teamsters pension fund to known mobsters.

Chuckie heard Hoffa discussing these topics with Fraley in Miami and in telephone conversations before the book was published. He also heard him threaten similar things in conversations with union allies. And he was not the only one who heard. In the fall of 1974, Hoffa began to talk loosely with union friends about how he planned to expose Fitzsimmons's cuddly relationship with the mob. "The thing I remember the most," Chuckie says, is when Hoffa said he would "get rid of the gangsters," which seemed, crazily, like something Bobby Kennedy would say. Hoffa was not always discreet about what he said or to whom he said these things. He appeared to want LCN to get the message, and it quickly did.

Hoffa was now juggling lit dynamite. He knew intimate details about mob relations with the Teamsters union. And he was openly threatening to provide a map and name names. This was a significant elevation beyond merely trashing Fitzsimmons. And it came at the worst possible time for the mob, which was under new pressure from the Feds since Hoover had died on May 2, 1972.

Richard Nixon's temporary replacement for Hoover, L. Patrick Gray, got caught up in the Watergate cover-up and resigned in April 1973 before he was confirmed. Under enormous political pressure, Nixon then nominated Clarence M. Kelley, a straitlaced FBI veteran and Kansas City police chief, to succeed Hoover. Kelley supported the FBI's relentless Watergate investigation and presided over the Bureau as Hoover's accumulated dirty deeds began to trickle out during the Watergate hearings. He weathered the storm by cleaning out Hoover's bureaucratic stables, apologizing for the FBI's past sins, and steering the Bureau's mission away from communists and toward organized crime. The FBI was assisted in this new focus by an array of new legal authorities and a 15 percent increase in manpower that Congress had given it in the late 1960s. The FBI's successful assault on the mob would not really get going until after Hoffa disappeared. But in the year before his disappearance, grand jury investigations and lawful wiretap initiatives had ramped up, and LCN was starting to feel the heat.

Against this background, Chuckie couldn't fathom what Hoffa was doing. "He was wrong, he was really wrong," Chuckie told me. "He was never that way. He got a lot of people nervous, a lot of people very nervous."

Chuckie said that many wiseguys he knew around the country expressed anxiety about Hoffa's antics. "I used to talk to Willie about it," he said, referring to William Cammisano, at the time a Kansas City capo and later its boss. "It's not good, Chuckie, it's not good," Willie told him. Sammy and Nunzi Provenzano, Tony Pro's brothers, expressed similar concern. So too did Joey Glimco, a Teamsters leader in Chicago who was also a capo in the Chicago Outfit. "Why can't you get the dog to stop barking?" he asked Chuckie. Chuckie heard from someone else—he wouldn't tell me who—that Santo Trafficante, a Florida don, said he was "getting up in age and 'I'm not going to die in that fuckin' jail, no way it's gonna happen.'" Chuckie says that Roy Williams, the mob-connected Kansas City Teamsters leader, warned Hoffa based on his conversations with the Kansas City crime family. And he says that Allen Dorfman pleaded directly with Hoffa in Miami to knock it off.

As he always did when he was not sure what to do, Chuckie sought Anthony Giacalone's advice. During the period when Hoffa was attacking only Fitzsimmons, Uncle Tony counseled him to lie low. "Stay put, keep quiet, and listen," he advised. "You cannot take sides in this deal. Hopefully Jimmy is going to come around, he's going to wake up."

But Uncle Tony, like everyone else, grew vexed when Hoffa threatened to finger LCN. He never spelled out the consequences, Chuckie says, but he didn't need to.

"You gotta tell the little guy to slow down," Uncle Tony advised. "Calm him down, get him interested in something else." Chuckie says that the "philosophy of the Sicilians," which Giacalone represented, was to "keep Hoffa close" so he wouldn't go "sideways."

Chuckie struggled with this assignment. "People expected me to keep him quiet," Chuckie said. "But I couldn't." Chuckie never expressly warned Hoffa that his threatening words would invite trouble. "It was not my place," he explained. "There are certain things I can do with him and certain things I couldn't do."

But Chuckie did beg Hoffa to stop. And he sometimes couched his pleas in personal terms. "You're putting a bonfire under me," Chuckie told Hoffa. "You know where I came from, you knew who my mother was, you know I'm from Kansas City."

Hoffa shrugged off this and every other concern. He just kept saying, as he had been for a while, that "when you're in a war you use every weapon you've got."

In one sense this was classic pragmatic Hoffa. His philosophy was always to use any tool, make any deal, no matter what or with whom, if it would bring him the ends he cherished. In another sense, however, lashing out at the mob made little sense. It had no power to remove the condition on Hoffa's commutation that was blocking his return to power. Linking Fitzsimmons publicly to the mob would exacerbate Fitzsimmons's pain by inviting scrutiny from the Feds and the press. But it wouldn't affect the legal bar on his return. And it came at an enormous cost: Hoffa would be deeply implicated, he would destroy the Teamsters, and he would place a bull's-eye on his forehead in the process. Perhaps Hoffa thought he could take care of the legal restriction himself, and his threats against the mob were designed to give him leverage to eliminate Fitz as an opponent and garner LCN votes for his election. But if so, that was an improbable, high-risk strategy.

Chuckie's theory is that Hoffa didn't care. Once he concluded he couldn't get his union back, he decided to demolish everything and everyone involved, including himself. "He was hell-bent," Chuckie said. "It's like Humphrey Bogart on the boat when he had the marbles back and forth, and the strawberries, the fuckin' boat's going down and we're all going with you," he explained, in an allusion to Captain Queeg's insanely destructive behavior in *The Caine Mutiny*.

"Do you think he was suicidal?" I once asked. It seemed to me that he was.

"He was blinded by his hate for Fitz," Chuckie replied. "When a person gets out of control, he sometimes will do stuff and not know he's doing it. His obsession to become general president came first before anything. Josephine pleaded with him. She'd say, 'Jimmy, please, please,' when he'd get all worked up and angry. He just got so pig-headed, he didn't give a shit. I just think them wheels were coming off his buggy. I think the years he did in prison really mentally destroyed him a lot."

"The ironic thing was, he became a rat," I said. I was referring to Hoffa's request that Chuckie drop a dime on Fitz, and his threats to expose the mob.

Chuckie bristled at this characterization. "He wasn't the kind of rat like Jackie Presser," he explained, referring to one of Hoffa's successors as Teamsters president who was a longtime government informant. "He wasn't himself talking to the government. He was trying to scare the shit out of everybody."

Hoffa succeeded in scaring the shit out of Chuckie, whose position at the side of a man who was attacking his union, his boss, and the Outfit was untenable. For his entire adult life he had lived at the crossroads of the Teamsters and LCN, between the Old Man and Uncle Tony. The only time that position had caused him heartburn was in the early 1960s, when his mother and Anthony and Vito Giacalone were exploiting Josephine. But that episode, which Chuckie got through, was nothing like the situation he now faced.

"I never tried to put myself in a position that I would do something to hurt Uncle Tony or the Outfit or the Old Man," he explained. "My mother raised me not to be a fool. She always taught me and taught me very well, schooled me, about both sides, don't put yourself in a position to hurt either side."

But now Chuckie was in just that position. He felt faithless to Hoffa in executing Uncle Tony's impossible assignment to keep him quiet. And he was failing in that assignment and thus not helping the Outfit. He was also unbearably miserable in Hoffa's presence. "Mr. Hoffa, when he started doing all that shit, I didn't want to be around him, because everything I thought that he should have been, he wasn't. He just became a human being that I loved and grew up with and would have done anything for him and then he—he broke my heart when he was doing that."

Chuckie's uncomfortable role between the Outfit and Hoffa, coming on top of his other troubles, made him more anxious and despondent than he had ever been in his life. "I had to deal with it the best I could," he told me. "My road got very narrow, which way I was going to go. It was hard."

It got even harder as several more jolting events over the course of a single month, beginning in early November 1974, caused Chuckie and Hoffa to part ways.

ALL YEAR LONG, and in the face of the Nixon condition, Hoffa had been publicly plotting to regain control of Local 299 in the December 1974 elections as a stepping stone to retaking the Teamsters presidency the following year. Winning that election became less plausible after Hoffa lost his legal challenge to the condition in the trial court in July. And so Hoffa shifted to plan B. He arm-twisted his friend Dave Johnson, then president of Local 299, to run for reelection in December against Fitzsimmons's son Richard, who announced his candidacy in August.

Johnson was not anxious to continue serving. As a result of power struggles in 299 he had been beaten to a pulp in 1970 and had his office windows blown out by a shotgun in 1972. "I wanted to retire and only stayed to help" Hoffa, who "had no hope of coming back as president of the international unless he had control of Local 299," Johnson told Dan Moldea. The plan was apparently for Johnson to win the presidency and then appoint Hoffa as a 299 business agent, which would qualify him to be a delegate at the 1976 national convention and thus run for president. (This plan flew in the teeth of Hoffa's commutation restriction.) The battle for the 299 presidency thus became a proxy war for the larger battle Hoffa was waging to rejoin the Teamsters.

All summer long, Chuckie had been urging Hoffa to let him run, and represent Hoffa's interests, in place of Johnson, who Chuckie knew was not keen to seek reelection. "My biggest dream was to one day become the president of 299, that was my fuckin' love," Chuckie told me. Chuckie had been pressing Hoffa to help him with his dream since the 1950s. Hoffa had pledged to do so but had also always put him off. "Just sit still, your time is coming," Hoffa would say.

But Chuckie had waited a decade before Hoffa went to Lewisburg, and then five years while Hoffa was in prison, and now several more after that. He waited and waited and waited. And he watched while several "incompetents," including "Dickie Bird" Fitzsimmons, rose up the ranks of Local 299. "'Sit still,' the Old Man told me, but all them assholes got in—Dickie Bird and all of them destroyed the local I had worked hard to build, and they didn't do nothing but play golf and they'd go to the bar and drink from twelve o'clock on."

Hoffa compounded Chuckie's despondency over the Local 299 presidency when, in late October 1974, he instructed Chuckie to rally support for Johnson among the union members he knew in town. "He wanted me to do stuff I normally did during elections—get stewards lined up, get business agents off their butt and behind him, stuff like that," Chuckie told me. It was the first time since jail that Hoffa asked Chuckie to openly work against Fitzsimmons. Chuckie viewed this task as more legitimate than the request to fink on Fitz to the IRS. But he knew the risks. Fitzsimmons's people were watching him closely, and many were urging him to support Dickie Bird. Chuckie nonetheless quietly did what Hoffa asked, because he was "loyal" and "loved the Old Man."

A few days later, Chuckie received a teletype "Directive" from Fitzsimmons that he was being reassigned to Teamsters Local 959 in Anchorage. "Chuckie O'Brien, the stocky adopted son of Jimmy Hoffa, has been transferred from his Teamster organizer job in Detroit—all the way to Alaska," *The Detroit News* reported on November 3, 1974. The story described Chuckie as "the latest casualty in the war of nerves" between Fitzsimmons and Hoffa, and attributed the transfer to his failure to support the Fitzsimmons faction.

After Fitzsimmons wielded his sword against Chuckie, Hoffa told a reporter: "I raised Chuck since he was a kid and I guess Fitz just doesn't want any symbols of me around Trumbull Avenue." But Hoffa offered Chuckie no plan to fight Fitz. And so Chuckie packed a travel bag and flew to Alaska the next day. "I wasn't happy," he told me. But he had no choice, since the alternative was being fired.

Chuckie spent only four days in Anchorage. "Fitz sent me to Alaska without clearing it," Chuckie told me. Uncle Tony had called Sammy Provenzano, Tony Pro's brother and then a member of the Teamsters Executive Board. "Tell Fitz to stop the bullshit and get that kid back here" was how Chuckie paraphrased the call. Fitzsimmons quickly reversed the transfer. But Chuckie got the message. "Fitz wanted to let me know that he was the general president, not Hoffa," he said.

Chuckie was back in Detroit, but in a worse position than ever. His loyalty still ran to Hoffa, whom he couldn't help without being fired, who was acting crazy, and who couldn't or wouldn't help Chuckie with his many problems. At the same time, Chuckie was under enormous pressure from Fitz and Uncle Tony to get Hoffa under control, which he had no means of doing.

"I was very upset," Chuckie told me. "I was like a fuckin' duck at a fuckin' shooting gallery," he said, describing how he felt going back and forth between Hoffa, Giacalone, and Fitzsimmons. "You go to a carnival and you shoot at it and it turns around and comes back the other way. I was like a duck. I would go from one end to the other. I was like a target. If he did something the wrong way, I'm the duck, they got upset."

A few days after his return from Alaska, Chuckie ran into Dave Johnson, whom he had known for decades, at Local 299. Chuckie knew that Johnson didn't want to run in the Local 299 election and pleaded with him to convince Hoffa to let Chuckie run in Johnson's place. We can speculate that Johnson had little patience for the unrealistic request. "Hoffa doesn't think you can handle 299," he said to Chuckie. Others, including Uncle Tony, had been hinting at this explanation for a while. But no one put it as bluntly as Johnson. The truth that everyone except Chuckie had known for decades had finally been aired without ambiguity.

Chuckie wouldn't tell me what his reaction was when he heard these words or how he felt in the interim few weeks before he joined the Hoffa family at the Lake for Thanksgiving dinner. Chuckie was already feeling down because on Thanksgiving morning he had broken off his relationship with his Playboy Bunny girlfriend, who lived in San Francisco. That afternoon, things got worse. He and Hoffa were sitting in the living room at the Lake before dinner, when Chuckie mentioned what Johnson told him.

"Someone told me that you said I can't handle the job," Chuckie said.

"Who said that?" Hoffa asked. "I never said that," he insisted.

"I don't understand," Chuckie responded. "Everything you've asked me to do when everybody else ran away, I did. What's the difference with me spending one solid year in Chattanooga? I handled that—why do you think I couldn't handle 299?"

"That's different," Hoffa responded, implicitly acknowledging the premise of Chuckie's question.

Chuckie did not follow up. He was quiet during Thanksgiving dinner. He left as soon as the meal was over.

"I realized that day, 'It ain't never going to happen,'" he told me, referring to 299.

"Did it piss you off?" I asked.

"It upset me," Chuckie said.

"Did you tell him?" I continued.

"No, I just kept it back in here," he said, tapping his heart and choking up.

Chuckie saw the Thanksgiving conversation as a turning point in his relationship with Hoffa because he finally understood that Hoffa would never help him advance in the union. But when he left the Lake and drove back to the Adells' home that evening, he had no plans to "leave" Hoffa. Fitzsimmons still wanted him to watch over Hoffa, and Chuckie didn't have any other job options. To the extent he thought about his future, he figured he would continue drifting aimlessly and miserably, as he had been for a while. "I had nowhere to go except be stuck in Detroit," Chuckie told me.

Chuckie's angst deepened considerably two nights later when he watched the ABC News special on Hoffa and the Teamsters relationship with LCN. The significance of this show has been missed by the FBI and all subsequent writers about the Hoffa disappearance, since Rosanova's mob connections and Teamsters tentacles had been aired in public before, and since Hoffa did not finger Rosanova on the program. But Rosanova and his friends, who had been hearing rumors that Hoffa was talking, believed Hoffa planted and approved the story and may have been involved in the earlier reports. That belief, whether true or false, was all that mattered. "When you get on national television and suggest Fitzsimmons is controlled by the Company—you've got people in New York that their hair was falling out," Chuckie told me.

Chuckie knew the danger in Hoffa's words, for he knew the rule with rats: *If there's any doubt, take 'em out.*

FIVE DAYS HENCE, when Chuckie was at the lowest point yet in his life—early forties, broke, divorced, alone, career dead, and trapped between the self-destructive Hoffa, his angry boss Fitzsimmons, and the menacing mob—his life changed sharply and unexpectedly.

He went into his office at Local 299 on the afternoon of December 5, 1974, for the first time in many weeks. On his desk he found a large pile of pink "While You Were Out" telephone messages. The slip on top of the pile rested for decades, faded and framed, on Chuckie's desk in Brenda's television room, just next to Jimmy Hoffa's photograph.

It was a message to "Chuck" from "Burger," a misspelling of my mother's maiden name, that included the phone number at my grandmother Clemmye's home in West Memphis, Arkansas, and a request to call. Brenda was just divorced and in a very dark place. She had telephoned Chuckie at the Detroit office of the AFL-CIO, thinking that was where he worked. The operator there happened to know who Chuckie was and gave Brenda the number at Local 299, which she called. "Please call this lady right away," Chuckie's secretary, Eleanor, advised him when she handed him the messages. "She sounded like she was desperate."

Chuckie is a Catholic with a detached but fatalistic religious sentiment. He saw the message as a gift from above. "I just was saying to myself, 'God gave me a second chance, and I'm not going to blow this,'" he told me. "God put your mother back in my life. There is no way that I ever thought I'd see your mother again."

Chuckie telephoned Brenda, who told him she was divorced and sad and wanted to see him. Chuckie bought a ticket with his Teamsters credit card and flew to West Memphis that day. "I got so excited that I went right to the airport and got on the airplane," he later told me. At the time I was twelve years old, and I only dimly remember the visit from a man whom my mother described as "a friend from Detroit." A few weeks later, just after Christmas, Brenda, my brothers, and I went to Detroit to spend a few days with Chuckie. On the second evening, my brothers and I stayed home with Chuckie's friends, the Adells, while he and Brenda went across the Detroit River to Canada for dinner. They barely knew each other, but they came back engaged.

The impulsive engagement is not hard to understand. Chuckie and Brenda were both deeply unhappy and (in different ways) deeply damaged. Each was frantically searching for change, and they each idealized, and saw salvation in, the other. For Brenda, Chuckie seemed like a stabilizing force, someone strong to take care of her and to be a father to her boys. She had no inkling of his volatile life or his enormous debts, and she never inquired. Nor could she have imagined the storm that would wreck our lives soon after Hoffa disappeared.

Chuckie saw my mother's return to his life as a "get-out-of-jail-free card, like in Monopoly," he told me. He mistook Brenda's mental illness for sorrow. He saw only a beautiful woman with three young boys, all vulnerable, thus giving him the chance to do what he did best and liked most—nurturing loved ones. Chuckie was smitten with my brothers and me. I discovered in the FBI's Hoffa files many summaries of interviews with Chuckie's acquaintances who said that during the first half of 1975 he obsessively displayed a photograph of the three of us and expressed his love for us.

When Brenda agreed to marry Chuckie on a below-freezing night in Canada, she told him she couldn't abide the frigid weather in Detroit. She preferred to live in Florida, near Fort Lauderdale, where I attended military school. Chuckie didn't resist. He desperately wanted out of Detroit too. Now he had an excuse.

The next day Chuckie flew to Washington and begged Frank Fitzsimmons for a transfer to the Southern Conference of Teamsters, which was in the midst of moving its offices to Hallandale Beach, Florida, just adjacent to Fort Lauderdale. Chuckie told Fitzsimmons about his new life and said he was serving no one's interests watching over the downward-spiraling Hoffa. Fitzsimmons had known Chuckie "since he was a kid," as he later told the FBI, and had been very close to his mother, Sylvia. He and Chuckie had had many ups and downs over the decades, including the Alaska transfer a month earlier. But Fitzsimmons appreciated better than anyone the difficulty of Chuckie's situation with Hoffa.

The FBI would later speculate that Fitzsimmons granted Chuckie's request as a payoff for his role in the Hoffa disappearance six months hence. They would have been more suspicious if they had known that Uncle Tony had advised Chuckie to "forget about Hoffa" and "get yourself established" in Florida with his new family, and had also counseled Fitzsimmons to grant his request. Nonetheless, the story Fitzsimmons told the FBI, in documents Chuckie never saw, dovetailed with Chuckie's account.

Fitzsimmons said that the "major factor" in his decision to transfer Chuckie was that he had recently "remarried and the woman he married resides in Pompano, Florida, and she doesn't want to leave that locale." Fitzsimmons noted that Chuckie's boss in Local 299 complained that "in the past O'Brien 'would screw off' and on a lot of occasions he did not know where the hell O'Brien was." As a result, Fitzsimmons says, he told Chuckie's new boss at the Southern Conference that "as soon as O'Brien 'screwed off' he is to fire him." With that understanding, he granted Chuckie his transfer.

Sometime in the late winter or spring of 1975 (Chuckie cannot remember precisely when), Chuckie went out to the Lake to see Hoffa to tell him about his new life. The two men spoke in the kitchen they had built together a few years earlier. Chuckie told Hoffa that he had grown close to a "girl from the South" and showed him pictures of Brenda and me and my brothers. "This is what my whole life is now," he said. He also told Hoffa that Brenda lived in Florida and didn't want to move to Detroit, and that Fitzsimmons had granted him a transfer. "There is nothing left in Detroit for me. I wanted to be a part of 299 and you said no. I've got an opportunity to go and work in the South, which I have always liked."

Hoffa was angry and dismissive, according to Chuckie. "What do you know about this girl?" he growled. Chuckie explained that he knew Brenda through his mother, and blew his chance with her the first time they met. Hoffa didn't like the fact that Brenda had been divorced twice and said it was a "mistake" to marry her. And he really didn't like the idea that Chuckie was leaving Detroit, which meant leaving him.

"You'll never make it in the South," he said. "You won't have a job in six weeks."

Chuckie pleaded for Hoffa's support. "I am tired, and I want a family," he said. "This is my chance to be happy."

"I don't want to hear about it," Hoffa said. "You do what you want to do."

Disheartened, Chuckie got up to leave.

"Watch the rats jump off the ship," Hoffa said, and scowled.

Chuckie looked at Hoffa in silent incredulity. He had seen Hoffa use this trope to denounce scores of opportunistic or insufficiently loyal men in the years after Lewisburg. But now he was charging Chuckie with infidelity. Chuckie says Hoffa knew he would never truly jump ship and was just lashing out in anger. But Hoffa's words broke Chuckie's heart nonetheless. Hoffa's wife, Josephine, broke into the painful moment and hugged Chuckie. "Everything is going to be okay, don't worry," she told him.

Chuckie was disconsolate about this last encounter with Hoffa but suppressed it during the next few months in which he was free of Hoffa's burden and spending his plentiful free time with our family. He did not speak to Hoffa during this period. On a few occasions Hoffa called him and left messages, but Chuckie did not return the calls. He was happy to be free of Hoffa and did not want to have a conversation in which he knew Hoffa would ask him to come back.

About a month before Brenda and Chuckie wed, sometime in May 1975, a few months before Hoffa was murdered, Hoffa finally got through to Chuckie when he managed to find the telephone number at my grandmother's home in West Memphis. My mother, who remembers the call well, answered the phone in her bedroom and handed the receiver to Chuckie. Hoffa pled with Chuckie to reconsider his decision and return to Detroit. According to my mother, Hoffa "put him down and told him he was making a mistake." Chuckie demurred, telling Hoffa he had a new life now. Hoffa hung up. It was their last conversation.

Hoffa's reaction to Chuckie's request for release from bondage and a new life made me think of Chuckie's melancholy but compassionate letter to me when I blew him off with much less cause as a young man.

"I hate to tell you this," I told Chuckie, after one of our discussions about this final meeting with Hoffa at the Lake. "Hoffa was a father figure to you when you were a young man and he gave and taught you a lot. But at the end of the day he only cared about himself. You gave your whole life to him and at the end of the day, when you needed him, he wasn't there for you. It was all about him."

"I think about that a lot," Chuckie acknowledged with obvious sorrow. "I think about my life and I think about things I did that the Old Man asked me to do. I did it because of what I thought about him and my love for him."

"It's a painful thing when he's your father," I continued. "The reality is that his love for you was very selfish."

"Yeah" was Chuckie's only response.

"Did you come to hate him?" I asked.

Chuckie gave me a puzzled look. "I didn't hate him, Jack," he said. "I loved him. To this day I still love him. I was hurt."

DURING CHUCKIE'S SEPARATION from Hoffa in the first seven months of 1975, relations between Hoffa and Frank Fitzsimmons and LCN continued to deteriorate.

"Hoffa is a bum, a has-been," Fitzsimmons said at a news conference in Cincinnati, Ohio, on March 1, when asked about Hoffa's charge, a week earlier, that the Teamsters were now run by "people more interested in playing golf than they are in the membership." Hoffa is "soft in the head," Fitzsimmons continued. "He's a liar and a stool pigeon. He doesn't pose any threat to the Teamsters or any other labor organization."

"No one has ever been disloyal like this rat Fitz," Hoffa parried to an interviewer for *People* magazine, referring to Fitzsimmons's role in the Nixon condition on his release. "All stool pigeons are rats. They scratch and bite you." Hoffa charged that Fitzsimmons and his Executive Board "like to divorce themselves from the rank-and-file, to have more time for the racetrack, golf course and sunning themselves."

The public spat between the two Teamsters was less worrisome to LCN than the rumors that Hoffa began to spread in May 1975 that the U.S. government was about to lift the restriction on his release, thereby freeing him to run for office against Fitzsimmons. The month before, a federal court heard Hoffa's appeal of the ruling that had rejected his challenge to the condition on his commutation. Hoffa was bullish about his chances and telling people that the court had signaled that he would win. This was a fabrication; his legal claim was weak and the court had sent no such signal.

Then on May 22, 1975, President Gerald Ford gave a full pardon to Dave Beck, Hoffa's predecessor who had been snared by Bobby Kennedy for tax evasion in the 1950s and finished his jail time in the mid-1960s. Hoffa began to spread rumors that Ford was going to pardon him too and wipe out the condition. "Edward Levi is looking at it," he told the journalist Charles Ashman a few months before he disappeared. "All the so-called constitutional law experts tell him I'm right."

Levi was the new, morally upright attorney general, the former president of the University of Chicago whom Ford had nominated in January 1975 to restore order to a Justice Department wracked by the Watergate scandal. While Hoffa's public suggestions about Levi's stance were understated and qualified, in private he was telling friends and journalists that Levi had decided to let him off. "In 1975 rumors began to circulate that Department of Justice lawyers who reviewed Hoffa's pardon agreement had concluded that the restrictions were in fact unconstitutional," writes Thomas Reppetto in his history of the Mafia, reporting the rumor. Levi "reportedly advised the President that the clause restricting Hoffa from union activity appeared to be illegal," Dan Moldea would later say, capturing another element of the rumor.

Hoffa was again lying. The Justice Department's experts on pardon issues had concluded over many years that Hoffa's constitutional arguments were baseless. A few months before Levi became attorney general, the Department's senior attorneys reached the same conclusion as they planned to enforce the condition against Hoffa for violating it. The Department defended the legality of the Nixon condition in court while Levi was in charge. And a Justice Department spokesperson in August 1975 stated that Levi "did not express" the view that Hoffa's restriction was unconstitutional, and added that such a view "would be counter to what the Justice Department has maintained for a long time."

The Levi rumor was false, but the mob did not know that, and it worried that Hoffa might soon be back in the Teamsters. There were also new rumors, beyond ABC's November 1974 outing of Lou Rosanova, that Hoffa was talking to the Feds about the mob's cozy arrangement with the Teamsters, perhaps in an effort to get his condition lifted. Hoffa himself was behind at least some of these rumors too. In June he told his old friend Jay Sarno and others that he believed "Fitzsimmons would be indicted in the near future." Sarno almost certainly took this as an indication that Hoffa was talking to the government about Fitzsimmons, or at least had highly unusual insight into the government's thinking. And he almost certainly told some of his many LCN friends—as Hoffa knew and must have hoped he would.

Hoffa was once again lying. Fitzsimmons was not at the time on the verge of being indicted, though he was secretly tattling to the IRS about some of his enemies in the Teamsters. (The Feds *would* go after Fitzsimmons hard after Hoffa disappeared.) And Hoffa was not talking to the government. After Hoffa disappeared, the Justice Department looked into the matter thoroughly. The chief of the Criminal Division, William F. Lynch, advised FBI headquarters "that he is unaware of any investigation within the Department regarding James R. Hoffa talking to anyone or planning to talk to anyone about illegal Teamsters activities."

Hoffa was leaving the false but unmistakable impression that the government would soon lift the legal bar keeping him from office and that he would rejoin the Teamsters and follow through on his threats to expose LCN's ties to the Teamsters and Fitzsimmons—and perhaps already had. It is very hard to understand Hoffa's motivation here in any other than self-destructive and perhaps suicidal terms. The legal bar was not going to be removed, and the only consequence of these false rumors would be to attract obvious and foreseeable danger to Hoffa himself. "He thought he was infallible," says Chuckie, trying to explain Hoffa's behavior. "He always had this intuition, 'I can handle it.'" But everybody else who knew about Hoffa's behavior saw the clear danger. "Dad was pushing so hard to get back in office," his son, James, would later say. "I was increasingly afraid the mob would do something about it."

As the anxiety was building around Hoffa, a violent proxy war seemed to break out in Detroit in July 1975. In the early morning of July 7, someone blew up the forty-five-foot yacht of Dave Johnson, the man Hoffa had chosen to run as his stand-in for the presidency of Local 299. The perpetrator was never identified, but many credible sources I spoke with say that Rolland McMaster, a Johnson enemy, was responsible. Three days later, Richard Fitzsimmons, Frank's son and Johnson's rival for the presidency of Local 299, had finished the last of several drinks at Nemo's Bar and was walking toward his parked white Lincoln Continental when he saw a bomb rip through it. Although this bombing was widely viewed as retaliation for the Johnson bombing, Chuckie and other credible sources insist that it was unrelated.

But even if the violence seemingly focused on Local 299 lacked a connection to Hoffa's kamikaze tactics against Fitzsimmons and the mob, not everyone knew this at the time. Thus the bombings—like the lies about Hoffa talking to the Feds, and about Levi's supposed pardon—contributed to the mob's anxiety about Hoffa.

"The Company was very worried about things," Chuckie acknowledged. "It started looking at the big picture. When you're in the garbage business, you're in the clothing business hauling all the dresses made in New York, and the cement business—you've got all this income coming in, big dollars, and it affected not just one guy but all the people in his group. So it's being threatened. You got a bunch of people in this country that make a lot of money and they've got to support a lot of people, they're going to start thinking, 'We're losing everything.'" Chuckie says that Hoffa understood the consequences of his actions to a point, but not fully. "He thought he was so connected with everybody that they wouldn't let it happen," he told me. "He got to a point he was not rational about a lot of things."

The person who tried the hardest to explain these consequences to Hoffa was Anthony Giacalone. The two men had been through a lot together since the 1940s and had done a lot for each other. Chuckie insists that they were friends and respected each other, despite the episodes in the early 1960s when Giacalone robbed Hoffa and facilitated his wife's affair. After Hoffa got out of jail in December 1971, he and Giacalone saw each other quite a lot, out of public view, in Miami Beach, where each had an apartment one block from the other's. When a reporter once saw them together in Miami in the early 1970s, Hoffa did not attempt to hide their relationship. "All I know is that Tony is a great guy and he's a friend of mine," he said. Near the end of Hoffa's life, in connection with Hoffa's unusual behavior, Giacalone would visit his old friend frequently.

After Hoffa disappeared, the FBI learned from Hoffa's son, James, that in the three months prior to Hoffa's disappearance, Hoffa, Anthony Giacalone, and his brother, Vito, met three times: on May 15 in James's law offices; on July 6 at the Lake; and on July 26, four days before the disappearance, also at the Lake. Hoffa's wife, Josephine, and Hoffa's friend Louis "the Pope" Linteau, the former president of Teamsters Local 614, confirmed these events.

Very little is known about those meetings. Linteau, who knew Giacalone and was a go-between in setting up some of the meetings, said he did not know what they were about. James says that the one in his office was an attempt to set up a meeting between Hoffa and Anthony Provenzano in order to "clear the air." Hoffa refused, according to his son. In the July 6 meeting, according to Hoffa's wife, the Giacalones sought Hoffa's help in securing a favor from Allen Dorfman. Nothing is known about what was said at the July 26 meeting, except that Giacalone and Hoffa apparently agreed to meet the following Wednesday, July 30, at a suburban Detroit restaurant.

Chuckie says there were more than three meetings between the Giacalones and Hoffa that grew out of Hoffa's antics. He says they began in the late summer of 1974, and occurred at the Lake that summer and fall, and continued in Miami in the winter, and then back in Detroit in the spring. Chuckie was at the Lake in the summer of 1974 for at least one of the meetings, but did not participate in it. He says he learned what the men discussed a bit from Hoffa but primarily from Giacalone. He would describe the conversations to me only in general terms.

"The house was on fire and the fireman's got to come to put the fire out— that's the best way I can explain it," he said of Giacalone's early visits. "He went out there as a friend, he didn't go out there to threaten him. I mean he went out there and would say to him, 'Jim, listen you've just got to calm down, this stuff will be all worked out.' Uncle Tony was a very meticulous person and he had a lot of responsibility on his end. He represents Detroit, and people outside of Detroit expected to get any information from Uncle Tony about a situation. He talked to him about people in this country that don't want any problems."

We can only guess what Hoffa thought about the visits. They showed that he had gotten the attention of the men whose attention he wanted to get. But to what end remains a mystery. Chuckie says that "Hoffa listened and never said nothing. He showed respect to Uncle Tony, but he just listened."

Chuckie also says that the meetings became tenser as time went on. "You have to understand Uncle Tony," he told me. "He didn't go out there to have a fuckin' dance with him. Uncle Tony was very calm when he said stuff, and I assure you that he told him about life. 'You've got to stop what you're doing, Jim. You're not only hurting yourself, you're hurting everybody.'"

I asked Chuckie what Giacalone thought he could accomplish, since Hoffa must have understood the consequences of his actions, and indeed must have seen Giacalone's presence as evidence that whatever strategy he had in mind was working. "He was trying to calm him down," Chuckie said. "Get him to start facing reality. He thought he could turn the wheel the other way—that Mr. Hoffa would listen to what he had to say and then he would stop all that shit."

In Chuckie's mind, Giacalone was trying to help Hoffa. "The heat was getting so bad, he was trying to do everything he could to save his friend," Chuckie said. "Let me tell you, if he wanted something to happen, he wouldn't waste his time going to these meetings, believe me."

Chuckie says that LCN through Giacalone offered Hoffa the world to stay quiet. "Uncle Tony would tell him, 'Jim, you gotta calm down. There's nothing you fucking need. You need something?'" Uncle Tony on behalf of his superiors "offered Hoffa anything he wanted outside the Teamsters," Chuckie said.

"Like what, money?" I asked.

"He didn't give a fuck about money," Chuckie said. Hoffa had millions, maybe tens of millions. "They'd make him a chairman of something, a company. Really, whatever he wanted, he coulda had it."

"He just wanted to get the Teamsters back," I suggested.

"He wanted to fuck over Fitzsimmons and get the general presidency back," Chuckie agreed. "He loved that title and that job. That was his life, Jack."

"And what about you, what was your position?" I asked.

"I just shut everything off. I shut it off because there was nothing I could do, there was nothing that I could change. I couldn't change it. Whatever happened, I didn't have the power to change it."

EIGHT

THE
DISAPPEARANCE

A T 3:15 A.M. on the morning of July 30, 1975, the day Jimmy Hoffa disappeared, Hoffa picked up the telephone in the kitchen in his Lake Orion cottage and called his old friend Morris Shenker at the Dunes Hotel in Las Vegas. Shenker had been Hoffa's principal attorney for a quarter century. He was also a go-between for many of Hoffa's Teamsters loans to finance Las Vegas casinos in the 1950s and 1960s. For his troubles, Hoffa and his LCN friends had made Shenker an owner of the Dunes.

Shenker would later tell the FBI that the typically no-bullshit Hoffa "uncharacteristically acted strangely" on the phone. He made small talk and asked for a reservation at the Dunes for the following month. The request astonished Shenker, who told Hoffa—the man who financed modern Las

Vegas—that he never needed a reservation. For the rest of the conversation Hoffa acted "haltingly as though he had a definite reason for calling him but could not unburden himself," according to Shenker. The conversation concluded without Hoffa "ever getting to the point of discussion he wanted to reach."

Hoffa had other telephone calls that morning. He spoke to loyalists in the union and to a business partner in Wilkes-Barre Pennsylvania, James Harding. And he twice spoke with Los Angeles talk show host Charles Ashman, on whose program he was due to appear in a few weeks. On one call, Ashman asked Hoffa whether, in light of the recent "rough stuff" at Local 299, he had protection. "Everybody knows where I am," Hoffa replied. "I never had bodyguards and I always drive myself. If anybody wants to get me, they know where I am."

Josephine Hoffa noticed during breakfast that Hoffa "acted in an uneasy manner," but she didn't question why. After breakfast Hoffa slept until 12:30 p.m., when Josephine woke him and the two had lunch together. Hoffa left the house at 1:15 p.m. for a meeting, wearing dark blue plaid pants and an open-neck, short-sleeve navy knit shirt with white stripes on each sleeve. He did not tell Josephine where he was going, but she later found taped to his lamp a list of appointments, one item of which read: "TG 230 Wed 14 Mile Tel Fox Rest Maple Road."

Hoffa drove his dark green Pontiac Grand Ville to Airport Limousine Services, a transportation company run by Louis Linteau. Hoffa and Linteau had a long and mixed relationship but had grown closer since Chuckie had left Hoffa's inner circle. Linteau also knew Anthony Giacalone. Chuckie had introduced the two men in early 1974 when Hoffa used Linteau as a go-between to buy Giacalone's apartment on Miami Beach. In the middle of the day on Saturday, July 26, Hoffa told Linteau at the Lake that he had arranged to meet with Giacalone at 2:00 p.m. on Wednesday, July 30, but did not indicate what the meeting was about.

Hoffa arrived at Linteau's place around 1:30 p.m., perhaps with the expectation that Linteau would join him for the 2:00 p.m. meeting. When Hoffa discovered that Linteau had just left for lunch, he grew "very loud and was obviously upset," and his "eyes were in a rage," as one of Linteau's employees recalled other employees saying. On his way out, Hoffa told an employee to tell Linteau that he was "meeting Tony Giacalone" and two other men at the Red Fox at 2:00 p.m. Linteau later noted how odd it was for Hoffa to discuss his business in public. "Hoffa was aware of something being very wrong," he later speculated, "and as a result of this, Hoffa acted completely out of character."

Hoffa then drove fifteen miles to the Machus Red Fox restaurant in Bloomfield Hills, a tony suburb in northwest Detroit. The Machus Red Fox was a popular steak and seafood joint at the front of the parking lot in a shopping mall known as Bloomfield Plaza. The restaurant abutted Telegraph Road, the most traveled street in Bloomfield Hills. "The number of individuals in the area of the restaurant and adjacent shopping center," the FBI would later write, "makes it one of the busiest areas to be found at the luncheon hour."

Hoffa probably arrived at the restaurant just before the 2:00 p.m. meeting. Although the notation on his lampshade indicated that the meeting was scheduled for 2:30 p.m., Hoffa all afternoon seemed to think it was set for 2:00 p.m. The attendees probably did not plan to meet inside the Machus, since Hoffa never went inside and was not dressed to meet its coat-and-tie rule. Instead, Hoffa parked his car on the north side of the restaurant and waited outside in the ninety-one-degree heat.

At 2:15 p.m., Hoffa telephoned his wife from a pay phone outside of Damman Hardware in Bloomfield Plaza, across the parking lot from the restaurant. "Did Tony Giacalone call?" he asked Josephine. When she said no, Hoffa asked her to tell Giacalone, if he did call, that he was waiting at the Machus Red Fox. Hoffa was an impatient man who ordinarily would not linger if someone was late for a meeting. But on that afternoon he would wait another hour.

Six people would later report that they saw Hoffa standing in the parking lot near the Machus between 2:00 and 2:45 p.m. All of them said that he appeared to be looking for someone. A few recognized Hoffa and spoke to him briefly. After waiting a bit longer, Hoffa telephoned Louis Linteau, who had by then returned to his office. Linteau said the call came at 3:30 p.m. "Son of a bitch Giacalone is an hour and a half late for the meeting," Hoffa said, according to Linteau. Hoffa told Linteau that he would be leaving "momentarily" and would stop by to see him at Airport Limousine Services on the way home.

And then, some time in the next few minutes, Jimmy Hoffa disappeared forever.

ABOUT SEVEN HOURS earlier, Chuckie had been sitting in a 1973 silver Lincoln Continental Mark IV with his best friend, Marvin Adell, on the north side of the same Bloomfield Plaza parking lot, about four hundred feet from the Machus Red Fox. It was a luckless beginning to a luckless day that would wreck Chuckie's life.

When he woke that morning, Chuckie was upbeat. He had a new wife and young family full of need, and he was set to start a new job in Florida with the Southern Conference of Teamsters that would for the first time give him real labor responsibility. He was, unfortunately, flat broke. He was behind on alimony payments to his first wife, the IRS had levied his wages, and creditors had foreclosed an apartment he owned near the Oakland Hills Country Club, just a mile from the Machus Red Fox. But the joy in Chuckie's life made his never-ending money problems less important. He and Brenda dreamed of a wonderful life together, and he planned to join his new family in Arkansas a few days hence to set out for Florida. For the first time since he went to work for Hoffa at age eighteen, Chuckie's life was full of possibility.

Chuckie was in Detroit to wrap up his affairs and say good-bye to the colleagues and friends he had garnered over a lifetime. He was staying at the Adells' home, where he had lived for the past fifteen months. His Teamsters-supplied Lincoln Continental was with my family in Hot Springs, Arkansas, and he could not afford a rental car. So he bummed rides around town.

On the morning Hoffa disappeared, Chuckie was scheduled to fly to a Teamsters gathering in Toronto with Detroit Local 337 president Robert Holmes Sr.—the same Bobby Holmes who had lost the coin flip to Fitz thirteen years earlier. Chuckie skipped the meeting because, as he later told the FBI, it involved business that no longer concerned him now that he was moving on to Florida. It was not unusual for Chuckie to skip meetings—he was notoriously unreliable in union affairs, and this time he had a decent excuse. But his life would have turned out much differently had he gone to Canada that morning.

Instead, Chuckie planned to spend the day at his office at Local 299 head-quarters in downtown Detroit, packing up his belongings. At about 8:30 a.m., Marvin Adell drove Chuckie in his Mark IV to the northeast corner of Bloom-field Plaza, at the intersection of Telegraph Road and Maple Road, where the two men waited a few minutes in Marvin's car before Bobby Holmes Jr., Bobby Sr.'s son, picked up Chuckie and gave him a ride to the office. This routine—Adell driving Chuckie to the northern segment of the parking lot from which Hoffa disappeared, where Holmes Jr. collected Chuckie and drove him to Local 299—had been going on for many days. In the evenings Chuckie would bum rides from various people back to the Adells' home or to a spot where Marvin could pick him up and take him home.

Chuckie fiddled around at the office until 11:30 a.m., when Airborne Freight Corporation delivered a four-foot cardboard box. The box contained a twenty-four-pound fresh-frozen salmon sent from a Teamsters official in Alaska to Bobby Holmes Sr. Chuckie signed for the delivery and, since Holmes was in Toronto, decided to take the fish to Holmes's residence in Farmington Hills, a northwest Detroit suburban town thirty miles away. Since Chuckie had no car, he called Joey Giacalone, Uncle Tony's twenty-two-year-old son, whom Chuckie had known since he was a baby and who considered Chuckie "like a brother to me." Chuckie asked Joey if he could borrow his maroon 1975 Mercury Marquis Brougham to deliver the fish.

Joey drove fifteen minutes from Lift-All Company, his heavy machinery firm in East Detroit, to collect Chuckie and the boxed salmon at Local 299. The box dripped a watery liquid as Chuckie carried it in the hot sun to Joey's car and placed it on newspapers on the back left seat. Joey drove Chuckie back to Joey's office (where Chuckie was seen by someone who worked in Joey's building). And then Chuckie took the salmon in Joey's car to the Detroit suburbs.

After driving twenty-eight miles to Holmes's residence in Farmington Hills, Chuckie with the box on his shoulder walked through the garage into the kitchen, where Holmes's wife, Violet, "got pissed" at him because liquid that appeared to be blood from the melting salmon had leaked onto her floor. Chuckie helped clean up the mess and then lingered for an hour. According to Violet, Chuckie chatted aimlessly, played with her toddler Robby, and "acted in a very normal manner," before departing between 2:20 and 2:30 p.m.

At this point Hoffa had been waiting outside the Machus Red Fox for about thirty minutes. The restaurant was a fifteen-minute drive from Violet's house. The FBI would later theorize that Chuckie left the Holmes house, drove to the Machus Red Fox, lured Hoffa into Joey's car sometime long after the scheduled meeting, and then drove Hoffa to his execution.

Chuckie tells a different story. He says that when he got in Joey's car he noticed that bloody liquid from the box had seeped through the box onto the seat and had dripped on the floor mat, where it formed a puddle. The car was also filthy and almost out of gas. Chuckie had a membership at the Jax Kar Wash, where he would have his car washed (when he had one) several times each week. He drove Joey's car to the closest Jax, a few miles away in Farmington, where he filled it with gas and purchased a standard wash and interior clean. Chuckie later produced a Standard Oil charge card receipt for gasoline purchased at that Jax Kar Wash that day, but it had no time stamp. He says he charged the wash to his personal Jax account, but Jax destroyed the records before the FBI asked for them. None of the employees at Jax remembered seeing Chuckie or cleaning a car with fish blood that day.

Chuckie says he then left the car wash and drove back for forty minutes to Joey's office, where he lingered a bit before Joey drove him back to Local 299. Several people saw Chuckie at Local 299 that afternoon, though at different times. Joe Valenti, the head of Teamsters Local 214, later drove Chuckie back to the northern suburbs to the Treasure House restaurant directly adjacent to, of all places, the Jax Kar Wash. Chuckie and Valenti spoke in the car about Chuckie's new family and his pending transfer to Florida. Around 5:30 p.m., Marvin Adell collected Chuckie at Jax and drove him home, where he and the Adell family spent the evening together.

The next morning, Thursday, July 31, Chuckie went in to work just as he had for several weeks. Adell drove him to the Bloomfield Plaza, but rather than waiting he dropped Chuckie off at the Sav-on drugstore at the north end of the plaza. Chuckie bought a *Detroit Free Press* newspaper at a nearby vending machine and walked across the lot to the northeast corner, where he usually met Holmes Jr. He placed his gray plaid sport coat over his briefcase—it was a sweltering morning that would become the hottest day of the year—and read the sports page while he waited.

Jack Milan, the owner of Jax Kar Wash, whom Chuckie knew because he had over the years so often washed his car at Jax, was driving south on Telegraph Road that morning. Milan saw Chuckie and slowed to ask if he needed a ride. Chuckie waved him on and continued to read the paper until Holmes arrived a few minutes later. He drove away in Holmes's car at about 9:00 a.m.—without noticing Hoffa's green Pontiac sitting beside the Machus Red Fox.

LOUIS LINTEAU WAS also in the parking lot of the Bloomfield Plaza that morning, looking for Hoffa. At about 10:00 p.m. the night before, he had called the cottage and learned from Josephine that Hoffa never came home. Linteau telephoned the Machus Red Fox, which paged Hoffa without success. He then called Anthony Giacalone to ask about the meeting and Hoffa's whereabouts. Giacalone told him that he had no meeting planned with Hoffa. Linteau then drove to the Lake and spent the night with a distraught Josephine.

Early the next morning, Linteau drove to the Machus and discovered Hoffa's Pontiac sitting alone and unlocked in the parking lot. Linteau telephoned the police. He then called Hoffa's son, James, who would later tell the FBI, as they reported it, that he "immediately thought his father had been killed." A few hours later, Linteau telephoned Chuckie.

Chuckie was out of the office helping a secretary fix a flat tire. When he returned the call, Linteau told him that Hoffa never came home last night. He also told him about the scheduled meeting with Giacalone at the Machus the day before. And he added that he had found Hoffa's car abandoned outside the Machus that morning.

The news hit Chuckie like a thunderclap. He instantly understood what had happened, and why. "Any time in the history of the Company they want to do something and they want to keep it quiet, they disappear you," he later explained to me. "They make it a complete mystery."

Neither a lifetime of LCN education nor knowledge of Hoffa's many sins had prepared Chuckie for the shock of the sudden vanishing of the man he had revered since he was nine years old and still loved deeply despite the disappointment and anger of the last few years.

"I didn't want him to go that way," he told me. "I wanted him to go normal, the way God wants it to happen."

Chuckie's first impulse was to blame himself for not being with Hoffa to protect him, as he had in many dangerous situations over two decades. *If I had driven him as I usually did*, Chuckie thought, *Hoffa would have made it home.*

At the same time Chuckie also must have believed that his other father figure, Anthony Giacalone, was somehow involved in in Hoffa's disappearance. In hundreds of conversations that he and I had about the disappearance, Chuckie never once pointed the finger at Uncle Tony. But he knew where Uncle Tony's ultimate commitments lay. He knew about Uncle Tony's visits to the Lake, and the reasons for the visits. He understood the rule for rats. The deed had happened in Detroit, which meant Uncle Tony almost certainly knew about it. And Linteau had said that Hoffa was supposed to meet Uncle Tony at the Machus.

These thoughts churned in Chuckie's mind as Linteau spoke. When Linteau was done, Chuckie unloaded on him.

"Where in the fuck were you!?" he screamed. Why wasn't Linteau with Hoffa when he went to the Machus? Why didn't Linteau protect Hoffa? Why didn't he call Chuckie sooner?

After the call with Linteau, Chuckie was paralyzed. What should he do? How should he act? For decades he had instinctively rushed to protect Hoffa. He had also instinctively reached out to Uncle Tony for counsel whenever he faced trouble. But Hoffa was now gone, and Chuckie sensed that Giacalone would not want a call from him at that moment.

After collecting himself, Chuckie called Hoffa's son, James P. Hoffa. James had been on vacation in Traverse City, Michigan. The distance and mutual animosity between him and Chuckie had grown in recent years with James's elevation as his father's legal advisor and with Chuckie's decline in influence. On July 30, 1975, Chuckie saw James as unworthy of the Hoffa mantle and James saw Chuckie as a useless mooch who had abandoned his father at his time of greatest need. Nonetheless, Hoffa's two very different sons had been family for more than thirty years, and so it was unsurprising that James asked Chuckie to watch over his wife and children that evening at his home in Troy, Michigan, while James stayed with his mother and sister at the Lake.

Chuckie didn't have a way to get to Troy. So just as he did on the day of the disappearance, he called Joey Giacalone, this time to ask for a ride from work to the Adells' home, where he planned to borrow one of their cars. Joey told Chuckie he was headed out to the northwestern suburbs early that evening but would need to make some stops on the way, including at his home.

Joey collected Chuckie in his maroon Mercury Marquis—the same car the FBI would soon claim Chuckie drove to pick up Hoffa at the Machus Red Fox. The two men drove to Joey's apartment in St. Clair Shores, where his parents were staying. While Joey showered, Chuckie chatted with Uncle Tony for the first time since the disappearance.

Chuckie would tell the FBI a few weeks hence that Giacalone told him that he had no meeting with Hoffa the day before and had no idea where he was. Giacalone also told Chuckie that he was at the Southfield Athletic Club when the event occurred. These statements accurately reflected what Giacalone told him, and the second statement, about Giacalone being at the club, was true. But forty-three years later, Chuckie added two details to me that he did not tell the FBI.

First, Chuckie says the usually cool Giacalone was agitated to the point of being rattled. "He was upset like I had never seen him," Chuckie told me. Giacalone was distraught, in Chuckie's mind, because Linteau was telling everyone that Giacalone was supposed to meet Hoffa at the Machus, because the deed had occurred on his turf in Detroit, and because he feared that the government's reaction to Hoffa's disappearance would have a huge impact on the Detroit family. There is no way to know if Giacalone was being himself or feigning for Chuckie's benefit, but in dozens of conversations over many years Chuckie insisted that Giacalone was very troubled. "This is going to kill us," he told Chuckie.

Second, Giacalone asked Chuckie for help with his alibi. He had learned from his son that Chuckie on the afternoon on July 30 was in the northern suburbs. He asked Chuckie to tell anyone who asked—and especially cops or journalists—that he (Chuckie) stopped by the Southfield Athletic Club in Southfield, Michigan, on the way back to Joey's office to pick up Uncle Tony's graduation presents—two one-hundred-dollar bills—for Chuckie's children from his first marriage. The club was owned by the Detroit mob associate Lenny Schultz, and had been Uncle Tony's business headquarters since he had sold Home Juice a few years earlier. It is unlikely that Giacalone would have made the request if he had imagined that the FBI would soon think Chuckie had picked up Hoffa on his orders and in his son Joey's car. To Chuckie at the time, it seemed like an inconsequential lie to tell, especially since he had no idea he would soon be a suspect.

Joey and Chuckie left Joey's apartment and went to the Adells' home, where Chuckie borrowed Betty's Lincoln Continental and made his way to Troy in the early evening to watch the Hoffa family.

Over the course of that afternoon and evening, James and Linteau grew suspicious of Chuckie's possible role in the disappearance. They learned that Chuckie had skipped his planned trip to Toronto, and they could not find anyone who had seen Chuckie between 2:30 p.m. (when he left Violet's) and 4:00 to 4:15 p.m. (when he was seen at Local 299), the period during which Hoffa vanished. They believed Chuckie had grown closer to Giacalone ever since (in their eyes) he had abandoned the elder Hoffa in November. And Chuckie was one of the few people whom James could imagine his father getting in a car with at the Machus.

At about 11:30 p.m. that evening, James called Chuckie and asked him to come to the Lake. Chuckie arrived just after midnight. He walked onto the porch he had built with Hoffa a few years earlier, and into the cottage that had been his second home for three decades. He had helped raise James in that cottage and had always been his superior there. But now the Old Man was missing and James was in charge. Years of pent-up mutual resentment filled the air as James greeted Chuckie from the kitchen and immediately began to interrogate him.

Why was his father supposed to meet Giacalone? Why hadn't Chuckie gone to Toronto? Why was he lurking yesterday morning near the Machus Red Fox? Why was he in the suburbs instead of at work? And why hadn't anyone seen him between 2:30 p.m. and when he arrived back at Local 299?

Chuckie was "really pissed off" by James's insolent badgering, but he answered his questions. James remained dissatisfied and continued to press. At some point he lost his temper and accused Chuckie of holding back, and of involvement in the disappearance.

Chuckie was floored by the accusation—because he wasn't involved in killing Hoffa and couldn't believe James thought he would be; because he felt guilty about what he might have done the year before to stop it; and because he *did* know more than he was saying, especially about the elaborate dance between Giacalone and Hoffa going back almost a year, and the reasons for it. He couldn't, and wouldn't, say a word about that to anyone. To do so would have been suicidal. But it never occurred to Chuckie for another reason: even with Hoffa as the target, he would have preferred death to betraying the mob.

As Chuckie's secret knowledge debilitated him, his exchange with James quickly descended into a screaming match about loyalty to Hoffa. James ordered Chuckie to leave the house and never come back. Chuckie complied and returned to the Adells' in the middle of the night.

AFTER A BRIEF SLEEP, Chuckie awoke on Friday, August 1, to "Jimmy Hoffa Is Missing" across the front page of the *Detroit Free Press*. His anxiety grew as he read *The Detroit News* headline above photos of his two father figures, Hoffa and Giacalone. "Mafia Chief Denies He Met Missing Hoffa," it said, and then detailed suspicions about Giacalone's involvement. Chuckie spent several hours aimlessly calling Teamsters officials for news about Hoffa's disappearance. In the middle of the afternoon, he borrowed a car from the Adells and went to see Anthony Giacalone at Joey's apartment.

In contrast to their meeting the day before, Chuckie says, Uncle Tony was calm and composed. Chuckie, by contrast, was distraught. Hoffa was gone, and Chuckie knew why. Giacalone was almost certainly involved, but Chuckie didn't dare inquire. James had accused Chuckie of involvement. And Chuckie *was* involved to the extent that he had been charged with calming Hoffa down at the Lake and had surmised what the consequences would be if he failed.

Chuckie had plenty to be upset about, and Uncle Tony noticed. "I had lost somebody that I really loved and Uncle Tony knew how much I loved that man because I went to the well for him," says Chuckie. "He was worried about me."

Uncle Tony was probably most worried about whether Chuckie could hold it together. Giacalone had plans that evening to attend the wedding of the daughter of William Bufalino, Hoffa's former lawyer and an attorney with LCN. But perhaps sensing Chuckie's confusion and anxiety, he changed plans and asked Chuckie to join him and his wife for an early dinner. "Let's take a ride and get away from all this shit," Giacalone told him.

Chuckie drove Giacalone and his wife, Zina, in Giacalone's Cadillac for fifty minutes to the St. Clair Inn in Port Huron, and got a table in the dining room facing the St. Clair River. The conversation in the car and at dinner was stilted, and no one discussed Hoffa's disappearance. But when Mrs. Giacalone excused herself to go to the restroom, Giacalone alluded to the disappearance.

"It was a terrible thing and I hope they can find him," Uncle Tony said, looking at Chuckie with the same grave stare that delivered the Omertà edict three decades earlier. "But life is very funny, Chuck. Very funny. Things happen, and you don't have control over it."

It was a bland statement that on its face was not incriminating. But Chuckie got the message. Giacalone was expressing affection for Hoffa out of respect for Hoffa and Chuckie. He was signaling the Outfit's role without conveying any details. And he was telling Chuckie that he, Uncle Tony, could not have stopped it from happening.

Uncle Tony then gave Chuckie some advice about how to act. "You need to be normal," he said. "You've been close to him your whole life. Just be normal. Don't talk about shit you don't know about."

Forty years later I asked Chuckie what he thought at that moment, listening to one father figure calmly talking to him about the killing of another.

"I didn't want to hear any of that shit," he explained to me. "If I hear it, then I'm stuck with the knowledge."

He was indeed stuck with knowledge, at least dim knowledge, from that point on.

"But what were you thinking when he told you what happened?" I asked.

"I never questioned it, Jack," he replied quietly.

"You couldn't have," I said. "You weren't in a position to."

"I was raised that way," Chuckie continued. "You just didn't question those old guys. I never questioned that shit."

"Even with something like Hoffa's disappearance?" I asked.

"It was not my place," said Chuckie.

"And Uncle Tony knew that you weren't going to say anything about it?"

"I'll take it to my fucking grave," he said.

"But you weren't upset that this happened to Mr. Hoffa?" I asked. "You must have been."

Chuckie was quiet for a long time. Then he looked at me intently and spoke slowly and hesitantly. "I wasn't . . . upset . . . in a way that . . . you'd be upset. . . . What was I going to do?"

There was nothing Chuckie could do.

In light of his intimacy with both Hoffa and Giacalone, and of his role in the middle of the Hoffa-Fitzsimmons-Giacalone machinations the previous year, Chuckie would have been implicated to some degree in the Hoffa disappearance even if he had an airtight alibi on July 30. But from the moment of his brief dinner conversation in the St. Clair Inn with Giacalone on August 1, and days before he became a suspect, Chuckie was more compromised because his understanding of the disappearance went beyond surmise to a twilight knowledge of LCN involvement. We can only speculate why Giacalone brought Chuckie into the loop. Perhaps he was trying to calm him down. Perhaps Chuckie knew enough about the run-up to the disappearance that Giacalone's faint acknowledgment of the crime was not a large step.

Or perhaps Giacalone needed Chuckie. After dinner, as the men walked to the car, he asked Chuckie for two favors. The first was to talk to *Detroit Free Press* reporters Chuckie knew well to underscore Giacalone's innocence. The second favor was to bring a message to Teamsters president Frank

Fitzsimmons in Washington, D.C. The message was that Fitzsimmons should lie low, stay off television, and "act normal."

Chuckie agreed to both requests and didn't ask any questions.

Late that evening Chuckie met with journalists for the *Detroit Free Press*. As they would report a few days later, he told them that Uncle Tony "could not have been involved in the disappearance" and added, falsely, that he "met Giacalone" at the Southfield Athletic Club "shortly after 2 p.m." that day. Chuckie also bragged that he "frequently acted as an intermediary when Hoffa and Giacalone wanted to meet," and would often "pick up Giacalone and drive him to Hoffa's cottage, or he would take Hoffa to Giacalone." It was a very strange thing to crow about if Chuckie had in fact picked up Hoffa for Giacalone and driven him to his death two days earlier.

The next day, Saturday, Chuckie met Giacalone for a haircut at the Southfield Athletic Club. That evening he attended the wedding of Marvin Adell's brother Bobby. Early the next morning, on Sunday, August 3, he returned to West Memphis to be with our family. He had no reason to stay in Detroit, especially since the Hoffa family had banished him. The following day, he flew to Washington, D.C., to deliver Giacalone's message to Fitzsimmons.

When Chuckie showed up unannounced in Fitzsimmons's office in Washington, D.C., on Monday morning, Fitzsimmons turned white. "Fitz didn't like no heat," says Chuckie. "And I was like a fuckin' rocket coming into the fuckin' front door."

"Holy shit, what the hell are you doing here, Chuckie?" Fitzsimmons said when he walked into his office.

"I got a message for you," Chuckie says he replied. The two men stepped into Fitzsimmons's bathroom to avoid bugs. Chuckie carried out Uncle Tony's task and then returned to be with our family in Arkansas.

NINE

LEADING
SUSPECT

J IMMY HOFFA'S DISAPPEARANCE was a national sensation that dominated newspaper headlines and nightly news broadcasts for weeks. In an era when the number of national news outlets was meager compared to today, dozens of reporters from around the country clustered outside the white aluminum picket fence surrounding the Hoffa cottage, many on a twenty-four-hour basis to keep a vigil with the Hoffa family. No one had a cell phone, and the closest pay phone was two miles away. So the journalists hooked field telephones into special jacks on a nearby telephone pole, through which they communicated with colleagues and sources around the nation.

The FBI hesitated to enter the case officially for the first few days. It was unsure of its jurisdiction. It was also reeling from Watergate, the Church Committee revelations, and its failure for a year and a half to find Patty Hearst's kidnappers, and it wanted to avoid another high-profile embarrassment. But the Hoffa children put enormous public and private pressure on FBI director Clarence Kelley. So did several of the FBI agents in Detroit. On the evening of Sunday, August 3, four days after the disappearance, Kelley announced that the FBI was entering the case based on threatening phone calls to the Hoffas. The Hoffa probe in Detroit was opened as a missing persons case, number 79-359. Jay Bailey, the assistant special agent in charge of the Detroit office, announced "an all-out investigation with considerable manpower," including scores of agents in Detroit and dozens more around the country.

The FBI interviewed thousands of people within a week of entering the case. The Bureau and state and local police were buried from the outset with hundreds of tips, rumors, and informant speculations, including dozens of crank calls, hoax theories, and psychic and "dreamer" reports about all manner of crazy things that supposedly happened to Hoffa. And they went on fool's errand upon fool's errand searching for Hoffa. He was seen in a yacht sailing around Lake Michigan. He was killed and deposited in a cornfield 100 miles west of Detroit. He was kidnapped and being held in a restaurant and poker club in Los Angeles. He was buried at a construction site near Marion, Michigan, 175 miles northwest of Detroit, or at a spot near Waterford Township, 15 miles from the Machus Red Fox. One informant said that Hoffa arranged his own disappearance, just as New York boss Joe Bonanno had done a decade earlier to avoid a federal grand jury. These were but a few of the leads that the cops took seriously but that did not pan out.

Amid the whirl of information and misinformation, the FBI from the beginning focused most intently on one person: Chuckie.

THE FBI WOULD have suspected Chuckie eventually, but it first focused on him because James P. Hoffa focused so intently on him. James told FBI agents Robert Kelley and Bob Neumann on Monday morning, August 4, all the reasons why he suspected Chuckie. He also told them that he believed Chuckie had switched loyalties from his father to Giacalone, and that Giacalone and Anthony Provenzano "utilized Charles O'Brien to 'set up' his father and have him killed," as the FBI would note in its records.

The FBI bought this version of events. "Young Jim put us on to Chuckie from the beginning," the lead Detroit FBI agent on the case, Robert Garrity, told me forty years after the event. "One of the things that bothers me most, I got convinced too early that the key to the case was Chuckie, to the exclusion of other things."

On the following evening, Tuesday, August 5, Chuckie was with our family as we watched the evening news in West Memphis, Arkansas, to catch up on the latest about the Hoffa disappearance. We looked at one another in disbelief when ABC's Ron Miller stated that there was "increasing concern and curiosity at the [Hoffa] family home about the whereabouts of Hoffa's adopted son, Chuck O'Brien," who had not been "seen or heard from" for four days. It was the first public mention of Chuckie's relevance to the case. He had been with us since Sunday morning except for the brief trip to Washington to see Fitz. But the Hoffa family was telling reporters that Chuckie had mysteriously gone missing. O'Brien "dropped out of sight last Friday," reported *The Detroit News*, adding that the Hoffa family "was puzzled by O'Brien's failure to communicate with them." It did not mention that James had banished Chuckie.

The next morning Chuckie flew to Detroit for what would be the first of two interviews with Garrity and his partner, the other lead FBI investigator in Detroit, Jim Esposito. He was the only suspect in the case who spoke to the FBI voluntarily. It was an extraordinary thing for him to do. Chuckie's distrust of the FBI went back to the 1950s. He had been taught by Hoffa, and Giacalone, and his mother, and bitter experience, to never cooperate, ever, since the FBI would always screw you.

But this time Chuckie felt he had no choice, since not cooperating would deepen the developing suspicions about him. He sought permission from Giacalone, who gave it but again counseled him to "not talk about shit you don't know about."

Chuckie's lawyer at the time was James Burdick, a former state prosecutor. Nearly forty years after the event, Burdick told me that he didn't know at first whether to believe Chuckie's protestations of innocence because of his reputation as "an absolute stranger to the truth" who would "make shit up about stuff for no reason at all." But he quickly came to believe Chuckie did not pick up Hoffa on the afternoon of July 30. Chuckie was convincing, Burdick says, in his adamant insistence that he loved Hoffa like a father and could never harm him. And he "really, really wanted to talk to the FBI" to clear his name, especially in light of James's accusations. Chuckie never would have been able to fulfill this wish if he had known anything at all about the disappearance, Burdick thought. He would have been killed first.

Agents Garrity and Esposito were in their early thirties and had been in the FBI for only a few years. Now fate had dropped one of the most important cases in FBI history in their laps. The two men were convinced from the outset that Chuckie was somehow involved. For that reason, they were pretty sure Chuckie would not talk to them. They were thus "shocked," as Garrity later told me, when Chuckie showed up for the interview in the late afternoon of August 6 at a windowless conference room at Teamsters Local 299. Garrity's heart was thumping loudly as "the main suspect in the disappearance" walked into the room to talk with them.

The ninety-minute interview was not hostile. Chuckie answered all the FBI's questions about his activities on July 30 and his whereabouts for the rest of the week, including the time he spent with Giacalone. He did not tell the agents about his trip to Washington to see Fitzsimmons (though he did soon after the interview), and he lied when he said that he stopped to see Giacalone at the Southfield Athletic Club. But he told them a lot that the agents did not know, including details about what he did in the suburbs the afternoon of the disappearance, and the extraordinary fact that he was driving in the area in Giacalone's son's car, which might have fish blood in the back seat. And at the end of the interview, Chuckie told the agents, "Whatever y'all need, I'll do."

"He told us incriminating stuff, things he didn't have to tell us," Garrity told me. Garrity and Esposito were puzzled why. It didn't occur to them that Chuckie was talking so freely because he did not see Hoffa on July 30. To the contrary, what Chuckie told them enhanced their suspicions. As Chuckie got up to leave at the end of the interview, one of the agents asked if he was worried about being killed. He said no. But as Chuckie walked out the door, Garrity thought to himself that "one of these days soon they're going to whack him, no doubt."

Chuckie called the Hoffa family at the Lake after the interview and spoke with James. He was calling to offer his support, to explain that he had been in West Memphis, and to reiterate that he was not involved. But James, convinced of Chuckie's involvement, called him a liar and demanded that he take a lie detector test. As soon as the call ended, James gave a press conference in which he claimed that Chuckie "has knowledge of what happened," appeared to be "lying" about his whereabouts on the day of the disappearance, and demanded that Chuckie be tested on a polygraph. Chuckie was deeply suspicious of a polygraph but wanted to take it then and for many decades hence to clear his name. But his lawyer, Burdick, like every lawyer Chuckie consulted for a while, advised against it. James treated the refusal as evidence that he had "something to hide" and was "withholding information from the authorities."

The news headlines and attention driven by James's accusations floored Chuckie, but he didn't know how to fight them. The next few days grew more Kafkaesque as the press began to report James's version of events as truth. On Thursday, August 7 the Detroit newspapers falsely reported that Chuckie had altered his alibi to the FBI and was refusing to further cooperate. The papers then began to draw contrasts between James, the polished University of Michigan law graduate and loyal son trying hard to find his father, and Chuckie, the ill-kempt, crime-prone, irresponsible son who wasn't cooperating.

On Friday, August 8, the FBI seized Joey Giacalone's car based on an affidavit that repeated James's accusations against Chuckie and noted that Chuckie's whereabouts on the afternoon of July 30 could not be confirmed. "I feel that probable cause exists to believe that CHARLES O'BRIEN has used JOSEPH GIACALONE's automobile to facilitate an abduction of HOFFA," swore the FBI's Esposito. The front-page headlines reported bloodstains in the car.

Chuckie viewed these events through the lens of his decades of experiences with Hoffa. "Since 1953 I had witnessed the Justice Department orchestrate incriminating scenarios as if they were directing a movie," he told me. "I knew the FBI liked to leak things to put suspicion on an individual. They use that psychology on people who are weak, so anybody that had something to do with it would contact them and drop a dime and become a rat."

Chuckie had seen the movie before, but this time it was a horror show and he was the victim. The day after his FBI interview in Detroit, FBI agents descended on sleepy West Memphis to interview everyone in my family and our neighbors. Journalists also started poking around town, forcing me and my brothers to stay indoors. My mother grew hysterical and my younger brothers were in tears. I remember crying once, after I thought I got my new stepfather in trouble by telling a journalist from *Time* who telephoned our home that Chuckie lived there.

Chuckie was outwardly steadfast and tried to calm us down, but in truth he was panicky, angry, and vulnerable. He thought he was being framed for a crime by the FBI or James or both. He worried that he might end up in the same situation as Hoffa. And he was wounding his new family and feared the ordeal might kill my mother. "My life was falling apart before my very eyes," he later told me.

A week later, Chuckie agreed to meet Garrity and Esposito for a second interview, this time at a conference room at the Detroit airport. In the interim, police dogs had detected Hoffa's scent in the back seat of Joey's car. The FBI agents were now convinced of Chuckie's guilt and "leaned on him a little," as Garrity told me. They interrupted him and openly doubted his explanations as he recounted his whereabouts during the week of the disappearance. They told him they knew Hoffa was in Joey's car. They called him the number one suspect. And they warned that he'd be killed by the mob but pledged that if he cooperated he could avoid jail and stay safe. Chuckie answered all the questions and volunteered more evidence they deemed incriminating, such as the fact that he telephoned Anthony Giacalone the night before the disappearance and then again from Violet Holmes's kitchen on July 30. But the agents thought Chuckie was being suspiciously careful about what he said and was holding back, especially since he was defending Giacalone and not helping them in the way James was.

Chuckie *was* holding back—not because of his guilt, but because of Omertà.

The following week the FBI found a three-inch brown hair in Joey's car that was sufficiently "similar" to the ones taken from Hoffa's hairbrush that the "possibility could not be eliminated that these hairs originated from the same person," as an FBI lab analysis concluded. The FBI lab underscored that the hair comparison was not "a basis for positive personal identification." But on top of everything else, the possible hair match convinced Garrity and Esposito that Hoffa had been in Joey's car.

Chuckie was bewildered in the face of the growing calamity, which he viewed as a frame job. "It's eating my guts out that I'm being made the number one fall guy in the case," he told *The Detroit News* on August 21. Uncle Tony was also "very upset" when the finger started to be pointed at Chuckie and his son Joey. "This is crazy," he told Chuckie. "They're gonna put you delivering him, for Christ's sake."

Chuckie invoked his Fifth Amendment right against compelled self-incrimination on Wednesday, September 3 at a grand jury convened on the Hoffa matter. James charged that Chuckie's action, "coupled with his continued refusal to take an FBI-administered lie detector test, makes it absolutely clear that he was involved in some way with my father's disappearance." That's how everyone else saw the matter as well.

WITHIN A FEW weeks after the disappearance, the FBI had settled on the theory of Hoffa's disappearance from which it has never publicly wavered: Chuckie, on Giacalone's instructions, and perhaps with other confederates in the car, picked up Hoffa and delivered him to his killers, probably without knowing in advance what was going to happen. No direct incriminating evidence supported this theory. But the FBI believed James that Chuckie was one of the few people who could lure Hoffa into a car. And lots of circumstantial evidence supported Chuckie's involvement—Hoffa's scent and possible hair in the car, Chuckie's last-second cancellation of the Toronto trip, his proximity to the Machus Red Fox the morning and afternoon of the disappearance, his visits with Giacalone after the disappearance, the time gap in which no witness saw him, his loyalty to Giacalone, his falling-out with Hoffa, and his seeming refusal to fully cooperate after the event. These were extraordinary coincidences if Chuckie was not involved, and much stronger evidence than the FBI had on any other suspect.

Under enormous pressure to make progress in the case, and lacking any better leads, the Bureau understandably zeroed in on Chuckie. Its early belief in Chuckie's role in driving Hoffa to his death became one of the few unquestioned certainties about the case. And through government leaks to the press and follow-on stories based on these leaks, the theory became unquestioned truth in the public mind and remains so to this day. But in reaching this conclusion, the FBI focused on facts that fit its theory and ignored or discounted the many countervailing facts and circumstances that did not fit its theory but that should have made it much less confident that Chuckie was involved.

Begin with Chuckie's day on July 30, 1975. He displayed no intention to go to the suburbs until the salmon unexpectedly showed up at Local 299 in the late morning, which led Chuckie to call Joey. Why had Chuckie not previously arranged for a car for his important assignment to pick up and deliver Hoffa? Perhaps, implausibly, he planned all along to use Joey's car and the salmon's arrival became a fortunate excuse. Or perhaps, also implausibly, the instructions to pick up Hoffa came out of the blue in the late morning, when the salmon arrived, and Chuckie decided to take the fish to the Holmes residence since he was already going in that direction.

But of all the automobiles available in the Motor City, why use the car of the son of a leading Detroit mobster and the man who supposedly arranged for the hit or likely knew it was coming? No one in the FBI ever imagined that Giacalone or any other Detroit family member who might have organized the hit would have wanted to whisk Hoffa away from the Machus Red Fox in Joey's car. But that means that the organizers must have left it up to Chuckie—who Giacalone and others knew had no car—to select the vehicle for the murder of the century.

To fit Chuckie's known behavior to its theory of the Hoffa plot, then, the FBI had to assume that the mob, in one of its most consequential hits ever, probably told Chuckie about the pickup only a few hours before the event, and definitely left it to Chuckie to find a car to use. It also had to explain why Chuckie would calmly and aimlessly chat in Violet Holmes's kitchen until almost 2:30, the time that Hoffa, fifteen minutes away, was due to be picked up. Chuckie was often a goofball, but he would not have been late for such an important assignment as picking up the Old Man for Uncle Tony. It is thus hard to understand why he would have been so casual at Violet's, and so tardy.

And then there is the supposed gap of time for which Chuckie had no alibi on the afternoon of July 30. The government's 1975 theory had Chuckie leaving Violet Holmes's house between 2:20 and 2:30 p.m. and Chuckie arriving back at Local 299 around 4:30 p.m. This gap in Chuckie's known whereabouts was the factual foundation for all suspicions that he picked up Hoffa at the Machus Red Fox and drove him to his death.

But as I explain in the Appendix, this theory for the disappearance focuses on the wrong time period. The relevant time period for assessing whether Chuckie could have picked up Hoffa at the Machus Red Fox should begin when Hoffa was last known to be alive and end when Chuckie was first seen at Local 299. Witness statements and grand jury testimony suggest that Hoffa probably disappeared around 3:30 p.m. These sources also reported that Chuckie arrived back at Local 299 before (and perhaps long before) 4:30 p.m. It would have taken Chuckie about an hour to drive from the Machus Red Fox back to Joey Giacalone's workplace, Lift-All, then pick up Joey, and then drive to Local 299, where Chuckie was seen before 4:30. On plausible assumptions, Chuckie would have no spare time to detour from this route to deliver Hoffa elsewhere.

Then there are the assumptions about why the mob used Chuckie to pick up Hoffa in the first place. Chuckie was deeply loyal to Anthony Giacalone, but many Detroit family members viewed him as unreliable. (Recall that Vito Giacalone had tacitly characterized Chuckie as follows: "Anything you ask, he says, 'Yeah, I can do it,' but he can't do it. No matter what it is, he can't do it.") Chuckie had also been deeply loyal to Hoffa all his life.

If the mob used Chuckie as an unwitting pickup man, it must have made a series of difficult assumptions. It must have assumed he would carry out his task competently, not try to defend Hoffa from attack, not attack the perpetrators after the hit or after he realized what was happening, and that he would remain silent after the deed was done. It is hard to see why Giacalone or his Syndicate partners would rest an event of this importance on these assumptions about Chuckie, especially if, as the FBI theorized, Chuckie was first told to pick up Hoffa on the morning of July 30.

But there was one very good reason to use Chuckie, on the conventional wisdom: he was supposedly one of the few people Hoffa would get in a car with that afternoon. This assumption drove a lot of the case against Chuckie. But there is no evidence at all that Hoffa voluntarily got in the car with anyone, much less Chuckie. The Bureau assumed he did because they assumed that witnesses would have noticed if Hoffa was overcome involuntarily. Perhaps so. But this assumption is no less speculative than the assumption that Hoffa, in an agitated and suspicious state of mind, would get in a car voluntarily with anyone, including Chuckie, after waiting more than an hour for a meeting, especially with someone other than the person he was supposed to meet and for a trip he was not supposed to take.

Then there is the evidence in Joey's car that the FBI impounded nine days after the disappearance. The car was full of Chuckie's fingerprints, but not Hoffa's, and it contained Hoffa's scent and a hair that in 1975 the FBI believed might have been Hoffa's. Why Chuckie's fingerprints and not Hoffa's? Why did Giacalone or whoever arranged for Chuckie to pick up Hoffa, once they discovered that Chuckie had used Joey's car for the pickup, not insist that Chuckie (or an agent) scrub or eliminate it entirely? Why disappear Hoffa but not the car full of possibly incriminating evidence that drove him to his death? The FBI had no explanations.

Chuckie's skittish behavior starting July 31, and especially his calls and visits to Anthony Giacalone, also attracted the FBI's attention. But it is at least puzzling that Chuckie would have contacted Giacalone so often—or that Giacalone would have agreed to meet him—if they were in league together on Hoffa's disappearance, precisely because of the suspicions it would have aroused.

A different explanation for Chuckie's nervous disposition was that he was in the precarious position of knowing generally what happened and why, of being terribly upset about it, of having no choice but to defend and be loyal to Giacalone, of being accused by James of involvement in the plot itself, and of not being able to be candid with James or the government about what he did know. Chuckie's apparent anxiety began only after he heard from Linteau on

Thursday morning that Hoffa was gone. Nobody claimed he acted nervous or abnormal before the disappearance or in the eighteen hours after he supposedly picked up Hoffa and helped eliminate him. And then one week after the disappearance Chuckie alone among the serious suspects volunteered to talk with the FBI and revealed a lot of information that they deemed incriminating but that Chuckie (and the mob) obviously did not, or else he would have stayed quiet.

Another revealing element of Chuckie's post-disappearance behavior occurred on the morning after the disappearance, when he appeared at the scene of the crime and blithely stood reading the newspaper awaiting a ride to work at Local 299 as Hoffa's abandoned car stood alone near the Machus, a little over a football field across the Bloomfield Plaza lot. "Either Chuckie O'Brien had veins of ice or he wasn't involved in the disappearance," an FBI agent who worked the Hoffa case in the 1970s said of Chuckie's casual appearance near where Chuckie allegedly picked up Hoffa the day before. "If he was involved, that is the gutsiest move I've ever seen."

Finally, and increasingly over time, no one in the FBI ever had a good explanation for why the mob did not kill Chuckie even though he alone among any of the suspects twice talked voluntarily to the FBI in August 1975. Garrity and Esposito thought that Chuckie would be killed in 1975, especially after he talked to them. And yet he lived.

These problems in the FBI's theory of the case do not by themselves exonerate Chuckie. But they stand as mysterious and unexplained counterpoints to the circumstantial evidence against him.

THE FBI DID not in 1975 or for decades thereafter ever make progress on what happened to Hoffa at the Machus on July 30. It had a few promising leads from eyewitnesses in the Machus parking lot, including one that purported to see someone who looked like Hoffa in the back seat of a car matching the description of Joey Giacalone's car. But these witness accounts were all determined to be either mistaken or made up or not credible for various reasons.

But while the events at the Machus remained a mystery, the FBI did develop pretty good reasons to think that "the prime movers behind the conspiracy were Anthony 'Tony' Giacalone and Anthony 'Tony Pro' Provenzano," as a 1978 Department of Justice memorandum stated. Giacalone was Hoffa's longtime intimate in the Detroit family. Provenzano was his old comrade in the East, the Genovese family captain who helped Hoffa gain control of the Teamsters in New York and New Jersey, and who served on the Teamsters Executive Board for many years.

Many clues pointed to Giacalone's involvement. He was known to have met with Hoffa thrice before the disappearance about an urgent matter, he was the man Hoffa thought and told others he was meeting at the Machus, and he had a conspicuous and, to the FBI, suspicious alibi at the Southfield Athletic Club. The main puzzle about Giacalone's involvement was why he used himself as bait, and thus volunteered himself as a suspect, to lure Hoffa to the Machus for his murder. Why not kill Hoffa at the Lake or by some less directly self-incriminating means? Why would Giacalone place the bull's-eye on his own forehead?

Provenzano had an alibi in Local 560 in New Jersey at the time of the disappearance, but he too quickly became a central suspect. Hoffa told the employees at Linteau's taxi service that he was going to meet "Tony P" in addition to Giacalone. Several witnesses testified that Provenzano and Hoffa had been fighting for years, since at least their days together at Lewisburg penitentiary, over (among other things) Pro's belief that the Teamsters had denied him his proper pension fund and Hoffa had done nothing to fix it. James P. Hoffa told the FBI that Anthony Giacalone told him in Miami Beach in December 1974 that his father should resolve his differences with Tony Pro, and that Giacalone told his father the same thing in May 1975. Josephine Hoffa told the FBI that Provenzano called Hoffa a few weeks before the disappearance asking for help, but Hoffa refused.

Then three months after Hoffa's disappearance, Ralph "Little Ralphie" Picardo started to sing. Picardo was a Provenzano associate—a wily five-feet-five thirtysomething with a body like a stump who was serving time in New Jersey for second-degree murder. In an effort to get out of jail and into witness protection, he gave the FBI a lot of information on (among other things) Provenzano's efforts to kill Hoffa. He says he saw the two men in a verbal fight in Miami in November 1973, after which, that day and then a year later, Provenzano ordered a hit on Hoffa. Those hits inexplicably never materialized. But Picardo told the FBI that some of Provenzano's associates told him in jail after the disappearance that Provenzano's men were involved in the disappearance and that Hoffa's body was brought to New Jersey by the Gateway Transportation Company. One of the killers, Picardo implied, was Salvatore Briguglio, a known Provenzano triggerman whom Picardo knew well. At the time, the FBI in Detroit had an eyewitness who claimed to have seen Briguglio in the Machus parking lot, though the Bureau later came to doubt the witness's veracity.

Despite initial excitement, the FBI was never convinced by Picardo's story, since Provenzano had been publicly proclaimed a suspect before he began to talk, and since over time it discovered corroboration holes in Picardo's story and little independent evidence to support it. Jim Dooley, the FBI agent in charge of handling Picardo, told me, "I would not believe a word that came out of his mouth, 'including *a* and *the*,' to quote Mary McCarthy, unless there was independent corroboration." But in late 1975, Picardo was the closest the FBI had to a witness. It thus took him seriously, especially in light of the other factors pointing to Provenzano.

And then there was the metadata information collected from the telephone call records of the players in the Hoffa drama. The Hoffa case was a pioneering effort to use computers to sort through telephone toll records and draw connections—a distant precursor to the metadata national security analyses of the types I worked on in the Department of Justice in 2003–2004.

The toll records revealed nothing about what happened on July 30. But they showed that Hoffa made calls to Allen Dorfman and his few remaining allies in the Teamsters in the run-up to the disappearance. They also showed a flurry of calls among New York, New Jersey, and Detroit mobsters, and included dozens of cross-cutting calls to Dorfman and Fitzsimmons. Most notably, they showed that Giacalone and Provenzano spoke dozens of times from April to July 1975—calls that ceased a few days before the disappearance and never recurred. (The toll records showed no pertinent calls from any of the suspects to or from Chuckie, but they did show three one-minute phone calls from Provenzano's Local 560 to the Teamsters office complex where Chuckie's office was, two days before the disappearance.)

But while the FBI believed that Giacalone and Provenzano organized the hit and used Chuckie as their instrument, they didn't understand the precise motive. The agents speculated that Hoffa was killed due to his efforts to reassume the Teamsters presidency, but early in the case they only dimly understood, if at all, how extensively LCN had infiltrated the Teamsters under Fitzsimmons. They also believed that perhaps Hoffa was knocked off due to Provenzano's personal vendetta against him, and that perhaps Provenzano himself ordered the hit, as Picardo told them.

CHUCKIE SAYS HE doesn't know what happened in the midafternoon of July 30, 1975, at the Machus Red Fox. But he knew plenty else. He knew about the tense run-up to the disappearance. He knew what Giacalone implied to him at dinner two nights later. And he knew intimate details about LCN membership and organization, how it used the Teamsters pension fund, and which locals were mob-controlled, and by whom.

After our family moved to Florida in September 1975, Anthony Giacalone and Anthony Provenzano—both of whom also lived in South Florida—worried a lot about Chuckie's knowledge. As Chuckie grew into a suspect in the case, and then a leading suspect, they feared that he might crack and tell what he knew. They worried more as the government pressure on him grew, as my mother's health deteriorated, and as his money troubles reached new heights. Their worries probably reflected the worries of their bosses. LCN doesn't like loose ends. And Chuckie was a very loose end. If he wanted to get the government off his back, he could have offered up quite a tale.

One afternoon about a month after we moved to Florida, Giacalone, then living in Miami, called Chuckie at his Teamsters office twenty miles away in Hallandale Beach. "Meet me in Pro's backyard in an hour," he said. Provenzano's house, on the intracoastal waterway in Hallandale Beach, was five minutes from where Chuckie worked.

Chuckie grew very anxious over the next hour because he had not seen Provenzano since the disappearance and because Giacalone did not explain the reason for the meeting. He knew the men would not be asking for a meet unless it was very serious business. He made his way to Pro's house an hour later and walked around the side to the backyard, where the two Uncles Tony were waiting in chairs beside Provenzano's pool—Giacalone in slacks and a colorful shirt, Provenzano shirtless and tanned in a bathing suit and slippers.

"Is this going to be good with me being here with you guys?" Chuckie nervously asked the two men he had known for decades. It wasn't clear whether he was afraid that the FBI might be watching, or for his life.

"We just want to talk with you and see how you're doing," Provenzano said, greeting Chuckie with a kiss and hug. Provenzano pointed with a laugh to a home across the water that he believed was filled with G-men monitoring him. It wasn't. But to play it safe and to avoid any bugs, Tony Pro directed Chuckie to join him and Giacalone behind some large bushes at the side of his backyard.

It was a warm day and Chuckie was sweating profusely. He wasn't afraid of Giacalone, but Provenzano was another matter. *Pro's testing me for a reason,* Chuckie thought. *To bring me to his house, at this time; it's like going into the furnace, he has so much heat on him.* And now Pro was leading Chuckie out of sight behind the bushes.

Only Provenzano, not Giacalone, spoke to Chuckie. He asked Chuckie about his wife and children. He asked how Fitzsimmons and Joe Morgan, his new boss in Florida, were treating him. And then he asked about how he, Chuckie, was doing.

"We just want to know that you're okay," Provenzano said.

"I got more heat on me than you got," Chuckie said.

"It'll go away," Provenzano replied.

"Life is funny," Chuckie replied after a silence. "I couldn't find a fucking car to deliver the fucking fish and I called Joey." If I hadn't delivered the salmon, he was saying, I wouldn't be in your backyard.

The salmon gave Provenzano an opening to talk about Hoffa's disappearance, which was the reason for the meeting.

"The little guy had lost his fucking mind and he was going to take everybody down," Provenzano said, referring to Hoffa. "He didn't give a fuck who he was going to take down."

Chuckie was very circumspect in telling me about the rest of the conversation. But he deduced that afternoon what he had suspected since the day of the disappearance: that the decision to kill Hoffa was made or approved in New York, possibly by Provenzano's Genovese family, or more probably by the Commission itself, which at the time was led by a declining Carlo Gambino. The organizational formalities that we associate with the way corporations and governments do business were not normally observed in LCN during this period. Very far-reaching decisions were made via trusted messengers or by men in Adidas warm-up pants standing on a warm summer afternoon in front of a Brooklyn, Manhattan, or Hoboken social club.

Chuckie also learned, or perhaps surmised, that Tony Pro played a role in the disappearance. He was not involved in the killing; he had an excellent alibi on July 30, 1975. And Provenzano never could have authorized Hoffa's disappearance on his own due to a mere personal vendetta against Hoffa, as many in the FBI once speculated. The implications of killing Hoffa were huge for LCN and must have been approved at higher levels. But Chuckie came away believing that Provenzano "had a lot to do with it," as he would tell me in the most unguarded conversation we had on the topic.

Provenzano conveyed this information to Chuckie in just a few general sentences. And he told him nothing at all about the disappearance itself. Chuckie was thrilled not to learn more. He wondered, and worried, why he was even being told this much.

By the end of the conversation, Chuckie believed that Provenzano conveyed why Hoffa was knocked off to make clear to Chuckie the stakes. "He was testing me to see how nervous I was, would I get conned by the FBI about what I knew," Chuckie said. Pro was telling Chuckie to keep his mouth shut about what he learned in the run-up to the disappearance, whatever he had learned since, and anything else about the Outfit. In a roundabout but unmistakably clear way, I think, Pro was telling Chuckie to keep quiet or Provenzano would have him killed. Giacalone's presence probably indicated that he intervened to protect Chuckie with Pro and his superiors and would vouch for his silence.

"*Nun si ni parla cchiu!*" Provenzano said in Sicilian to indicate that the meeting was over. We're done talking, he was saying, implying that Chuckie should keep his mouth shut about what was just said. The two men escorted Chuckie back to his car, and he went back to work.

Forty years later I asked Chuckie what he thought when Provenzano told him what happened and why.

"Nothing," Chuckie told me. "The Old Man was getting crazy." And then after a pause, he added, "I . . . I . . . I know what the rules are, Jack."

"Did they apologize for what happened?" In nearly a decade of talking with Chuckie and asking many stupid questions, this was without a doubt the stupidest.

"No," he said, looking at me with a combination of disbelief and anger. "These guys don't fucking apologize. Are you crazy?"

"Weren't you pissed off about it when you learned what happened?" I asked.

Chuckie paused for a long time. "No," he eventually said.

"What do you think happened to him?" I continued.

"I don't know," Chuckie said. "I wish I knew," he added, and then fell silent for several seconds. "And then I'm glad I didn't know"—because his ignorance about the details gave him forty-five more years of life.

"It happened because he . . . he . . . he was losing control of himself," Chuckie continued.

"And they thought that he was . . . ," I started to say.

"He was going to take everybody down," Chuckie said, cutting me off. "*Crazy*," he added, shaking his head, still barely able to fathom Hoffa's behavior at the end.

TEN

TRAGEDY OF ERRORS

FOR A YEAR AFTER HOFFA'S DISAPPEARANCE, I read, or watched on television, news story after news story claiming that witnesses and evidence proved that Chuckie was involved in the disappearance. The one I remember distinctly was a long and widely discussed *Newsweek* feature that came out in August 1976, just shy of my fourteenth birthday.

"Federal investigators are now satisfied they know who was responsible for Hoffa's abduction and presumed murder and will soon have evidence for indictments," *Newsweek* reported in an article titled "A Break in the Hoffa Case." The story explained that investigators had new information that Hoffa "was kidnapped and spirited to the basement of a private residence only four minutes away—where he was garroted." The kidnapping "was arranged with the help of Charles L. 'Chuckie' O'Brien, 42, a ne'er-do-well union operative regarded as Hoffa's foster son," it continued, as if Chuckie's involvement were settled fact. It added that Chuckie "has been living in fear of his life," and had been "running scared" from Anthony Provenzano, the supposed mastermind of Hoffa's demise, and other mobsters. "Frankly," an unnamed federal agent told the magazine, "I am surprised that Chuckie is still walking around."

The *Newsweek* story expressed a new level of confidence about Chuckie's involvement in the disappearance, and was the first one to give me pause about his innocence. It also scared me since it suggested in public, for the first time I noticed, at least, that Chuckie's life was in jeopardy. And it caused my mother enormous stress, since if Chuckie's life was in jeopardy, our family's safety might be as well.

Chuckie always insisted that the story was nothing more than "the usual FBI bullshit," which he had experienced since the 1950s, of false government leaks designed to pressure him. Four decades later, when I interviewed former government officials and got my hands on the relevant government documents, I learned that Chuckie was right.

A confidential FBI memorandum written seven months after the *Newsweek* story acknowledged that the government had a "troublesome . . . lack of evidence" about what happened to Hoffa. "It is not known who was actually responsible," the memorandum stated, "and if JRH was killed, where it was done and where his body was taken." The supposedly new information incriminating Chuckie was a lie.

Nor was the government close to indicting Chuckie at that time. An internal Justice Department memorandum written just a few months after the *Newsweek* story reviewed the assumptions and inference chains that would have to be overcome to nail Chuckie for the disappearance. "The prospects of obtaining a conviction are not encouraging," it concluded. "Departmental attorneys are unanimous in recommending against a prosecution of O'Brien at this time." The mendacious leaks to the press to the contrary, several retired government officials confirmed to me, were what Chuckie said they were: efforts to scare him into cooperating.

The *Newsweek* article's claim that Chuckie was running scared from

Provenzano seemed odd to me at the time, since we frequently visited Tony Pro's home in Hallandale Beach, and he was always generous and gracious. Chuckie may well have been anxious after his October 1975 meeting in Provenzano's backyard, which I learned about much later. But at the time he never displayed any hint of it and never took steps—at least that I knew about—to protect our family from any harm. I also later learned that Pro's wife often asked Chuckie to collect her husband, a hard drinker who was frequently too sotted to drive home from his beloved bar at the Shore View Hotel on the Atlantic Ocean, ten minutes from Chuckie's office. If the FBI had known how often Chuckie saw Tony Pro, it might have deployed different types of pressure. Instead, it assumed antagonism and tried to play Provenzano against him.

Chuckie's attempts to fight back against the false rumors against him were invariably self-defeating. His first effort came on the CBS show *60 Minutes* on November 7, 1976. I was fourteen years old by then, and was excited and proud that my famous stepfather was on the program. As I watched his interview with Morley Safer, I thought he successfully refuted the allegations against him. My mother framed the publicity placard for the interview—a sketch of her tough-looking husband under the headline "Chuckie," the title of the interview segment—and hung it in our living room, as if CBS had produced a glowing biopic.

Watching the video of the interview four decades later, I realized that Chuckie came off as complicit. Safer asked if he picked up Hoffa's killers in Joey Giacalone's car. Chuckie denied that he "ever picked up anyone in that Mercury," and added, "If Jimmy Hoffa was ever in that Mercury, there's no steers in Texas, and Texas is a big cow country."

Asked who killed Hoffa, Chuckie looked calculating to the point of guilty as he stated: "I couldn't answer that, because I don't know." After a long hesitation, he added: "If I knew, if I knew, if I knew and I cooperated, as long as I cooperated with the authorities, we'd find out."

Chuckie also let linger Safer's implication that his loyalty had migrated from Hoffa to Fitzsimmons, Provenzano, and Giacalone. Chuckie ended the interview by agreeing with Safer's suggestion that the government's harassment was designed to make him crack. "But, you know, unfortunately, I was born of heritage of half being Sicilian and half being Irish," Chuckie said. "They're not gonna crack me."

The *60 Minutes* interview was typical of the tragedy of errors that defined Chuckie's efforts to clear his name in the years after the disappearance.

IN ADDITION TO the bullying leaks, the government squeezed the main Hoffa disappearance suspects through prosecutions for crimes unrelated to the disappearance. Government lawyers "would sit around and think about how we could fuck people," as Paul Coffey, the head of Detroit's Organized Crime Strike Force in the late 1970s, explained to me. The government sent Anthony Giacalone to jail for ten years in the mid-1970s for tax evasion, and was prosecuting him for racketeering and extortion when he died in 2001. Anthony Provenzano was convicted for the 1961 murder of his Local 560 rival, Anthony Castellito, and died in 1988. Other leading suspects all did significant jail time.

The Feds also plowed through decades of Chuckie's tax and financial records, labor dealings, and shadier antics. It convicted him for accepting a car from a dealership where he represented union workers and for inflating his net worth on a bank loan application. Amazingly, in light of Chuckie's suspect past and associations, the government couldn't find other ways to pressure him through courts.

Before Chuckie went to jail in January 1979, the FBI tried to squeeze him in a different way. On March 21, 1978, Sal Briguglio, Provenzano's button man who some believed might have pulled the trigger on Hoffa, was murdered when two gunmen pumped four shots into his head and one into his chest after he walked out of a restaurant on a rainy night in New York's Little Italy. The rumors were that Sally Bugs was killed because he was cooperating with the Feds in the impending trial of Tony Provenzano for the 1961 Castellito murder, but some thought he may also have been talking about Hoffa.

"Hours after Briguglio was gunned down," reported Pete Yost of the Associated Press, "FBI agents offered O'Brien protection in Florida but he refused." As Chuckie tells it, the morning after the hit, two FBI agents phoned him at his office and said that for his safety they needed to speak with him immediately. Chuckie met them at a nearby deli. One of the agents said that Stephen and Tommy Andretta—Provenzano thugs who were also suspects in the Hoffa disappearance—had killed Sally Bugs and were going to kill Chuckie next.

"Do you think I'm going to start sweating just because you throw these names out?" Chuckie says he asked the agents. The agents offered to put Chuckie and our family in a witness protection program if he told them what happened to Hoffa. "You tell me, because I don't know," Chuckie replied. Chuckie later scoffed at the notion that the agents could scare him with threats about Giacalone and Provenzano, whom he had known his whole life and with whom he had an explicit understanding. "I used to think to myself, 'What are these morons doing?'" he told me. "Tony Pro told me Sally had so many enemies in New York, and was a stool pigeon," Chuckie said. "They don't kill you if you're not a stool pigeon."

I don't remember Briguglio's murder, but I do remember an event that occurred at my school, Pine Crest, two mornings later. The principal's office received an anonymous call that "the O'Brien children are going to be kidnapped." Jim Byer, the principal, removed me from English class and brought me and my two younger brothers to his office, where my mother, Brenda, met us thirty minutes later. We stayed home for several days, and Pine Crest asked my parents to consider removing us from the school before reversing itself and letting us return. "People were afraid to have Chuckie around," Byer told me much later.

The kidnapping threat rattled Chuckie like nothing before because it threatened our family. "At first I felt that our love was strong and piss on them, we'll survive and we'll make it," Chuckie told me. But the threat on top of everything else made Chuckie realize he had "no control to stop all the bullshit." Years of stories about his involvement in the Hoffa crime made his new job hard, since many union members shunned him. They also shattered the image he sought to present to the world.

The core commitment in Chuckie's life was loyalty. Omertà was loyalty. And the decades of unquestioned service to Hoffa, and his love for him, were the greatest and costliest expressions of his loyalty. It was enraging to

Chuckie that everyone thought he betrayed and then killed Hoffa. But even worse was the horrendous impact the Hoffa drumbeat had on my mother's fragile physical and mental health. After the kidnapping scare sent my mother into a "tailspin," as he put it, Chuckie began to consider leaving our family to spare us the pain.

Also in a tailspin was the government's investigation into the Hoffa disappearance. "The Hoffa investigation has reached an impasse," an attorney on the Hoffa case in Buffalo wrote in the first sentence of a long memorandum in April 1977. The impasse was "not due to any dearth of investigative leads," it insisted, "but rather to problems of policy, commitment, authority, coordination, and manpower" by the Department of Justice. One month earlier, Detroit FBI agents had written a memorandum that similarly complained that the Justice Department and FBI were not making the "necessary manpower and time commitments" to solve the case.

But the view from Washington looked quite different. For two years the government had conducted the most extensive investigation in its history for someone believed to be dead. (The only larger one to that point was the nineteen-month search for Patricia Hearst.) The Detroit field office alone had expended tens of thousands of man-hours following hundreds of leads, and government lawyers in Detroit had called more than 116 people before the grand jury. Smaller but still intensive investigations had been undertaken in New York, New Jersey, Buffalo, and many other cities. The government conducted literally thousands of interviews, but still didn't have a single piece of evidence about who knocked off Hoffa, or how.

For Justice Department officials in Washington, the expensive, single-minded focus on Hoffa grew hard to justify, especially in light of what the FBI had learned about organized crime due to its investigation of Hoffa's disappearance. That investigation uncovered what the Justice Department described in a 1977 memorandum as "pervasive Syndicate control of the Teamsters—a malignancy which rages and ravages as if the McClellan Committee's work of exactly twenty years ago had never existed."

In fact, the problem had grown significantly worse since Kennedy's day, as Hoffa's departure in 1967 had led to a decade of much greater LCN dominance of the Teamsters union than anything that happened before. It was the Hoffa disappearance that led the Feds to truly understand and crack down on this corrupt arrangement. Though other factors were in play, one can plot a straight line from the Hoffa investigation in 1975–77 to more than 2,500 mob-related indictments, including convictions of nineteen bosses, thirteen underbosses, and forty-three capos, in the 1980s. The Hoffa case "had a tremendously positive impact on the FBI's focusing on labor racketeering," and it "definitely had a long-range positive impact on our investigations into organized crime," said Paul Coffey, then the deputy chief of the Organized Crime and Racketeering Section of the Justice Department, in 1985.

The ironies abound. Bobby Kennedy's crusade against Hoffa, which was designed to eliminate mob influence over the Teamsters union, actually deepened mob control over it and gave it greater access to Teamsters cash. Hoffa threatened this arrangement in the mid-1970s in his bid to win back the union. The mob's decision to kill Hoffa in order to protect its Teamsters assets had finally roused the FBI and Justice Department to commit the resources and imagination needed to understand the problem of labor racketeering and to break the mob's hold on the union and its power more generally. In the process, the executive branch for the first time aggressively deployed the powerful weapons Congress had given it in the late 1960s to fight organized crime, including the Racketeer Influenced and Corrupt Organizations Act, expanded wiretapping authority (under court supervision), and a well-financed witness protection program.

As Al Sproule, an FBI agent who worked the Hoffa case from New York in the 1970s, told me, "If Jimmy was left in the street, a lot of people would not have gone to prison and the Teamsters Union and 'organized crime' would not have been affected as dramatically as they have been."

But while the effort to find the killers of Jimmy Hoffa bore significant collateral fruit, it did not discover who killed Jimmy Hoffa. "It really is an extraordinary case in that the closer we approach the event that set everything into motion, the less certainty as to specifics obtains, until the event goes almost completely dark," FBI agent Jim Dooley told me. By the late 1970s the Hoffa matter went from an active investigation looking for the killers to a reactive one that responded to events. But unfortunately for Chuckie, the original public narrative about his involvement in the disappearance never waned.

BY THE FALL of 1976, Chuckie was growing weary of the public lies about him. He wanted to speak out to proclaim his innocence and defend his honor. He pleaded with Anthony Giacalone for permission to talk, citing his innocence, loyalty, trustworthiness, and the impact on his family and job.

Even if Chuckie knew nothing about the July 30 plot, however, he knew lots of other stuff, including what he had learned from years at Hoffa's and Giacalone's side, and at the Lake with Hoffa in 1974, and in Provenzano's backyard. Giacalone was not a sentimental man, and he and his LCN superiors typically would assume no risk about such matters. And yet Uncle Tony came through. According to Chuckie, Giacalone used his considerable influence at the top. It is unclear precisely who gave Chuckie permission to defend himself. But Chuckie came under "New York's protection," as he told me.

It is unclear why Giacalone went out on a limb for Chuckie. Perhaps he was motivated by love for Chuckie, or by remorse that Chuckie was accidentally in the FBI's cross hairs. Or perhaps he saw little risk because he had confidence in Chuckie's Omertà commitment and he knew he could reveal nothing about the actual event.

Another possibility, as one former FBI agent suggested to me, is that letting Chuckie talk was a calculated move by LCN to deflect attention from the real culprits. LCN never would have let Chuckie speak publicly—indeed, it would have killed him—if there were any chance he could slip up and offer details about what actually happened on July 30. "These Mafia guys would kill you over a bone with no more remorse than a crocodile," Dooley once explained to me. But if Chuckie flailed about trying to defend himself about July 30, that might keep the public and FBI spotlight on him and keep it off the actual conspirators.

Whatever the reason, by the late summer of 1976, Chuckie had a green light. "Do what you have to do to protect yourself," Giacalone advised Chuckie. But, he made clear, never come close to betraying the family or talking about what you're not supposed to talk about. Chuckie understood the stakes. "When Uncle Tony put me with the Old Man, his word, his name, was on the line." (The "Old Man" here is a senior organized crime figure in New York, not Hoffa.)

The *60 Minutes* interview in November 1976 was Chuckie's first effort at vindication. It didn't go well. But if LCN had set Chuckie loose as a misdirection play, it got a huge return in his first outing.

A Detroit radio interview two days later with Jerry Stanecki, the last journalist to interview Hoffa, went a little better for Chuckie. He denied in a straightforward way any involvement in the disappearance and repeated his version of events on July 30. He said he "would never let anything happen" to Hoffa, adding that if he were around Hoffa that day "they'd have to do it to me first." He then answered the charge that the FBI dogs had detected Hoffa's scent in the car nine days after the disappearance, saying, "If I could have one of their cars for a week I'd put Adolf Hitler or J. Edgar Hoover in that car," and emphasized that "there's just no way that Jimmy Hoffa was in Joey Giacalone's car, period."

"Chuckie O'Brien is very convincing," pronounced Stanecki after the interview. But Chuckie's Omertà commitments also led him to say some unconvincing things. "I couldn't in my wildest dreams ever say why would somebody want [to] do harm to him," he replied, when asked why Hoffa was killed. He denied that he knew "who the Mafia is" and said that "whoever you think the Mafia is is not involved in the Teamsters." He described Provenzano as a "hardworking officer of the local union in New Jersey," paid compliments to thugs who worked for Provenzano, and denied bad blood between Hoffa and Fitzsimmons. Chuckie's care not to lay blame anywhere near his organized crime friends made him look suspicious, or worse.

Despite Chuckie's obeisance to the mob in these and other public interviews, the government thought he was running a risk in talking. "Investigators are watching [O'Brien] closely," a Justice Department attorney wrote in a 1976 memorandum. "His recent TV and radio appearances must certainly have annoyed his co-conspirators." During this period of the investigation, the government never seriously considered the alternative explanation for why Chuckie could speak out with impunity: he was not involved in the disappearance, and he had permission to talk to clear his name.

But Chuckie's efforts made little headway in the years after Hoffa's disappearance. Book after book, aping elements of the leaked Hoffex Memorandum, the leaked Picardo story, and other early government leaks, insisted that Chuckie drove Hoffa to his death.

Dan Moldea's 1978 book *The Hoffa Wars* reported that unnamed "government agents" believed Chuckie picked up Hoffa at the Machus Red Fox and drove him to the nearby home of a friend, where Frank Sheeran and the Tony Provenzano associates Salvatore and Gabriel Briguglio, and Thomas Andretta, were waiting to kill Hoffa. That same year, Steven Brill in *The Teamsters* relied on a "study of the government's investigation" and other sources to place Salvatore Briguglio and either Gabriel or Andretta in the car with Chuckie. Brill said Hoffa was knocked out within minutes and later either strangled or shot. The self-styled "mob lawyer" Frank Ragano claimed in a 1994 book that Chuckie alone picked up Hoffa and delivered him to a gas station, where Salvatore and Gabriel choked Hoffa to death in Chuckie's and Andretta's presence. And Frank Sheeran claimed in Charlie Brandt's 2004 book *I Heard You Paint Houses* that he and Salvatore were in the car when Chuckie picked up Hoffa and drove him to the home near the Machus Red Fox, where he was murdered. (Brandt's book is being made into a major motion picture.)

Through these mutually inconsistent variations of the original leaks, the public heard one constant over the years: Chuckie picked up Hoffa and drove him to his death.

As the bad publicity continued, the home front worsened for Chuckie. His money problems hit a new low during that first terrible year with our family in Florida. The IRS repossessed his Teamsters car. Never inclined to prudence, Chuckie withdrew decades of accumulated pension savings to pay off debts and build my mother an extravagant "dream home" in Plantation, Florida. After eighteen months one of his pensions was depleted, and he couldn't make the payments. When Chuckie went to jail for his bribery and bank fraud convictions in early 1979, we abandoned the dream home to move into a small apartment nearby. And then the IRS went after him again, this time for paying insufficient taxes on his withdrawn pension.

When Chuckie got out of jail a year later, he was forty-five years old and financially and emotionally destitute. "My family has been through a lot," he told the local Florida newspaper just after his release. "I've gone through a lot. I'm tired." He went back to work for the Teamsters, and the next several years were relatively quiet. The Hoffa investigation seemed to fizzle, and Chuckie stayed out of the headlines. On the tenth anniversary of the disappearance, in August 1985, the FBI seemed to be giving up. "I believe there are very few, less than five people probably, who actually know for sure what happened," said FBI spokesman John Anthony. "We've done everything we could do through our investigative efforts and still haven't broken the case. Someone will have to talk."

Although the FBI's interest in Chuckie was dissipating, he continued to inspire writers and film producers. In 1969 Mario Puzo had modeled the Godfather's consigliere Tom Hagen on Chuckie, and in the 1972 film Robert Duvall played the role. In 1981, it was Paul Newman's turn to play a character based on Chuckie's life. Newman was cast as Michael Gallagher in the film *Absence of Malice*. Gallagher was a Miami liquor wholesaler with mob ties who awakes one day to find himself falsely accused on the front page of the local newspaper of involvement in the disappearance of a local union official. The story was concocted. The federal prosecutor in charge of the Justice Department's Organized Crime Strike Force in Miami had planted it with the reporter to try to coerce Gallagher into telling what he knew about the murder. The ordeal ruined Gallagher's life.

"In America can a man be guilty until proven innocent?" asked the movie's tag line. "Suppose you picked up this morning's newspaper and your life was a front page headline . . . And everything they said was accurate . . . But none of it was true." This was exactly how Chuckie felt. And it was how the screenplay writer, Kurt Luedtke, viewed Chuckie's situation. Luedtke, who also wrote *Out of Africa*, was in a position to know. He was the executive editor of the *Detroit Free Press* in July 1975 and thus had a front-row seat for the shenanigans the Feds pulled with the press. Luedtke witnessed them "squeezing Chuckie," and he modeled the Gallagher character "in part on Chuckie and his experiences with the government after the Hoffa disappearance," he told me. "The movie was about the press being used by the Feds in a way that damaged lives." Chuckie was no straight arrow. But that is what happened to him.

The relative quietude in Chuckie's life did not last. On December 3, 1987, my mother, Brenda, divorced him. The break had been a long time coming because of Chuckie's endless debts and unreliability, but more than anything else because of his Hoffa troubles and mob associations. This was about the time when I was stiff-arming Chuckie for similar reasons and also berating my mother for staying with him. Other members of Brenda's family were sending the same message. My mother said that all she wanted in life was "peace"—peace from her mental distress and from anxiety. She didn't find it with her first two husbands, and Chuckie, though he adored her and tried very hard, couldn't give it to her either. The divorce did not mark a permanent break—after a few months' separation, Chuckie returned and they continued to live together for the rest of their lives. But in 1987 their relationship was at its nadir.

SIX MONTHS AFTER the divorce, on June 28, 1988, an ambitious young New York federal prosecutor named Rudy Giuliani filed a novel lawsuit against the Teamsters union, its Executive Board, the LCN Commission, and twenty-six alleged LCN members. The lawsuit built on a decade of investigative work into labor racketeering and organized crime that began with the Hoffa investigation. It alleged that the Teamsters union was a "captive labor organization, which La Cosa Nostra figures have infiltrated, controlled and dominated through fear and intimidation and have exploited through fraud, embezzlement, bribery and extortion." The government sought the authority to essentially take over the union to enforce its disciplinary rules and rid it of the corrupt influence of organized crime.

Giuliani's team of lawyers summoned Chuckie for an interview. On the morning of November 16, 1988, he appeared in a dinky windowless room at the U.S. Attorney's Office in downtown New York for a deposition by Assistant U.S. Attorney Ed Ferguson. Chuckie showed up voluntarily and without an attorney, which he could not afford. He didn't really understand the nature of the proceedings against him and had not read the government's charges. It was a legally fraught situation, since Chuckie would be answering questions under oath without any concrete idea of his legal vulnerabilities. Ferguson felt sorry for Chuckie. He remembers him as "erratic," "rambling," and "out of his depth." Chuckie was "not operating pursuant to strategy," he told me.

The main point of Ferguson's interview was to establish Chuckie's relationships with organized crime figures. Chuckie was proudly unapologetic in acknowledging that he knew well the many individuals Ferguson named, including half a dozen senior Detroit family members and Anthony Provenzano. "I wasn't going to walk away from my life and deny my friendships," Chuckie explained to me.

But Chuckie grew quiet when Ferguson asked whether these gentlemen were in the mob, since a candid answer would be a death sentence.

"Was Anthony Giacalone ever a member of La Cosa Nostra?" asked Ferguson.

Chuckie paused. "I'm going to invoke my right of the Fifth Amendment," he answered.

Ferguson asked the same question about Anthony Provenzano. He also asked whether "individuals who have been members of La Cosa Nostra [had] ever been employees or officers of the International Brotherhood of Teamsters." To all of these questions, Chuckie gave the same answer: "I'm going to invoke my right of the Fifth." Chuckie was no legal eagle, but he knew enough to invoke his right against self-incrimination when answering a specific question would force him to choose between telling the truth and Omertà.

Chuckie took a revealingly different tack, however, when Ferguson moved on to ask about the Hoffa disappearance. Chuckie saw no conflict between Omertà and the truth in that context, and he answered Ferguson's questions without invoking the Fifth. He directly denied in several different ways that he was involved in the Hoffa disappearance.

Ferguson asked again. "Just so we are clear, on July 30, 1975, did you see or meet Mr. Hoffa?" he asked.

"No, I sure didn't," Chuckie responded.

Especially in light of Chuckie's frequent invocation of the Fifth Amendment on other topics, Ferguson was surprised by his straightforward answers about Hoffa. "Since he had been a suspect I would have expected him to 'take five' touching on disappearance, but he didn't," Ferguson told me. It should have been surprising as well, and relevant, for the Hoffa disappearance investigators, since Chuckie had sworn under oath that he was not involved. But they never learned about his statements.

Giuliani's legally controversial suit forced a settlement in which the Teamsters Executive Board agreed to an "independent administrator" who would investigate and discipline corrupt union agents. Chuckie was soon hauled before the administrator, Frederick B. Lacey. Lacey cited Chuckie for his misdemeanor convictions, for using $12,000 in unauthorized union funds to fly Johnny Cash in a private plane to a disaster relief concert in Texas, and for "knowingly associating" with dozens of organized crime figures. He had little trouble concluding that Chuckie should be expelled from the Teamsters. On September 11, 1991, a federal judge agreed, and Chuckie at age fifty-seven was gone from the union to which he had devoted his life for forty years. To make matters worse, under the government takeover of the Teamsters, he could not talk to or associate with his many friends and acquaintances who remained in the union.

As 1992 dawned, Chuckie was out of a job and out of his second marriage, at least nominally. He thus found little solace from his third portrayal on the Hollywood big screen, this time in the movie *Hoffa*, which premiered in December. Jack Nicholson played the Old Man, and Danny DeVito, the movie's producer and director, played his sidekick, Bobby Ciaro, a composite character based largely on Chuckie in a creative screenplay written by David Mamet. Chuckie didn't like the "bullshit" movie, which portrays Ciaro as the unwitting set-up man who is killed along with Hoffa in the final scene.

It takes a special life and a special character to be portrayed by Robert Duvall, Paul Newman, and Danny DeVito in three quite different roles in three major motion pictures. (Chuckie would later be played in a fourth major motion picture, *The Irishman*, by Jesse Plemons.) And it is very bad luck, or worse, to generate that kind of interest in one's life and not make any money off it. Chuckie tried to interject his story into the making of DeVito's *Hoffa* movie, but he couldn't convince DeVito to purchase the legal rights. Once again, Chuckie lost out.

The *Hoffa* movie did, however, provide Chuckie with an opportunity to accidentally but credibly exonerate himself from suspicion in the Hoffa disappearance. When the movie came out, the Detroit FBI was in the midst of blanketing the Detroit mob with wiretaps and bugs as part of an operation, known as Gamtax, to bring it down. One bug was placed in Vito Giacalone's black Cadillac in Morgantown, West Virginia, where he was visiting a girlfriend in January 1993 on his way to Florida for the winter.

A few months later, after the bug had been renewed, Chuckie, as he often did, drove Vito back to Detroit from Florida. The FBI listened to all of their conversations during the two-day trip. The men chitchatted the entire time but discussed nothing of note until Chuckie brought up the recent *Hoffa* movie out of the blue. Chuckie blabbed away, offering various theories of who might have done it and why, in a way that implied he had no idea what actually happened. Vito, by contrast, went uncharacteristically silent and did not engage. One former FBI agent told me that the conversation made him "absolutely convinced beyond possible doubt" that Chuckie was not involved in Hoffa's disappearance. (I sought the transcripts of these recordings from the FBI, which declined to produce them or even to acknowledge their existence, even though I showed them proof of the government's application for the surveillance.)

Chuckie didn't learn until decades later that the FBI was listening in to that conversation, but the *Hoffa* movie did induce him and my mother to write a book about his life with Hoffa called *The Agony of Justice*. In contrast to others connected with the mob or the Hoffa disappearance who wrote books in the 1980s and 1990s, Chuckie found no publishers who were interested in his manuscript. It's not hard to see why. He wouldn't dish any dirt at all on the "so-called mafia," as he said in the manuscript. And he denied that there was any dispute between Hoffa and the mob in the mid-1970s. "The blaring headlines and misinformation campaign implicating Tony Giacalone, Tony Provenzano and myself," he wrote, "were mere smokescreens orchestrated by certain government factions to cover the truth." The truth, according to Chuckie, was that the CIA had knocked off Hoffa.

The theory actually had a sliver of circumstantial support. The summer of 1975 was the height of the Church Committee investigation into disreputable U.S. intelligence activities in the previous decades. One of the most salacious secrets to emerge from the investigation, and there were many, was that the CIA worked with LCN members with Cuban connections in several plots to assassinate Fidel Castro.

In June 1975, six weeks before Hoffa disappeared, former CIA director Richard Helms testified in secret before the Committee about the plots. Chicago mobster Salvatore Giancana—who had once shared a mistress with President John F. Kennedy—was scheduled to testify on the matter, but before he could, he was shot in the head and neck in the kitchen of his Oak Park, Illinois, home while cooking sausage and spinach. The assassination was widely seen as a mob hit, and the timing made many believe that it was related to the Church Committee investigations. A similar inference was drawn when Los Angeles wiseguy Johnny Rosselli, who did testify on the assassinations, was found the following year chopped up in a metal drum in Miami harbor.

Some have speculated that the mob knocked off Hoffa too because he was going to spill the beans on what he knew to the Church Committee. There's no evidence for this theory. Chuckie certainly didn't provide any evidence in *The Agony of Justice*, though he did change the tale to place the responsibility for silencing Hoffa not on LCN but rather on the CIA. In Chuckie's retelling, Hoffa was knocked off not just because of his knowledge of the Castro plots, but also because he was involved in CIA efforts to discredit the Kennedy brothers. This was all made up. Chuckie later told me that Hoffa wasn't to his knowledge involved in any way with the Cuban assassination schemes, though he did play a role in arranging arms and munitions for his Mafia friend to give to the Cubans in the early 1960s.

Chuckie had read so many untrue or made-up things about him and his life over so many decades, in newspapers and books, that he thought truth was irrelevant when he wrote his book. "Everybody that's written these books, they all surmise what happened," he explained to me. "They have no facts on them, they have no truth on them. The book gets printed and it goes out and they sell 'em, and that's it." That's a pretty good description of many books written about Hoffa's disappearance. But Chuckie, uniquely among

Hoffa friends and acquaintances, still couldn't get his book printed. It was too contrived even for the Hoffa genre.

AFTER CHUCKIE WAS expelled from the union, he took on several odd jobs to eke out a living. By January 1993, he decided to make a final, desperate effort to clear his name.

Chuckie appeared on the January 7 episode of *The Maury Povich Show* wearing a too-tight white sweater, large tinted eyeglasses, and a menacing look. "I am tired of headlines coming out in this country saying that I drove this man to his death," Chuckie told Povich. "I have had it, I have got a family, it's destroyed them."

Povich asked Chuckie directly whether he "took [his] adopted father in a car unwittingly to a meeting with 'some connected people' in Detroit?" Chuckie gave his standard denial and explanation. "If this was true, I would not be sitting here today. I would be gone." When asked if he knew where the body was, he replied, "I don't know, I wish I knew. . . . It's been very difficult."

Povich then turned to another guest, Kenneth Walton, the FBI agent in Detroit who oversaw the Hoffa investigation from 1985 to 1988. Walton said Chuckie was lying and claimed to have proof that Chuckie had driven Hoffa to his death. "There are two men in this room who know what happened to Jimmy Hoffa," explained Walton. "I'm not talking because I don't want to get other people killed. And Chuckie knows and he's not talking because he doesn't want to be killed."

The false statement infuriated Chuckie. "I almost got out of my chair and leveled him," he told me. Instead, Chuckie told Povich that to rebut Walton, he would "take a lie detector test on your program, conducted by whoever you want to bring in here, about where I was that day." Chuckie had been wanting to take a lie detector test since 1975, but lawyer after lawyer had advised him against it. He had finally found one who said it was okay.

Povich asked Walton whether a lie detector test by Chuckie would satisfy him.

"I wouldn't recommend that he do it, to tell you the truth," he replied. "If Chuckie keeps talking about this, I'm very concerned about Chuckie's welfare, as he ought to be. Chuckie, you should get ahold of the FBI and tell them the truth for the first time in a whole lot of years and then do what they tell you to do, don't take a polygraph on TV."

Chuckie decided to take the polygraph test. The Povich program hired Natale Laurendi, the New York Police Department's longtime "star lie detector," whose "expertise with lie detectors helped convict the guilty and clear the innocent for many years," according to *The New York Times*. Laurendi had retired from public service and ran his own firm when Povich called. He was one of the most respected polygraphers in the country.

On the show the following week, Povich asked Laurendi if Chuckie passed.

"Yes, indeed, he passed," Laurendi responded. "As far as I'm concerned he was telling the truth when he claimed he was not in an automobile with James Hoffa on the afternoon of July 30, 1975. Neither was he involved in any conspiracy to do harm to James Riddle Hoffa. As far as I'm concerned, Chuck O'Brien today is a nonentity in the disappearance of James Riddle Hoffa."

Povich then played the tape of the questions and answers:

LAURENDI: "Have you agreed with anyone to drop off James R. Hoffa someplace on Wednesday, July 30, 1975?"

CHUCKIE: "No."

LAURENDI: "Were you in any automobile with James R. Hoffa on that afternoon of Wednesday, July 30, 1975?"

CHUCKIE: "No."

LAURENDI: "Were you involved in any conspiracy to harm James R. Hoffa?"

CHUCKIE: "No."

Chuckie, who on the second show was wearing a Teamsters jacket even though he was barred from the union, teared up with emotion when the results were announced. He couldn't collect himself to answer Maury's question about what the polygraph results meant to him. But inside he was overcome with relief and joy. The truth, he thought, had finally come out. He had taken the lie detector test so many people for eighteen years had insisted that he take. After eighteen miserable years, in Chuckie's mind, there was now objective evidence of his innocence.

The only problem was that no one seemed to notice. The headlines of exoneration that Chuckie expected did not appear. In article after article and book after book, the same public narrative—that Chuckie had driven Hoffa to his death—continued unabated as if he had never taken the test.

Nothing appeared to change inside the FBI, either. An FBI agent in New York alerted the Organized Crime Strike Force in Detroit and the FBI Polygraph Unit about the test Laurendi administered to Chuckie. The chief of the Polygraph Unit concluded that only FBI polygraph examiners are relevant in cases like Chuckie's, and recommended against giving Laurendi's examination any credence.

Chuckie had come up empty, again.

ELEVEN

FAILED
VINDICATION

DURING MY FIRST INTERVIEW with Chuckie for this book, in the spring of 2012 at our usual spot in my mother's television room, he handed me two letters from Detroit FBI agent Andrew Sluss. "These letters prove I wasn't involved in Mr. Hoffa's murder," Chuckie told me.

Sluss was the agent in charge of the Hoffa case for about a decade, beginning in October 1993, nine months after Chuckie's polygraph test on *The Maury Povich Show*. The first letter he wrote, on February 13, 1995, asked Chuckie for a meeting to discuss the Hoffa disappearance. "I am well aware that you are probably not the biggest fan of the FBI," Sluss said, "but nonetheless your assistance in this case will be helpful."

That wasn't a very appealing offer, but the next sentence got Chuckie's attention: "I do not consider you a suspect in this matter."

I was astonished to read that an FBI agent on the Hoffa case had told Chuckie he did not consider him a suspect. But the letter seemed like a trick or a prank to get Chuckie to talk—as the topic of Sluss's second letter seemed to confirm.

The second letter was written six and a half years later, in August 2001, a few weeks after Sluss and his partner had succeeded in meeting Chuckie near his home in Boca Raton to try to convince him to take an FBI polygraph test to clear his name. On September 7, *The Detroit News* reported that the FBI had used a previously unavailable DNA test to match the hair found in Joey Giacalone's car in 1975 to Hoffa. The new evidence "calls into question the repeated claim by O'Brien that Hoffa was never in the car," the story said. It added that the government might soon bring charges in the Hoffa case.

The DNA story made Sluss's claims about Chuckie's innocence, and his efforts to polygraph Chuckie, seem like a double cross. Sluss's second letter was written the moment the story appeared in print. It explained to Chuckie that the newspaper story was factually inaccurate, that he still believed in Chuckie's innocence, and that he still wanted to help him clear his name by conducting a polygraph test.

Chuckie was "pissed off" by the revelations about the hair in Joey's car, and pissed off at Sluss. Larry King knew Chuckie from his days as Hoffa's sidekick and invited him to defend himself on *Larry King Live*, in Los Angeles, on the evening of September 12, 2001. Chuckie accepted the invitation but never made it to the interview. His flight from West Palm Beach on September 11 turned around midmorning and landed in Tampa as part of the response to the national emergency. King canceled the interview and never invited Chuckie back.

The 9/11 attacks shoved the new allegations against Chuckie off the headlines. They sent Sluss to Pennsylvania for two weeks to gather evidence in Somerset County, where flight 93 crashed. And they eventually drew me from the University of Chicago Law School, where I was teaching at the time, to work in the Department of Defense. After Sluss returned to Detroit, he telephoned me early in my tenure at the Pentagon, in the fall of 2002, for help to convince Chuckie to take a polygraph to clear his name. At the time I was not in contact with Chuckie and knew nothing about Sluss's letters or approaches to Chuckie. I was focused on getting a security clearance, and I was suspicious of Sluss's phone call, so I curtly refused his request.

But when I read Sluss's letters a decade later in my mother's television room, I immediately wanted to contact him to see why he believed Chuckie was innocent and whether I could do anything to help clear Chuckie's name.

SLUSS HAD BECOME an FBI agent in September 1986 after receiving a law degree from the University of Nebraska and serving as a law clerk and Nebraska police officer for nearly a decade. He was a soft-spoken and outwardly modest man with a stocky build, full beard, and shambling gait that made him seem like a gentle bear. But Sluss's Boy Scout disposition masked an intensely analytical approach to criminal mysteries. "Assumptions are scary things," he once chastised me when we were bouncing around theories about the Hoffa case. "They mislead. Always fight assumptions."

At Sluss's going-away party from his first FBI assignment in Kentucky in 1991, his supervisor predicted that when he got to Detroit, Sluss would solve the Hoffa case. Everyone laughed, but Sluss secretly hoped that he might be assigned to the case. When he arrived in the Motor City, Sluss lucked into working on Gamtax, the Detroit corner of the government's post-Hoffa-disappearance effort to kneecap the mob. His specialty was writing the wiretap affidavits that helped lead to the 1996 arrest of the entire leadership of the Detroit family and later to the conviction of most of them.

Sluss was thus familiar with Detroit organized crime when the case agent on the Hoffa file transferred to another squad in the summer of 1993. Sluss asked Joe Finnegan, the supervisor of the FBI's Organized Crime Squad in Detroit, if he could take over the Hoffa case. "There was no line for the job," Sluss later told me. The Hoffa case was moribund and deemed unsolvable, and time spent on it was seen as a career-killer. But Sluss had no ambitions to be a supervisor. He liked to work cases and "wanted to work the Hoffa case."

Finnegan assented and assigned the investigation to him on October 6, 1993. He gave Sluss "tremendous freedom" to pursue the case as he wished and no pressure to solve it.

During the next six months, in his spare time from Gamtax, Sluss read the entire Hoffa file—four file drawers full of FBI interviews, evidence, and analysis, and several banker's boxes full of material gleaned from 106 grand jury witnesses. He was the first person not involved in the original investigation, and maybe the only person ever, to read it all through. He did so with twenty-twenty hindsight, with no preconceived notions, and with no pressure to reach a result. He also did so with relevant collateral knowledge—about how organized crime worked in Detroit, of subsequent events related to the Hoffa matter, and about information about the Hoffa disappearance picked up on wiretaps in Gamtax—that the original investigators lacked in the 1970s.

When Sluss entered the Hoffa case, the FBI possessed what he described as an "institutional belief" that Chuckie picked up Hoffa at the Machus Red Fox. Within a year, Sluss had concluded that this belief was erroneous and that Chuckie was not in the Machus Red Fox parking lot that afternoon.

Sluss was first drawn to this conclusion by the same basic circumstantial reasons to doubt Chuckie's involvement in the crime that I had been drawn to for years—especially the ways that Chuckie's behavior the week of the disappearance belied his involvement in it, and the reasons the mob would have for not employing Chuckie and Joey Giacalone's car for the job. He also found it implausible that Chuckie could be involved in the disappearance and still be alive almost twenty years after the event. The fact that the mob did not kill Chuckie even though he alone among the suspects twice talked voluntarily to the FBI in August 1975, and spoke on TV and radio about the disappearance after 1975, made Sluss doubt that Chuckie had any firsthand knowledge to give up.

Sluss also apparently studied the timeline of Chuckie's activities during the afternoon of July 30 more carefully than the original investigators, and concluded that it was practically impossible for Chuckie to have picked up Hoffa at the Machus Red Fox based on his known whereabouts that afternoon. (Sluss never revealed to me his reasons for this conclusion, but he advised me to study the timeline closely.)

Sluss also came to doubt the validity of the hair and scent evidence in Joey Giacalone's car. This evidence would have been hard to use against Chuckie in a trial because it was sketchy on its own and because nine days passed between the last time he drove the car and the time the FBI impounded it, and the evidence might have been introduced during that interim period. But Sluss discovered explanations for this evidence that attenuated its significance further.

One thing the initial investigation team missed was that three weeks before the disappearance, during one of Anthony Giacalone's visits to the Lake, Josephine Hoffa asked Anthony Giacalone to help lay what she later described as a "large rug" in the main house that had previously been in the guesthouse, where Hoffa worked out. According to Josephine, Giacalone helped her in "putting the rug down."

Individuals shed approximately one hundred head hairs each day. Thousands of Hoffa's hairs could have been on the rug, a number of which would have been transferred to Giacalone's clothes when they laid the rug together, and perhaps during their earlier discussions as well. This is known as a "secondary hair transfer" in FBI lingo, since the hair is transferred to a "suspect" not from the "victim" directly but from some environment where the victim shed hair. "Contact between a victim and a suspect's environment can easily cause a secondary transfer of hair," explains an FBI academic treatment of the subject. So it is possible that Giacalone himself brought Hoffa's hair into his son's car in the weeks before the disappearance, when he was often in the car.

A similar explanation may account for why Hoffa's scent was detected in the car: through transfer to the car by Anthony Giacalone after his time with Hoffa, especially his removal of the rug. "Human scent is easily transferred from one object to another so that relationships between objects and people are sometimes unknowingly established," explains an FBI study. The study cautions that "a suspect identification made by a scent-discriminating canine only establishes that some form of relationship to the scent object exists," and not that the originator of the scent was present where the scent was picked up.

By late 1994, these and many other considerations had persuaded Sluss that the early Hoffa investigation's obsessive focus on Chuckie was misplaced and indeed had thrown the investigation off track. He thought the matter went "off the rails" on August 4, 1975, when James pointed the finger at Chuckie and offered the FBI a theory, accepted then and ever since, about the gap in Chuckie's day and about how Chuckie was one of the few people Hoffa would get in the car with.

Sluss wanted to focus the moribund Hoffa investigation in a more profitable direction based on other clues the FBI had developed. That meant moving Chuckie off the FBI's priority list. Sluss's idea was to approach Chuckie, tell him that he believed he was innocent, ask him to take a lie detector test in order to eliminate him as a suspect, and then, having gained his trust, hopefully get him to talk about what he might know about the disappearance. Sluss was aware of the test on Maury Povich's show. His reaction was the same one as the official FBI reaction to all privately conducted polygraph tests, even if done by a former government professional. He trusted only FBI polygraphs. Nonetheless, the Povich show "piqued my interest and certainly influenced my desire to polygraph Chuckie," Sluss told me.

One hurdle to this approach was that the Hoffa case was so low on the priority list that the Detroit field office was not willing to pay for even Sluss's trip to Florida to see Chuckie. So Sluss decided to vacation near Boca Raton and make an approach then. He got the sign-off from both the Detroit and Miami FBI offices and on February 13, 1995, knocked on Chuckie's door in Boca Raton, Florida. When no one answered, Sluss left the letter in which he told Chuckie he wanted to talk about the disappearance and announced that he did not think he was a suspect.

Chuckie was pleased to get the letter. But he did not call Sluss, who was hugely disappointed. Chuckie was finished dealing with the FBI.

About five years later, sometime in November 2000, and unbeknownst to the public, the FBI used techniques unavailable in 1975 to conclude that the hair found in Joey Giacalone's car did in fact share nuclear DNA with Hoffa (though the test could not make a more discriminating nuclear DNA match). The details of the test were never revealed, and the same old problem with using the hair evidence persisted: the nine-day gap between the Hoffa disappearance and the impoundment of the car, and the possibility of hair transfer via Anthony Giacalone. Nonetheless, the leadership of the FBI in Detroit discussed whether Chuckie should be prosecuted in light of the DNA evidence. Sluss resisted this course of action since he believed Chuckie was innocent, he believed the alternative explanation for the hair's discovery in the car, and he remained convinced that it was impossible for Chuckie to have picked up Hoffa on July 30.

But his bosses' persistent focus on Chuckie, and the Bureau's "institutional belief" in Chuckie's guilt, made it all the more important, in Sluss's mind, to clear him with a polygraph so he could refocus the investigation. When Anthony Giacalone died on February 23, 2001, Sluss decided to try again. He believed Chuckie could elucidate some elements of the case even if he was innocent of the crime due to his long association with Giacalone, and he hoped that Chuckie's lips might be looser since Uncle Tony had died, especially if Sluss could clear him as a suspect.

At 11:06 a.m. on August 13, 2001, with the approval once again of both the Detroit and Miami FBI, he knocked on the door of my mother's condominium, the venue for most of my conversations with Chuckie for this book. Sluss introduced himself and asked to chat. Chuckie had a doctor's appointment, but two hours later the two men and another agent, Steve Ferrari, met at a nearby hotel lobby and talked for several hours.

Chuckie insisted over and over to Sluss that he was "not involved in the Old Man's disappearance," and he berated Sluss for all of the evils that had befallen him in the last quarter century as a result of FBI harassment. Sluss told Chuckie that he agreed that he was innocent and asked him to take a lie detector test to prove it so he could move him off the suspect list. Chuckie took an improbable liking to Sluss, whom he started referring to affectionately as "Slush." Sluss was the first FBI representative in fifty years who treated Chuckie with respect and seemed to be on his side. Chuckie was desperate to clear his name and felt he had little to lose. So he told Sluss he would take the test.

That evening my mother had an allergic reaction to the idea. Chuckie had been out of the news for years. She didn't trust the FBI, which had treated him badly for decades. And she worried that taking a lie detector test, especially if he failed, would bring the world down on him, and her, again. She telephoned my younger brothers, who agreed. Chuckie wasn't going to do something Brenda didn't support. And so he called Sluss and declined the following day. "Due to personal problems with his wife and family he wanted to cancel the polygraph examination but he agreed he would take one at a later date concerning Hoffa's disappearance," Sluss wrote in his report.

My mother's worries seemed confirmed when, a month later, on September 7, 2001, *The Detroit News* reported the DNA hair match from a year and a half earlier. According to *The New York Times*, "Federal investigators said that the DNA work contradicted" Chuckie O'Brien's account of events and that "they could envision finally bringing charges in the case within the next couple of years." In light of this information, the Sluss visit the previous month seemed like an elaborate double cross, just as my mother had suspected. The Feds seemed to have new evidence, and to be on the verge of prosecuting Chuckie.

Sluss was furious that the DNA story leaked because he believed it had destroyed his credibility with Chuckie that he had been trying for years to build. And so he quickly wrote Chuckie the second, three-page handwritten letter, with a copy of the story, the morning it came out. "Many of the facts are wrong in the paper," Sluss wrote in his letter. "I have known the results of the DNA test for over a year and a half. This article really changes nothing." Sluss asked Chuckie once again to take a polygraph test in order to "allow me to focus the investigation in the proper direction." He then ended the letter: "*Except for you and your family* no one is ticked off as much as Steve and I are that this came out in the paper. I promised you this wouldn't happen, someone somewhere is responsible. I'm sorry."

Sluss's letter had much less impact on Chuckie than the new round of bad publicity about his involvement in Hoffa's disappearance. Chuckie still wanted a way to clear his name, but everyone around him thought the polygraph was a bad idea. In December, Chuckie told Sluss that he had decided not to take the test because, as Sluss reported in his memorandum on the matter, it was a "family consensus" that "the FBI was just trying to set him up." Sluss added that Chuckie "understood how our last visit got in the newspaper," since "some people always leak stuff they like to see in the newspaper." But Chuckie was not so sanguine. He told Sluss that if his family decided he should take it, he would. And he suggested that Sluss should contact his children—including me, a "professor at the University of Chicago Law School." (This was the suggestion that led Sluss to call me when I was in the Department of Defense.)

Over the next several months, at the request of the Detroit U.S. attorney and the special agent in charge in Detroit, Sluss wrote the summary of the evidence against Chuckie, including the grand jury information. The memo was the basis for his senior leadership in Detroit to make a final decision whether Chuckie should be prosecuted in light of the new DNA information. Sluss's original draft concluded that it was essentially impossible for Chuckie to have had the time to pick up Hoffa. "The original conclusion was practically unequivocal and very strongly worded," he told me.

But Sluss's superiors ordered him to change the conclusion to weaken the bottom line. The final, compromise language was as follows: "The evidence in this case does not provide a clear-cut answer to Charles Lenton O'Brien's guilt in this matter. Giving O'Brien the benefit of the doubt and using his statements regarding the times and locations he traveled to on July 30, 1975 leaves a narrow window of time when he could have picked up James Riddle Hoffa, and driven Hoffa to a nearby location."

After examining Sluss's memo and the evidence, including the new hair evidence, federal and state authorities decided that they lacked sufficient evidence to prosecute Chuckie. On March 28, 2002, the special agent in charge of Detroit's FBI office announced that "there is no viable federal prosecution at this time." In August, Oakland County (Detroit) prosecutor David Gorcyca announced that state officials would not bring a prosecution against Chuckie either.

Chuckie was out of legal jeopardy. But Sluss was not able to clear him from suspicion.

A DECADE LATER, soon after Chuckie first told me about Sluss's letters to him, I contacted Sluss to find out what the letters signified. On April 25,

2012, I found myself in a cramped, box-filled conference room with three agents in the FBI building in dilapidated downtown Detroit.

One agent was Sluss, who wore a white shirt and thin tie, and had a jocular open face behind his close-cropped silvery hair and beard. Sluss had by then left the Hoffa case and was now an associate division counsel in the Detroit office, but was present in the room because he was my contact and was also the office expert on all things Hoffa. Next to him sat Louis Fischetti, the organized crime squad supervisor for the Detroit office. Fischetti was wearing jeans and a goatee and packing a pistol on his belt. He was both ornery and sarcastic and had a self-deprecating manner. "I'm just a guy who got lucky and passed the test," he told me then and in several subsequent meetings. The boyish-looking third agent, Neil Gavin, was now the case agent for the Hoffa file.

I sat down, briefly apologized to Sluss for being short on the phone a decade earlier, and explained my business. "I am not here as an attorney, but rather as a son," I said. "I don't think Chuckie had anything to do with the disappearance, and I want to learn why you sent him those letters and why you asked him to take a polygraph."

Sluss responded in a slow, deliberate manner, smiling as he spoke. "When I was the Hoffa case agent in the early to mid-1990s, I reread the entire Hoffa case file, including the grand jury testimony," he explained. "I discovered when and why Charles O'Brien became a suspect, and I think it was a mistake that put the investigation on the wrong track."

The other agents were watching me closely, apparently for my reaction.

"I do not think Mr. O'Brien was involved in the disappearance," Sluss continued. "The FBI knows where he was that day and it knows where Jimmy Hoffa was that day. It is a physical impossibility that Mr. O'Brien was with Hoffa when he disappeared." Sluss then explained that Chuckie might be able to help the FBI in the investigation by telling what he knew about others who might be involved. He said he hoped Chuckie would agree to an interview and to take a polygraph examination so that the FBI could "formally eliminate O'Brien as a suspect."

I was stunned. *A physical impossibility that Chuckie was with Hoffa when he disappeared.* That was a definitive statement from an FBI agent without weasel words. *Formally eliminate O'Brien as a suspect.* That sounded even better.

"Do you agree with that?" I asked Fischetti. He was the senior person in Detroit assigned to the Hoffa investigation. I would later learn that he had been obsessively seeking Hoffa's killers since 1993, when he entered the Bureau. "All I can say now," he responded cautiously, "is that it would help us to eliminate Mr. O'Brien as a suspect if he agrees to answer a few questions on the polygraph." He also emphasized that an interview with Chuckie could help the FBI better understand the disappearance even if he weren't involved.

The agents didn't say anything concrete about how they might clear Chuckie's name, and I walked out of the FBI building with little optimism. I telephoned Chuckie that evening to tell him that the FBI no longer thought he was involved but it wanted him to take a lie detector test.

I advised against it. "I doubt we can trust them to do anything in return," I said.

Chuckie felt like the FBI had been screwing him for five decades, especially since the Hoffa disappearance, and he didn't question my judgment. "Okay" was all he said in reply.

Over the course of the next year, however, Chuckie often asked me, in roundabout ways, how he could clear his name. "Your only option is through the FBI" was my standard reply. By the beginning of 2013, with his diabetes worsening and his life seemingly drawing to a close, this option grew more attractive. He had for many reasons declined to take an FBI lie detector test in August 1975. But now, at the end of his life, he had nothing to lose.

"Fuck, I took a lie detector test on nationwide television, why the fuck wouldn't I do it with the FBI?" he said to me one day. "Maury Povich had the best guy in that business. I just don't want to make a big thing out of it. I don't want to get Mom all worked up."

I met with Fischetti and Sluss on April Fool's Day of 2013 and explained that Chuckie might be prepared to answer questions and take a lie detector test, depending on what they were offering in return. The agents told me that if Chuckie was truthful he would receive a letter stating that he is not a target or subject of the investigation. I told them that if that was the official offer from the entire Justice Department, including the lawyers in the U.S. Attorney's Office, we might be able to do business.

While waiting to hear back, I did due diligence on Chuckie's legal exposure.

I spoke with several former prosecutors, including my friend the future FBI director James Comey, who was then working at Bridgewater Associates. Most were skeptical. They doubted the efficacy of polygraphs, they said the FBI held all the cards, and some speculated that the government might use Chuckie's words against him. Mike Morganroth, an experienced Detroit lawyer whom I would soon hire to represent Chuckie, was against the idea at first for just these reasons.

My Harvard colleague the criminal defense maven Alan Dershowitz agreed with the pessimistic assessments, but was more pragmatic. "I doubt there's much of a realistic downside," Dersh told me. "If he really wanted to do it for his legacy, I wouldn't say absolutely no." Morganroth began to change his mind when he learned that the offer had come from the FBI in Detroit rather than in Florida. He grew more open to it when I told him that I had learned that the assistant U.S. attorney who was working with the FBI agents to offer Chuckie the deal was Eric Straus, a prosecutor Mike trusted. After Mike spoke with Straus, he saw relatively little downside. "Eric is a man of his word and the possibility of an exonerating letter in exchange for a truthful interview is real," he told me. "I don't think this is a setup."

I also worried about Chuckie's health. He was seventy-nine. He used a walker to get around. Stress made his sugar go through the roof. And as I had learned from many national security officials of undoubted integrity who had taken polygraphs, strapping on wires and answering questions is enormously stressful even when one has nothing to hide. Morganroth gave me some comfort when he said that the government probably wouldn't put Chuckie through the polygraph if he spoke truthfully in his interview. But even the interview worried me—not because I thought Chuckie had anything to hide at this point, but because the experience of being grilled by officials he mistrusted in a legally risky, adversarial context is inherently traumatic. I wasn't sure he would hold up, emotionally or physically.

ON APRIL 17, 2013, Mike and I met Eric Straus in the Detroit federal building. Straus explained that the FBI and the U.S. Attorney's Office would like to interview Chuckie about the disappearance and, if necessary following the interview, conduct a lie detector test. "If Mr. O'Brien answers the questions truthfully and to our satisfaction, my office is prepared to send a letter stating that he is not a target or suspect in the investigation," Straus said. He acknowledged that such a letter would be unusual, but he said that the circumstances were unusual. He added without prompting that he was personally confident that Chuckie was uninvolved in the disappearance. "My office might be prepared to send Mr. O'Brien the requested letter even without the FBI," Straus said.

After Straus and Mike discussed further ground rules for the interview, I made one additional point. "Chuckie is old and frail, and this will be a very traumatic experience for him," I said. "I want to make sure that everyone in the government is on board for this, all the way to the Justice Department, before I put him through this." Straus assured me that he had approval in his office, and he said he would get it from all other appropriate authorities, including the Criminal Division in the Justice Department, before our meeting.

I left Straus's office thinking for the first time that this might actually work. My optimism grew when we received an email from Straus a few weeks later, on May 2, 2013. In it Straus said that he "envision[ed]" a letter that would "include language—approved by the U.S. Attorney—stating that Mr. O'Brien is not a subject, target, or suspect in the disappearance of Hoffa," as long as the government was satisfied that Chuckie "made truthful statements" and concluded that he "was not involved in the disappearance of James Riddle Hoffa on July 30, 1975." Straus also implied the government would get Chuckie an answer quickly. "We only ask that after the interview we have time to review and discuss" what Chuckie said, to determine whether a "follow-up or polygraph is necessary," and to "meet with my Office's leadership." These were not tentative or preliminary views. They were the settled position of the government before the interview, which would occur the following day, on May 3.

I flew to Detroit from Boston the morning before the interview and met Chuckie at the airport. When I saw him entering the baggage claim area in a wheelchair, I thought the interview and lie detector test might be a mistake. I don't know if it was his seventy-nine years, the stress of a three-hour flight from West Palm Beach, or anxiety about talking with the government. But his face was grayer, his eyelids lower, and his eyes more sunken than I had ever seen. He was also quieter than usual as I struggled to get him in the rental car.

"They are going to ask the same kind of questions you've been asked before," I said during the ride to our hotel in the Detroit suburbs. "Not only the FBI guys but the prosecutor as well told me that they think it's impossible that you were involved and that there was a mistake made forty years ago. They're willing to give you this letter, but you've got to go through this process."

"No problem. I want that fucking letter," Chuckie said.

Chuckie scowled when I told him the interview would take place in the downtown federal building. He hated the idea of walking into the enemy's camp, but what he really hated was that someone might see him walking in and think he was a rat. And he still didn't understand why he might have to take a lie detector test since he had already taken and passed one on *The Maury Povich Show* two decades earlier.

"I know the guy was an expert, but the government can't rely on it," I said.

"Fuck the government," Chuckie shot back, in his usual form.

"Don't get in that mood," I said. "These guys tomorrow are your friends. This is a very unusual thing that is happening."

"They owe it to me," Chuckie said. "Thirty-eight years of my life they tried to fuck me around."

I couldn't disagree with that statement.

Chuckie and I spent our free day together visiting places in and around Detroit he hadn't seen in almost four decades. After driving by the building that used to house Tocco's fruit and vegetable business, where his mom, Sylvia, got her first Detroit job and met the Detroit family, we stopped by Holy Trinity Church on Porter Street. Chuckie occasionally attended this church as a boy and used to listen, mesmerized, to Father Clement Kern, the famous "labor priest." When he took the alabaster statue of St. Theresa from the customhouse that landed him an indictment in 1963, he donated it to Kern at this church.

We then drove a mile to the cluster of Teamsters office buildings on Trumbull Avenue that served as Jimmy Hoffa's bustling headquarters back in the day. Chuckie remembers the offices at labor's apex in the late 1950s as "beehives of activity." Union members parked their semis for blocks in every direction to congregate and socialize at the union hall, and Hoffa would often come out of his office and greet "the men." By 2013 membership had dropped off sharply from Local 299's heyday. The parking lots were nearly empty and the area around the buildings seemed deserted. "Look at those fuckin' union halls, nobody around them," Chuckie said, shaking his head.

The next stop was Hoffa's unassuming home on 16154 Robson Street. The neighborhood was a bit run-down, but the house looked pretty much the same as when Chuckie's young family lived there with the entire Hoffa family in the late 1950s and early 1960s. Chuckie told me how they all squeezed into the tiny abode, and how his mom would sometimes come over and cook for everyone, and how Barbara dressed there for her wedding. The Robson house was a place of happy memories.

We then traveled further north to the suburbs, to the Bloomfield Plaza, where the Machus Red Fox still stood, renamed Andiamo. Chuckie showed me the spot where he sat most mornings in July 1975, including the mornings of and after the Hoffa disappearance, awaiting Bobby Holmes Jr. We then entered the restaurant for lunch. Chuckie used to eat often at the Machus Red Fox, since Marvin and Betty Adell lived nearby, and it was once a place for fun times. But of course since July 30, 1975, that building had a different meaning to him. He seemed sanguine when we first walked in, noting that the restaurant was a "popular joint" in the 1970s and explaining how the internal decor had changed in the new restaurant. But as we sat at our table, his mood changed. I asked what was wrong.

"You have to remember I'm going to be eighty years old and I'm shaking my brain, I'm going back to when I was nine and ten," he said. "This morning, I sat in that car and I kept looking at everything and I went back to when I was young and when I'd go to Father Kern's church and it's all changed. I got frightened."

We made small talk for a bit and ate, and then Hoffa's disappearance came up.

"Is this the first time you have been here since the disappearance?" I asked.

He nodded slowly.

"Is it weird to be here?" I continued.

"Definitely," he replied, sarcastically. "I'll sleep with one eye open now."

I asked why. Chuckie grew more serious. But he couldn't articulate his feelings very well.

"This brings a lot back, Jack," he said slowly. "This morning, all the changes. Now here. If you were in my body you'd understand. I'm going back in my life."

"And?" I pressed him.

"Tough to go back, Jack," he said, with one of the saddest faces I had ever seen. "I miss him so much. It breaks my heart."

By the time we finished lunch, I had concluded that our tour down memory lane was a mistake and proposed that we call it a day. But Chuckie insisted that we drive twenty miles north to our final destination, Hoffa's cottage in Lake Orion, along the same basic route that Hoffa traveled, in the opposite direction, on his last day on earth. The Lake was the place of Chuckie's happiest memories with Jimmy Hoffa—his first weekend with Hoffa as a young boy, and the decades there during the good ol' days. It was also a spot of his most miserable moments—the years stuck at the Lake with the cantankerous, self-destructive Hoffa after prison, and the late-night confrontation with James the evening after the disappearance in 1975.

Chuckie was nonetheless excited as we drove to the end of the long road that opened at the Lake. When we pulled up, he saw that everything had changed for the worse. He would point with pride over the next fifteen minutes to the things still standing that he helped build over the years— the many additions to the cottage itself, now in disrepair; a barn for Barbara's daughter's pony, also in terrible shape; a seawall "you couldn't move with dynamite." But he felt the place looked like "trash." The buildings were run-down, the tennis court was gone, and the lawn that he and Hoffa had manicured over the years to look "like Augusta National" was now

279 | FAILED VINDICATION

unkempt and marked by large dirt spaces, tire tracks, and old, seemingly abandoned cars.

Chuckie was unhappy and agitated as we returned to our hotel in Birmingham.

THE NEXT MORNING we drove down Woodward Avenue, the traditional thoroughfare to downtown that is known as "the spine of Detroit." I wish I had taken Interstate 75 instead, for it turned into yet another bad experience. Chuckie had known Woodward Avenue in its heyday, and his, from the 1940s through the 1960s, when it was dotted with bustling retail stores, crowded museums, and beautiful churches and apartment buildings that reflected Detroit's prosperity. He had not traveled down Woodward in decades, and what he saw—block after block of razed, abandoned, or burned-out buildings, as well as run-down churches and unkempt, out-of-place museums—shocked and saddened him even more than what he saw the day before.

"Jesus Christ, this is terrible," he said. "A disgrace. I never want to see this again." Chuckie was nervous about the interview, and the trip down Woodward didn't help. I imagined that the tough memories the day before followed by the ruins of Detroit reminded him of the arc of his life as he journeyed to a meeting that would be his final shot to redeem himself.

We reached the federal building downtown and parked. Wearing maroon sweatpants, a white T-shirt, a dark leather jacket, and dark glasses, Chuckie shuffled inside for his first formal interview with the government about the Hoffa disappearance in almost thirty-nine years. We met Mike Morganroth and took the elevator to the twenty-first floor, where we were taken to a bright conference room overlooking the Detroit River to Canada.

On one side of the long table sat Assistant U.S. Attorney Eric Straus, FBI agent Louis Fischetti, and Fischetti's "student," which was Chuckie's term for the young FBI agent in charge of the Hoffa case, Marc Silski, who took notes on a legal pad but otherwise remained quiet. "Slush" was not there because he was no longer on the Hoffa case.

As Chuckie walked in, the three government officials rose. Fischetti, who was wearing a tie for the first time in our many meetings, grinned wide-eyed at Chuckie, as if he were meeting a favorite rock star for the first time. Straus too had a pleased smile on his face. Chuckie shuffled by, shook everyone's hands, made a few FBI jokes, and sat down across the table from the officials, next to Mike. I sat at the end of the table with my back to the window.

Straus started the meeting by opening a large white roll of paper that contained a detailed timeline of Chuckie's whereabouts on the day of the disappearance. He reiterated the old concern about an unaccounted-for block of time when no witnesses saw Chuckie. "What can you tell us about that day?" he asked.

Chuckie told them quite a lot. He complained about his "fucked-up memory," but he went over much of the day in long digressive detail on the same terms as thirty-eight years earlier. He talked about "sitting like a jackass" at the end of the Bloomfield Plaza, and what an idiot he would be to go there the day after the disappearance if he had done the crime. He talked a lot about the "fucking fish" that he delivered to Violet Holmes and which, he said, ruined his life by bringing him to the suburbs that afternoon. Of the trip to Jax Kar Wash to get Joey's car cleaned, he said, "Thank God I kept that ticket." He also recounted the confrontational argument with James at the Lake the evening after the disappearance.

This was all warm-up. Straus then asked him directly if he saw Jimmy Hoffa on July 30, 1975, or was involved in any way in the disappearance. Chuckie said no straightforwardly, and then added, "If I were with him I wouldn't be here today." After a pause, Chuckie then fell into a meandering, unstoppable twenty-five-minute tangent about Jimmy Hoffa—what a great labor leader he was, his most successful organizing techniques, how popular and smart he was, how he "didn't drink or mess around," how the government "fucked him," about Chuckie's visits to see Hoffa in Lewisburg prison, how Hoffa knew very well about the Nixon condition but pretended he didn't, and how he, Chuckie, would always do "anything he could to protect him."

At this point Fischetti interjected to ask a series of questions that were, unbeknownst to Chuckie, probably the most important of the meeting. He first asked if Chuckie ever drove Anthony Giacalone from Detroit to Miami or in the other direction. "Sure," Chuckie said, describing in detail the trips he and Uncle Tony took, and how he would drive while Uncle Tony would

sing Frank Sinatra songs all day long. Fischetti later said that he had been following Chuckie on two of those trips.

Fischetti then asked Chuckie whether he drove Uncle Tony's brother,
Vito, in South Florida or between South Florida and Detroit, to which
Chuckie responded once again in the affirmative and explained in detail. (I
did not realize it at the time, but Fischetti was asking in part about the car trip
where Chuckie spoke about the *Hoffa* movie in a way that seemed exonerating to one FBI agent.) It appeared to me that Fischetti was testing Chuckie to
see if he would tell the truth about matters involving mobsters that he might
not have known the FBI knew about. Chuckie was candid in answering those
questions and acknowledged that he knew numerous LCN members, though
he never described them that way.

The interview lasted four hours and covered dozens of topics. Chuckie
answered every question without hesitation. Near the end, Fischetti, who appeared to be in a very good mood, told Chuckie a story about when he surveilled
him from inside an FBI truck at Anthony Giacalone's funeral, at St. Michael's
Catholic Church in Sterling Heights, Michigan, on February 27, 2001.

The truck was parked with a view of the church entrance and had a side
window through which Fischetti was watching the comings and goings of
attendants at the funeral and snapping pictures. As Chuckie and two other
gentlemen emerged from the church after the funeral and came into view,
Fischetti's camera jammed and he missed the picture. At just that moment,
Fischetti said, Chuckie looked at the truck and, realizing it was a surveillance
vehicle, flipped the FBI his middle finger. Everyone in the conference room at
the U.S. Attorney's Office howled with laughter.

At the end of the interview, as Mike had predicted, Eric Straus said there
would be no need for a lie detector test that day. "We will deliberate as soon as
possible and get back to you about next steps," he said. Chuckie, Mike, and I
walked out of the federal building confident that Chuckie had upheld his end
of the bargain.

SEVERAL WEEKS PASSED and we heard nothing. Mike finally contacted
Straus. He acknowledged that Chuckie had done well in the interview and

said that his office had had trouble finding a time when all the relevant attorneys could meet to discuss the case.

After a few more months of delay, good news came on July 15. Mike left me a voice mail that said Straus had told him that the U.S. Attorney's Office had agreed that Chuckie had spoken truthfully, and it was prepared to issue a letter stating that Chuckie was not a target or suspect in the Hoffa investigation. "All three people in U.S. attorneys panel, and the U.S. attorney, approved it," Mike told me. Straus told Mike that his office was "waiting for the FBI to sign off," which "hopefully will happen sometime today."

To my amazement, Chuckie's exoneration seemed imminent. But Chuckie's lifelong bad luck bit him once again.

A month earlier, and about six weeks after Chuckie's interview, the FBI had spent three days digging for Hoffa's remains based on a tip from Anthony Zerilli, a former Detroit underboss. Zerilli had been in prison at the time of the disappearance but claimed to have learned after he was released that Hoffa was abducted and taken to a farm twenty miles north of the Machus Red Fox, where he was buried alive. The FBI pursued the tip, but as with scores of similar digs in the nearly four decades since Hoffa's disappearance, it found nothing. "We did not uncover any evidence relevant to the investigation on James Hoffa," an embarrassed Robert Foley, the head of the FBI in Detroit, told the press.

Foley's humiliation could not have come at a worse time for Chuckie, because he was the man who needed to approve the letter from the FBI. Foley would retire a few months later. He was already going out on a down note after the failed dig, and, Straus implied to me, he didn't want to add to his humiliation by making his last major act an acknowledgment that the FBI had been pursuing the wrong man in the Hoffa investigation for nearly thirty-nine years.

Foley's failure to sign off followed by his transfer killed the momentum to clear Chuckie. The federal prosecutors told Mike they would need to wait for a new head of the FBI's Detroit office to be appointed and get up to speed. Paul Abbate was named to the post in October, but for the six months following his arrival the government gave one excuse after another for delaying a decision.

Finally, in early March 2014, ten months after Chuckie's interview, the U.S. attorney in Detroit, Barbara McQuade, called Mike to say that she had met with Abbate and a final decision had been made: Chuckie would not get a chance to take a lie detector test, and he would not receive an exonerating letter. McQuade did not explain why she had changed her mind from the previous summer, and she did not suggest that Chuckie had not been truthful. Rather, she said that the FBI had decided not to sign off on the letter, and she had agreed. The only reason she gave was that Andrew Sluss had never been authorized to contact Chuckie with the offer of a polygraph test to clear his name.

I didn't know at the time what behind-the-scenes machinations derailed Chuckie's chances, but this was a laughable excuse. Sluss was my initial point of contact. But Chuckie's agreement to interview with the government, and the expectations surrounding that interview, had nothing to do with Sluss. The agreement had been made with the U.S. Attorney's Office and approved by the FBI office in Detroit. Sluss was not in the four-hour interview that took place a few doors down from McQuade's office. Rather, the FBI had been represented there by the agent officially assigned to the Hoffa case and the Detroit office's organized crime squad supervisor. In phone calls with Mike Morganroth over many months after the interview, McQuade and Straus sent only positive signals about their belief in Chuckie's innocence, and never suggested any problem due to Sluss's involvement two decades earlier.

When Mike called to tell me the bad news about McQuade's decision, I was enormously disappointed. I knew that Chuckie was out of options—there could be no further appeal. But Mike also told me that McQuade, whom I had never met, was willing to talk with me about her decision. I called her up and told her I would prefer to speak in person rather than on the phone, and she very reluctantly agreed. And so on March 11, 2014, I flew to Detroit and went to the federal building. I entered a conference room adjacent to McQuade's office, where the U.S. attorney for Detroit and Eric Straus were waiting.

McQuade seemed exasperated from the outset of our meeting, probably since she was not in the habit of having to explain decisions of this sort at any length, much less twice.

"Mr. O'Brien was promised consideration by the U.S. Attorney's Office, and he received that consideration," she said. "I am sorry it did not work out, but my decision is final."

"But I understand that everyone in the meeting believed Chuckie was truthful, and we were told that if he was truthful about his involvement in the disappearance, he would get the letter," I replied.

McQuade didn't deny that Chuckie had been truthful, and she acknowledged that Straus had lobbied hard for the letter. But she repeated that Chuckie had been promised only a consideration for the letter, nothing more. And she added that Andrew Sluss had not been authorized to make the contact on behalf of the FBI.

"That's a preposterous reason," I said. I noted that the arrangement for Chuckie's interview had not been made with Sluss, but rather with her office and Sluss's superiors in the FBI.

McQuade's face reddened. "I will tell you that the reason it took so long for us to decide was that we worried a lot about the perception that the U.S. Attorney's Office does not abide by its promises, and the impact that might have on the willingness of people under investigation to talk to us," she said.

This was a damning admission, for it implied that the government had agreed to give Chuckie the letter in exchange for a truthful interview and had reneged on that promise. I was on the verge of asking McQuade to explain that discrepancy. I also wanted to ask why she had been prepared to sign the letter last summer but had now changed her mind, and why Chuckie was never given his promised chance to state his innocence while examined on a polygraph. But I didn't see the advantage in "gotchas" at this point, especially since McQuade, who had absolute power over the matter, was growing more impatient by the moment. And so I made only a final request.

"Chuckie is not well, he is at the end of his life, he came up here and did everything you asked, and no one thinks he lied," I said. "Is there any mechanism short of a letter in which you could convey to him that you do not believe he was involved in the Hoffa disappearance?" I asked. "We are not going to make any of this public anytime soon, if that is what you are worried about," I added. I suspected that was precisely what they were worried about.

"I have already told Mike Morganroth that Chuckie is not a target or subject in this investigation," said Eric Straus, speaking for the first time, and in the present tense.

"Do you agree with that?" I quickly asked McQuade. Her face was by now very dark red. "That's his opinion," she snapped. "And the decision is mine."

I rarely get angry. But as I descended in the elevator, I was furious at the government's bait and switch. "Snookered" was the subject heading of my email to Morganroth that summarized the meeting.

Chuckie had been so close to receiving the exoneration he had sought for thirty-nine years. He had fallen short even though the career officials who had been working the case for many years thought he was innocent. And he had fallen short, it seemed, only because political appointees in the FBI and the U.S. Attorney's Office didn't want to take the political heat from admitting the government's errors during the last four decades.

I always worried that at the end of the day no one in the government would want to take responsibility for letting Chuckie off the hook. But I had allowed myself to have some hope because so many officials told me and Mike that they thought Chuckie was innocent and that he would be exonerated if he told the truth. I never discovered exactly what happened to deny him exoneration, and I don't know enough to claim that any particular person in the government acted in bad faith. But there is no doubt that the government as a whole acted outrageously in representing to Chuckie the belief that he was innocent; in inviting him in his ill health to Detroit for a protracted and legally fraught interview with a promise that he could vindicate himself before a lie detector and that a decision would come shortly; in representing after the interview that he did well and that the exoneration was forthcoming; and then in delaying ten months before informing him, without any good reason, that it would not in fact give him a chance to take the test to clear his name.

Still fuming on my way to the airport after my meeting with McQuade and Straus, I telephoned Louis Fischetti at the FBI to talk about what had just happened.

"You told me over and over again that you weren't a bullshitter, and I believed you!" I screamed at Fischetti. "Chuckie did everything you asked, and you believed him, but you didn't follow through as promised," I added.

"I was not bullshitting you," he replied. "I got my wings clipped."

"I can understand why the political guys wouldn't want to take the heat," I said. I was just about to add that I didn't understand why they had put Chuckie through all this at his age when Fischetti interrupted.

"I can't understand it," he said in the middle of my sentence, acknowledging that politics was the reason the letter never came.

The next day I called Chuckie to tell him the bad news. He hid what must have been colossal disappointment. "Those motherfuckers have been screwing me for fifty years," he said with resignation. "I never thought they were going to give me the letter."

TWELVE

OMERTÀ

T HE NOVEMBER AFTER THE MEETING IN DETROIT, I flew to Boca Raton because Brenda was in the hospital. She and my brother Brett had been on a fishing trip on Lake Ouachita in Arkansas, twenty miles from the spot where, thirty-nine years earlier, our family was fishing when Jimmy Hoffa disappeared. Brenda grew short of breath near the end of the trip and suffered a "silent" heart attack on the plane ride home. When I walked into her room the following morning in the Boca Raton Regional Hospital, she was weak, punctured with tubes, and still had trouble breathing. She was upbeat, however, since the doctors had told her she would recover.

But Chuckie, who was also in the room, was a wreck. Every time I saw him his face was grayer, his stoop lower, and his gait slower. This time he was also panicky and weepy about Brenda's health. "Why did she have to go on that fucking fishing trip?" he asked with a crumpled face. Chuckie was distraught not just about my mother's health, I sensed, but also about the prospect of life without her, and maybe about the short time he believed he had left.

"Take him to lunch," my mother whispered, when Chuckie went to the bathroom. "The food will calm him down."

I drove Chuckie to his favorite eating spot in Boca Raton—Seasons 52. He liked to go there because he knew the staff. "Hey, Red, how ya doing, honey?" he said to the auburn-haired receptionist as he shuffled with his walker through the restaurant entrance. "How's your boy?"

Chuckie's need to be chummy and appear in the know with his many "friends" once bugged me. But when "Red" seemed pleased to see him and asked about his family, I shook my head and laughed.

After we were seated in a booth in the middle of the busy restaurant, I ordered grilled salmon and Chuckie ordered a cup of black bean soup and a turkey burger. For the next fifteen minutes, we discussed Brenda's health, my family, and the weather. Chuckie's mood picked up when the conversation moved to our time together when I was a boy—my "Jack O'Brien" period.

"We had some fun in those days," he said wistfully. I agreed.

The conversation meandered to my middle school years, and to the times that Anthony Giacalone had picked up me and my brothers at Florida Air Academy and taken us to lunch. The mention of Giacalone, in turn, led me to make a stray remark about the FBI interview in Detroit.

"Those FBI guys in Detroit, that week you were there, it's pretty clear they think Uncle Tony and Uncle Billy [i.e., Vito Giacalone] did it, and they don't think that Provenzano had anything to do with it," I said.

Chuckie continued to eat his soup and didn't respond for several seconds.

"Provenzano had a lot to do with it," he finally said in a low voice, talking through the spoonful of black beans in his mouth, staring intently at the bowl. "I'm just telling you this," he added, again in a low voice, still looking down.

I was gobsmacked. Chuckie had deflected talk about Provenzano's role in Hoffa's disappearance so assuredly for so many years that I couldn't believe he had uttered those words.

"And Uncle Tony didn't?" I asked, after another silence, unsure if Chuckie would continue. I was referring to Giacalone. "How could Provenzano do something in Detroit?" Provenzano was a capo in the Genovese family in New York. He wasn't supposed to act in Detroit, Giacalone's territory, without permission from the Detroit bosses.

"He'd get the okay," Chuckie said, still looking away from me.

"But who'd he get the okay from if it wasn't Uncle Tony?" I continued. My heart was starting to race, since Chuckie was for the first time being candid about what he knew about the disappearance.

"He got the okay from the guys that run his people," he said.

"From Uncle Tony's bosses? I thought you had to get the okay from someone in . . ." I was trying to ask whether the Detroit family had approved a hit in Detroit.

"New York," Chuckie said, referring either to one of the crime families headquartered there, probably the Genovese family, or the Commission itself. "New York had to approve it. The decision would be made in New York. They didn't give a shit once they made the decision."

Prior to this conversation, Chuckie had told me a lot of things about the run-up to the disappearance—especially about Hoffa's irrational actions in the year before he vanished, and the difficult spot he, Chuckie, was in at the time. But in hundreds of conversations about the disappearance itself he had said practically nothing of interest other than to deny his involvement along the basic lines of what he told the FBI in 1975.

In our entirely unexpected seventy-five-minute conversation at Seasons 52, however, Chuckie told me most of what I have reported in this book about what he knew or believed about Hoffa's disappearance: who ordered it, Tony Pro's role, the tasks Anthony Giacalone gave him after the disappearance, the real reason for his trip to Washington to see Fitz after the disappearance, his meeting with Provenzano and Giacalone at Provenzano's Hallandale Beach home, and more.

I couldn't believe it when Chuckie began to reveal thirty-nine-year-old secrets. He spoke plainly and directly, and with unusual calm and focus and clarity, about at least some of what he knew about the disappearance.

Why now? Was it my mother's illness? His fear of death?

I never figured that out. But after this lunch, I knew more about the disappearance conspiracy, I believed more intently that Chuckie did not pick Hoffa up on July 30, 1975, and I understood much more clearly Chuckie's tragic predicament after the disappearance. I also now faced a predicament of my own.

ABOUT A YEAR after my Seasons 52 lunch with Chuckie, I met the four original FBI investigators on the Hoffa case in New York City. They were all retired, and an impressive lot: Robert Garrity, the thoughtful, highly respected agent who led the case in Detroit, where he interviewed Chuckie twice within weeks of the disappearance; his physically imposing but taciturn Detroit colleague, Jim Esposito, who publicly swore in August 1975 that he believed Chuckie drove Hoffa to his death; Al Sproule, the chisel-jawed expert on East Coast crime families who led the New York corner of the investigation; and the thin, bespectacled Jim Dooley, the brainiest of this unusually brainy bunch, who covered the case in New Jersey.

The four agents had been young men in their late twenties and early thirties, about a decade younger than Chuckie, when they were assigned to the Hoffa investigation in 1975. For several years they worked the case hard, day after frustrating day, pursuing Chuckie and other suspects. They never discovered what happened, of course, and they eventually moved on to other matters in their long and successful careers. But throughout those careers, and deep into retirement, they never stopped thinking about the Hoffa case, never stopped trying to solve it, and never stopped being haunted by their inability to do so.

"It's been 39 years since Hoffa disappeared," Garrity said in an email to me and his colleagues on the morning of July 30, 2014. "What the hell have you been doing?" he joked. "We should know what happened by now."

To which Dooley responded, more seriously: "39 years later and only the shadow knows for sure; but at least I've managed to shrug off some of the guilt for not knowing what the shadow refuses to reveal."

Guilt might seem like a strong emotion for failure to solve one of the most brilliantly executed murders in American history. But the four agents were, even in retirement, idealistic about the FBI's mission. "The FBI at its best solves puzzles," Sproule told me. "We were on the biggest puzzle of all time, a huge puzzle, and we didn't solve it. We made accomplishments along the way, but we never got to the heart of the matter."

I had met the agents several years earlier through Garrity, whose passion for solving the Hoffa case never abated. "I don't think about the disappearance every day, but I think about it every week," he told me at age seventy-seven.

The five of us learned a great deal from one another about the Hoffa case during several lunches in New York City over many years, usually at Keens Steakhouse. Improbably, we became friends.

On this occasion, I greeted the FBI men at the Harvard Club, where I'd reserved a room for a full day of conversations to discuss a slew of old government documents I'd obtained about the Hoffa case.

When I met the agents in the lobby, they were better dressed than usual, decked out in sports coats they had mothballed at retirement but that the club's dress code required. As we walked through the building, the former G-men gawked at the trappings of the stuffy club—the wide staircase and high chandeliered ceilings, the deep crimson walls and wing chairs and carpet, the dozens of portraits of serious-looking men, most from another era, and the long shelves of old books in grand rooms. It was not exactly their scene. They were intelligent and learned, but they were not Ivy Leaguers. They were practical, unpretentious men who had spent their lives not in clubs and academic halls, but in faceless government offices and in the streets, working informants, running wires, writing reports, tracking leads, hunting thugs.

Our day together was productive. Near the end I explained in detail why I did not believe Chuckie was involved in Hoffa's disappearance. Garrity and Esposito, who pursued Chuckie in Detroit, remained unconvinced but seemed to be having doubts. "If you are right, we made a giant mistake," Garrity told me. "We glommed on to a guy and failed to focus on other theories."

(Four and a half years later, after reading a draft of this book, Esposito told me that he no longer believed Chuckie was involved in Hoffa's disappearance.)

By the time of the Harvard Club meeting, Sproule and Dooley, who saw the case from a wider lens, had come to believe that Chuckie played no role. Dooley expressed regret about the pain the FBI caused Chuckie over the decades. "For some reason the gods just decided to position him where so much of his life would be chewed up in the clash between an implacable government and an implacable Mafia," he told me. "He was trapped in a web of fate and I honestly don't believe that, given where Chuckie found himself by circumstance, we had any choice but to try to figure out how those circumstances fit into the larger picture of Hoffa versus the Mafia, Fitzsimmons, and the Teamsters."

Just as clearly, Dooley believed, Chuckie had no choice but the course of silence that he took after July 30, 1975. "What was the alternative for Chuckie? The rest of his and his family's life in South Dakota with the Marshal's Service on his speed dialer. If Chuckie had come to be viewed as a threat of any kind, Giacalone would have been no more able to protect him than he was able to protect Hoffa. There is only so much that can be asked of one man."

CHUCKIE AND THE FOUR original agents on the Hoffa case were not the only ones whose lives were changed "down to the roots," as Dooley put it, by the unresolved mystery of the Hoffa disappearance.

Hoffa's immediate family had a terrible time. Starting in late 1976, Chuckie occasionally visited Josephine Hoffa in Miami before she died in 1980. He would take her to church some Sundays, help her buy groceries, and chat about the good old days and her missing husband. Josephine was declining, and would often cry and ask Chuckie over and over, "Where's my Jimmy?" Chuckie told her over and over that he didn't know.

"Did that break your heart?" I asked Chuckie, almost forty years later.

"Yeah," he told me. "What are you gonna do, Jack? I knew this woman my whole life, I loved her like a mother." When I was a teenager, a downhearted Chuckie would return home from visiting Josephine and tell us how lonely and defeated she was.

Hoffa's two children were outwardly stoic in dealing with decades of sadness, anxiety, and humiliation following their father's disappearance. They suffered through a roller-coaster ride of recurrent hope and disappointment—in 2003, when Frank Sheeran, a Hoffa associate, "confessed" to killing Hoffa; in 2009, when the mob contract killer Richard "the Iceman" Kuklinski "confessed" to the same crime; in 2013, when Anthony Zerilli identified three other men who supposedly buried Hoffa alive in a field twenty miles north of the Machus Red Fox; and many other times over the years, as scores of other "informant" tips led to more than a dozen other high-profile digs in farms, pools, and fields, only to find nothing of relevance.

James and Barbara also suffered through the endless jokes about their father, and through the many widely repeated rumors about his fate: that he was brought to a fender factory in Detroit where he was thrown in boiling zinc that was used to make sheets of metal; that he was run through a cardboard shredding machine at a garbage disposal service near Detroit, or crushed in a trash compactor at a restaurant five miles from the Machus; that he was chopped up and put in an oil drum delivered to a New Jersey landfill or the Florida Everglades; that he was shot, dismembered, and buried in the end zone at the old Giants Stadium in the Meadowlands; and many more.

"It would be a comfort to find his body," Barbara said a few decades after the disappearance, "but I don't think we will."

Neither Barbara, a retired administrative law judge, nor James, the president of the Teamsters union now for a much longer period than his father, would speak to me for this book. They remain bitter at Chuckie for what they see as his role in the disappearance, and for his silence ever since. "If you were accused of doing something so heinous, so reprehensible, wouldn't the first thing you'd want to do if you were innocent is get in touch with family members and reassure them?" Barbara asked in 1991. "We've never heard from him. No letter, no call . . . I think of him now as a completely amoral person."

Barbara's bitterness is understandable, but she forgets that Chuckie did reach out to the Hoffas right after the disappearance, only to be banished by James, and then again a week later, only to be publicly accused by James, then and thereafter, of having been involved in their father's disappearance. Chuckie saw no reason to think the Hoffas would welcome him or even want

294 | IN HOFFA'S SHADOW

to hear from him after that, especially in light of the public narrative that developed and James's continued attacks on him. Chuckie hasn't missed James. But he was very close to Barbara. He adored her and often says, with affection, that she is "just like her father." One of the many awful consequences of the Hoffa case is Chuckie's estrangement from her.

The dean of Hoffa journalists, Dan Moldea, has been gripped by the disappearance since literally the day after it occurred, when he was twenty-five years old. Like so many longtime observers, he no longer believes, as he claimed in his 1978 book *The Hoffa Wars*, that Chuckie was involved in the disappearance. Moldea interviewed many of the leading suspects and players in the case, including Sal Briguglio, the Andretta brothers, and Brother Moscato, a Provenzano protégé. Moldea knew more details about the Hoffa case than anyone I met outside the government, has offered many theories of the disappearance over the years, and is always close by with analysis when a new rumor or ostensible piece of evidence pops up. "Even though the FBI hasn't located Hoffa's body," Moldea told me in August 2018, at the start of his forty-fourth year on the case, "I still hope to find it."

Other government officials besides the original four have also agonized over the Hoffa investigation, which has quietly moved in a very different direction from the public narrative that has prevailed since the 1970s. In the course of my research for this book, I learned that current and former officials in the Detroit office of the FBI and the Detroit U.S. Attorney's Office have for two decades believed that Vito Giacalone, Anthony's brother, was directly involved in Hoffa's disappearance and was probably the person who picked him up at the Machus Red Fox. These officials also believe they know who murdered Hoffa. The killer was a low-level family member in 1975, someone entirely off the early investigators' radar screen. His status in the Detroit family rose almost immediately after the disappearance, and he died in January 2019. But the government remains frustrated because its informed suspicions about this person cannot be proven.

NO ONE I spoke to for this book was more consumed or frustrated by the Hoffa case than Andrew Sluss, who worked it for fifteen years. Low points for him included his failure to clear Chuckie and his failure to control the widespread public acceptance of the supposed deathbed claims by Frank Sheeran that he was involved in Hoffa's murder, which Sluss viewed as preposterous. The lowest point on Sluss's watch as case agent came when in May 2006 the FBI undertook a high-profile two-week dig for Hoffa's body at the eighty-acre Hidden Dreams Farms in Milford Township, almost forty miles northwest of Detroit. The farm had been owned by the former Teamsters official Rolland McMaster, who had been an ally and then a rival of Hoffa's in the union. A dying federal inmate who once lived on the farm told a credible story, confirmed by a polygraph, that Hoffa was buried under or near a barn.

For two weeks, dozens of FBI agents, with the assistance of sniffing dogs, archaeologists, surveyors, anthropologists, and students and professors from Michigan State University, spent a quarter of a million dollars tearing down the barn and digging up the farm looking for Hoffa's remains. The carnival atmosphere that has always characterized the Hoffa investigation descended on sleepy Milford Township. Helicopters whirled overhead as locals tromped to the farm to try to catch a glimpse of the dig. A "Hoffa steak salad"—a strip steak cut up and buried in greens—became the bestselling item at the local bar and grill. And funny T-shirts—"Milford Digs Hoffa, Do You?" and "Milford: A Great Place to Meet Your Friends . . . and Bury Your Enemies"—popped up everywhere. Sluss was "cautiously optimistic" when the dig began. But embarrassingly, the FBI found nothing and gave up after two weeks. The dig was widely criticized as a waste of taxpayer money.

"I failed," Sluss told me, reflecting on the Hoffa case in 2018. "It's my white whale," he added, with a frustrated laugh. "Only one case caused me to shed tears—Hoffa."

I felt the intensity with which Sluss wanted to solve the case when he blamed *me* in part for his failure to do so. I once asked Sluss a tough question about his 2002 memorandum summarizing the evidence about Chuckie, and how it squared with what he told me about his belief in Chuckie's innocence. I tried to make clear that I was not questioning his good faith, but that I had to resolve every tension because I was "very cynical about the government's treatment of Chuckie in light of many past events."

Sluss took offense at my suggestion and gave me a sharp rejoinder.

"Your cynical view regarding the government's treatment of Chuckie is well founded," he wrote back. "Yet never forget that cynicism is a jealous taskmaster," he added. "Your cynical distrust in 2002 prevented me from clearing Chuckie."

Sluss was referring to my refusal to do more to encourage Chuckie to take a lie detector test in 2002 when I was at the Department of Defense. Sluss led the case then, unlike in 2013 during Chuckie's FBI interview fiasco. He believes that the Detroit FBI and U.S. Attorney's Office easily would have cleared Chuckie if Chuckie had done an official interview in 2002 as he did in 2013. Sluss saw my brusque refusal to help him as a cause for that failure.

I am not sure I could have convinced Chuckie to take a lie detector test in 2002 had I tried. But Sluss's charge still stung. It reminded me that I wasn't looking out for Chuckie in 2002. And it, among other things, made me wonder how much I was looking out for him in writing this book.

WHEN I BEGAN this project, my main aim was to figure out what I could about Chuckie's actual involvement in the disappearance, and to try to set out a fair-minded account that, I hoped, would put him in a better light. I believe I have accomplished that. But I have not done another thing that over time I grew fixated on: *solving the case*, in the sense of figuring out what actually happened at the Machus Red Fox on July 30, 1975.

I read every document I could get my hands on, by the government and others, about Hoffa and his disappearance. And then I read them all again and again, like Champollion trying to decode the Rosetta Stone, convinced that I would find the hidden clues that had eluded everyone else. I met with the FBI agents who worked the case in the 1970s ten times, with Sluss a dozen times, and with nearly a dozen other agents and prosecutors who worked it, pressing them over and over for what they knew. And I tried to interview everyone else alive—including journalists and people who knew Hoffa or Chuckie or his mother or Giacalone—who might be able to shed light on the case.

I came to believe I could solve the mystery that had eluded everyone else because I alone had access to a crucial observer: Chuckie. One reason I pored over the official documents so intently was to collect information that might trigger Chuckie's memory or spark a reaction or otherwise help me find a back door through the thick wall of Omertà around his knowledge of the disappearance.

While I learned enough from Chuckie and other sources to be convinced that he did not pick up Hoffa in the Machus Red Fox parking lot on July 30, 1975, I also suspected that he did not tell me everything he knew, or at least that he believed. At Seasons 52, he slipped into telling me at least some of what he learned after the disappearance, and about his predicament between the mob and the FBI. But even those remarks were guarded.

Chuckie's main approach over many years was to steer our conversations away from the disappearance or his business with organized crime and toward his early time with Hoffa and his involvement with the labor movement. He had an unusually precise memory on topics he wanted to talk about, such as his role in the 1950s and 1960s as Hoffa's faithful servant. When I brought up the disappearance, however, he would typically utter bromides, or feign forgetfulness, and then change the subject.

But while Chuckie tried to be faithful to his Sicilian commitments, he was torn. "I love you and I want you to write a good book," he said more than once. He knew, because I told him, that writing a truthful book was important to me, and he wanted to help me and not disappoint me. And so he told me as much as he could, sometimes more than he believed he was supposed to.

Chuckie seemed to hope that I would figure out what he knew from the interstices of our conversations, without him having to tell me directly. "You're hitting the nail on the head now," Chuckie once said with clarity and excitement when I correctly speculated about the answer to a small puzzle that was distantly implied by his remarks. "I know you'll figure it out," he often said, usually at a crucial point in a conversation about the disappearance or the mob, just before his mother's visage popped into his head and he retreated into his Omertà shell.

Just as Chuckie tried to control our agenda even as he tried to help me, I did the same in return. I wanted to know everything he could tell me, including things I knew he couldn't tell me. I always backed away when Chuckie drew a red line, and I never tried to trick or coerce him into telling me things.

At the same time, I tried to make sure that whatever he was holding back did not undermine the truth about what he did tell me, especially since he was not candid in some of our conversations. Over time my determination not to be misled morphed into a strong desire, and then an obsession, to uncover Chuckie's deep secrets.

The intensity of my obsession did not manifest itself in our years of conversations until after Chuckie's unexpected revelations to me at Seasons 52. When I returned to Boston after that visit, Chuckie became uncharacteristically reticent—especially about any topic related to his life—when I telephoned Boca Raton to check on him and my mother. "I just don't feel like talking about it," he said dejectedly more than once. I believed he was stewing about what he told me over lunch, but I didn't raise the topic on the phone.

When I saw Chuckie during my next visit to Boca Raton a few months later he seemed taciturn, embarrassed, and obviously unhappy. I suspected that bringing up the source of his unhappiness would lead to a painful conversation. But I finally forced the issue, one afternoon in the television room, as Jimmy Hoffa and Anthony Giacalone stared down at us from the wall of fame.

"Why did you tell me all that stuff at Seasons 52?" I asked. After receiving no answer, I continued, "You said that Provenzano had a lot to do with it—with the disappearance."

After another pause, Chuckie exploded. "That makes me a stool pigeon, Jack, and I don't want to be considered a stool pigeon," he said.

I grimaced. Chuckie had told me nothing concrete about Provenzano's role in the Hoffa disappearance. Nor did he add anything to the circumstantial and informant evidence that had long led the FBI to make Provenzano a suspect.

"You can make all the faces you want," Chuckie said. "I just don't want to be considered a fucking rat this late in life." Chuckie recounted his many friends and relatives who were still connected to organized crime or who were related to deceased crime figures. "Even though people are gone, I'm not gonna get stung for saying something about Provenzano."

"That's bullshit," I said. "Everybody and their uncle have been talking about this. Nothing happened to anybody." And then after a bit, I asked,

"Why did they even tell you this stuff?" I was asking why Uncle Tony brought him barely into his circle of confidence a few days after the disappearance, and about the things Giacalone and Provenzano implicitly revealed on the hot afternoon in Pro's backyard.

"Because they trusted me, Jack. Uncle Tony would believe in me and my trust because he knew how my mother raised me. I mean, I would never rat anybody out, period. I just wouldn't do it. It's something, there's a code of honor, if you're going to be part of something, you can't do it. You know that I avoided telling you a lot of shit. Because I know your ability and what you think about the law and things. So I got as close to what I could do to help you write the book. But I would never betray Tony Giacalone. Never. I would never do that. I mean, shit. I can't do it, Jack."

Chuckie was speaking deep truths here. He avoided telling me a lot during our conversations. He was deeply loyal to Anthony Giacalone, long after his death. And more than anything else, he could not abide having ratted someone out.

"You told me you'd be honest," I reminded him.

"I was just talking to you as a father to a son," said Chuckie, explaining why he opened up at Seasons 52. "I wanted you to know the position I'm in."

On this point, Chuckie succeeded. That conversation helped me to understand much better the wretched pressures he faced in 1975 and beyond. But his revelation and then regret about Provenzano and the other matters created a problem for me. If I did not include what I learned from Chuckie at Seasons 52, my explanation for the disappearance, and especially for Chuckie's innocence, and for many other things in this book, would be incomplete to the point of misleading. In my mind, that meant I could not tell Chuckie's story at all if I could not include what I learned in that conversation.

"I've been telling you for years that I have to write a true and credible book," I explained to Chuckie.

"Not about Provenzano," Chuckie snapped.

"About the Hoffa disappearance," I said.

"I had nothing to do with the Hoffa disappearance," he replied. "I sat with you for four hours in the fucking federal building [in Detroit] with those jackasses, and not one of them said I had anything to do with it."

I agreed with this assessment, but I couldn't resist pressing on.

"And there's nothing you could have done to save him, to stop what was going to happen?" I asked.

"No," said Chuckie. "Only the Good Lord could have saved him. Only the Good Lord."

WHEN I STARTED this book seven years ago, I viewed Chuckie's Omertà fixation as a self-serving, crime-hiding, responsibility-evading excuse. Over the years, and especially after witnessing his painful anguish at inadvertently spilling secrets, I came to understand how much Omertà ordered his life, and indeed was the very thing he had suffered for forty-five years to preserve.

I grew to admire the honor in his commitment. Chuckie had lost everything else in his life after July 30, 1975—Hoffa, his career, his reputation for loyalty, and most other elements of his dignity. But he held on hard to Omertà, the last but most important remnant of his identity and self-esteem. For a long time I struggled with whether publishing what I learned from him would dishonor him. I feared it would be an act of selfishness and betrayal akin to blowing him off when I was twenty-one years old—and maybe worse, since I had set out to write the book to help Chuckie, and to make up for the past heartaches I had caused.

My predicament brought to mind Janet Malcolm's book *The Journalist and the Murderer*. Malcolm claimed that journalism, especially the individual profile, is "morally indefensible" because the author draws on the subject's vanity, loneliness, or ignorance to dupe him into thinking she will write the story he wants, when all along the author intends to write her own story, one that invariably casts the unwitting subject in a light he loathes. "Journalists justify their treachery in various ways according to their temperaments," Malcolm explained. "The more pompous talk about freedom of speech and 'the public's right to know'; the least talented talk about Art; the seemliest murmur about earning a living." None of these excuses, Malcolm suggests, are really persuasive.

My situation with Chuckie was much more precarious. We were a son and a father with a long and sometimes painful history. And now we were working on a project at a time when our mutual affection was most intense.

Despite (or perhaps because of) our intimacy, we were well aware of the other's mixed motives. Chuckie was committed to Omertà, I was committed to its opposite, but we were both committed to each other. And so we both tried hard, out of affection, to help or accommodate the other. We were trusting of each other, but not fully so. I was always on guard for mendacity or deflection. He was always on guard for forbidden topics, and was brilliant, when he wanted to be, at resisting my probes. And while in the end Chuckie told me a lot, he was never drawn out by narcissism or self-importance to "[blather] on and on, apparently oblivious of the notebook or tape recorder that is catching the words on which he is later to be impaled," as Malcolm describes the typical subject. The only time Chuckie uttered words he later deemed "impaling" was during his unprompted disclosure at Seasons 52.

What was my justification for reporting these words—for my treachery, as Malcolm might have it? Unlike the journalists Malcolm described, I cannot invoke freedom of speech, or the public's right to know, or Art, or the need for income, as an excuse for writing the book I wanted to write about Chuckie rather than the one he wanted me to write about him. I included some things in this book that I was pretty sure would displease Chuckie because I believed that these details were necessary to give a true picture of his life—especially his relationship with Hoffa and Giacalone, and his knowledge of the disappearance. I felt strongly that telling the truth about these matters as well as I could discern it was the best way of achieving my and Chuckie's mutual goal of clearing him from the ghastly stain of patricide.

Chuckie had for a while asked me when this book would be published. He hoped it would come out before the release of a 2019 movie about Hoffa's disappearance, *The Irishman*, which promised once again to humiliate him publicly by portraying him as the person who collected and delivered Hoffa on July 30, 1975. Before I decided to publish, I traveled to Florida to show him a copy of the manuscript and ask for comments. I prayed that he would see the book as an act of love. I also hoped that he would think I portrayed him fairly and honorably, and would appreciate my efforts to clear his name. But I worried, and told him, that he might not like some things in the manuscript. And I reminded him that I needed to write a truthful and credible book.

I watched Chuckie over the next three days as he occasionally picked up and read the spiral-bound draft. He made a few stray comments about it, but said little of substance. As I was leaving for Boston, he handed me the document. He asked me to remove three very small things, including one "out of respect" for the Hoffa children, especially Barbara.

And then Chuckie told me a noble lie.

"I read every word," he said halfheartedly. "You wrote a great book."

I doubt that Chuckie read every word. I saw him frown and then scowl two days earlier at about the place in the book where I described how others viewed his work in the Teamsters. He barely dipped into the manuscript after that—at least when I was watching. I wonder if he even looked at the last half.

Why might Chuckie not have wanted to know what I wrote? Maybe he thought he wouldn't live to see the words published and wanted to spare himself any pain. Maybe he wanted the secrets out, but didn't want the knowledge of, and thus the responsibility for, their publication. Maybe he wanted to clear his name at any cost. Or maybe he knew how long and hard I had worked on the book, and he decided to sacrifice his honor and pride out of love for me.

I never asked.

YEARS EARLIER, BUT after our revelatory lunch at Seasons 52, Chuckie and I visited Detroit for the last time. We went there mainly to see his old-timer friends. Chuckie asked me whether we could also see "Slush" and "the Italian kid"—by which he meant former FBI agent Andrew Sluss and FBI agent Louis Fischetti. Chuckie had taken a shine to both men. And both were delighted to meet with him.

We had lunch the first day in town with Sluss, at a diner adjacent to our hotel. It was the first time the two men had seen each other since August 2001, when Sluss had tried, in his capacity as the head of the Hoffa case, to convince Chuckie to take a polygraph. It was a strange lunch. Early on Sluss apologized to Chuckie for what happened in 2001 with the DNA evidence leak, which he described as "distasteful" since the government had publicly let Chuckie down in the media.

At that point Chuckie began weeping uncontrollably. Through his tears he mumbled about how hard the relentless pressure and publicity had been. And after a pause, he added, "I miss him so much." I had never before seen Chuckie "crack" over the weight of the investigation. It was an awkward moment followed by a long, awkward silence.

We moved on to pointless talk. I eventually asked Sluss whether he had any questions for Chuckie. I knew he did; he had been very keen to see Chuckie since he was still trying to solve the case, even in retirement. With this opening, Sluss asked a series of questions about the various occasions when Hoffa had meetings. He was trying to understand what happened on the afternoon of July 30, and how out of character Hoffa's actions were. Chuckie gave him plenty of stories, but they didn't seem to lead anywhere. When lunch ended—Chuckie and I had to leave after an hour—Sluss seemed gravely disappointed, as if he had missed his last chance to solve the case.

The following day we met Lou Fischetti and his partner, Marc Silski, at the Redcoat Tavern in Royal Oak, a bar with good burgers, which we all ordered. The conversation was genial and for the most part not about business. A wide-eyed Fischetti asked Chuckie lots of questions about his days with Hoffa, about growing up in Italian neighborhoods, and about some of the Detroit family members he knew.

Chuckie was emotionally more secure in this meeting, and he enjoyed the banter with Fischetti. He got a kick, after all these years, out of having the upper hand with the seemingly adulatory FBI agents. About halfway through the conversation, Chuckie asked Fischetti point-blank whether he thought he, Chuckie, had anything to do with Hoffa's disappearance.

"I don't think you did," Fischetti responded. "I wouldn't be here like this if I did." And then, after a pause, he added: "Well, I might, but that is not why I am here." Fischetti told Chuckie that he was "appalled by the way you were treated" by the U.S. Attorney's Office and the FBI the year before. He added that "I got my ass ate out" over the ordeal, but did not explain further.

Fischetti then sought to turn Chuckie's question around. "What do *you* think happened to Hoffa?" he asked.

"Nope," I interjected, placing my arm across Chuckie's chest to indicate that he should not answer. "You had your chance to hear the answer to that question, and didn't come through as you promised."

The night before, I had pressed Chuckie on that same question, at the back of a Mediterranean restaurant, Elie's, near our hotel in Birmingham, Michigan. I told myself before our meal that this would be the last time, the very last time, I ever asked him about Hoffa's disappearance—a vow I kept. By this point I was near certain that he was not at the Machus Red Fox on the afternoon of July 30, 1975. But I still suspected that he knew more than he had told me—things he had perhaps learned, or inferred, from his time after the disappearance with Anthony and Vito Giacalone, and with Tony Provenzano. I decided to lay my cards on the table like never before.

"You've already told me kind of what happened," I said, referring to our Seasons 52 conversation. "I cannot believe that you're not going to lay out in complete detail everything you know about what happened. Are you sure you even know?"

Chuckie smiled at me skeptically and with a tad of derision. "Is the Pope a Catholic?" he said. "Do you think that I don't know?"

"Pappy, you've told me so many different stories . . . ," I said, laughing.

"Jack, I tell you different stories to try to avoid the true meaning," he said.

This was an honest statement about Chuckie's relationship to the truth. I was pressing him to report on facts about what happened to Hoffa and why. But Chuckie operated with a different conception of truth—one that was not about factual reality, but rather about fidelity to a principle of honor, Omertà. This is why he dissembled on matters he was not supposed to talk about.

"Do you really know?" I pressed.

"Yeah," he said.

"In detail?" I asked.

"Not in detail, but I know," he said. I interpreted this to mean, and I believed, that he knows why Hoffa disappeared, but not how or by whom.

After a long pause, Chuckie continued: "Anyway, Jack, I love you to death, but there are some things I'm not going to do. I know you'll get pissed off, but I'm not gonna do it."

"I am not pissed off," I said honestly. "Do I look mad?"

I wasn't mad. I wanted him to tell me. But then again, I didn't. I was in awe of his eccentric integrity.

"No, but internal you are," he said. "Inside your stomach, you're mad. You're grinding right now."

Chuckie was poking fun at me.

"No," I replied. "I am frustrated, but not mad at you. I can't believe you're going to take this to your grave without telling the world what happened to him."

"I'll leave that to somebody else," Chuckie said, seemingly indifferent. "You don't know these guys, Jack," he added, referring to the people he would betray if he told me more.

"People have been talking about the Hoffa disappearance for forty years," I said. "Nothing's happened to anyone. But listen, I obviously don't want you to do anything that's going to cause you any fear or physical harm."

"It's not fear," Chuckie said firmly. "It's my honor."

"I don't know what to say about that, because you're the only honorable person involved in this whole matter," I continued.

I was thinking about the mob guys and thugs who knew Hoffa or had some connection to him and tried to make a buck off it, and the made men who wrote Omertà-defying tell-alls. And I was thinking of the many secrets that I suspected Chuckie hid from me.

"I'm not being critical," I continued. "And I know why keeping your mouth shut is so important. But I don't understand why you're the only person who has to take it to your grave. There are so many things that would be served by you telling the truth. I just cannot believe that you hold the secret to the greatest mystery in American history in your head and you're not going to tell the world. I can't believe it."

"Believe it, Jack," Chuckie said.

AFTERWORD TO THE PAPERBACK EDITION

I N EARLY SEPTEMBER 2019, a few weeks before this book was published in hardcover, I returned to Boca Raton to give Chuckie an advance copy. He was more subdued than usual. He had trouble eating due to the painful aftereffects of a procedure for esophageal cancer. And he was worried about the impending premiere, later that month, of Martin Scorsese's *The Irishman*, which he knew would portray him as the man who drove Jimmy Hoffa to his death.

On this trip, Chuckie read the book all the way through, slowly and carefully, over a few days. He pronounced that he was fine with it, but he did not seem enthusiastic. I knew why. He had little confidence that the public would pay attention to what I wrote. But he knew his aging mob friends would read it, as would Sylvia Pagano's grandchildren and great-grandchildren and the living relatives of Anthony Giacalone and of Anthony Provenzano, who were also close friends. He didn't like that I had "put all that personal shit" in the book.

But Chuckie's worries proved to be unfounded. In fact, he came to regard the book's reception as miraculous. To a person, everyone he cared about—the wiseguys, the friends and family of the wiseguys, his family in Kansas City—told him they loved it. I wasn't sure why. Perhaps they overlooked Chuckie's accidental indiscretions and admired the commitment to Omertà he showed to the last page. Perhaps they loved the book's history and critique of government malfeasance—and especially the portrayal of Bobby Kennedy's defects and misdeeds. Perhaps they were pleased to see my case for why Chuckie should be cleared of the crime.

And then, in Chuckie's mind, more miracles came. For forty-four years, he had watched himself portrayed in the news and in books as the unquestionably treacherous ne'er-do-well who drove Hoffa to his death. It had been a bizarre experience, and a grim one, to read so many made-up things about himself over so many decades and not be able to do anything about it.

But the reviewers of this book told a different story. Chuckie was amazed to read their assertions that he was innocent of the crime he had been tagged with since 1975. Just as miraculous to Chuckie, and almost as satisfying: some of the reviews recounted the federal government's mistakes, its lies about his role in Hoffa's disappearance, and its indifference to correcting the record once it knew the truth. Many reviews portrayed Chuckie as a loving father and a man of honor. One Detroit columnist lobbied for his exoneration.

Chuckie had no smartphone or computer. So as the reviews and other notices of the book came out, I sent them to my mother, Brenda, so she could show him. She told me how pleased he was about it all. But when Chuckie and I spoke on the phone, he didn't bring up the book. Neither did I.

About ten days after the book was published, Chuckie's precarious health—not just the esophageal cancer, but also the ravages of decades of diabetes and many collateral problems—took a turn for the worse. At the start of this decline, just before he went into a rehabilitation center, he called me. He was worked up. Chuckie was the toughest tough guy, and he kept his emotions down deep. But he was hesitant and weeping as he began to speak.

"Son, I've read the book three times now," he said. "You figured everything out; you got it all right." His heaving sobs rose. "I don't know how you did it, and I'm sorry I was such a pain in the ass," he added, referring to some of our difficult interviews, when his commitment to Omertà came between us. "I am so grateful. I love you so much."

I worked on this book for seven years in the hope that I would one day hear these words.

"I love you so much too, Dad," I replied. "And I'll forever be sorry for what I did to you."

CHUCKIE'S PUBLIC EXONERATION didn't last long. *The Irishman* premiered at the New York Film Festival on September 27, 2019, a few days after this book was published. It began to stream on Netflix two months later, on November 27. Over twenty-six million people watched the movie during its first week on Netflix.

Chuckie had dreaded the release of the film. It is based on *I Heard You Paint Houses*, by Charles Brandt, a book that contains a supposed end-of-life confession by the former Teamsters official Frank Sheeran. Sheeran claimed to be Hoffa's murderer, and the book wove Sheeran's tale into the publicly known elements of the early FBI theory of the case, including Chuckie's alleged role in picking up Hoffa. Chuckie had long worried that Scorsese's adaptation of the book would give his supposed involvement in the Hoffa disappearance a reality in popular culture that prior books and headlines had not. This concern was the main reason he urged me to publish this book in September 2019, despite his anxieties about it.

The Irishman turned out to be worse for Chuckie than he feared.

In the movie, the actor Jesse Plemons plays Chuckie. On the surface, the film tracks reality. There really was a Teamsters union official named Frank Sheeran (played by Robert De Niro), who really was an associate of an eastern Pennsylvania crime boss named Russell Bufalino (Joe Pesci). Hoffa (Al Pacino) really did act self-destructively toward the mob in the mid-1970s as he tried but failed to regain control of his union. And the mob clearly came together to knock him off.

But beyond these surface truths, and despite the "true crime" feel, the movie is high fiction. "One of the greatest fake movies I ever saw," Chuckie told me.

As I have explained elsewhere in greater detail, it is clear Sheeran was not involved in Hoffa's murder.* There is significant evidence that he was not in Detroit the day of the disappearance, and there are a number of large discrepancies between the known facts and his "confession." The mob never would have used Sheeran to commit the crime under the cockamamie circumstances recounted in the movie (and in the book it's based on). It's not just Sheeran's implausible private plane flight into and out of Detroit to pull off a crime with associates he had never met. It's also Russell Bufalino's dubious involvement. "It would be the first time that a La Cosa Nostra boss drove the 'shooter' en route to a hit—and the boss even took his wife along for the ride!" a former FBI agent told me. And finally, secret FBI surveillance of Sheeran after the disappearance has him on tape credibly disclaiming that he was in Detroit on the fateful day, or had any involvement in the crime.

The character based on Chuckie appears occasionally in the film. As Hoffa's disappearance nears at the end of the film, Scorsese follows the scenario Brandt lays out in his book. We see Chuckie drive with Sheeran and Sal Briguglio in a car that reeks of the salmon he'd delivered to Violet Holmes. The three men pick up Hoffa, then Chuckie drives them all to a house where Sheeran shoots him. In this scene, Chuckie is portrayed as an affable but bewildered simpleton as Briguglio and then Hoffa kid him about the fish smell. "What kind of fish?" asks Briguglio. "I don't know," says Chuckie. "The kind you eat? A fish."

This scene, and much of the movie, are pure fiction. And yet, as Chuckie expected, the fiction became a reality for the tens and maybe hundreds of millions who watched the film. I spoke with dozens of people who watched

---

* Goldsmith, Jack, "Are the Claims in the New Film *The Irishman* True?," *Lawfare*, November 26, 2019, https://www.lawfareblog.com/are-claims-new-film-irishman-true; Goldsmith, Jack, "Jimmy Hoffa and *The Irishman*: A True Crime Story?," *The New York Review of Books*, September 26, 2019, https://www.nybooks.com/daily/2019/09/26/jimmy-hoffa-and-the-irishman-a-true-crime-story/.

the movie but had not read my book. Almost all of them assumed that the movie told a true story—including the part where Chuckie picks Hoffa up on the day of his death.

There was a different aspect of the film that Chuckie did not expect, and that for him was even more humiliating. Even more than the book, the movie portrayed Sheeran as a close associate of Hoffa—as his right-hand man during trials, as his troubleshooter in the office, and as his intimate companion in union halls and in the evenings on the road.

Sheeran, whom Chuckie knew, was none of those things. He ran a Delaware Teamsters local, and Hoffa had business dealings with him over the years, but their relationship went little further. "The Irishman was never that close to Hoffa," Chuckie told me. "He was a drunk, he couldn't run a union, he got thrown out finally, and the only thing he would do was set a building on fire now and then."

What Scorsese did, in effect, was to place Sheeran in Chuckie's role in Hoffa's life. It was Chuckie, not Sheeran, who for decades served as Hoffa's intimate companion and troubleshooter. Chuckie expected to be "tagged with the disappearance" in the movie, he told me. He did not expect Scorsese to appropriate his close relationship with Hoffa—the precious blood, sweat, tears, and joy of a three-decade father-son relationship, the apex of his life—and give it to Sheeran for all the world to see and believe.

Scorsese has been mostly indifferent about the truth of his film when speaking about it in public. "I don't really care about that," he said, when asked about the veracity of his portrayal of Hoffa's death. "The point is, it's not about the facts." According to Scorsese, the film is about "the world" his characters inhabit and "the way they behave." And yet much of the frisson of the film comes from its "true crime" feel—it depicts characters based on real people who are embedded in a narrative that self-consciously weaves itself into actual events. This is now a convention of the genre: films grounded in history often take license with the facts to serve the larger drama. Even so, the imprimatur Scorsese gave to Sheeran's tale falsely implicated Chuckie and had a devastating impact on him.

The impact was akin to that of the illegal FBI surveillance recordings described in chapter 5—the tapes that picked up the most intimate details of Chuckie's relationships with his mother, Sylvia; Josephine Hoffa; the Giacalone brothers; and, indirectly, Hoffa. When the government leaked some of the transcripts in 1976, in an effort to pressure Chuckie and others, it not only violated his privacy but also deprived him of the power to define and shape these relationships for himself and the world.

Scorsese did something similar—not by listening in illegally and publishing humiliating truths, as the FBI did, but by usurping Chuckie's relationship with Hoffa, giving it to someone else, and then broadcasting the untruth. The effect on Chuckie in both instances is the same. "I had no control," he told me during our recent conversation. His control over his life, and the presentation of his life to the world, was snatched from him in ways he could never recover.

Chuckie had grown resigned to the lies told about him over the years. "Mr. Hoffa always taught me, you can't change what they print," he told me. "Put it on the side and keep going forward." This is easier said than done, he also acknowledged. "It hurts a lot, because you're in the ring and getting the snot kicked out of you, and you cannot fight back."

Still, Chuckie's portrayal in *The Irishman* as a "dim jackass" driving Hoffa to his death made him livid. "To see this happen, it just makes me so mad," he told me. "I'd like to get hold of that Scorsese and choke him like a chicken. And then after I get through with him, I'd grab that other pip-squeak, the guy who played the Irishman."

Chuckie was too frail when he uttered these words for them to be a threat, and indeed he did not mean them as such. It was the end-of-life cri de coeur of a man whose being, despite this book's efforts, had been enveloped and ruined by demeaning public untruths that he lacked the power to rectify.

THE LAST TIME I saw Chuckie alive was in late January 2020. I'd flown to Boca Raton to assist Chuckie during two days of intense interviews for what might later become a film. He was out of the rehabilitation center and back home. But all of his ailments had grown worse, and he was in extraordinary pain due to diabetic neuropathy in his left leg. He struggled in the interviews to focus and to remember events, but he still did a good job.

The evening after the second day of filming, on January 24, an exhausted Chuckie pronounced that he wanted to go see his friends at his favorite local Italian restaurant. We had been to this restaurant many times before. It is a boisterous place frequented by aging wiseguys wearing very dark tans and colorful sport coats. Chuckie loved it. The food reminded him of his mother's cooking. He enjoyed being greeted with kisses and hugs by his friends—a throwback to the world where he was most at home. He liked the special attention that the waiters, at the behest of the maître d', always gave him. And he especially liked it when his closest friend in the Outfit was there. This friend was a senior wiseguy who served as Chuckie's "goombah"—his patron and adviser—after Giacalone died.

I never liked going to this restaurant. The food was fine, but I didn't enjoy hanging out in a place where so many people looked like mobsters, and some in fact were. I was especially anxious about going to the restaurant that night, since it would be the first time I had been there since this book had been published.

Chuckie had told me that his friends had no problems with this book, and he didn't seem to worry about it. I still worried, though. The book disclosed that Chuckie had told me that the Commission had organized the Hoffa hit and that Giacalone and Anthony Provenzano were involved in the crime at some level. It also disclosed that government officials in Detroit believed that Vito Giacalone and another man had actually carried out the hit in 1975. I assumed that no one in the mob cared about these revelations forty-five years after the event. But I wasn't sure. And I wasn't keen to conduct a live experiment in a restaurant full of old-timers.

As I pushed Chuckie in a wheelchair into the restaurant, his face lit up. He pointed to a table in the middle of the main room and said, "Take me over there." I rolled him toward a square table that hosted four well-dressed elderly gentlemen, including Chuckie's goombah, whom I had met a few times before. The men at the table spoke to one another as we approached. They then rose and greeted Chuckie with warm affection. At that point, the burliest of the four men, not his goombah, turned to me.

"Are you the author?" he asked, in what seemed like a thick New Jersey accent.

I hesitated for a moment. Was it a good idea to answer? How could I not? "I am," I said.

He smiled and gave me an enthusiastic handshake. "You wrote a great book!" he said. "Those government assholes."

The other gentlemen shook my hand and congratulated me. It was the most bizarre and least anticipated reaction I had received to this book. We proceeded to our table and had a fine meal. Chuckie's goombah picked up the tab. And the next day I returned to Boston.

ALMOST THREE WEEKS later, on February 13, 2020—one day shy of Jimmy Hoffa's 107th birthday—Chuckie had a heart attack and died.

I was distraught by Chuckie's passing but heartened by the hundreds of people who wrote me to say, in various ways, how much they treasured getting to know him in the pages of this book, and how much they admired him despite his ever-so-human flaws.

I was also so grateful for the outpouring of love at his funeral.

I gave a brief eulogy, where I spoke about Chuckie's greatness in four related qualities: "First, Dad never knew a stranger . . . Second, the thing that gave Dad the most pleasure in life was to do for others . . . Third, despite a life that was in some respects filled with frustration and heartache, Dad invariably had an upbeat, humorous, and even cheerful presence . . . Fourth, and finally, he was a great Dad." I explained the fourth point as follows:

He became my father, and Brett and Steven's, when we were young and vulnerable. This was also in the midst of the Hoffa disappearance, which unjustifiably enveloped his life. And yet in the midst of all that pressure, he gave us undying love, security, support, encouragement, and even inspiration. Whatever success and happiness we have achieved in life would not have occurred but for his love and strength.

May this great man rest in peace.

It is impossible to fully reconstruct and corroborate Chuckie O'Brien's whereabouts on the afternoon of July 30, 1975. But a review of the evidence reveals problems with the FBI's early theory that Chuckie picked up Hoffa at the Machus Red Fox and drove him to his death. The evidence consists of witness statements and references to grand jury testimony that are included in a comprehensive 2002 FBI report on Chuckie's alleged role in the Hoffa disappearance. This evidence has not previously been considered in public debates about the Hoffa affair.

The FBI's early theory, as reflected in numerous internal memoranda, was premised on the following facts. On the morning of July 30, 1975, a frozen salmon was delivered to Teamsters Local 299 at 2801 Trumbull

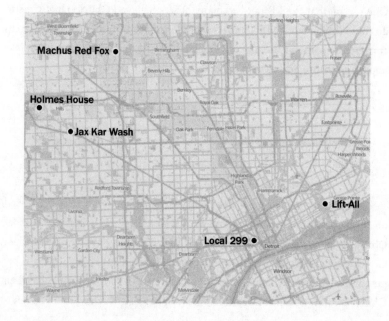

Avenue in Detroit. The fish was a gift from a Teamsters official in Alaska for Bobby Holmes Sr., a Detroit Teamsters official who was out of town on business. Chuckie was at Local 299 when the fish was delivered. He signed for it and volunteered to take it to Violet Holmes, Bobby's wife, at the Holmes residence at 36045 Congress Court in Farmington Hills, Michigan. In the middle of the day, Chuckie borrowed his friend Joey Giacalone's Mercury Marquis for this task. Joey drove the car to Local 299 from his workplace at Lift-All, at 2679 Conner Street, Detroit. Chuckie drove Joey back to Lift-All, dropped him off, and then drove the car with the salmon to the suburbs. In her interviews with the FBI and in her grand jury testimony, Violet stated that Chuckie delivered the fish to her home, lingered for a while, and then departed between 2:20 and 2:30 p.m. Chuckie was later seen in downtown Detroit at Local 299, sometime around 4:30 p.m.

For many years, the FBI theorized that during this two-hour-and-ten-minute period, Chuckie left the Holmes residence, drove to the Machus Red Fox at 6676 Telegraph Road in Bloomfield Hills, picked up Hoffa, and drove Hoffa to his death. Chuckie eventually drove back to Lift-All to return Joey's car, after which Joey drove Chuckie to Local 299, arriving there around 4:30. One reason that the FBI and so many others believed Chuckie had time to do these things during this period is because the FBI found no witnesses to corroborate some of the places Chuckie claimed to be after he left Violet's house and before he was seen at Local 299.

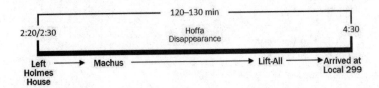

The central problem with the FBI's original theory is that it focused on the wrong time period. The relevant time period for assessing whether Chuckie picked up Hoffa at the Machus Red Fox does not commence when Chuckie left the Holmes residence between 2:20 and 2:30 p.m. Rather, it begins at the later time when Hoffa was last known to be alive, and it ends when Chuckie was first seen at Local 299. A review of FBI interviews and FBI references to grand jury testimony provides reason to think that Chuckie lacked sufficient time to have picked up Hoffa and driven him to his death, and also to have returned to the Teamsters offices by the time he was observed there. It is impossible to know exactly when the relevant events occurred. But based on plausible interpretations of witness statements and grand jury testimony, Chuckie arrived back at Local 299 too early to have been able to collect and deliver Hoffa after Hoffa was last known to be alive.

According to the available witnesses, the last time Hoffa was known to be alive was when he called and spoke with his friend Louis Linteau—who was at his workplace, Airport Limousine Services—from a pay phone in the strip mall near the Machus Red Fox. Linteau said that Hoffa told him on this call that he was tired of waiting to meet Anthony Giacalone and would be leaving the Machus Red Fox "momentarily."

In his first interview in August 1975, Linteau told the FBI that this call came at "approximately" 3:30 p.m. In his November 1975 interview, he said that he was "positive" that the call came at 3:30 p.m., and was "vehement" for various reasons that it could not have been earlier or later. The FBI was originally doubtful about Linteau's statements concerning the 3:30 p.m. specification for the call. But Linteau and three of his employees also testified before the grand jury. According to the FBI summary of that testimony, Linteau again said that the call came at 3:30 p.m. Two other employees, Cynthia Green and Elmer Reeves, testified that the call came between 3:00 and 3:30 p.m. And the third employee, Marita Crane, testified that the call was received between 3:20 and 3:25.

Hoffa Calls Linteau from Machus Red Fox Strip Mall

🕐	👤
3:30 "approximately"	Linteau August 1975 interview
3:30 "positive" and "vehement"	Linteau November 1975 interview
3:30	Linteau grand jury testimony
3:00–3:30	Green grand jury testimony
3:00–3:30	Reeves grand jury testimony
3:20–3:25	Crane grand jury testimony

It is thus plausible, based on the FBI interviews and the grand jury testimony, to infer that Hoffa was alive between 3:20 and 3:30, and that his killers must have picked him up no earlier than after the call ended—around 3:30. Even assuming Chuckie was not seen at Local 299 until 4:30 p.m., as the FBI's theory reflects, the window of time Chuckie would have had to pick up Hoffa, drive him to his death, drive to Lift-All to pick up Joey, then drive to Local 299, is considerably narrower than the FBI's original theory suggests.

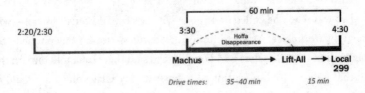

But the actual time interval was likely even shorter. The grand jury testimony also indicates that Chuckie was back at the Trumbull Avenue complex of Teamsters offices that included Local 299 before 4:30 p.m., and likely many minutes before. Destine Kyff, a Local 458 office manager, told the FBI and testified at the grand jury that she saw Chuckie at 2:30 or 3:00 p.m., and again between 3:30 and 4:00 p.m. Jacqueline Flowers, a secretary, testified that she saw Chuckie there between 2:30 and when she left work, which was normally 4:30 p.m. Joey Giacalone testified that he drove Chuckie from his company, Lift-All, and dropped him off at Local 299 between 4:15 and 4:45 p.m. Finally, Joseph Valenti, then the president of Teamsters Local 214, told the FBI in an interview that he received a telephone call from Chuckie between 4:00 and 4:10 p.m. requesting a ride home at the end of the day, that Chuckie appeared at his office next door to Local 299 five minutes later (i.e., between 4:05 and 4:15 p.m.), and that Chuckie stayed in Valenti's office until they departed at 4:30 or 4:35 p.m. Hoffa's son, James, confirmed Valenti's basic account. James told the FBI that the day after the disappearance, Valenti told him that Chuckie telephoned on July 30 to ask for a ride home between 4:00 and 4:15 p.m., and that he (James) believed Chuckie had been observed back at Local 299 by 4:00 p.m.

Collectively this testimony supports the inference that Chuckie arrived back at Local 299 before 4:30 p.m., and likely many minutes before. There is no suggestion in the 2002 FBI report, or in any of the FBI files examined for this book, that any of these witnesses lied to the FBI or perjured themselves in order to help Chuckie. Indeed, some of these statements—most notably James Hoffa's and Linteau's—came from people who were very critical of Chuckie to the FBI.

Chuckie Seen at Local 299	
🕐	👤
2:30–3:00 and 3:30–4:00	Kyff August 1975 interview and grand jury testimony
2:30–4:30	Flowers grand jury testimony
4:15–4:45	Joey Giacalone grand jury testimony
4:05–4:15	Valenti August 1975 interview

If Hoffa was picked up at the Machus around 3:30 p.m., and Chuckie was back at Local 299 before 4:30 p.m.—two witnesses, Kyff and Valenti, say that they saw Chuckie at 4:15 p.m. or earlier—then Chuckie would have had practically no extra time to pick up and deliver Hoffa. The drive from the Machus Red Fox to Lift-All on a typical Wednesday midafternoon would take thirty-five to forty minutes today. Chuckie would have spent at least a minute or two picking up Joey at Lift-All. The drive back to Local 299 would have taken (according to the FBI in 1975) fifteen minutes. And it would have taken at least a minute or two for Chuckie to have been seen by the three people who testified that they observed him at Local 299 before 4:30 p.m.

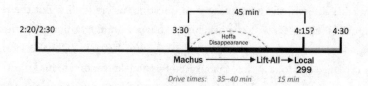

In sum, if Chuckie arrived at Local 299 before 4:30 p.m., as the interviews and grand jury testimony suggest, the available time for him to pick up Hoffa at the Machus Red Fox, drive Hoffa to his death, and still arrive and be seen at Local 299, is small to nonexistent.

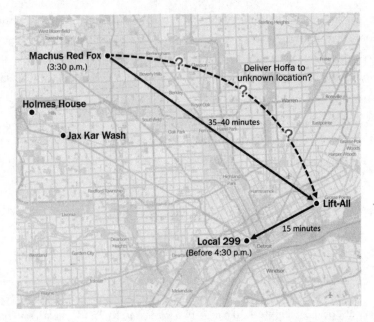

The testimony of Joey Giacalone presents another anomaly for the timeline that casts Chuckie as the driver who picked up Hoffa at the Machus Red Fox. As summarized by the FBI, Joey Giacalone testified before the grand jury that Chuckie returned his car to Lift-All between 2:30 and 3:45 p.m. and lingered for forty-five minutes before Joey drove him to Local 299, to arrive between 4:15 and 4:45 p.m. If Chuckie arrived at Lift-All at 3:45 p.m. at the latest, as Joey testified, he could not have picked up Hoffa at the Machus Red Fox at 3:30 p.m., since Lift-All was at least thirty-five to forty minutes away. Since Joey is the son of Anthony Giacalone and has close personal ties to Chuckie himself, there are reasons to question his credibility. But the testimony is consistent with the conclusion drawn from the testimony of three witnesses who place Chuckie at Local 299 before 4:30 p.m.: Chuckie lacked time to pick up Hoffa at the Machus Red Fox and deliver him to his killers.

Consider, finally, Chuckie's own account of his activities on the afternoon of July 30. His account is self-interested, and he admitted during research for this book that he falsely told the FBI in 1975 that his travels in the suburbs included a stop at the Southfield Athletic Club. But even if one subtracts that falsehood, the remainder of Chuckie's alibi is consistent with the

FBI witness statements and the summary of the grand jury testimony. Violet Holmes says Chuckie left her house between 2:20 and 2:30 p.m. According to Chuckie's account of his route that afternoon, it would have taken him ten minutes to get to Jax Car Wash, fifteen to twenty minutes to gas up and get the car washed, and thirty-five to forty minutes (on today's roads) to get to Lift-All. This would have placed Chuckie at Lift-All between 3:20 and 3:45 p.m., which fits squarely with Joey Giacalone's testimony, and after a stay at Lift-All and a fifteen-minute drive to Local 299, Chuckie would have arrived back at Local 299 before 4:30 p.m., as many witnesses recall.

This timeline analysis by itself does not settle whether Chuckie O'Brien picked up Hoffa at the Machus Red Fox on July 30, 1975. A great deal of additional circumstantial evidence bears on whether Chuckie did the deed. The aim here is simply to address problems in the government's original theory, and to show, based on FBI interviews and grand jury testimony, that there are plausible reasons to doubt that Chuckie had time to commit the crime that has been attributed to him for decades.

NOTES

This book is based on interviews with dozens of people, many of whom I recognize in the acknowledgments. Unless otherwise noted with citations below, all quotations are from these interviews, or from personal recollection confirmed when possible by participants in the conversation.

INTRODUCTION

4   *"massive amount of chatter"*: Shane Harris, "The Time U.S. Spies Thought Al Qaeda Was Ready to Nuke D.C.," *Daily Beast* (Sept. 10, 2016).

6   *"O'BRIEN is described by even his closest friends as a pathological liar"*: FBI Memorandum, Hoffex Conference, FBI Headquarters (Jan. 27 and 28, 1976), at 31 (in author's possession). This document is widely known as the Hoffex Memorandum.

10   *"Live and let live"*: "Inside Jimmy Hoffa," *David Brinkley's Journal* (NBC television special, Apr. 1, 1963), transcript at 14.

1. CHUCKIE AND ME

12 *"The Plantation Inn was a family place"*: Robert Gordon, *It Came from Memphis* (2001), at 50.

17 *wanted to interview Hoffa's "foster son"*: William K. Stevens, "Investigators in Hoffa Case Trying to Find Foster Son," *The New York Times* (Aug. 6, 1975).

17 *bloodstains in the back seat*: The Detroit papers attributed the discovery of bloodstains in the car to anonymous sources. *See, e.g.*, "FBI Seizes Hoffa Case Car; Bloodstains Found on Seat," *Detroit Free Press* (Aug. 10, 1975). The Detroit FBI agents on the case in 1975 told me in 2019 that no bloodstains were found in the car, and I found no reference to a finding of bloodstains in the car in any of the internal FBI documents.

17 *Chuckie had given "conflicting accounts"*: "Hoffa Presence in Car Is Hinted," *The New York Times* (Aug. 28, 1975).

18 *"a large sum of money"*: Hoffex Memorandum, *supra*, at 30.

18 *"appalling when a man like this"*: Agis Salpukas, "Hoffa Case Figure Reported Silent," *The New York Times* (Sept. 4, 1975).

18 *"coupled with"*: "O'Brien Balks at Hoffa Quiz," *Detroit Free Press* (Sept. 4, 1975).

19 *"a lead-pipe cinch"*: Id.

19 *"hysterical neurosis"*: Pete Yost, "Hoffa Son Mulls Union Politics," *Lansing State Journal* (Sept. 18, 1975).

20 *"propensity for violence is legendary"*: Unsigned, Undated FBI Memorandum, in Wayne State University, Archives of Labor and Urban Affairs, Jimmy Hoffa FBI Files, Box 1, Folder 3 [hereinafter "Wayne State Archives, Jimmy Hoffa FBI Files"].

22 *"consider plea bargaining"*: Agis Salpukas, "Foster Son Held in Hoffa Inquiry," *The New York Times* (July 9, 1976).

25 *In college I read for the first time*: The books I read in college were Dan E. Moldea, *The Hoffa Wars: The Rise and Fall of Jimmy Hoffa* (1978) and Steven Brill, *The Teamsters* (1978).

31 *"intellectual-in-residence"*: Victor S. Navasky, *Kennedy Justice* (1971), at 424.

32 *"Special Agent with experience"*: Airtel from Director, FBI, to FBI Richmond/Priority (Sept. 5, 1989), obtained through a Privacy Act request.

33 *"GOLDSMITH advised he lived with his mother"*: Memorandum from Special Agent in Charge, Richmond, to Director, FBI, *Subject: Jack L. Goldsmith III, Security Clearance Investigations Program* (Oct. 5, 1989), obtained through a Privacy Act request.

40 *"Judge not, that you be not judged"*: Matthew 7:1.

40 *speck of sawdust*: Id.

2. TWO LOYALTIES

44 *"O'Brien was generally considered"*: Moldea, *supra*, at 391.

45 *Black Hand gangs in Kansas City*: On Black Hand gangs and the growth of underworld governance in Kansas City in the first third of the twentieth century, see William Ouseley, *Open City: True Story of the KC Crime Family, 1900–1950* (2008); Frank R. Hayde, *The Mafia and the Machine: The Story of the Kansas City Mob* (2007).

45 *Binaggio's "chauffeur"*: Memorandum from Special Agent John L. Shelburne to Special Agent in Charge, Detroit, *re: Vito Giacalone*, 92-438, ELSUR 92-470-1442 (June 12, 1963), at 1. This document, and many of the FBI documents that I reviewed from

the early 1960s, can be found on the website of the Mary Ferrell Foundation, www
.maryferrell.org.

46 *"fled to Kansas City"*: David Critchley, *The Origin of Organized Crime in America: The
New York City Mafia, 1891–1931* (2008), at 247 n.49. The memoir in question is Nicola
Gentile, *Vita di Capomafia* (1963), at 83–85.

48 *Hoffa was born on Valentine's Day*: The account of Hoffa's childhood and early adult
life in this chapter is drawn from discussions with Chuckie and from the treatments
in Arthur A. Sloane, *Hoffa* (1991); James R. Hoffa and Donald I. Rogers, *The Trials of
Jimmy Hoffa* (1970); Thaddeus Russell, *Out of the Jungle: Jimmy Hoffa and the Remak-
ing of the American Working Class* (2001); Jim Clay, *Hoffa! Ten Angels Swearing* (1965);
James R. Hoffa and Oscar Fraley, *Hoffa: The Real Story* (1975). I owe a debt to these
books.

48 *"The culture of Brazil"*: Russell, *supra*, at 11, 13.

49 *"We learned that unless you were willing"*: Hoffa and Rogers, *supra*, at 20–21.

49 *"remarkable independence"*: Id. at 17.

50 *"the kind of guy who causes unions"*: Clay, *supra*, at 53.

50 *"outrageous meanness"*: Hoffa and Rogers, *supra*, at 45.

50 *"the open shop capital of America"*: Sloane, *supra*, at 13.

51 *the workingman's "constant insecurity"*: Hoffa and Rogers, *supra*, at 42.

51 *at a propitious time*: The labor history treatments that I found the most fruitful for this
and subsequent periods were Philip Dray, *There Is Power in a Union: The Epic Story of
Labor in America* (2010); Melvyn Dubofsky and Foster Rhea Dulles, *Labor in America:
A History*, 8th ed. (2010); Nelson Lichtenstein, *State of the Union: A Century of Ameri-
can Labor* (2002); Russell, *supra*; and Robert H. Zieger, *American Workers, American
Unions, 1920–1985* (1986).

52 *"wants you to join a union"*: Dray, *supra*, at 421.

52 *In the decade of labor's resurgence*: On the history of trucking in the 1930s, see David
Witwer, *Corruption and Reform in the Teamsters Union* (2003), at 63–65; Stier, Ander-
son & Malone, LLC, *The Teamsters: Perception and Reality; An Investigative Study of
Organized Crime Influence in the Union* (2002), at 111–12.

52 *"By 1942, less than a decade after"*: Russell, *supra*, at 96.

53 *"Mob guys had muscle"*: Hoffa and Fraley, *supra*, at 92–93.

53 *"They hired thugs"*: Ralph C. James and Estelle Dinerstein James, *Hoffa and the Teamsters: A Study of Union Power* (1965), at 86.

53 *"The police would beat"*: Id.

53 *"a savage decade for labor"*: Arthur M. Schlesinger Jr., *Robert Kennedy and His Times*
(1978), at 140.

54 *"every day of the average individual"*: *David Brinkley's Journal*, *supra*, at 14.

54 *The organization that became known as the "Mafia"*: On the origins of the post-Prohibition
Italian Syndicate, including the origins of "the Commission," I am indebted to many of
my interview subjects, as well as Nigel Cawthorne, *Mafia: The History of the Mob* (2012);
John Dickie, *Cosa Nostra: A History of the Sicilian Mafia* (2004); Stephen R. Fox, *Blood
and Power: Organized Crime in Twentieth-Century America* (1989); Thomas Reppetto,
American Mafia: A History of Its Rise to Power (2004); Selwyn Raab, *Five Families: The
Rise, Decline, and Resurgence of America's Most Powerful Mafia Empires* (2005); and Stier,
Anderson & Malone, *supra*.

55 *"no direct executive power"*: Joseph Bonanno, *A Man of Honor: The Autobiography of Joseph Bonanno* (1983), at 159.

56 *"One must remember that in the economic sphere"*: Id. at 78.

56 *"not as hired specialists but as partners"*: Humbert S. Nelli, *The Business of Crime: Italians and Syndicate Crime in the United States* (1981), at 243.

56 *"perversions of the search for economic security"*: Walter Lippmann, "The Underworld: Our Secret Servant," *The Forum* (Jan. 1931).

58 *a Teamster picket named Arthur Queasbarth*: Russell's invaluable account of this period says that the brick that killed Queasbarth was thrown by an employer's "guard." Russell, *supra*, at 78. Schramm says he was killed by "an undetermined source." LeRoy H. Schramm, "Union Rivalry in Detroit in World War II," 54 *Michigan History* 3 (1970): 201, 204. Chuckie says one of Giacalone's men did the deed.

59 *"I've never been able to understand"*: Hoffa and Fraley, *supra*, at 92.

65 *"my other son"*: Hoffa and Rogers, *supra*, at 114–15.

66 *"biggest small man in Detroit"*: Sloane, *supra*, at 38.

3. UNIONISM, HOFFA-STYLE

69 *"The main but not exclusive"*: "The Rise and Fall of the American Labor Movement," Harvard Law School Course Catalog, 2012–13.

71 *"an initially hostile audience"*: Sloane, *supra*, at 256.

71 *"regarded capitalism as a racket"*: Schlesinger, *supra*, at 140.

72 *Union membership peaked*: Gerald Mayer, *Union Membership Trends in the United States*, Congressional Research Service (Aug. 31, 2004), at app. A.

72 *"We are going backward"*: Dubofsky and Dulles, *supra*, at 346.

72 *In the decade before he became president*: On Hoffa's decade in labor before he became president of the Teamsters, see Sloane, *supra*, at 35–41; Russell, *supra*, at 147–70; Witwer, *supra*, at 138–43; James and James, *Hoffa and the Teamsters*, *supra*, at 117–27. The 132,000 figure is from Sloane, *supra*, at 136.

73 *"If it moves, organize it"*: Chuckie said this in the Harvard class. *See also* Sloane, *supra*, at 35 (noting that Hoffa posted a sign at Local 299 that read: "If it moves, sign it up").

73 *"policy of non-discrimination"*: Letter from James R. Hoffa to All Local Unions (April 16, 1958), at http://teamsternation.blogspot.com/2013/02/jimmy-hoffa-letter-on-discrimination.html, perma.cc/R5M6-D7C8. On Hoffa's attitude toward organizing women and African American workers, see Witwer, *supra*, at 146–49.

73 *"a rough, brawling, extremely competitive battle royal"*: Paul Jacobs, *The State of the Unions* (1963), at 6.

74 *"ingenious" organizing techniques*: Ralph James and Estelle James, "Hoffa's Leverage Techniques in Bargaining," 3 *Industrial Relations* (Oct. 1963): 73. *See also* Witwer, *supra*, at 140–43.

74 *"First, we close down"*: Roy Rowan, "What Hoffa's Up To, as Jimmy Himself Tells It," *Life* (May 25, 1959).

75 *"single-minded dedication"*: Sam Romer, *The International Brotherhood of Teamsters: Its Government and Structure* (1962), at 47.

75 *"the boys who pay me"*: Conversation with Chuckie; and James and James, *Hoffa and the Teamsters*, *supra*, at 46.

76 *"I don't care what Jimmy Hoffa does"*: Romer, *supra*, at 142–43.

76 *"one of the most significant labor developments"*: John D. Pomfret, "Teamsters Achieve First National Pact in Truck Industry," *The New York Times* (Jan. 16, 1964).

77 *"hardly left Hoffa's side"*: FBI Interview with Barbara A. Crancer, Detroit 79-359 (Aug. 5, 1975) (in author's possession).

77 *"Tom is sort of a rough model"*: Steve Dunleavy, "Did Chuckie Take Sides Against the Family?" *New York Post* (Sept. 8, 2001).

78 *"intimate companion, driver, bodyguard"*: Victor Riesel, "Hoffa Is Free for '65," *Detroit Free Press* (Jan. 1, 1965).

80 *"the business sense of an industrial tycoon"*: James and James, *Hoffa and the Teamsters*, supra, at 36.

80 His time at Hoffa's side gave him *"much knowledge"*: FBI Interview with Frank Fitzsimmons, Washington, D.C., 79-431 (Aug. 15, 1975) (in author's possession).

80 *"would screw off"*: Id.

81 described Chuckie to the FBI as a *"bullshit artist"*: FBI Interview with Vincent Angelo Meli, Detroit, 79-359 (Aug. 1975) (in author's possession).

81 *"a big show-off"*: FBI Interview with Dominic Peter Corrado, Detroit, 79-359 (Aug. 6, 1975) (in author's possession).

81 *"extreme loyalty"*: Teletype from Las Vegas FBI to Director, FBI, 97-359 (Aug. 9, 1975), in Wayne State Archives, Jimmy Hoffa FBI Files, Box 1, Folder 25.

82 *"Hoffa loved Chuck"*: FBI Interview with Jackie Presser, Cleveland, 79-193 (Aug. 7, 1975) (in author's possession).

82 Hoffa *"completely trusted"* Chuckie: FBI Interview with Charles Ashman, Los Angeles, 9-5682 (August 7, 1975) (in author's possession).

82 *"started stomping and kicking"*: Nellie Kenyon, "Hoffa Attacker Confined," *The Tennessean* (Dec. 6, 1962).

82 *"spectators who had previously feared"*: Jim Ridley, "The People vs. Jimmy Hoffa, Part 2," *Nashville Scene* (Apr. 4, 2002).

83 *"My man Chuckie"*: Gavin Scott, "Mental Patient Fires 3 Shots at Hoffa in Court," *Atlanta Constitution* (Dec. 6, 1962).

83 *$1,000 for a cadaver's head*: Chuckie told me this story years before I read about it in confirming detail in David Maraniss's book, *Once in a Great City: A Detroit Story* (2015), at page 336. Maraniss reports in his book that this event occurred in 1977. But in correspondence Maraniss told me that he got the 1977 date (and other aspects of the story) from the Detroit journalist Pete Waldmeir, and added that the event might have occurred earlier. I contacted Waldmeir, who told me that upon reflection, "the head incident must have occurred in the 1960s."

83 *"paramount consideration, surpassing competence"*: James and James, *Hoffa and the Teamsters*, supra, at 64.

84 *"Puerto Rican boarding house"*: Clay, supra, at 79.

84 Chuckie was *"highly devoted"*: FBI Interview with Barbara A. Crancer, supra.

84 *"fun-loving and personable"*: Sloane, supra, at 59–60.

84 *"She stamped her foot"*: Jean Sharley, "Barbara Hoffa Wed in Exuberant Setting," *Detroit Free Press* (Oct. 22, 1961).

85 *"We go to him"*: Detroit FBI, ELSUR 92-438-Sub1-85, DE-0919-C* (Apr. 15, 1963), at 3.

86 *"You can't choose your associates"*: James and James, *Hoffa and the Teamsters*, supra, at 66.

86 a pact he struck with Johnny Dioguardi: For a review of the evidence of Dioguardi's

involvement, see James Neff, *Vendetta: Bobby Kennedy versus Jimmy Hoffa* (2015), at 20–22.

88 *"the product where it really counts"*: James R. Hoffa, *Chairman's Report*, 1958 Central Conference of Teamsters, *quoted in* Romer, *supra*, at 45.

89 *"Twenty years ago"*: Rowan, May 25, 1959, *supra*.

90 *"to reward friends and make new ones"*: Sloane, *supra*, at 275.

90 *"hailed like a Caesar"*: David G. Schwartz, *Grandissimo: The First Emperor of Las Vegas* (2013), at 87, 96.

91 *"the Teamsters Union did not participate"*: Stier, Anderson & Malone, *supra*, at 198.

93 *"is your key to Jimmy Hoffa"*: Detroit FBI, ELSUR 92-438-Sub1-327, DE-919-C* (June 3, 1963), at 13.

93 *"What she has done for us"*: Detroit FBI, ELSUR 92-438-Sub1-327, DE-919-C* (Dec. 13, 1963), at 11.

94 *"with some objectivity"*: James J. Healy, "Are Unions Coming of Age?," *Harvard Business School Bulletin* 35 (June 1959).

95 *"a man at war"*: Eric Sevareid, "Bloodied but Unbowed," *The Reporter* (Oct. 2, 1958) (reproduction of CBS radio broadcast).

4. BOBBY, JIMMY, AND CHUCKIE

97 *"Make sure he signs for every damned piece"*: Hoffa and Fraley, *supra*, at 91. Chuckie told me this story long before I discovered Hoffa's version of it, and some of the details are from Chuckie's recollection. *See also* James R. Hoffa, "The Day Hoffa Threw Out RFK," *Detroit Free Press* (Oct. 7, 1975) (giving more detail of Chuckie's involvement in this episode). Hoffa claimed that this event occurred in the summer of 1956, but for various reasons it is much more likely that it occurred in the summer of 1957.

97 *"conspiracy of evil"*: Robert F. Kennedy, *The Enemy Within: The McClellan Committee's Crusade Against Jimmy Hoffa and Corrupt Labor Unions* (1960), at 162.

98 propensity to pick fights had grown *"manic"*: Evan Thomas, *Robert Kennedy: His Life* (2000), at 67.

98 *"Without quite realizing why"*: *Id.* at 70.

99 *"There is a sinister criminal organization"*: Third Interim Report of the Special Committee to Investigate Organized Crime in Interstate Commerce, U.S. Senate (May 1, 1951), at 2.

99 *"the greatest potential threat"*: Letter from John L. McClellan to President Dwight D. Eisenhower, December 3, 1957, *quoted in* Anthony Baltakis, *Agendas of Investigation: The McClellan Committee, 1957–1958* (1997), at 39.

99 He was disgusted when he learned: The best accounts of the Hoffa-RFK relationship and feud, from which I have learned much, are Thomas, *supra*; Schlesinger, *supra*; Neff, *supra*; and John Bartlow Martin, *Jimmy Hoffa's Hot* (1959).

99 *"betrayed honest workingmen"*: Schlesinger, *supra*, at 154.

100 *"I know what I done wrong"*: Martin, *supra*, at 49.

100 The dinner at Cheyfitz's was *"foredoomed"*: Schlesinger, *supra*, at 154.

100 *"I do to others what they do to me . . . only worse"*: *Id.* at 153.

100 *"Here's a fella"*: *Id.*

101 *"damn spoiled jerk"*: *Id.* at 154.

101 253 separate investigations and hear 270 days of testimony from 1,526 witnesses: Moldea, *supra*, at 99.

101 *"jump off the Capitol"*: Schlesinger, *supra*, at 154.

102 *"Kennedy's sloppy practices"*: Neff, *supra*, at 84.

102 *"as a lifetime friend"*: Schlesinger, *supra*, at 155.

102 *"I feel deeply"*: Martin, *supra*, at 13.

102 *"besmirch Hoffa"*: Neff, *supra*, at 96.

103 *343 in all, pleaded the Fifth*: Larry Tye, *Bobby Kennedy: The Making of a Liberal Icon* (2017), at 76.

103 *"morally . . . yellow," lacking "guts"*: Investigation of Improper Activities in the Labor or Mgmt. Field: Hearings Before the Select Committee on Improper Activities in the Labor or Mgmt. Field, Part 49, 85th Congress 17848 (1958).

103 *"little girl[s]"*: Investigation of Improper Activities in the Labor or Mgmt. Field: Hearings Before the Select Committee on Improper Activities in the Labor or Mgmt. Field, Part 53, 86th Congress 18681 (1959).

103 *"were obviously designed"*: David Kaiser, *The Road to Dallas* (2009), at 22.

103 *"subvert the integrity of the administration of justice"*: Alexander M. Bickel, "Robert F. Kennedy: The Case Against Him for Attorney General," *The New Republic* (Jan. 9, 1961).

104 *"to the best of my recollection"*: Investigation of Improper Activities in the Labor or Mgmt. Field: Hearings Before the Select Committee on Improper Activities in the Labor or Mgmt. Field, Part 36, 85th Congress 13668 (1958).

104 *"to be something of a joke"*: Neff, *supra*, at 147.

104 *"to campaign against any candidate"*: "McClellan's Electioneering," *The Washington Post* (Sept. 25, 1957).

105 *"serve the cause"*: "The Pressures on Hoffa," *The Wall Street Journal* (Sept. 23, 1957).

105 *"Something is wrong"*: Sloane, *supra*, at 96.

105 *"a steady stream of inflammatory press"*: Robert A. Caro, *The Passage of Power: The Years of Lyndon Johnson* (2013), at 66 (internal quotations omitted).

105 *"a dragnet, working backwards"*: Neff, *supra*, at 135.

106 *"with every indication of sincerity"*: A. H. Raskin, "Why They Cheer for Hoffa," *The New York Times Magazine* (Nov. 9, 1958).

106 *"devastating impact"*: Lichtenstein, *supra*, at 162–63.

108 *"depicted the problem"*: Witwer, *supra*, at 183–84.

108 *"In my judgment, an effective Attorney General"*: Question and Answer Period Following Speech of Senator John F. Kennedy, Mormon Tabernacle, Salt Lake City, Ut. (Sept. 23, 1960).

109 *"I'm not satisfied"*: First Kennedy-Nixon Debate, Chicago, Ill. (Sept. 26, 1960).

109 *"The prosecutor has more control"*: Robert H. Jackson, "The Federal Prosecutor," delivered at the Second Annual Conference of United States Attorneys, Washington, D.C. (Apr. 1, 1940).

110 *"From the moment he was named attorney general"*: Nicholas deB. Katzenbach, *Some of It Was Fun: Working with RFK and LBJ* (2008), at 96.

110 *"became the public policy of the United States"*: Monroe H. Freedman, "The Professional Responsibility of the Prosecuting Attorney," 55 *Georgetown Law Journal* 1030 (1967).

110 *"files, records, and documents requested by him"*: Quoted in *Political Intelligence in the Internal Revenue Service: The Special Service Staff: A Documentary Analysis*, United States Congress, Senate Committee on the Judiciary Subcommittee on Constitutional Rights (1974), at 185. On the use and abuse of the IRS during the Kennedy administration and

other presidencies, I learned a good deal from this government analysis and from John A. Andrew III, *Power to Destroy: The Political Uses of the IRS from Kennedy to Nixon* (2002); David Burnham, *A Law Unto Itself: Power, Politics, and the IRS* (1990); and Neff, *supra*.

110 *"'saturation type' investigation"*: Schlesinger, *supra*, at 283.

111 *RFK first indicted Hoffa*: Neff's thorough account of Hoffa's two trials was indispensable to my understanding of them. Neff, *supra*.

111 *"Never in history had the government"*: Navasky, *supra*, at 417.

111 *"I knew where he was"*: *Id.* at 409.

111 *"The Man"*: *Id.* at 413.

111 *"On the other side, you had a group of criminal defendants"*: *Id.* at 410.

112 *"was dominated by his fear"*: James and James, *Hoffa and the Teamsters*, *supra*, at 62.

112 *"shameful" jury tampering efforts*: Neff, *supra*, at 275.

113 *Hoffa Squad memorandum*: Memorandum from James F. Neal to Nathan Lewin, *Re: Hoffa Jury Tampering—Joinder Problems* (Mar. 27, 1963), Lyndon B. Johnson Library, Personal Papers of Ramsey Clark, Box 95, Hoffa v. United States.

114 *"I know a way to get out of here"*: Quoted in Hoffa v. United States, 385 U.S. 293, 318 n.2 (1966) (Warren, C. J., dissenting).

114 *"report to the federal authorities any evidence"*: *Id.* at 298 (majority opinion).

115 *"My God, it's Partin"*: "Edward Partin, 66; Union Aide Became Anti-Hoffa Witness," *The New York Times* (Mar. 13, 1990).

115 *"the colored male juror"*: Quoted in *Hoffa*, 385 U.S., at 296 n.3.

117 *"Hoffa wouldn't be in this trouble"*: Detroit FBI, ELSUR 92-438-Sub1-536, DE-919-C* (July 9, 1964), at 8.

118 *"Bobby Kennedy is just another lawyer"*: Walter Sheridan, *The Fall and Rise of Jimmy Hoffa* (1972), at 300.

118 *"the kind of guy everybody knew"*: Moldea, *supra*, at 427–28 n.13.

118 *"the motive, means and opportunity"*: House Select Committee on Assassinations, 95th Congress, Final Report, No. 95-1828 (1979), at 176–79.

119 *"silent, melancholy"*: Caro, *supra*, at 577.

119 *"allowed existing rackets"*: Stier, Anderson & Malone, *supra*, at 190.

121 *"the greatest dangers to liberty"*: Olmstead v. United States, 277 U.S. 438, 479 (1928) (Brandeis, J., dissenting).

5. SURVEILLANCE BACKUP

123 *"Forty years ago, another Attorney General"*: Speech by Attorney General John Ashcroft, U.S. Conference of Mayors (Oct. 25, 2001).

123 *"extraordinary campaign"*: Elisabeth Bumiller, "Putting Name to Bush Justice Dept.: Kennedy," *The New York Times* (Nov. 21, 2001).

123 *"pushed in front of"*: Annex to the Report on the President's Surveillance Program, vol. III (July 10, 2009), at 30.

123 *"Don't ever let this happen again"*: John Ashcroft, *Never Again: Securing America and Restoring Justice* (2006), at 130.

123 *Ashcroft took this remark "personally"*: *Id.*

124 *"critically important"*: Annex to the Report on the President's Surveillance Program, *supra*, at 30.

124 *the godfather of the American surveillance state*: On Hoover and the FBI, I have learned from Tim Weiner, *Enemies: A History of the FBI* (2012); and Curt Gentry, *J. Edgar Hoover: The Man and the Secrets* (2001).

125 *"Justice Department Bans Wire Tapping"*: "Justice Department Bans Wire Tapping; Jackson Acts on Hoover Recommendation," *The New York Times* (Mar. 18, 1940).

125 *"under ordinary and normal circumstances"*: Confidential Memorandum, President Franklin D. Roosevelt to Attorney General Robert Jackson (May 21, 1940), *reproduced in* Senate Select Committee to Study Governmental Operations with Respect to Intelligence Activities, 94th Congress, Final Report, Book III (1976) [hereinafter "Church Committee Report Book III"], at 279.

126 *"flagrantly" violated the Fourth Amendment*: Irvine v. California, 347 U.S. 128, 132 (1954) (Jackson, J., plurality opinion). *Irvine* was a state court decision in which the government prevailed, but a majority of justices made clear that the police practice in that case violated the Fourth Amendment. The Supreme Court in the earlier 1942 decision of Goldman v. United States, 316 U.S. 129 (1942) had implied that such microphone surveillance premised on trespass violated the Fourth Amendment. In 1952, on the basis of *Goldman*, Truman's attorney general, J. Howard McGrath, banned the FBI practice of bugging via trespass. Hoover complied with McGrath's directive until he got a different ruling from Attorney General Brownell two years later (as explained in the text). *See* Church Committee Report Book III, *supra*, at 295–97.

126 *"informal draft"*: Gentry, *supra*, at 406.

126 *"espionage agents"*: Confidential Memorandum, Attorney General Herbert Brownell to FBI Director J. Edgar Hoover, *Re: Microphone Surveillance* (May 20, 1954), *reproduced in* Church Committee Report Book III, *supra*, at 296–97.

127 *"is not authorized to conduct"*: Testimony of J. Edgar Hoover, Investigation of Organized Crime in Interstate Commerce: Hearings Before the Senate Special Committee to Investigate Organized Crime in Interstate Commerce, 82nd Congress (1951), at 526.

127 *rural southern New York town of Apalachin*: On the Apalachin event, see Michael Newton, *The Mafia at Apalachin, 1957* (2012). Newton notes that while some sources say that Anthony Giacalone was a "probable" Apalachin attendee, "no solid evidence confirms his presence at the meeting." Chuckie says that Giacalone was at the meeting.

127 *"One microphone was worth a thousand agents"*: Gentry, *supra*, at 456.

128 *"national safety"*: Memorandum, FBI Assistant Director Alan Belmont to FBI Associate Director Clyde Tolson (July 2, 1959), *reproduced in* Athan Theoharis, *From the Secret Files of J. Edgar Hoover* (1993), at 142–43.

128 *"pushed, ordered, cajoled"*: Navasky, *supra*, at 46.

128 *"microphone surveillances"*: Memorandum, FBI Director J. Edgar Hoover to Deputy Attorney General Byron White (May 4, 1961), *reproduced in* Theoharis, *supra*, at 144.

129 *great deal of other evidence*: Much of this evidence is contained in Hoover's file for Fred B. Black Jr. in Hoover's Official and Confidential Files. J. Edgar Hoover, Official and Confidential Files, Fred B. Black, Jr., Cabinet 6, Drawer 1, copy available in Lamont Library, Harvard University. A few months after Hoover wrote to White, FBI assistant director Courtney Evans, the Bureau's liaison with RFK, wrote in a memorandum that he told Kennedy that the FBI was using microphones in organized crime cases, and that RFK

was "pleased." Memorandum from Courtney Evans to Alan Belmont (July 7, 1961), *reproduced in* Church Committee Report, *supra*, at 113–14. A month later, Kennedy approved a special telephone arrangement "in connection with microphone surveillances," though the approval did not distinguish between bugs deployed with and without trespass. *See* Navasky, *supra*, at 90.

129 *"To the extent that Kennedy was ignorant"*: Navasky, *supra*, at 71. As noted later in the text, the Department of Justice acknowledged in an artfully worded submission to the Supreme Court that it authorized Hoover's microphone practice, including during Kennedy's time as attorney general.

129 *842 wiretaps and installed 374 bugs*: Statement of Honorable Edward H. Levi, Attorney General of the United States, Electronic Surveillance Within the United States for Foreign Intelligence Purposes: Hearings Before the Subcommittee on Intelligence and the Rights of Americans of the Senate Select Committee on Intelligence, 94th Cong. 25 (1976). These figures are based on the full years 1961–1964. Kennedy served as attorney general from January 1961 through September 1964.

129 *"frightening paraphernalia"*: Silverman v. United States, 365 U.S. 505, 509 (1961).

130 *"were very real to Hoffa"*: James and James, *Hoffa and the Teamsters, supra*, at 63.

130 *"knew of any irregularities on the part of Bobby Kennedy"*: Informal Memorandum, FBI Assistant Director Cartha DeLoach to FBI Associate Director Clyde Tolson (June 14, 1966), *reproduced in* Theoharis, *supra*, at 268–71.

131 *"accomplished by means"*: Silverman, *supra*, 365 U.S. at 509.

132 *"Informant" of a "sensitive nature"*: One of scores of examples is Memorandum from Special Agent Harry R. Lunt to Special Agent in Charge, Detroit, *re: Anthony Giacalone*, ELSUR 92-470-1455, DE-92-228-Sub2 (July 11, 1963).

133 *criticized an associate as a "miniature Chuck O'Brien"*: Detroit FBI, ELSUR 92-438-Sub1-403, DE-919-C* (Feb. 27, 1964), at 11.

133 *"Trouble seems to follow both of them around"*: Detroit FBI, ELSUR 92-438-Sub1-443, DE-919-C* (Apr 7, 1964), at 2.

134 *"is in a state of shock"*: Detroit FBI, ELSUR 92-228-Sub1-159, DE-925-C* (Aug. 14, 1963), at 3.

134 *"She can't stand it no more"*: Detroit FBI, ELSUR 92-438-Sub1-354, DE-919-C* (Jan. 9, 1964), at 15.

134 *"had dinner at the Living Room Lounge"*: Detroit FBI, ELSUR 92-438-Sub1-359, DE-919-C* (Jan. 14, 1964), at 2.

134 *"belongs in an institution"*: Detroit FBI, ELSUR 92-438-Sub1-404, DE-919-C* (Feb. 28, 1964), at 1.

134 *"I love you, Josephine"*: Detroit FBI, ELSUR 92-228-Sub1-129, DE-925-C* (July 15, 1963), at 1.

134 *"if Josie didn't drink"*: Detroit FBI, ELSUR 92-228-Sub1-97, DE-925-C* (June 13, 1963), at 4.

134 *"I could have beat"*: Detroit FBI, ELSUR 92-228-Sub1-167, DE-925-C* (Aug. 22, 1963), at 1.

135 *"You can't watch her"*: Detroit FBI, ELSUR 92-438-Sub1-404, Feb. 28, 1964, *supra*, at 1.

135 *"I love you," she tells him*: Detroit FBI, ELSUR 92-228-Sub1-140, DE-925-C* (July 26, 1963), at 1.

135 *kicked the dispute up to his "confessor":* ELSUR 92-438-Sub1-318, DE-919-C* (Dec. 4, 1963), at 43.

135 *"one of the first requisites": Id.* at 28.

135 *"we are not connected with Hoffa": Id.* at 29.

136 *"talk to Gillis":* Detroit FBI, ELSUR 92-438-Sub1-292, DE-919-C* (Nov. 8, 1963), at 7.

136 *"wait till this thing is over":* Detroit FBI, ELSUR 92-438-Sub1-NR, DE-919-C* (Dec. 13, 1963), at 29.

136 There *"ain't nobody sharp enough": Id.* at 50.

136–37 *"grab that Jimmy Hoffa":* Detroit FBI, ELSUR 92-438-Sub1-311, DE-919-C* (Nov. 27, 1963), at 33.

137 *"Sylvia is the only person":* Detroit FBI, ELSUR 92-438-Sub1-356, DE-919-C* (Jan. 11, 1964), at 3.

137 Josephine *"got drunk and gave":* Detroit FBI, ELSUR 92-438-Sub1-360, DE-919-C* (Jan. 15, 1964), at 17–18.

137 *"zoop it up":* Detroit FBI, ELSUR 92-438-Sub1-383, DE-919-C* (Feb. 7, 1964), at 5.

140 *"They don't care about Hoffa":* Detroit FBI, ELSUR 92-228-Sub1-97, June 13, 1963, *supra,* at 1.

141 *"more resources, more power":* Tye, *supra,* at 143.

141 *"those officials at the highest levels of government":* Senate Select Committee to Study Governmental Operations with Respect to Intelligence Activities, 94th Congress, Final Report, Book II (1976) [hereinafter "Church Committee Report Book II"], at 139.

142 *"armory of electronic snooping devices":* "Congress Hopes to Cut Government Snooping," *Los Angeles Times* (Jan. 18, 1966).

142 *"referral fees":* William Lambert, "A Reply to the Senate Ethics Committee's 'Vindication' of Senator Long," *Life,* vol. 63 (Nov. 10, 1967), at 38. The original *Life* article critical of Long was William Lambert, "Ed Long's Help—Hoffa Campaign," *Life,* vol. 62 (May 26, 1967), at 26. On the FBI's manipulation and retaliation, see Ronald Kessler, *The Bureau: The Secret History of the FBI* (2002), at 103–104; Alexander Charns, *Cloak and Gavel: FBI Wiretaps, Bugs, Informers, and the Supreme Court* (1992), at 92; Gentry, *supra,* at 92. On the IRS's role, see Burnham, *supra,* at 296–99.

142 *"clearly illegal":* Do Not File Memorandum, FBI Assistant Director William Sullivan to FBI Assistant Director Cartha DeLoach (July 19, 1966), *reproduced in* Theoharis, *supra,* at 129.

142 *"The AG apparently feels":* Memorandum from A. H. Belmont to Clyde Tolson, Special Investigative Techniques, 62-12114-3398 (Sept. 28, 1965), *cited and quoted in* Charns, *supra,* at 155 n.26.

143 *"extremely concerned" about the loss of microphones:* Memorandum, FBI Director J. Edgar Hoover to Attorney General Nicholas Katzenbach (Sept. 14, 1965), *reproduced in* Theoharis, *supra,* at 148.

143 *"no specific statute or executive order":* The relevant portion of the Marshall memorandum is reproduced in Charns, *supra,* at 63–64.

143 *"FBI Had Sanction in Eavesdropping":* Fred P. Graham, "FBI Had Sanction in Eavesdropping," *The New York Times* (July 14, 1966).

143 *"Lawless Lawmen"*: Alan Barth, "Lawless Lawmen," *The New Republic* (July 30, 1966).

144 *"An extensive review"*: Supplemental Memorandum for the United States, Schipani v. United States, No. 504, October Term, 1966, at 5.

144 *"any information"*: Response to Application for Order, Kolod v. United States, No. 133, October Term, 1967, at 2.

145 *JUNE file*: "FBI Reveals It Has Special Wiretap File," *Detroit Free Press* (Aug. 20, 1969).

145 *"was not a surreptitious eavesdropper"*: Hoffa v. United States, 385 U.S. 293, 302 (1966).

145 *instructions from federal authorities to report "anything illegal"*: Id. at 319–21 (Warren, C. J., dissenting).

146 *"although many of the practices"*: Memorandum from law clerk to Justice Abe Fortas, *Hoffa v. United States*, Abe Fortas Papers, Yale University, Group No. 858, Series No. 1, Box 22, Folder 469.

146 *"pushed to the limit of propriety"*: Memorandum from law clerk to Justice John Marshall Harlan, *Hoffa v. United States* (Jan. 7, 1966), *in* John Marshall Harlan II Papers, Seeley G. Mudd Manuscript Library, Princeton University, *Hoffa v. United States*, Folder 32.

146 *"domestic security"*: U.S. v. U.S. District Court for Eastern District of Mich., 407 U.S. 297 (1972).

147 *"Martin Luther King, Jr., Security Matter—Communist"*: Memorandum for Attorney General, *re: Martin Luther King, Jr., Security Matter—Communist* (Oct. 7 1963) (in author's possession).

6. THE CONDITION

152 *"abuse of the Internal Revenue Service"*: Richard Nixon, *RN: The Memoirs of Richard Nixon* (2013), at 247.

153 *"I feel a little bit denied"*: White House Tapes: Sound Recordings of Meetings and Telephone Conversations of the Nixon Administration, Conversation No. 683-020 (Mar. 13, 1972), National Archives at College Park, College Park, MD [hereinafter "Nixon Tapes"].

153 *"Fellow sitting there"*: Nixon Tapes, Conversation No. 698-002 (Mar. 30, 1972).

153 *"Some people hate [Hoffa]"*: Nixon Tapes, Conversation No. 017-061 (Dec. 25, 1971).

155 *"the puppet"*: See, e.g., Detroit FBI, ELSUR 92-438-Sub1-451, DE-919-C* (Apr. 15, 1964), at 2.

157 *"chief concern was about his adjustment"*: Memorandum from J. J. Clark, Associate Warden, to J. J. Parker, Warden, *Preliminary Interview with James Hoffa*, U.S. Penitentiary, Lewisburg, Pennsylvania (Mar. 8, 1967), *in* Personal Papers of Ramsey Clark, *supra*, Bureau of Prisons, Box 84.

157 *"is not capable"*: Id.

157 *"I don't think I can judge"*: David R. Jones, "Fitzsimmons, Head of Teamsters, Fights Off Move to Oust Him and Strengthens His Hand," *The New York Times* (Aug. 27, 1967).

158 *"Most Teamster officials are happy"*: Id.

159 *"strong" and "uneducated working people"*: Nixon Tapes, Conversation No. 541-002 (July 21, 1971).

159 *"strong, vigorous pro-American"*: Nixon Tapes, Conversation No. 495-021 (May 7, 1971).

160 *"practically can't string"*: Nixon Tapes, Conversation No. 541-002, *supra*.

160 *"I like him"*: Nixon Tapes, Conversation No. 015-058 (Nov. 20, 1971).

160 *"I believe in the president"*: Nixon Tapes, Conversation No. 301-025 (Nov. 3, 1971).

160 decried countercultural *"agitators"*: Harry Bernstein, "Hoffa's Aide Confounds Observers, Develops Own Personality," *The Sunday Oregonian* (Apr. 27, 1969).

160 *"We've been getting"*: Nixon Tapes, Conversation No. 014-012 (Nov. 10, 1971).

160 *"was hopeful that he would not be here very long"*: Memorandum from J. J. Clark, *supra*.

161 Hoffa was *"buried alive"*: Sloane, *supra*, at 333.

161 Hoffa as a *"political prisoner"*: Ronald J. Ostrow and Murray Seeger, "Full Board to Consider Hoffa Parole," *Los Angeles Times* (Mar. 21, 1971).

162 *"made good political sense"*: Stephen Ambrose, *Nixon*, vol. 2, *The Triumph of a Politician, 1962–1972* (1989), at 491.

162 *"Mr. President, we've been playing"*: Nixon Tapes, Conversation No. 506-013 (May 28, 1971).

164 *"as assertive as ever"*: A. H. Raskin, "What the 'Little Fellow' Says to the Teamsters Is What Counts," *The New York Times Magazine* (May 30, 1971).

164 *"I'm going to run for president in July"*: This conversation is drawn from what Chuckie recalled about the event and from what Frank Fitzsimmons told Richard Nixon about it. *See* Nixon Tapes, Conversation No. 698-002 (Mar. 30, 1972).

165 *"almost surely would win"*: Raskin, *supra*.

165 *"because of my present legal problems"*: Philip Shabecoff, "Hoffa Is Stepping Aside as Teamsters' President," *The New York Times* (June 4, 1971).

165 *"My door is always open"*: Ambrose, *supra*, at 492.

165 *"it was the greatest"*: Nixon Tapes, Conversation No. 528-001 (Jun. 23, 1971).

165 *"I agree not to be in organized labor"*: Fitzsimmons made public the note six months after Hoffa disappeared. Rachelle Patterson, "Teamsters Chief Says Employers Face Big Increase in Pension Costs," *The Boston Globe* (Dec. 4, 1975).

166 *"We have got Mr. Fitzsimmons"*: This and the conversation in the next few paragraphs comes from Nixon Tapes, Conversation No. 558-003 (Aug. 9, 1971).

166 Chuckie had *"tears in [his] eyes"*: Ralph Orr, "Hoffa Loyalists Shocked," *Detroit Free Press* (Aug. 21, 1971).

167 *"I don't want him out"*: Nixon Tapes, Conversation No. 301-025 (Nov. 3, 1971).

167 *"Fitz wants to get Hoffa out"*: Nixon Tapes, Conversation No. 016-053 (Dec. 8, 1971).

167 *"strings" or "wraps"*: Nixon Tapes, Conversation No. 307-027 (Dec. 8, 1971).

167 *"The P apparently met"*: Harry R. Haldeman, *The Haldeman Diaries: Inside the Nixon White House* (1994), at 382.

167 *"enter the educational field"*: Hoffa v. Saxbe, 378 F. Supp. 1221, 1224 (D.D.C. 1974).

167 *"not engage in direct or indirect"*: Executive Grant of Clemency to James Riddle Hoffa and others (Dec. 23, 1971) (signed by President Richard Nixon) (in author's possession); *see also* Grant of Executive Clemency for James R. Hoffa (Dec. 23, 1971) (signed by Attorney General John Mitchell) (in author's possession).

168 *"The power of the President"*: Memorandum for Attorney General John Mitchell from John Dean, Counsel to the President, *Conditional Commutations* (Dec. 21, 1971) (in author's possession).

168 *"Now that solves"*: Nixon Tapes, Conversation No. 640-011 (Dec. 22, 1971).

169 *"I have no intention"*: "Nixon Frees Hoffa," *Detroit Free Press* (Dec. 24, 1971).

169 *"Whatever [the conditions] are"*: Gary Ronberg, "Hoffa Here for Christmas," *St. Louis Post-Dispatch* (Dec. 24, 1971). Hoffa's discussion with his probation officer is recounted in Brief of Appellee United States, Hoffa v. Saxbe, No. 74-1743 (Sept. 24, 1974), at 16 (in author's possession).

170 *"As a child O'Brien used to play"*: FBI, Interview with Frank Fitzsimmons, Washington, D.C., 79-431 (Aug. 15, 1975) (in author's possession).

173 *"What I mean is"*: Nixon Tapes, Conversation No. 886-008 (Mar. 21, 1973).

173 *"account for almost all of the money"*: Memorandum from Robert C. Stewart, Attorney in Charge, Buffalo Strike Force, to Kurt W. Muellenberg, Acting Chief, Organized Crimes and Racketeering Section, Department of Justice (Apr. 18, 1977), in Wayne State Archives, Jimmy Hoffa FBI Files, Box 1, Folder 6.

173 *Mitchell would "handle it"*: Nixon Tapes, Conversation No. 016-060 (Dec. 8, 1971).

178 *"almost no Hoffa interviewer"*: Sloane, *supra*, at 353.

179 *"Information would be our first line"*: Nixon, *supra*, at 357.

179 *"The president created"*: Weiner, *supra*, at 296.

180 *"the Watergate bugging incident"*: Carl Bernstein and Bob Woodward, "FBI Finds Nixon Aides Sabotaged Democrats," *The Washington Post* (Oct. 10, 1972).

180 *"bitter and widening rift"*: Philip Shabecoff, "Rift in Teamsters Dilemma to Nixon," *The New York Times* (Feb. 5, 1973).

180 *"To what extent is Fitz"*: Nixon Tapes, Conversation No. 849-001 (Feb. 5, 1973).

180 *"gradually violating"*: Id.

180 *"going to go back to jail"*: Nixon Tapes, Conversation No. 862-006 (Feb. 23, 1973).

180 *"move quickly to enforce all aspects"*: "U.S. Won't Budge on Hoffa Union Ban," *Detroit Free Press* (Feb. 27, 1973).

181 *"traveling all over the country"*: "Hoffa Criticizes 'Golfing Fitzsimmons,'" *Lansing State Journal* (Feb. 25, 1974).

181 *"I would not have accepted"*: Greg Walter, "Did Hoffa Err in Nixon Appeal?," *The Philadelphia Inquirer* (Mar. 13, 1974).

181 *The lawsuit "could produce"*: Philip Shabecoff, "Hoffa Sues Nixon for Free Role in Union," *The New York Times* (Mar. 14, 1974).

182 *It was widely reported*: See, e.g., Raskin, May 30, 1971, *supra*; Ralph Orr, "Fitzsimmons Wins in Landslide," *Detroit Free Press* (July 9, 1971). On the Justice Department's proposed legal bar, *see* Rowland Evans and Robert Novak, "Parole Held Likely for Jimmy Hoffa," *Hartford Courant* (July 15, 1970).

182 *"particularly displeased"*: Affidavit of Olymp Dainoff, Hoffa v. Saxbe, No. 74-424 (D.D.C.) (April 26, 1974) (in author's possession). Dainoff originally thought he spoke to James P. Hoffa, not Crancer.

182 *"insisted"*: FBI Summary of Interview with Morris Shenker, *reproduced in* Unsigned Insert for the File, Summary of the Evidence in the Hoffa Case, FBI, New Jersey (1979) [hereinafter "Unsigned 1979 Insert"] (in author's possession).

183 *"reasonable" in light of Hoffa's conviction*: Hoffa v. Saxbe, 378 F. Supp. 1221, 1222 (D.D.C. 1974) (internal quotations omitted).

183 *"Nothing is lost until the final round"*: Ralph Orr, "Hoffa's Union Ban Upheld," *Detroit Free Press* (July 20, 1974).

183 *"unwilling to alienate"*: Hoffa's thinking was attributed to a "source close to Hoffa" in William A. Clark, "How Hoffa Figures to Get Teamster Driver Seat Back," *The Pittsburgh Press* (Nov. 21, 1974).

183 *"retake and recommit"*: Memorandum from Henry E. Petersen, Assistant Attorney General, Criminal Division, to the Deputy Attorney General, *Re: James R. Hoffa* (Nov. 29, 1974) (in author's possession).

183 *"violated the terms and conditions"*: President of the United States, undated Draft Letter to the Attorney General to Apprehend and Return James R. Hoffa (in author's possession).

184 *"supreme realist"*: Unsigned 1979 Insert, *supra*.

7. "HE GOT NUTS"

186 *"All or some of the information"*: Complaint, Rosanova v. ABC-TV, James R. Hoffa et al., *filed in* Chatham County Superior Court (Jan. 27, 1975).

186 *"At that point"*: Report of Detroit Special Agent Andrew Ray Sluss, Case 281A-DE-67821 (May 13, 2002) (in author's possession).

188 *"Money is just a commodity"*: Patricia Burstein, "Tough Jimmy Hoffa Fights to Take Over the Teamsters Again," *People* (Mar. 3, 1975).

189 *"should not be allowed"*: Ralph Orr, "Hoffa Hits Back at Fitz on TV," *Detroit Free Press* (June 14, 1974).

189 *"I understand from reliable sources"*: Id.

191 *"Hoffa is going to try"*: Billy Bowles, "Hoffa Tries to Assist in Calif. Kidnap Case," *Detroit Free Press* (July 21, 1974).

192 *offered LCN leaders $10 million*: Unsigned 1979 Insert, *supra*.

192 *"'used to be guy'"*: Id.

194 *"almost like a son to me"*: Hoffa and Fraley, *supra*, at 91.

194 *"I charge"*: Id. at 15.

198 *"I wanted to retire"*: Moldea, *supra*, at 364.

199 *"Chuckie O'Brien, the stocky adopted son of Jimmy Hoffa"*: "Hoffa's Adopted Son Is Banished to Alaska," *Detroit Free Press* (Nov. 3, 1974).

200 *"I raised Chuck"*: "Hoffa's 'Son' Gone 4 Days," *The Detroit News* (Aug. 5, 1975). This story was published after Hoffa's disappearance but recounted Hoffa's earlier statement.

204 *"since he was a kid"*: FBI Interview with Frank Fitzsimmons, *supra*.

204 *"major factor"*: Id.

206 *"Hoffa is a bum"*: "Teamsters Chief Backs President," *Wilmington News Journal* (Mar. 3, 1975).

207 *"No one has ever"*: Burstein, *supra*.

207 *"Edward Levi is looking"*: Charles Ashman, "Hoffa Said No One Would Remember Him When He Was Gone," *The Boston Globe* (Aug. 13, 1975).

207 *"In 1975 rumors"*: Thomas Reppetto, *Bringing Down the Mob: The War Against the American Mafia* (2006), at 170.

207 *"reportedly advised the President"*: Moldea, *supra*, at 378.

208 *Levi "did not express"*: "FBI Moves into Hoffa's Home," *Detroit Free Press* (Aug. 5, 1975). An attorney who worked for Levi and handled his pardon matters—Mark Wolf—told me that he recalled nothing at all about considering, much less concluding, that the Hoffa condition was illegal.

208 *"Fitzsimmons would be indicted in the near future"*: Unsigned 1979 Insert, *supra*.

208 *"that he is unaware of any investigation"*: Memorandum from Special Agent in Charge, Detroit, to Director, FBI, Hoffex (Mar. 5, 1976), in Wayne State Archives, Jimmy Hoffa FBI Files, Box 2, Folder 19.

209 *"Dad was pushing so hard"*: Sloane, *supra*, at 371.

210 *"All I know is that Tony"*: Id.

210 *"clear the air"*: FBI Interview with James Phillip Hoffa, Detroit 79-359 (Aug. 4, 1975) (in author's possession).

8. THE DISAPPEARANCE

213 *"uncharacteristically acted strangely"*: Unsigned 1979 Insert, *supra*.

214 *"rough stuff" at Local 299*: Charles Ashman, "Hoffa Shared Thoughts Readily, Shrugged Off Fear," *Dayton Daily News* (Aug. 24, 1975).

214 *"acted in an uneasy manner"*: FBI Interview with Josephine Hoffa, Detroit, 79-359 (Aug. 4, 1975) (in author's possession).

214 *"TG 230 Wed"*: Hoffex Memorandum, *supra*.

214 *"very loud and was obviously upset"*: FBI Interview with Cynthia B. Green, Detroit 79-959 (Aug. 7, 1975) (in author's possession).

215 *"Hoffa was aware of something being very wrong"*: FBI Interview with Louis Clark Linteau, Detroit 79-359 (Aug. 4, 1975) (in author's possession).

215 *"The number of individuals in the area"*: Hoffex Memorandum, *supra*.

215 *"Did Tony Giacalone call?"*: FBI Interview with Josephine Hoffa, *supra*.

215 *"Son of a bitch Giacalone"*: FBI Interview with Linteau, Aug. 4, *supra*.

217 *"like a brother to me"*: FBI Interview with Joseph Giacalone, Detroit 79-359 (Aug. 8, 1975) (in author's possession).

218 *"acted in a very normal manner"*: FBI Interview with Violet Holmes, Detroit 79-359 (Sept. 3, 1975) (in author's possession).

219 *"immediately thought his father had been killed"*: FBI Interview with James Philip Hoffa, *supra*.

223 *"Jimmy Hoffa Is Missing"*: "Jimmy Hoffa Is Missing," *Detroit Free Press* (Aug. 1, 1975).

223 *"Mafia Chief Denies"*: "Mafia Chief Denies He Met Missing Hoffa as Police Hunt Mystery Man," *The Detroit News* (Aug. 1, 1975).

226 *"could not have been involved"*: "Hoffa's Stepson Reappears, Talks to FBI," *Detroit Free Press* (Aug. 7, 1975).

9. LEADING SUSPECT

228 *"an all-out investigation"*: "FBI Probing Hoffa Case," *The Detroit News* (Aug. 4, 1975).

229 *"utilized Charles O'Brien to 'set up' his father and have him killed"*: FBI Interview with James Philip Hoffa, *supra*.

229 *"increasing concern and curiosity"*: ABC Evening News (ABC television broadcast, Aug. 5, 1975).

229 *"dropped out of sight last Friday"*: "Hoffa's Family Sure O'Brien Is 'All Right,'" *The Detroit News* (Aug. 6, 1975).

231 *"has knowledge of what happened"*: "Hoffa's Foster Son Stalls on Demand for Lie Test," *Detroit Free Press* (Aug. 7, 1975).

231 appeared to be "lying": "O'Brien Is Lying, Says Hoffa's Son," *The Detroit News* (Aug. 7, 1975).

231 "something to hide": "Hoffas Suspect Union Tie to Disappearance," *The Detroit News* (Aug. 8, 1975).

231 "I feel that probable cause": United States v. Giacalone, 541 F.2d 508 (6th Cir. 1976).

233 sufficiently "similar" to the ones: Hoffex Memorandum, *supra*.

233 "It's eating my guts out": Robert M. Pavich and Michael F. Wendland, "'I'm the Fall Guy,' O'Brien Says," *The Detroit News* (Aug. 21, 1975).

233 "coupled with his continued refusal": "O'Brien Balks," *supra*.

238 "the prime movers": Unsigned Department of Justice Memorandum, Re: *Unknown Subjects; Anthony Giacalone; Anthony Provenzano; James Riddle Hoffa—Victim Missing Person* (Nov. 24, 1978), Wayne State Archives, Jimmy Hoffa FBI Files, Box 1, Folder 6.

10. TRAGEDY OF ERRORS

244 "Federal investigators are now satisfied": Tom Joyce and Anthony Marro, "A Break in the Hoffa Case," *Newsweek* (Aug. 30, 1976).

245 "troublesome . . . lack of evidence": Unsigned Department of Justice Memorandum, Detroit, Michigan, Re: *Unknown Subjects; Anthony Giacalone; James Riddle Hoffa—Victim* (Mar. 29, 1977), in Wayne State Archives, Jimmy Hoffa FBI Files, Box 5, Folder 19.

245 "The prospects of obtaining a conviction": Memorandum from Robert C. Stewart, Attorney in Charge, Buffalo Strike Force, to Kurt W. Muellenberg, Acting Chief, Organized Crimes and Racketeering Section, Department of Justice (Nov. 26, 1976), in Wayne State Archives, Jimmy Hoffa FBI Files, Box 1, Folder 6.

246 denied that he "ever picked up anyone": *60 Minutes* (CBS television broadcast, Nov. 7, 1976).

247 "Hours after Briguglio was gunned down": Pete Yost, "Hoffa's Disappearance Still Mystery, Thee Years Later," *The Morning News* (July 27, 1978).

249 "The Hoffa investigation has reached an impasse": Stewart Memorandum, Apr. 18, 1977, *supra*.

249 "necessary manpower and time commitments": Unsigned Memorandum, March 29, 1977, *supra*.

249 "pervasive Syndicate control of the Teamsters": Stewart Memorandum, Apr. 18, 1977, *supra*.

250 2,500 mob-related indictments: These figures come from James B. Jacobs, *Busting the Mob: The United States v. Cosa Nostra* (1994), at 5.

250 "had a tremendously positive impact": James Risen, "But FBI Thinks It Knows Killers: After 10 Years, Hoffa Case Still Shrouded in Mystery," *Los Angeles Times* (July 27, 1985).

252 "would never let anything happen": Interview with Chuckie O'Brien, *The David Newman Show* (WXYZ radio broadcast, Nov. 9, 1976).

252 "Investigators are watching": Stewart Memorandum, November 26, 1976, *supra*.

253 "government agents" believed: Moldea, *supra*, at 400–401.

253 "study of the government's investigation": Brill, *supra*, at 69–70.

253 "My family has been through a lot": "The Jimmy Hoffa Mystery—Five Years Later," *Pensacola News* (July 30, 1980).

254 *"I believe there are very few"*: Risen, *supra*.

254 *"In America can a man be guilty until proven innocent?"*: *Absence of Malice*, Taglines, *at* www.imdb.com/title/tt0081974/taglines, *archived at* perma.cc/V9Y3-MLVS.

255 *"captive labor organization"*: Complaint, United States v. Int'l Bhd. of Teamsters, No. 88 Civ. 4486, Southern District of New York (1988). The relevant portions of the Complaint are reproduced in James B. Jacobs, *Breaking the Devil's Pact: The Battle to Free the Teamsters from the Mob* (2013), from which I learned much.

256 *"Was Anthony Giacalone ever a member"*: Deposition of Chuckie O'Brien, by Edward Ferguson, Assistant U.S. Attorney, Southern District of New York, 88 Civ. 4486 (Nov. 16, 1988) (in author's possession).

258 *"The blaring headlines"*: Charles O'Brien, *The Agony of Justice* (in author's possession).

260 *"I am tired of headlines"*: *The Maury Povich Show* (Jan. 7, 1993).

261 *"star lie detector"*: Wolfgang Saxon, "Natale Laurendi, 75; Investigator and Expert with the Lie Detector," *The New York Times* (Jan. 4, 1999).

261 *"Yes, indeed, he passed"*: *The Maury Povich Show* (Jan. 14, 1993).

262 *In article after article and book after book*: Dan Moldea is an exception. In his book *Confessions of a Guerilla Writer* (2013), he noted that Chuckie took and passed a polygraph test administered by Laurendi, the "New York Police Department's top lie-detector expert until 1975."

11. FAILED VINDICATION

264 *"calls into question the repeated claim"*: Norman Sinclair and David Shepardson, "New Clue Might Mean Charges in Hoffa Death," *The Detroit News* (Sept. 7, 2001).

267 *"large rug"*: FBI, Interview with Josephine Hoffa, Detroit 79-359-Sub G (Sept. 19, 1975) (in author's possession).

267 *"Contact between a victim"*: Douglas W. Deedrick, Unit Chief, Trace Evidence Unit, FBI, *Hairs, Fibers, Crime, and Evidence, Part 3: Crime and Evidence*, 2(3) Forensic Science Communications (July 2000).

267 *"Human scent is easily transferred"*: Rex A. Stockham, Dennis L. Slavin, and William Kift, *Specialized Use of Human Scent in Criminal Investigations*, 6(3) Forensic Science Communications (July 2004).

270 *"Due to personal problems"*: FBI, Memorandum by Stephen J. Ferrari and Andrew Ray Sluss, No. 281A-DE-67821 (Aug. 14, 2001), in Wayne State Archives, Jimmy Hoffa FBI Files, Box 1, Folder 23.

270 *"Federal investigators said that the DNA"*: Sinclair and Shepardson, *supra*.

270 *it was a "family consensus"*: FBI, Memorandum by Stephen J. Ferrari and Andrew Ray Sluss, No. 281A-DE-67821 (Dec. 11, 2001), in Wayne State Archives, Jimmy Hoffa FBI Files, Box 1, Folder 23.

271 *"The evidence in this case does not provide"*: Sluss, May 13, 2002, Report, *supra*.

271 *"there is no viable federal prosecution"*: "No Federal Charges to Be Filed in Hoffa Case," *Lansing State Journal* (Mar. 29, 2002).

282 *"We did not uncover"*: Joseph Lichterman, "FBI Ends Search for Jimmy Hoffa's Body," *Chicago Tribune* (June 20, 2013).

12. OMERTÀ

293 *"It would be a comfort to find his body"*: John Wisely, "40 Years Later, Jimmy Hoffa Mystery Endures," *Detroit Free Press* (Aug. 18, 2015).

293 *"If you were accused"*: Paul Hendrickson, "The Fighting Spirit of Jimmy Hoffa's Kids," *The Washington Post* (July 17, 1991).

295 *"Hoffa steak salad"*: Steve Neavling, "Barn Shredded in Hoffa Search," *Detroit Free Press* (May 25, 2006).

300 *"morally indefensible" because the author*: Janet Malcolm, *The Journalist and the Murderer* (1990), at 3.

APPENDIX

317 *would be leaving the Machus Red Fox "momentarily"*: FBI Interview with Linteau, Aug. 4, *supra*.

317 *call came at "approximately" 3:30 p.m.*: Id.

317 *"positive" that the call came at 3:30 p.m., and was "vehement" for various reasons*: FBI Interview with Louis Clark Linteau, Detroit 79-359 (Nov. 6–7, 1975) (in author's possession).

318 *Joey Giacalone testified that he drove Chuckie*: One limitation in the evidence is the absence of corroboration or contradiction in the FBI record for the testimony by Chuckie and Joey Giacalone that Chuckie stopped at Lift-All, rather than proceeding directly to Local 299 and having the car returned to Joey by some other means. Nevertheless, the FBI's 2002 report does not challenge this testimony. And even the direct route from the Machus Red Fox to Local 299 would have required almost thirty minutes, which would still leave Chuckie little time for a detour to drop off Hoffa and be back at Local 299 by the times he was seen there by Destine Kyff and Joseph Valenti.

ACKNOWLEDGMENTS

I am thankful for the help I received from so many people during the seven
years that it took to research and write this book.

I received very generous support from two Harvard Law School deans,
Martha Minow and John Manning, and two directors of the Hoover Institution, John Raisian and Tom Gilligan.

I am especially grateful to the amazing FRIDA staff at the Harvard Law
School Library for its years of help in tracking down legal and factual materials for this book. George Taoultsides and Mallory Heath deserve special
mention for helping me obtain materials from other libraries and collections.
I also thank the staff of the Walter P. Reuther Library at Wayne State University, especially Kristen Chinery.

Many people, including students at several universities, provided vital research help over the seven years: Ahson Azmat, Lauren Bateman, Lavinia Borzi, Nina Cohen, Cameron Etchart, Andrew Ferguson, Kayla Ferguson, Jonathan Gartner, Isaac Gelbfish, Justin Gilio, Mark Gillespie, Jenya Godina, David Husband, Kevin Keller, Marissa Lambert, Harold Lee, Maddie McMahon, Daniel Melling, Evan Meyerson, Jack Middough, Ben Miller-Gootnick, Joseph Nawrocki, Jason Neal, Daniel Nessim, Branton Nestor, Kevin Neylan, Sara Nommensen, Catherine Padhi, Todd Pierce-Ryan, Deema Qashat, Chris Rendall-Jackson, Paul Rogerson, Andrew Rohrbach, Michael Roig, Neha Sabharwal, Garrett Schuman, Lauren Schwarzenholzer, Andrew Smith, James Strickland, Frank Tamberino, David Thoreson, Sean-henry VanDyke, JB Ward, Derek Woodman, and Victor Zapana.

For helping me to better understand the many topics and events covered by this book, I thank Marvin and Betty Adell, David Ashenfelter, Mike Bane, Marvin Berke, Jules Bernstein, John Bies, Robert Blakey, Larry Brennan Jr., Steven Brill, James Burdick, Jim Byer, Pete Catalano, Ramsey Clark, Paul Coffey, Keith Corbett, John Dean, Michael DeFeo, Jim Dooley, Jim Esposito, Edward Ferguson, Richard Freeman, Robert Garrity, William Hagner, Phil Heymann, James Jacobs, Michael Katz, Larry King, Joe Koenig, Nathan Lewin, Nelson Lichtenstein, Kurt Luedtke, David Maraniss, Dan Moldea, Clyde Pritchard, Thaddeus Russell, Fritz Schwarz, Charles Shaffer, Arthur Sloane, Andrew Sluss, Al Sproule, Gregory Stejskal, Jody Valet, Pete Waldmeir, Mark Wolf, Jon Wolman, and Richard Zuckerman. I also thank those who did not want to be mentioned.

For valuable comments on all or part of the manuscript, I thank Mike Bane, Andrew Crespo, Jim Dooley, Tim Edgar, Jim Esposito, Robert Garrity, Orin Kerr, Marty Lederman, Larry Lessig, Daryl Levinson, Sam Moyn, Brett O'Brien, Steven O'Brien, Michael Roig, Peter Romatowski, Kerri L. Ruttenberg, Al Sproule, Paul Stephan, Alex Whiting, Leslie Williams, and Andrew Woods. Toby Lester deserves special mention. He gave me excellent detailed and structural comments on the entire manuscript, and he helped me think through a number of hard issues in the book during many fun lunches.

Peter Romatowski provided superb legal and other advice in connection with the book. Elisa Rivlin also provided great legal advice. Kerri L. Ruttenberg designed the maps and graphics in the Appendix, and Kim Levine produced them.

For the second book in a row, Blakey Vermeule gave me an idea that proved important.

My agent, Andrew Wylie, provided his usual sage counsel, and also had a crucial conversation with Chuckie.

Farrar, Straus and Giroux was wonderful in every way. Over seven years my editor, Alex Star, provided essential help on every element of the book that improved it enormously. He was also patient and supportive at every step. I am also thankful for the help of others at FSG, especially Scott Auerbach and Ian Van Wye.

My extraordinary assistant, Jan Qashat, helped me in ways that are too numerous to list. Jan, thanks for everything.

I am confident I have neglected to mention others who helped me along the way. I thank you all, and apologize for the omissions.

Finally, I want to thank my family.

My wife, Leslie, and sons, Jack and Will, gave me all manner of loving support, including tolerating without complaint my dozens of out-of-town trips to work on this book. As the writing dragged out, my sons developed a standard retort—"When are you going to finish the Hoffa book?"—when I chastised them for being behind on schoolwork.

Writing this book required me to dig up, remember, and relive some painful experiences that my mother, Brenda, and my brothers, Brett and Steven, lived through. My work on the book has also led them to relive some of these experiences. We have grown closer as a result, and my love and respect for all of them has deepened. Writing this book led me to appreciate much more than before how difficult Brenda's life has been. But she was always extraordinarily resilient, and she worked fiercely despite her difficulties to give my brothers and me every opportunity to succeed. You made everything possible, Mom.

No one has had more painful remembrances due to this book than Chuckie. And yet he soldiered through seven years of discussions with me, answering question after question, almost always with humor and good cheer. The hundreds of hours we spent together talking about this book brought us much closer than ever, despite occasional hard moments. And it made me realize what a great man he is, and what greatness in a father means. I don't have much to add on that score beyond what I have said in this book. But I thank you once again, Dad, and dedicate this book to you.

INDEX

Abbate, Paul, 282–83
ABC (TV network), 229
ABC News Close Up, 185–86, 202, 208
Absence of Malice, 254
Accardo, Anthony "Big Tuna," 93
ACLU (American Civil Liberties Union), 111, 145
Addington, David, 37, 148
Adell, Betty, 172, 185, 191, 201, 203, 221–23, 277
Adell, Bobby, 226
Adell, Lawrence, 191
Adell, Marvin, 172, 185, 191, 201, 203, 216–18, 221–23, 226, 277

AFL (American Federation of Labor), 51, 52, 72
AFL-CIO, 72, 106
African American workers, 73
Agony of Justice, The (O'Brien and O'Brien), 258–60
Alaska, 199–200, 204
alcohol, 24, 55; Prohibition and, 45, 46, 49, 54, 55, 57, 58, 110
Allen, Charles, 176
al-Qaeda, 4, 37
Ambrose, Stephen, 162
Andretta, Stephen, 248, 294
Andretta, Thomas, 248, 253, 294

Anthony, John, 254
Apalachin meeting, 60–61, 127, 128
Ashcroft, John, 38, 120, 122–24, 147–49
Ashman, Charles, 82, 207, 214
Attorney's Office, U.S., *see* U.S. Attorney's Office

"backup," 98, 121, 124, 150
Bailey, Jay, 228
Baker, Barney, 117, 118
Baker, Bobby, 143
Baker, Jim, 147–48
Bane, Michael, 81–82
Barbera, Joe "the Barber," 127
Beck, Dave, 96–97, 101, 207
Bellino, Carmine, 97, 110
Belmont, A. H., 142–43
Bender, Tony, 87
Berger, Clemmye, 13–17, 21, 172, 202
Berger, Morris, 12
Berger v. New York, 4
Berke, Marvin, 130
Bernstein, Carl, 180
Bickel, Alexander, 103
Biddle, Francis, 125
Binaggio, Charlie, 45–46, 47
Black, Fred, 143–44
Black Hand gangs, 45
Bonanno, Joseph, 55, 56, 228
Boudin, Leonard, 181
Brandeis, Louis, 121
Brandt, Charlie, 253, 309, 310
Brazil, Ind., 48
Brennan, Larry, 165
Brennan, Owen "Bert," 48, 58, 66, 67, 81; funeral for, 154, 155
Bridges, Harry, 73
Briguglio, Gabriel, 253
Briguglio, Salvatore "Sally Bugs," 239, 247–48, 253, 294, 310
Brill, Steven, 253
Brinkley, David, 54
Brown, Harold, 116

Brownell, Herbert, 126–28
Bufalino, Russell, 94, 309, 310
Bufalino, William, 224
Burdick, James, 229–31
Burns, Larry, 136, 144
Bush, George W., 35–38, 122; Stellarwind program of, 3–4, 123–24, 147–51
Byer, Jim, 248

Caesars Palace, 90–91
Caine Mutiny, The, 197
Cammisano, William, 195
Campbell, Larry, 112
Campo, Paolo, 46, 47
Caplin, Mortimer, 110
Capone, Al, 16, 54, 55, 57, 120
Card, Andrew, 149
Caro, Robert, 105, 119
Cash, Johnny, 80, 257
Castellammarese War, 54
Castellito, Big Anthony "Three Fingers," 87, 247
Castro, Fidel, 259
CBS, 95; *60 Minutes*, 246–47, 252
Central States Drivers Council, 53, 66
Chavez, César, 172
Cheasty, John Cye, 101, 102
Cheney, Dick, 37–39, 148–49
Cheyfitz, Eddie, 100, 101
Chicago, Ill., 57, 85, 89, 93–94, 186, 195
Chicago Waste Handlers Union, 89
Church Committee, 141, 146, 228, 258–59
CIA (Central Intelligence Agency), 32, 38, 258–59
Cimini, Anthony, 135, 139–40
CIO (Congress of Industrial Organizations), 52, 53, 58, 59, 72
Civella, Carl "Cork," 94
Civella, Nick, 94
civil rights movement, 73, 141
Clark, J. J., 157

Clark, Ramsey, 111
Clinton, Bill, 16, 120
Clinton, Ind., 48–49
Coffey, Paul, 247, 250
Colson, Chuck, 153, 159–60, 162, 166–68, 173–74, 178, 181–82
Comey, James, 148–49, 274
Commercial Appeal (Memphis), 18
communism, 71, 73, 124, 126, 128, 129, 147–48, 195
Congress, U.S., 146, 178, 195, 250; *see also* Senate, U.S.
"Convoy," 23
Corallo, Antonio "Tony Ducks," 86, 94
Corrado, Dominic Peter, 81
Cosa Nostra, *see* Mafia
Costello, Frank, 16, 101
Cox, Archibald, 181
Crancer, Barbara Hoffa, 64, 65, 77, 82–84, 293, 294, 302
Crancer, Robert, 84
Crane, Marita, 317
Crater, Joseph, 188
Curtis, Carl, 108

Dainoff, Olymp, 182
Dalitz, Morris "Moe," 60, 90
Dean, John, 168, 173, 181
Defense Department, U.S., 35, 36, 264, 296
DeLoach, Cartha, 130
De Pasco, Lanie, 191, 201
Depression, Great, 47, 50–52, 55
Dershowitz, Alan, 274
Detroit, Mich., 49–50, 66, 276–77; author's visits to, with O'Brien, 276–78, 287, 302–303; Mafia in, 47, 57–61, 63, 67, 81, 84–85, 87, 135, 221, 258, 265, 266; Teamsters in, 52–53, 57–60, 154; Teamsters Local 299 in, *see* Local 299; UAW-General Motors contract in, 72; violence in, 53, 209, 214; Woodward Avenue, 279

Detroit Free Press, 84, 131, 166, 191, 218–19, 223, 225, 226, 254
Detroit Lumber Company, 57–59, 84
Detroit News, The, 83, 139, 183, 200, 223, 229, 233, 264, 270
Detroit Red Wings, 80
Detroit River, 80–81, 144
DeVito, Danny, 257
Dioguardi, Johnny ("Johnny Dio"), 86, 88, 92, 104
Dooley, Jim, 239, 250, 251, 290–92
Dorfman, Allen, 89–93, 112, 117, 119–20, 158, 163, 170, 175, 176, 195, 210, 239
Dorfman, Paul "Red," 89, 117
Dunes Hotel, 91, 213
Dunlop, John, 70
Duvall, Robert, 77, 254, 257

Eisenhower, Dwight D., 99, 126, 128, 129
Eglin Air Force Base, 22, 25
Ehrlichman, John, 162, 180, 181
Ellsberg, Daniel, 159
Enemy Within, The (Kennedy), 97, 111
Ervin, Sam, 108
Esposito, Jim, 229–33, 237, 290–92

FBI (Federal Bureau of Investigation), 7, 45, 77, 80, 81, 84, 85, 93, 99, 101, 116, 117, 149, 170, 173, 176, 180, 182, 184, 186, 193, 195, 208, 213, 215, 216, 219, 310; and ABC News special on Hoffa, 202; author's meeting with Hoffa case investigators, 290–92; author's security clearances and, 32–34; and failed vindication of O'Brien, 263–86; on Giacalone, 20–21; Hoffa disappearance investigation of, 227–40, 249–50, 254, 255, 260; Hoffa disappearance theory of, 17–18, 233–37, 268, 291, 309, 315–21; Hoffa's remains searched for by, 282, 295; Hoover at, 124–29; JUNE file of secret recordings, 131–40, 144, 145; Mafia under increased pressure from,

FBI (cont.)
194–95; and O'Brien as suspect in
Hoffa's disappearance, 5, 6, 17–18, 22,
39, 218, 221, 222, 245–48, 269–70,
315–21; O'Brien interviewed by, 17,
229–32, 237, 266, 296; O'Brien's Florida
relocation and, 204; O'Brien's refusal
to take lie detector test with, 18, 36;
organized crime discoveries made by,
249–50, 255; surveillance by, 125–29,
143, 311–12; surveillance of Hoffa by,
111, 112, 129–42, 145–46; surveillance
of Mafia by, 127–29, 138, 141–43
Ferguson, Ed, 255–57
Ferrari, Steve, 269, 270
Field, Sally, 23
Fields, Gratin, 112–15
Fifth Amendment, 103, 105, 233, 256
Filardo, Joseph, 61
Finazzo, Sam, 144
Finnegan, Joe, 265–66
Fischetti, Louis, 272, 273, 279–81,
285–86, 302, 303
F.I.S.T., 23
Fitzsimmons, Frank, 23, 154–55, 184,
230, 241; as Brennan's successor,
154–55, 216; and conditions of Hoffa's
release, 164–69, 182, 207; elected
president of Teamsters, 165–66;
Giacalone and, 155, 171; Giacalone's
message to, 225–26, 289; golf playing
of, 158–59, 171, 181, 206–207; Hoffa's
feud with, 178–81, 185, 188–90,
193–97, 200, 206–207, 212, 252;
Hoffa's prison furlough and, 163–65;
Hoffa's reelection plans and, 163–65;
Hoffa's requests to O'Brien to turn
against, 193–94, 197, 199; IRS and,
193, 199, 208; Mafia and, 17, 156, 158,
163, 171, 185–86, 192, 240; Mitchell
and, 173–74; Nixon and, 159–62, 165,
166, 178–81; and Nixon's deliberations
about Hoffa's release, 162–63; O'Brien

and, 157, 158, 161, 170–72, 174–76,
187, 189, 190, 192–94, 197, 200, 201;
O'Brien relocated to Alaska by,
199–200, 204; Pagano and, 170;
Rosanova and, 186; as Teamsters
head in Hoffa's absence, 155–65;
as Teamsters president, 17, 23, 80,
119–20, 165–66, 170, 171, 192, 240;
Teamsters pension fund and, 158
Fitzsimmons, Richard "Dickie Bird," 190,
193, 198, 199, 209
Florida, 16, 18, 20, 204–205, 216
Florida Air Academy, 14, 19–20, 204
Flowers, Jacqueline, 318
Foley, Robert, 282
Ford, Gerald, 183, 207
Foreign Intelligence Surveillance Act
(FISA), 146–48
Fortas, Abe, 130, 145–46
Fourth Amendment, 126, 128, 131, 138,
145, 146, 150
Fraley, Oscar, 194
Frank & Cedar's Dry Goods, 49, 50
Freedman, Monroe, 110
Freedom of Information Act, 141–42
Fremont casino, 91, 142
Frontier casino, 133, 135

Gambino, Carlo, 242
Gambino crime family, 63
Gamtax, 258, 265, 266
Garrity, Robert, 229–33, 237, 290, 291
Gavin, Neil, 272
General Motors, 72
Genovese crime family, 17, 86, 87, 238,
242, 289
Giacalone, Anthony "Uncle Tony,"
20–22, 43–44, 57–58, 60–61, 85,
92, 93, 127, 131–33, 135–37, 140,
187, 191, 193, 200, 210–12, 223, 267,
280–81, 288, 292, 299, 304, 308, 313;
conviction and imprisonment of,
247; death and funeral of, 247, 269,

281; FBI surveillance and, 131–38, 144, 145, 312; Fitzsimmons and, 155, 171; Fitzsimmons's message from, 225–26, 289; Hoffa's disappearance and, 16–18, 20, 43, 44, 139, 214–16, 219–26, 229–43, 258, 267, 269, 288–89, 317, 320; Hoffa robbery plotted by Pagano and, 137–39, 210; Hoffa's meetings with Vito and, 210–11; Hoffa's wardrobe and, 136; Home Juice Company headquarters of, 131, 133, 144, 145, 222; Josephine Hoffa and, 135, 197, 210; O'Brien and, 17, 18, 33, 43–44, 61–64, 67–68, 133, 170–71, 175, 177, 187, 195–98, 200, 222, 235, 248, 299; O'Brien given permission to talk by, 251–52; O'Brien's meeting with Provenzano and, 240–43, 289, 299; and O'Brien's questioning by Ferguson, 256; Pagano and, 60, 62, 93, 131, 135; Southfield Athletic Club headquarters of, 222, 226, 230, 238, 320; wiretapped conversations of, 258, 281

Giacalone, Giacamo, 58

Giacalone, Joey, 217, 221, 222, 235, 318, 320, 321; car of, 17, 217, 218, 221, 222, 230, 232–34, 236, 237, 241, 246, 252, 264, 266–68, 280, 316

Giacalone, Vito, 133, 134, 136–39, 191, 197, 281, 288, 304, 313; Hoffa's meetings with Tony and, 210–11; as suspect in Hoffa's disappearance, 294

Giacalone, Zina, 20, 224

Giancana, Salvatore, 93, 259

Gibbons, Harold, 165

Gillis, Joseph, A., 136

Giuliani, Rudy, 255–57

Glimco, Joey, 195

Godfather, The (film series), 98

Godfather, The (Puzo), 77–78, 254

Goldsmith, Jack: birth of, 12; at boarding school, 14, 19–20, 204; brothers of, 12–14, 16, 19–20, 24, 27, 29, 30, 203, 232, 248, 270; career of, 3, 5–7, 30–32, 34,

36–40; childhood of, 12–16; children of, 34, 35, 40; Christian faith of, 40; at Defense Department, 35, 36, 264, 296; education of, 25–27, 30–31; as Harvard Law School professor, 6, 39, 43; Harvard Law School seminar taught by, 69–71, 75; Hoffa's disappearance investigated by, 8–9, 296–97; at Italian restaurant with O'Brien, 313–14; at Justice Department, 3, 5, 7, 36–40, 122, 147–51, 239; kidnapping threat and, 248; mother of, see O'Brien, Brenda; name changes of, 21, 26–30; O'Brien as stepfather of, 5, 9, 11, 15–16, 20–37, 40, 42–43, 203, 288, 314; O'Brien renounced by, 5, 25–40, 98, 255; O'Brien's conversations with, 7–10, 42, 62–64, 174–77, 206, 220, 224–25, 243, 263, 288–90, 297–302, 304, 309; O'Brien's correspondence with, 27–30, 40, 206; O'Brien's reaction to book of, 307–9; O'Brien's reconciliation with, 6, 38, 40–41, 42; O'Brien's revelations to, at Seasons 52, 288–90, 297–99, 301, 302, 304; O'Brien's visits to Detroit with, 276–78, 287, 302–303; political views of, 30; security clearances of, 32–37, 265; as University of Chicago professor, 34, 35, 264; wife of, 34, 35, 40

Goldsmith, Jack, Jr. (father), 11–16, 26; Andrew and, 11–12; Brenda's marriage to, 12–14

Goldsmith, Jack, Sr. (grandfather), 26

Goldwater, Barry, 99, 108

Gonzales, Alberto, 36–38, 148–49

Goodfellas, 62

Gorcyca, David, 271

Gordon, Robert, 12

Gotti, John, 63

Graham, Billy, 75

Gravano, Salvatore "Sammy the Bull," 63

Gray, L. Patrick, 195

Grecian Gardens, 67

Green, Cynthia, 317

Haggerty, James, 130

Haldeman, H. R., 162, 166, 168–69, 181

Harding, James, 214

Harlan, John Marshall, 146

Harvard Business School Bulletin, 94

Harvard Law School, 6, 39, 43; author's seminar at, 69–71, 75; Hoffa's speech at, 70–71

Hastings, Al, 50–51

Hayden, Martin, 83

Healy, James, 94

Hearst, Patricia, 228, 249

Helms, Richard, 259

Hidden Dreams Farms, 295

Hitler, Adolf, 125

Hoffa (film), 257–58, 281

Hoffa, Barbara (daughter), 64, 65, 77, 82–84, 293, 294, 302

Hoffa, Billy (brother), 49

Hoffa, James P. (son), 18, 64, 65, 83, 84, 118, 181, 182, 190–91, 209, 210; Jimmy's disappearance and, 219–23, 228–33, 236, 231, 232, 238, 293, 318, 319; O'Brien and, 190–91, 220–23; O'Brien suspected by, 228–33, 236, 268, 278, 280, 293–94

Hoffa, James R. "Jimmy": on *ABC News Close Up*, 185–86, 202, 208; Adell kidnapping and, 191; arrests of, 99–101, 103; assassination attempt on, 82–83; assumed to be O'Brien's biological father, 44, 59–60, 82; author's Harvard Law School seminar and, 69–71, 75; autobiography of, 65; authoritarian control by, 4, 74–75, 170, 171; birth of, 48; Cheasty and, 101, 102; commutation restriction rumors spread by, 207–209; criminal trials of, 77, 81, 83, 94, 106, 111–17, 130, 132, 135, 137, 145, 154; dedication to union members, 75, 94, 179; *Detroit News* and, 83; early jobs of, 49–50; early life of, 48–49; education of, 49, 70; elected

president of Teamsters, 72, 79, 86, 88, 96, 104–106; FBI surveillance of, 111, 112, 129–42, 145–46; first union organizing by, 50–51; Fitzsimmons as Teamsters head during imprisonment of, 155–65; Fitzsimmons's feud with, 178–81, 185, 188–90, 193–97, 200, 206–207, 212, 252; Giacalone and, *see* Giacalone, Anthony "Uncle Tony"; government investigations of, 77, 83, 94, 99–100; grocery stores and bars organized by, 75, 99–100; Harvard Law School speech of, 70–71; health problems of, 157, 162; *Hoffa v. United States*, 4, 145–46, 150–51; interviews with, 178, 185–86, 202, 208, 189–90; IRS and, 102, 105–106, 110, 121, 193; JFK and, 108–10, 120; JFK's assassination and, 117, 118; Josephine's affair and, 139–40, 210; jury tampering conviction of, 115–16, 119, 130, 145–46, 150, 178, 181; at Kroger, 50–51, 154; labor philosophy of, 71; Lake Orion cottage of, 64–65, 179, 186–89, 201, 204, 206, 210–11, 213–14, 219–24, 227, 267, 278–79; Las Vegas and, 90–91, 213–14; Local 299 and, 51, 53, 180, 183–84, 189, 198; Mafia and, 9, 49, 54, 57–60, 74, 75, 84–95, 99, 117, 119, 135–37, 158; Mafia rules and traditions and, 92; Mafia-Teamsters exposure threatened by, 185–87, 194–98, 202, 208–12; McClellan Committee and, 101–108, 110; mental state after release from prison, 162, 184, 193–94, 197, 210, 241, 243, 289; money of, 75–76, 187–88, 192, 212; move to Washington, 83; national bargaining obstacles and, 74; National Master Freight Agreement of, 76–77, 115, 132–34, 139–40; Nixon and, 153, 160–62; Nixon administration payoff rumors and, 172–77; Nixon's commutation of sentence and conditions of release, 5, 153–54, 162–69, 172–84, 189, 191, 196, 198–99, 207, 280; Nixon supported by, 109; O'Brien as assistant of, 79, 169–70, 187, 190; O'Brien asked to turn against Fitzsimmons by, 193–94, 197, 199; O'Brien's career advancement and, 79–80, 199–201; O'Brien's falling-out with, 5, 15, 18–19, 198, 233; O'Brien's family living at home of, 83–84, 277; O'Brien's finances and, 191–92; O'Brien's last conversation with, 206; O'Brien's meeting of, 5, 43, 44, 64; O'Brien's message-carrying for, 93–94, 190; O'Brien's relationship with, 5, 7, 10, 15, 18, 34, 64–68, 77–84, 140, 186–88, 190–92, 197–98, 200–201, 220–22, 230, 235, 311, 312; and O'Brien's relationship with Brenda, 5, 205–206; organizing techniques of, 74; Pagano and, 48, 57–61, 64, 65, 86, 90, 92–93, 137, 140, 154; pension fraud conviction of, 4, 116–17, 178; post-prison union comeback efforts of, 163–65, 177–78, 180, 183–84, 189–94, 198–99, 207–209, 212, 240, 250; post-prison image of, 178; power and, 54, 188, 189, 192; in prison, 5, 77, 89, 119, 156–57, 160–72, 178, 181, 197, 199; prison furlough of, 163–65; prison reform and, 178–79; prison release of, 177, 187, 187, 188; prudishness and morals of, 19, 24, 49, 90–91, 191; reelected as Teamsters president before imprisonment, 156; reelection plans after release, 163–65, 177–78; resignation as Teamsters president, 165, 166; RFK's crusade against, 5, 9, 31, 38, 95, 96–98, 101–21, 123, 130, 132, 153, 250; RFK's Hoffa Squad and, 109–12, 114; RFK's meeting of, 100–101; rise to power in Teamsters, 5, 52–53, 60–61,

66; Rosanova and, 186, 202, 208; Sheeran and, 311; Teamsters' eastern expansion and, 84–88; Teamsters' funds and, 89–93, 99, 119, 135, 142, 157, 158, 178, 185–86; Teamsters' growth under, 71–73, 84–88, 94, 106; Test Fleet trial of, 111–17, 153, 154; violence and, 53; work ethic of, 49, 73

Hoffa, James R. "Jimmy," disappearance of: 4, 5, 7, 15–17, 22, 23, 34, 170, 195, 203, 207, 213–26, 227–43, 244–62, 288–305; and ABC News special, 202; author's investigation of, 8–9, 296–97; author's meeting with FBI investigators of, 290–92; books and articles about, 8, 25, 39, 253, 258, 259, 262; Brenda O'Brien and, 15, 18–19, 232, 249; and conditions of prison release, 153–54, 168, 183; Crater story and, 188; DNA evidence in, 264, 268–71, 302–303; FBI investigation of, 227–40, 249–50, 254, 255, 260; FBI's discoveries about organized crime due to investigation of, 249–50, 255; FBI's theory of, 17–18, 233–37, 268, 291, 315–21; Fitzsimmons and, 208; Anthony Giacalone and, 16–18, 20, 43, 44, 139, 214–16, 219–26, 229–43, 258, 267, 269, 288–89, 317, 320; grand jury and, 18, 19, 233, 235, 271, 317, 318, 320; "informant" tips on, 293; James P. Hoffa and, 219–23, 228–33, 236, 231, 232, 238, 268, 278, 280, 293–94, 318, 319; Joey Giacalone's car and, 17, 217, 218, 221, 222, 230, 232–34, 236, 237, 241, 246, 252, 264, 266–68, 280, 316; jokes about, 293, 295; Josephine Hoffa and, 214, 215, 219, 221, 238, 292; Local 299 and, 217, 218, 222, 223, 234, 235, 237, 315–16, 318, 319, 321; Machus Red Fox and, 215, 216, 218–23, 228, 233–35, 237–40, 253, 266, 277, 282, 293, 294, 296, 297, 304, 315–21;

Hoffa, James R. "Jimmy," disappearance
of (*cont.*)
O'Brien and, *see* O'Brien, Charles
"Chuckie," Hoffa's disappearance
and; Provenzano and, 229, 238–43,
245–46, 253, 258, 288–89, 298; public
knowledge, narratives, and rumors
about, 7–8, 253, 262, 293; search for
remains, 282, 295; suspects convicted
of crimes unrelated to, 247; telephone
records and, 239–40; timeline analysis
of, 315–21; Vito Giacalone as suspect,
294
Hoffa, John (father), 48, 65
Hoffa, Josephine Poszywak (wife), 43,
59, 60, 65, 79, 83, 84, 132, 133–34,
136, 137, 163, 172, 181, 190, 197, 205,
210, 267, 280; affair of, 135, 139–40;
alcoholism of, 60, 132–34, 136–40;
death of, 292; FBI surveillance and,
131–35, 312; Giacalone and, 135,
197, 210; hospitalization of, 133–35;
Jimmy's disappearance and, 214, 215,
219, 221, 238, 292; O'Brien and, 133,
170, 292; Pagano and, 60, 64, 84,
132, 134–35, 137–38, 140, 197; Vito
Giacalone and, 134, 137, 139, 197
Hoffa, Viola (mother), 48–49, 51
Hoffa v. United States, 4, 145–46, 150–51
Hoffa Wars, The (Moldea), 44, 253, 294
Hoffman, Clare, 100
Holmes, Robert "Bobby," Jr., 217, 219, 277
Holmes, Robert "Bobby," Sr., 154–55,
216, 217, 316
Holmes, Violet, 217–18, 222, 232,
234–35, 280, 310, 316, 321
Holy Trinity Church, 144, 276, 277
Home Juice Company, 131, 133, 144, 145,
222
Hoover, J. Edgar, 117, 124–29, 143, 153,
179; death of, 194–95; Mafia and,
127–29; surveillance and, 125–29,
140–41, 143, 147, 150

Hotel Employees and Restaurant
Employees Union, 65
Hot Springs, Ark., 16, 18
Humphrey, Hubert, 109, 153
Hunt, E. Howard, 173

Ianniello, Matthew "Matty the Horse," 86
I Heard You Paint Houses (Brandt), 253,
309, 310
Inciso, Angelo, 191
International Brotherhood of Teamsters,
see Teamsters union
Interstate Commerce Commission, 76
Intruders, The (Long), 142
Iran-contra affair, 32
Irishman, The, 257, 301, 307, 309–312
IRS (Internal Revenue Service), 120–21;
Fitzsimmons and, 193, 199, 208; Hoffa
and, 102, 105–106, 110, 121, 193;
Ideological Organizations Project, 121;
Nixon and, 121, 152; O'Brien and, 21,
191, 216, 253; wiretapping and, 110
Irvine v. California, 126
Issues and Answers, 178
Italian organized crime, *see* Mafia

Jackson, Robert, 109–10, 120, 125, 126,
149–50
Jacobs, Paul, 73
James, Estelle and Ralph, 74, 80, 83, 112, 130
Jax Kar Wash, 218, 219, 280, 321
Johnson, Dave, 198–201, 209
Johnson, Lyndon B., 111, 142, 143, 160
Journalist and the Murderer, The
(Malcolm), 300, 301
Justice Department, U.S., 38–39, 106,
109, 117, 120, 124, 152, 153, 161,
207–208, 238, 245, 252, 273, 275;
Ashcroft at, 38, 120, 122–24, 147–49;
author at, 3, 5, 7, 36–40, 122, 147–51,
239; and conditions of Hoffa's release,
182, 183; Hoover at, 124–26; Long
and, 142; O'Brien and, 6, 26, 38–39,

43, 98, 231; Office of Legal Counsel (OLC) in, 3, 36–38, 110, 147; RFK at, 31, 38, 104, 109–10, 120, 122, 132, 151; Stellarwind and, 3–4, 123–24, 147–51; *see also* FBI; Kennedy, Robert F.

Kaiser, David, 103
Kansas City, 45–46, 54, 57, 61, 63, 94, 195, 196
Katzenbach, Nicholas, 110, 142–43
Kefauver, Estes, 99, 100
Kefauver Committee, 99, 107, 127
Kelley, Clarence M., 195, 228
Kelley, Robert, 228
Kennedy, Ethel, 101
Kennedy, John F., 98, 99, 108–109, 152, 153, 162, 259; assassination of, 117, 119; Hoffa and, 108–10, 120
Kennedy, Joseph, 110
Kennedy, Robert F., 97–99, 157, 162, 189, 194, 207, 249, 259, 308; Ashcroft and, 123; assassination of, 152–53; childhood of, 98; crusade against Hoffa, 5, 9, 31, 38, 95, 96–98, 101–21, 123, 130, 132, 153, 250; Hoffa's meeting of, 100–101; Hoffa Squad of, 109–12, 114, 119, 121, 144, 151; IRS and, 102, 105–106, 110, 121; JFK and, 98, 99, 108–109, 152; JFK's assassination and, 117, 119; at Justice Department, 31, 38, 104, 109–10, 120, 122, 132, 151; King wiretapping and, 147–48; McClellan Committee and, 99, 101–108, 110, 119; Nixon and, 152–53; O'Brien and, 26, 38, 96–98, 121; press manipulated by, 101–102, 107, 110–11; surveillance and, 9, 128–29, 140–41, 143, 147–48, 150; Test Fleet trial and, 111–17, 153
Kern, Clement, 144, 276, 277
Kincaid, Jim, 186
King, Ewing, 112, 114, 115
King, Larry, 264
King, Martin Luther, Jr., 73, 141, 147–48

Kleindienst, Richard, 180, 181
Kovens, Calvin, 92, 188
Kroger (grocery store), 50–51, 154
Kuklinski, Richard "the Iceman," 293
Kyff, Destine, 318, 319

labor unions, 9, 30, 44, 50–52, 71, 72, 178; anti-labor forces and, 72, 106–108; Hoffa's philosophy of, 71; Kroger and, 50–51; Landrum-Griffin Act and, 108; Mafia and, 55–57, 85; membership rises and falls, 72, 108; Nixon and, 159–60; racketeering and, 56–57; and RFK's crusade against Hoffa, 106–108, 119–20; "salting" and, 48; strikes and, 49–51, 53, 55–59, 65–66, 72; Taft-Hartley Act and, 72, 111; violence and, 53; Wagner Act and, 52, 53
Lacey, Frederick B., 257
La Cosa Nostra, *see* Mafia
Lake Hamilton, 16, 18
LaMare, Chet, 57
Landrum-Griffin Act, 108
Lansky, Meyer, 16, 94
Larry King Live, 264
Las Vegas, Nev., 60, 90–91, 133, 135, 142, 143, 153, 170, 213–14
Laurendi, Natale, 261–62
LCN, *see* Mafia
legal system, 9, 95, 120; Giacalone's view of, 136; O'Brien's view of, 30, 33
Leitch, David, 37
Levi, Edward, 207–209
Levinson, Edward, 142
Lewin, Nathan, 31, 112, 146
Lewis, John L., 52
Lichtenstein, Nelson, 106
Liddy, G. Gordon, 180
Life, 142
Lift-All Company, 217, 235, 316, 318–21
Linteau, Louis "the Pope," 210, 214–16, 219–22, 236–38, 317, 319
Lippmann, Walter, 56

Local 299, 51, 53, 66, 67, 79, 96, 154,
    158, 169–70, 180, 183–84, 186, 187,
    189, 193, 198–201, 204, 205, 209, 277;
    Hoffa's disappearance and, 217, 218,
    222, 223, 234, 235, 237, 315–16, 318,
    319, 321; O'Brien at, 67, 79, 169–70,
    186, 187, 199–201, 204, 205; violence
    and, 209, 214
Long, Edward, 141–44
Long Committee, 142, 144
longshoremen, 73
Louis, Joe, 102
Lucchese crime family, 57, 86, 94
Luciano, Charles "Lucky," 16, 54–55, 127
Luedtke, Kurt, 131, 254
Lynch, William F., 208

Machus Red Fox, 215, 216, 218–23, 228,
    233–35, 237–40, 253, 266, 277, 282,
    293, 294, 296, 297, 304, 315–21
Mafia (the mob; La Cosa Nostra; LCN;
    the Outfit; Italian organized crime),
    44, 53–57, 110, 310; Apalachin meeting
    of, 60–61, 127, 128; Castellammarese
    War and, 54; Castro and, 259; in
    Chicago, 57, 85, 89, 93–94, 186, 195;
    Chicago meeting of leaders of, 55;
    Commission of, 55, 88, 127, 242, 255–57,
    289, 313; in Detroit, 47, 57–61, 63, 67,
    81, 84–85, 87, 135, 221, 258, 265, 266;
    FBI's discoveries about, due to Hoffa
    disappearance investigation, 249–50,
    255; FBI's increased pressure on,
    194–95; FBI's surveillance of, 127–29,
    138, 141–43; Fitzsimmons and, 17,
    156, 158, 163, 171, 185–86, 192, 240;
    Gambino family, 63; Genovese family,
    17, 86, 87, 238, 242, 289; Giuliani's
    lawsuit against, 255–57; Hoffa and, 9,
    49, 54, 57–60, 74, 75, 84–95, 99, 117,
    119, 135–37, 158; Hoffa's commutation
    restriction claims and, 207–209; Hoffa's
    lack of affinity with, 92; Hoffa's loaning

of funds to, 89–93, 135, 137, 142, 158;
    Hoffa's plans to expose Teamsters
    infiltration by, 185–87, 194–98, 202,
    208–12; Hoover and, 127–29; IRS and,
    121; JFK's assassination and, 117; in
    Kansas City, 45, 46, 54, 57, 61, 63, 94,
    195, 196; Kefauver Committee and,
    99, 127; labor unions and, 55–57, 85;
    Lucchese family, 57, 86, 94; in New
    York, 54, 55, 57, 63, 85–88, 94, 127,
    289; O'Brien's denial of existence of,
    22, 25, 34; O'Brien's permission to talk
    and, 251–52; Omertà in, see Omertà;
    pretextual prosecutions against, 120;
    racketeering and, 56–57; Teamsters
    and, 22, 23, 44, 56–57, 119–20, 158,
    185–86, 240, 249–50
Magaddino, Stefano, 55
Malcolm, Janet, 300, 301
Mamet, David, 257
Maranzano, Salvatore, 54, 55
Marcello, Carlos, 94, 117, 118, 178
Marshall, Thurgood, 143, 144
Masseria, Giuseppe, 54
Maury Povich Show, The, 260–61, 263,
    268, 273, 276
McCall, C. W., 23
McCarthy, Joseph, 98, 101, 103, 107
McClellan, John, 99, 108, 110
McClellan Committee, 99, 101–108, 110,
    119, 121, 249
McCord, James W., Jr., 180
McLean, Malcolm, 74
McMaster, Rolland, 209, 295
McQuade, Barbara, 283–85
McVittie, Gerald R., 140
Meli, Angelo, 58, 81
Meli, Frank, 81
Meli, Vince, 81
Meyer, John, 70
Milan, Jack, 219
Miller, Cassidy, Larroca & Lewin, 31
Miller, Ron, 229

Miller, William E., 111, 112

Mitchell, John, 159, 162, 163, 166–68, 176, 182; Fitzsimmons and, 173–74

mob, see Mafia

Moldea, Dan, 44, 198, 207–208, 253, 294

Morgan, Joe, 28, 241

Morganroth, Mike, 274–75, 279, 281–83, 285

Morton, Rogers C. B., 153

Moscato, Phillip "Brother," 294

Mueller, Robert, 149

Mundt, Karl, 108

Nashville Banner, 112

National Guard, 53

National Master Freight Agreement, 76–77, 115, 132–34, 139–40

National Security Agency, 4, 147

National Security Council, 123

Navasky, Victor, 111, 128, 129

Neff, James, 102–105

Nelli, Humbert, 56

Ness, Eliot, 194

Neumann, Bob, 228

New Deal, 52

New Jersey, 86, 87

Newman, Paul, 254, 257

New Republic, The, 143–44

Newsweek, 78, 244–46

New York, N.Y.; Mafia in, 54, 55, 57, 63, 85–88, 94, 127, 289; Teamsters in, 57, 85–88

New York Times, The, 22, 77, 106, 125, 143, 158, 164, 165, 180, 182, 261, 270

Nicholson, Jack, 257

9/11 attacks, 38, 122–24, 264

1984 (Orwell), 129

Nixon, Richard M., 109, 189, 195; Fitzsimmons and, 159–62, 165, 166, 178–81; Hoffa and, 153, 160–62; Hoffa released with conditions by, 5,

153–54, 162–69, 172–84, 189, 191, 196, 198–99, 207, 280; Hoffa's support of, 109; IRS and, 121, 152; labor and, 159–60; payoff rumors for Hoffa's prison release, 172–77; reelection campaign of, 159–60, 173, 174, 179, 180; resignation of, 183; RFK and, 152–53; Teamsters and, 153, 159–60, 162–63, 165, 166, 180, 181; Watergate scandal of, 159, 163, 173, 174, 179–83, 189, 195, 207, 228

O'Brien, Brenda (mother of Jack Goldsmith), 16, 24, 27, 31–36, 40, 177, 308; author's name change and, 29, 30; book written by Chuckie and, 258–60; Chuckie divorced by, 31, 33, 255, 257; Chuckie's lie detector test and, 269–70; Chuckie's marriage to, 5, 14–16, 18–19, 24, 31, 33, 203–205, 216, 255, 257; Chuckie's meeting of, 14, 172, 205; and Chuckie's rift with Hoffa, 5, 18–19; Chuckie's 60 Minutes appearance and, 246; electroshock therapy of, 19, 20; health problems of, 21, 249, 287–88, 290; Hoffa's disappearance and, 15, 18–19, 232, 249; kidnapping threat and, 248; marriage to Jack Goldsmith Jr., 12–14; marriage to Robert Rivet, 13–14, 16, 172; mental health problems of, 13–15, 18–21, 203, 249; return to Chuckie's life, 187, 202–203; suicide attempt of, 13–14

O'Brien, Brett (brother of Jack Goldsmith), 12–14, 16, 19–20, 24, 27, 29, 30, 203, 232, 248, 270, 287, 314

O'Brien, Charles "Chuckie": as associate in the Outfit, 67–68; author's book and, 307–9; author's conversations with, 7–10, 42, 62–64, 174–77, 206, 220, 224–25, 243, 263, 288–90, 297–302, 304, 309; author's correspondence with, 27–30, 40, 206; at author's Harvard Law School

O'Brien, Charles "Chuckie" (*cont.*)
seminar, 69–71, 75; author's name changes and, 21, 26–30; author's reconciliation with, 6, 38, 40–41, 42; author's renunciation of, 5, 25–40, 98, 255; and author's security clearances, 32–34; as author's stepfather, 5, 9, 11, 15–16. 20–37, 40, 42–43, 203, 288, 314; author's visits to Detroit with, 276–78, 287, 302–303; Barbara Hoffa and, 65, 82–84, 294; birth of, 47; book written by Brenda and, 258–60; Brenda's divorce of, 31, 33, 255, 257; Brenda's marriage to, 5, 14–16, 18–19, 24, 31, 33, 203–205, 216, 255, 257; Brenda's meeting of, 14, 172, 205; Brenda's return to life of, 187, 202–203; bumper stickers and, 171; convictions on minor charges, 22; death of, 314; early life of, 43–44, 47, 61–62, 64–65; expelled from Teamsters, 35, 257, 260; father of, *see* O'Brien, Charles Lenton; FBI surveillance and, 131–33, 138–40, 144, 311–12; financial troubles of, 18, 21, 24–26, 39, 191–92, 203, 216, 240, 253, 255; first wife of, *see* O'Brien, Mary Ann Giaramita; Fitzsimmons and, 157, 158, 161, 170–72, 174–76, 187, 189, 190, 192–94, 197, 200, 201; and Fitzsimmons/Holmes coin flip, 155, 216; Fitzsimmons's relocation of, 199–200, 204; funeral for, 314; Giacalone and, 17, 18, 33, 43–44, 61–64, 67–68, 133, 170–71, 175, 177, 187, 195–98, 200, 222, 235, 248, 299; Giuliani's lawsuit and, 255–57; on government "backup," 98, 121, 124, 150; health problems of, 35, 42, 46, 274, 275, 284, 285, 307, 308, 312; high school years of, 66; Hoffa and career advancement of, 79–80, 199–201; Hoffa assassination attempt and, 82–83; Hoffa assumed to be biological father of, 44, 59–60, 82; Hoffa home as home of, 83–84, 277; as Hoffa's assistant, 79, 169–70, 187, 190; Hoffa's criminal trials and, 77, 81; Hoffa's disappearance and, 7; Hoffa's falling-out with, 5, 15, 18–19, 198, 233; Hoffa's imprisonment and, 156, 161–63, 166, 169–72, 199; Hoffa's last conversation with, 206; Hoffa's meeting of, 5, 43, 44, 64; as Hoffa's message-carrier, 93–94, 190; and Hoffa's plans to expose Mafia infiltration of the Teamsters, 185–87, 194–98, 202, 208–12; Hoffa's relationship with, 5, 7, 10, 15, 18, 34, 64–68, 77–84, 140, 186–88, 190–92, 197–98, 200–201, 220–22, 230, 235, 311, 312; Hoffa's requests to turn against Fitzsimmons, 193–94, 197, 199; on Hoffa's ties with Mafia, 84–94; *The Irishman* portrayal of, 257, 301, 307, 309–12; IRS and, 21, 191, 216, 253; at Italian restaurant, 313–14; James P. Hoffa and, 190–91, 220–23; Josephine Hoffa and, 133, 170, 292; Justice Department and, 6, 26, 38–39, 43, 98, 231; kidnapping threat and, 248; legal system as viewed by, 30, 33; as liar, 6, 24, 26, 81, 230; at Local 299, 67, 79, 169–70, 186, 187, 199–201, 204, 205; Mafia existence denied by, 22, 25, 34; mother of, *see* Pagano, Sylvia; movie roles inspired by, 77–78, 254, 257; *1984* and, 129; *O'Brien v. United States*, 4, 38, 144, 146; old-school values of, 24; Omertà and, 6, 10, 61–64, 67, 177, 232, 248, 251, 252, 256, 297, 299–301, 304, 308; and payoff to Nixon administration for Hoffa's release, 174–77; in prison, 22, 25, 247, 253; professional limitations of, 80–81, 133, 170, 235; Provenzano and, 17, 33, 245–46; RFK and, 26, 38, 96–98, 121; St. Theresa statue taken by, 4, 144, 276; Seafarers International Union and, 80–81; Teamsters job in Florida, 16, 18, 20, 204–205, 216, 254; Teamsters joined by, 66, 77, 78; Test Fleet trial and, 112–16; truck driving of, 66

O'Brien, Charles "Chuckie," and Hoffa's disappearance: 34, 43, 44, 216–26, 288–305; actions on day of disappearance, 17, 216–19, 222, 225, 230, 231, 234–36, 256, 266–68, 271, 272, 280, 297, 315–21; CIA involvement postulated by, 258–59; denial of involvement and exoneration attempts, 6, 230, 246–47, 251–53, 260–62, 289; failed vindication, 263–86, 294–96; FBI interviews with Chuckie about, 17, 229–32, 237, 266, 296; Florida relocation and, 16, 18, 204; and Giacalone's tasks for Chuckie, 225–26, 289; grand jury appearance, 18, 19, 233; James P. Hoffa and, 228–33, 236, 268, 278, 280, 293–94; and lack of mob hit on Chuckie, 237, 266; meeting with Provenzano and Giacalone, 240–43, 246, 289, 299; news of disappearance, 219–20, 236–37; polygraph tests about, 18, 36, 231, 233, 260–62, 263–65, 268–70, 272–76, 281, 283, 296, 302; public exoneration following publication of author's book, 308, 309; revelations to author at Seasons 52, 288–90, 297–99, 301, 302, 304; Sluss and, 36, 263–73, 279, 283, 284, 294–96, 302–303; as suspect, 5, 6, 8–9, 17, 19, 20, 22, 25, 32, 35–37, 39, 70, 133, 139, 186–87, 218, 221–23, 225, 228–40, 244–62, 269–70, 291–92, 315–21; television appearances and, 246–47, 252, 260–61

O'Brien, Charles Lenton (father of Chuckie), 44–47; disappearance and death of, 47; Sylvia's marriage to, 46–47

O'Brien, Josephine (daughter of Chuckie), 84

O'Brien, Mary Ann Giaramita (first wife of Chuckie), 15, 24, 66, 84, 134; Chuckie's divorce from, 172, 191

O'Brien, Steven (brother of Jack Goldsmith), 12–14, 16, 19–20, 24, 27, 29, 30, 203, 232, 248, 270, 314

O'Brien v. United States, 4, 38, 144, 146

Office of Legal Counsel (OLC), 3, 36–38, 110, 147

Omertà, 55, 62–63; O'Brien and, 6, 10, 61–64, 67, 177, 232, 248, 251, 252, 256, 297, 299–301, 304, 308

On the Waterfront, 107

Orwell, George, 129

Oswald, Lee Harvey, 117

Outfit, the, see Mafia

Oxford University, 30

Pagano, Sylvia (mother of Chuckie O'Brien), 14, 15, 17, 46–49, 54, 60–61, 63, 67, 84, 93, 117, 131, 133, 140, 172, 193, 196, 198, 205, 276, 308; Brennan and, 48; death of, 172, 177; Detroit family and, 57–60; FBI surveillance and, 131–38, 145, 311–12; Fitzsimmons and, 170; Giacalone and, 60, 62, 93, 131, 135; Hoffa and, 48, 57–61, 64, 65, 86, 90, 92–93, 137, 140, 154; Hoffa robbery plotted by Giacalone and, 137–39; Josephine Hoffa and, 60, 64, 84, 132, 134–35, 137–38, 140, 197; marriage to O'Brien, 46–47; as mother, 61

Parker, J. J., 157

Parks, Thomas, 112

Partin, Edward Grady, 113–15, 145, 146, 150–51, 178

People, 207

Perrone, Santo, 58

Petersen, Henry, 183

Picardo, Ralph "Little Ralphie," 238–40, 253

Plantation Inn, 12, 13, 19

Plemons, Jesse, 257

police, 53, 95

Povich, Maury, 260–61, 263, 268, 273, 276

Pratt, John H., 183

Presser, Jackie, 23, 82, 197

Prohibition, 45, 46, 49, 54, 55, 57, 58, 110

Provenzano, Anthony "Tony Pro," 17, 22, 86–88, 92, 105, 157, 195, 200, 210, 252, 294, 304, 308, 313; author given pool table by, 22, 33; conviction and imprisonment of, 247; death of, 247; Hoffa's disappearance and, 229, 238–43, 245–46, 253, 258, 288–89, 298; O'Brien and, 17, 33, 245–46, 248; O'Brien's meeting with Giacalone and, 240–43, 246, 289, 299; and O'Brien's questioning by Ferguson, 256

Provenzano, Nunzi, 195

Provenzano, Sammy, 195, 200

Puzo, Mario, 77–78, 254

Queasbarth, Arthur, 58

Racketeer Influenced and Corrupt Organizations Act (RICO), 250

racketeering, 56–57

Ragano, Frank, 253

Raskin, A. H., 106, 164, 165

Reed, Jerry, 23

Reeves, Elmer, 317

Rehnquist, William, 37

Reppetto, Thomas, 207

Reuther, Walter, 71, 72

Reynolds, Burt, 23

Ricca, Paul "the Waiter," 93

Richardson, Elliot, 181

Ridley, Jim, 82–83

Riesel, Victor, 78, 86

River Gang, 57, 58

Rivet, Robert, 13–14, 16, 32, 172

Roemer, William, 128

Rogers, William, 128

Romer, Sam, 75

Roosevelt, Franklin D., 52, 125–26, 146, 149–50

Rosanova, Louis "the Tailor," 93–94, 186, 202, 208

Rosselli, Johnny, 259

Ruby, Jack, 117, 118

Ruckelshaus, William, 181

Russell, Thaddeus, 48, 49, 53

Safer, Morley, 246

Sarno, Jay, 90, 193, 208

Saxbe, William, 181

Scaglia, Mariano, 46, 47

Scalia, Antonin, 37

Schlesinger, Arthur, Jr., 53, 71, 100

Schultz, Lenny, 222

Schwartz, David G., 90

Schweder, Bernard A., 140

Scorsese, Martin, The Irishman, 257, 301, 307, 309–12

Seafarers International Union (SIU), 80–81

Seigenthaler, John, 111

Senate, U.S., 95; Church Committee, 141, 146, 228, 258–59; Long Committee, 142, 144; McClellan Committee, 99, 101–108, 110, 119, 121, 249; Permanent Subcommittee on Investigations, 97

September 11 attacks, 38, 122–24, 264

Sevareid, Eric, 95

Shaffer, Charles, 117

Sheeran, Frank, 253, 293, 295, 309–11

Shenker, Morris, 81, 142, 165, 181, 182, 184, 213–14

Sheridan, Walter, 111, 114, 117

Shultz, George, 159, 165

Silberman, Laurence, 183

Silski, Marc, 279, 303

Sirhan, Sirhan, 152–53

60 Minutes, 246–47, 252

Sloane, Arthur, 71, 84, 178

Sluss, Andrew, 36, 263–73, 279, 283, 284, 294–96, 302–303

Smith, Bertha, 15

Smith v. Maryland, 150, 151

Smokey and the Bandit, 23

Southern Christian Leadership Conference, 141, 147

Southfield Athletic Club, 222, 226, 230, 238, 320

Spindel, Bernard, 111

Sproule, Al, 250, 290–92

Squires, Al "Pop," 78

Stallone, Sylvester, 23

Stanecki, Jerry, 252

Starr, Ken, 120

Stellarwind, 3–4, 123–24, 147–51

Stewart, Potter, 129

stock market crash of 1929, 49–50

Straus, Eric, 274–75, 279–84

Sullivan, William, 142

Supreme Court, U.S., 3, 34, 38, 130, 181; *Berger v. New York*, 4; *Hoffa v. United States*, 4, 145–46, 150–51; *Irvine v. California*, 126; *O'Brien v. United States*, 4, 38, 144, 146; *Smith v. Maryland*, 150, 151; surveillance and, 4, 125–26, 131, 143–46

surveillance, 37–39, 122–51; *Berger v. New York* and, 4; Church Committee and, 141, 146; by FBI, 125–29, 143; by FBI, of Hoffa, 111, 112, 129–42, 145–46; by FBI, of Mafia, 127–29, 138, 141–43; Foreign Intelligence Surveillance Act, 146–48; Gamtax wiretapping operation, 258, 265, 266; *Hoffa v. United States* and, 4, 145–46, 150–51; Hoover and, 125–29, 140–41, 143, 147, 150; IRS and, 110; *Irvine v. California* and, 126; of King, 141, 147–48; Long's exposure of, 141–44; metadata in, 123, 150, 239; *O'Brien v. United States* and, 4, 38, 144, 146; Partin and, 145, 146, 150–51; reform in 1960s, 146; RFK and, 9, 128–29, 140–41, 143, 147–48, 150; *Smith v. Maryland* and, 150, 151; Stellarwind program, 3–4, 123–24, 147–51; Supreme Court and, 4, 125–26, 131, 143–46

Swanson, Warren, 82–83

Taft-Hartley Act, 72, 111

Teamster (magazine), 77

Teamsters, The (Brill), 253

Teamsters union (International Brotherhood of Teamsters; IBT), 44; AFL-CIO and, 106; African American workers in, 73; author's Harvard Law School seminar and, 69–71, 75; author's youthful veneration of, 22; Central Conference of, 88; Central States Pension Fund of, 89–90, 116–17, 119, 135, 142, 157, 158, 178, 185–86, 240; in Chicago, 57; in Detroit, 52–53, 57–60, 154; Detroit Lumber Company strike and, 57–59; *Detroit News* and, 83; eastern expansion of, 84–88; Executive Board of, 140, 154, 163, 165, 170, 171, 200, 207, 238, 255–57; Fitzsimmons as president of, 17, 23, 80, 119–20, 165–66, 170, 171, 192, 240; Fitzsimmons as Teamsters head during Hoffa's imprisonment, 155–65; formation and early years of, 51; Giuliani's lawsuit against, 255–57; golf and, 23, 158–59, 171, 181, 206–207; growth of, 71–73, 84–88, 94, 106; Hoffa elected president of, 72, 79, 86, 88, 96, 104–106; Hoffa reelected president prior to imprisonment, 156; Hoffa's authoritarian control of, 4, 74–75, 170, 171; Hoffa's control of funds of, 88–93, 99, 119, 135, 142, 157, 158, 185–86; Hoffa's dedication to members of, 75, 94, 179; Hoffa's organizing techniques for, 74; Hoffa's plans to expose Mafia infiltration of, 185–87, 194–98, 202, 208–12; Hoffa's post-prison ban on returning to, 5, 153–54, 162–69, 172–84, 189, 191, 196, 198–99, 207; Hoffa's post-prison comeback efforts, 163–65, 177–78, 180, 183–84, 189–94, 198–99, 207–209, 212, 240, 250; Hoffa's resignation as president of, 165,

Teamsters union (*cont.*)
166; Hoffa's rise to power in, 5, 52–53, 60–61, 66; International Executive Board, 88; Local 299, *see* Local 299; Local 541, 66; Local 560, 86, 87; Mafia and, 22, 23, 44, 56–57, 119–20, 158, 185–86, 240, 249–50; national bargaining obstacles and, 74; National Master Freight Agreement and, 76–77, 115, 132–34, 139–40; in New York, 57, 85–88; Nixon and, 153, 159–60, 162–63, 165, 166, 180, 181; Nixon administration payoff rumors and, 172–77; O'Brien expelled from, 35, 257, 260; O'Brien's Florida job with, 16, 18, 20, 204–205, 216; O'Brien's joining of, 66, 77, 78; and RFK's crusade against Hoffa, 5, 9, 31, 38, 95, 96–98, 101–21; Southern Conference of, 22–23, 204, 216; White Tower strike and, 65–66; women workers in, 73
Tennessean, The, 111, 112
Test Fleet, 111–17, 153, 154
Thomas, Evan, 98
Time, 18, 78, 232
Tobin, Dan, 66
Tocco, William "Black Bill," 47, 48, 57, 61, 276
Tolson, Clyde, 130, 143
torture, 39, 123
Trafficante, Santo, 117, 195
Traylor, Lawrence, 168
truckers, truck driving, 23, 52, 171; O'Brien and, 23, 66
trucking industry, 52, 71; national bargaining and, 76–77; organization of, 73–74
Tye, Larry, 141

United Automobile Workers (UAW), 52–53, 72, 86
United Farm Workers, 172, 187

United Mine Workers, 49, 52
University of Chicago, 207; author at, 34, 35, 264
Untouchables, The (Ness and Fraley), 194
U.S. Attorney's Office, 255, 273–75, 281–85, 294, 296, 303

Valenti, Joseph, 218, 318, 319
Vietnam War, 169–61

Wagner Act, 52, 53
Wallace, George, 159
Wall Street Journal, The, 78, 104–105
Walton, Kenneth, 260
Warren, Earl, 145
Warren Commission, 117, 118
Washington Post, The, 104, 180
Watergate scandal, 159, 163, 173, 174, 179–83, 189, 195, 207, 228
Wayne County Morgue, 83
Weiner, Tim, 179–80
White, Byron "Whizzer," 128
White Tower, 65–66
Wholey, Dennis, 189
Wilkinson, J. Harvie, 32
Williams, Edward Bennett, 101–103, 136, 142
Williams, Leslie Anne, 34, 35, 40
Williams, Roy, 23, 195
Witwer, David, 108
Wolfgang, Myra, 65
women workers, 73
Woodward, Bob, 180
World War I, 124
World War II, 52, 71, 72, 149–50
WXYZ-TV, 189–90

Yale Law School, 26, 30–31
Yost, Pete, 247

Zerilli, Anthony, 85, 135–37, 282, 293
Zerilli, Joseph, 57, 58, 61, 67, 85, 127, 135
Zwingle, C. G., 77